Probing Human Dignity

Stephanie N. Arel • Levi Cooper •
Vanessa Hellmann
Editors

Probing Human Dignity

Exploring Thresholds from an Interdisciplinary Perspective

Springer

Editors
Stephanie N. Arel
Theology
Fordham University
New York City, NY, USA

Levi Cooper
Law
Bar-Ilan University
Ramat Gan, Israel

Vanessa Hellmann
Law
University of Bielefeld
Bielefeld, Germany

ISBN 978-3-031-42436-6 ISBN 978-3-031-42437-3 (eBook)
https://doi.org/10.1007/978-3-031-42437-3

This Springer imprint is published by the registered company Springer Nature Switzerland AG
The registered company address is: Gewerbestrasse 11, 6330 Cham, Switzerland

Paper in this product is recyclable.

Foreword by Ulrike Davy and Michal Linial

This edited volume grew out of a joint initiative of ours when we held, for one, the post of the managing director of the Zentrum für interdisziplinäre Forschung, Bielefeld (ZiF), and, for another, the post of the director of the Israel Institute for Advanced Studies, Jerusalem (IIAS). The idea of launching an IIAS-ZiF-funded endeavor began in March 2013 at a conference convened by a network of institutes for advanced study (University-Based Institutes for Advanced Study, UBIAS) in Jerusalem, where directors of those institutes from around the globe met to discuss new forms of cooperation between two or more of those institutes. One such new format was the Intercontinental Academia, a thematically focused scholarly endeavor carried out by two institutes located in differing world regions, aimed to attract young scholars from various countries who were enthusiastic about doing research across disciplines and borders. The IIAS and ZiF were happy to volunteer. Yet, it took another two and a half years until the idea of pairing ZiF and the IIAS became a reality. When, in our discussions, the concept of "human dignity" first arose as a candidate for a thematic focus for the Intercontinental Academia, we were thrilled. It was immediately clear to both of us that we could not imagine something more appropriate for a collaboration between an Israeli and a German institute of advanced study. Also, we have been acutely aware that questions of human dignity did not only relate to antisemitism in Europe and the Holocaust perpetrated by Nazi Germany, but also to the conflict between Jews and Arabs over land, representation, and equality in contemporary Israel. The more we thought about human dignity and its fragility, the more we realized that there has not been, in the past few years, a day when human dignity has not been at the center of news events across the globe. That still holds true in 2024.

Even though the fellowships were open to young scholars from all countries (and many in fact applied and attended), it was clear that, with ZiF and IIAS joining in a common effort, Israeli and German scholars would be bringing in their own unique sensitivities to this area of inquiry. Germans and Israelis have struggled to define the parameters of human dignity after 1945 and after 1948, respectively, from the purely theoretical aspects to the reality of facts on the ground, which cannot be ignored and should be addressed.

In 2019, again under the aegis of UBIAS, the Johannesburg Institute of Advanced Study (JIAS), headed by Peter Vale and, later, by Bongani Ngqulunga, partook in the endeavor, bringing in a new venue for a further session, new scholars, and new perspectives, such as slavery, apartheid, freedom of speech, and reconciliation.

Indeed, the balance of power between legal, political, and governmental authorities, on the one hand, and the individuals living under those authorities, on the other, has always been a delicate one, vulnerable to abuse. It is a balance which needs to be continually negotiated and redefined and strengthened when under duress.

We are delighted that our undertakings continue to bear fruit. When the first session of the fellows of the Intercontinental Academy on Human Dignity took place in Jerusalem in the spring of 2016, we had high hopes. Clearly, somehow, we wanted to change the lives of the young scholars participating, coming from diverse backgrounds and family histories. Yet, the outcome by far exceeded our hopes and dreams. We saw friendships being formed that were reinforced and intensified in the following sessions in Bielefeld in the summer of 2016 and in Johannesburg in January 2019. The sessions created relationships among the fellows that were inspiring and strong enough to make them engage in an effort of their own. The project of a joint book tied them together even as the Intercontinental Academia had formally been closed. The fellows of the Academia embarked on a follow-up journey, sometimes straight, sometimes winding—a journey that eventually led to the publication of an edited volume. Congratulations! Seeing all this emerge and grow and, eventually, fully blossoming was certainly a unique and most pleasant experience. Thank you, Fellows of the Intercontinental Academia on Human Dignity!

Bielefeld, Germany — Ulrike Davy
Johannesburg, South Africa
Jerusalem, Israel — Michal Linial

Preface by the Editors

Probing Human Dignity from multiple disciplinary backgrounds by a cadre of scholars from a variety of countries and different cultures is an intense intellectual and emotional venture. Encountering Human Dignity challenges individuals, communities, and society at large to navigate different spheres of human action, including ethical, moral, religious, and legal realms. Difficulties emerge in the attempt to bridge the discourse about Human Dignity across cultural contexts, traditions, and vantage points. This volume confronts such difficulties exploring new horizons of the discourse and offering a mosaic of the universal quest for Human Dignity.

In philosophy and law, Human Dignity is discussed as an individual right, as a principle or a value, or as the source of human rights in general. Scholars in philosophy and theology extract the term from the legal context and explore Human Dignity as a value intertwined with the vulnerability of human beings. Scholars of religion often view Human Dignity as a divinely mandated, religious imperative. Despite the widespread recognition of Human Dignity, the denial of a person's dignity continues to manifest in contemporary life, through injustices often related to personal hardship, crisis, unrest, or upheaval. The present volume brings these injustices to light engaging academic discourses on Human Dignity to develop a sensitive, complex, and nuanced understanding of the term.

Each chapter in the volume begins from the understanding that recognizing and investigating Human Dignity often occurs "at the threshold," where in times of societal crisis or individual hardship questions of Human Dignity turn into ethical, moral, and legal dilemmas. The quest of this volume is to draw on theoretical and conceptual distinctions of Human Dignity in order to inform new perspectives that probe its ambiguity. The contributors offer greater clarity and push beyond thresholds to develop new paradigms that cross disciplinary lines while speaking to the goals and needs of post-modern societies and individuals. Each chapter crosses into new territory in an effort to examine a pressing legal or societal issue with a new lens.

Following the introduction, the volume turns to legal approaches examining Human Dignity as it emerges from the fields of Constitutional Law and Jewish legal tradition. The third part of the volume moves to various aspects of dignity in threshold spaces. Connecting Human Dignity to trauma lies at the heart of part four of the volume. Part five concludes with different examinations of Ubuntu, as the sub-Saharan moral principle that has been equated with Human Dignity. This section includes recent reflections on Human Dignity and Ubuntu in the early stages of the Covid-19 pandemic.

All the authors worked together as an international and interdisciplinary research group within the framework of the 2nd Intercontinental Academia of the UBIAS network (University-Based Institutes for Advanced Studies). This volume reflects their journey, their fruitful collaboration, and their scholarly endeavors. The result is a collection that serves as a fresh and exciting contribution to the contemporary Human Dignity discourse.

Acknowledgements

Ultimately, Phases 1, 2 and 3 of the 2nd Intercontinental Academia on Human Dignity were all successful examples of international academic cooperation, pushing the boundaries, academically and personally, of everyone involved. The Academia has been a truly unique endeavor which would not have been possible without the ongoing support of several institutes and their members. The 2nd Intercontinental Academia on Human Dignity was a joint initiative of the Israel Institute for Advanced Studies (IIAS) in Jerusalem and the Center for Interdisciplinary Research (Zentrum für interdisziplinäre Forschung, ZiF) in Bielefeld, under the rubric of the Intercontinental Academia program of the UBIAS network (network of University-Based Institutes for Advanced Study).

Thus, on behalf of the fellows of the 2nd Intercontinental Academia on Human Dignity, we would like to thank IIAS and IIAS' Directors Eliezer Rabinovici and Yitzhak Hen as well as Nadiv Mordechay, who worked as a project coordinator for our Phase 1 in Jerusalem, and IIAS' Administrative Director Iris Avivi, who did an amazing job coordinating the fellows and being available on the ground in Jerusalem. They all were essential to Phase 1 becoming such a huge success. Being part of the steering committee kicking off Phase 1 of the Academia, we thank Alon Harel, who also contributed a chapter to this book (see Chap. 4), Hannah Lerner, Benny Porat, and everyone else working at or being associated with IIAS who made this journey possible. We also thank IIAS and the IIAS Board of Directors for their contribution to Phase 3 of the Academia. Your ongoing support meant a lot to us. Regarding ZiF, our deepest thanks go to ZiF's Director Véronique Zanetti, for being such a huge part of our endeavor regarding Phase 3 of the Academia in South Africa. Thank you to ZiF's Managing Director Britta Padberg for doing everything in her power to make Phase 2 of the Academia in Bielefeld such a huge success, and all ZiF staff members for working similarly in this regard. Among them, we recognize Manuela Lenzen, who had also been part of Phase 1 of the Academia, and Marc Schalenberg, who took responsibility during our Phase 2 at ZiF and is a great singer. We thank the UBIAS network and especially, the (Chairman) Coordinator of

UBIAS' Guilherme Ari Plonski and the Institute for Advances Studies in São Paulo (IEA-USP) in Brazil. Guilherme Ari Plonski and the IEA-USP also supported Phase 3 of the Academia for which we are grateful. Regarding Phase 3 of the Academia, we thank JIAS and JIAS' Directors Peter Vale and Bongani Ngqulunga and all JIAS' staff members, especially Emelia Kamena, Reshmi Singh, and Christian, the photographer. On behalf of the fellows, we would also like to thank everyone who taught us about human dignity during the Academia as Marcus Düwell, Bernadette Brooten, Christine Hayes, Raya Morag, Aharon Barak, Michael Rosen, Ami Ayalon, Mordechai Kremnitzer, Bana Shoughry-Badarne, Sari Nusseibeh, Michael Karayanni, Menahem Ben-Sasson, Mayer Brezis, Gertrude Lübbe-Wolff, Ralf Poscher, Lynn Hunt, Anna Konik, Aleida Assmann, Sasha Stevenson, Mbongiseni Buthelezi, Shireen Motala, Eddie Webster, Johan Froneman, Maria Frahm-Arp, Barney Pityana, Rabbi Sa'ar Shanked, Moulana Ebrahim Bham, Fred Khumalo, Ismail Mohammed, Michelle Constance, Emilia Potenza, and Ian McKay.

The fruit of the 2nd Intercontinental Academia on Human Dignity is this book: "Probing Human Dignity: Exploring Thresholds from an Interdisciplinary Perspective". Thus, we would like to thank the authors featured in this book: Ralf Poscher, Alon Harel, Caterina Drigo, Michael Kolocek, Ulrike Davy, Sima Kramer, Marius von Staden, Connor M. Ewing, Caterina Preda, Ron Roth, Ernst J. Marais, Roxan Venter, Nontando M. Hadebe, and Ben Davy. The road to this book has neither been a fast nor an easy one. Thank you for taking all the time and bearing with us. Your contributions are very much valued. Ben Davy deserves a special thanks. Not only did he and Ulrike with their chapters do the greatest job in working with the format of this book, but after being part of Phase 3 of the Academia Ben also agreed to contribute to this book a chapter on COVID-19 (see Chap. 17). The Covid Pandemic impacted us a year after Phase 3 in South Africa and touched upon human dignity in a whole new way.

On behalf of the authors of this book who are hereby "Probing Human Dignity", we would like to thank Springer Nature, and namely Brigitte Reschke, Kay Stoll, Peter Pushpanathan, and Kali Gayathri, for emotional, technical, and personal support. Thank you for publishing this book. Your endless support and patience have been very much appreciated.

This we saved for last. The biggest thanks are due to Ulrike Davy and Michal Linial, who were the founders of the Academia and together served as the fellow's academic parents so to speak. Ulrike Davy, as Director of ZiF, came up with the idea of "Human Dignity" as the topic of the Academia, and Michael Linial, as Director of IIAS, seconded it immediately. Ulrike and Michal invested more than a year of planning to make their vision come true. Your vision has become a huge success for all of us, academically and personally. For this, we will be forever grateful.

New York City, NY, USA Stephanie N. Arel
Ramat Gan, Israel Levi Cooper
Bielefeld, Germany Vanessa Hellmann

Contents

Part I Introduction

1 **Learning from Dignity** 3
Vanessa Hellmann

Part II Solving Dignity: Solutions in Constitutional Law and Jewish Legal Thought

2 **A Sin for the Sake of Heaven: Vigilante Heroes in Law and Culture. An Old-New Paradigm** 23
Levi Cooper

3 **Human Dignity as Taboo: The Hidden Rationality Behind the Absolute Legal Prohibition of Torture** 49
Ralf Poscher

4 **Dignity-Enhancing Constitutionalism** 61
Alon Harel

Part III Fields of Dignity as Threshold Spaces

5 **Human Dignity, Poverty and Social Exclusion Challenges for Europe** 75
Caterina Drigo

6 **The Human Right to Housing Through the Lens of Human Dignity as Non-humiliation** 103
Michael Kolocek

7 **Asylum Seekers' Dignity: Elusive in Europe and Lost in Crisis. At the Threshold of Universality** 117
Ulrike Davy

8 Human Dignity and the Law of Work: Between Collectivism and Individualism 153
Sima Kramer

9 Human Dignity and Labor Protection in South Africa 167
Marius van Staden

10 Same-Sex Marriage: The Structural Articulation of "Equal Dignity" 183
Connor M. Ewing

Part IV Human Dignity and Trauma

11 The Role of Art in Restoring Human Dignity at the Threshold of Forgetting Traumatic Pasts 205
Caterina Preda

12 Shame, Trauma, and Guilt: Restoring Dignity Through Empathy 223
Stephanie N. Arel

13 Standing at the Threshold, Standing on the Edge: Intersections of Human Dignity and the Holocaust 241
Ron Roth

Part V Human Dignity and Ubuntu (Including Recent Reflections on COVID-19)

14 Human Dignity and Ubuntu in Eviction Law 263
E. J. Marais

15 Dignity, Freedom of Expression and the Battle over Hate Speech: A Case Study in Post-Apartheid South Africa 289
Roxan Venter

16 Reclaiming African Dignity through Ubuntu and Decolonization as Dangerous Memory 309
Nontando M. Hadebe

17 Gently, But Firmly: Human Dignity and Public Responses to COVID-19 321
Benjamin Davy

Contributors

Stephanie N. Arel Fordham University, New York City, NY, USA

Levi Cooper Bar-Ilan University, Ramat Gan, Israel

Benjamin Davy TU Dortmund University, Dortmund, Germany
University of Johannesburg, Johannesburg, South Africa

Ulrike Davy University of Bielefeld, Bielefeld, Germany
University of Johannesburg, Johannesburg, South Africa

Caterina Drigo University of Bologna, Bologna, Italy

Connor M. Ewing University of Toronto, Toronto, ON, Canada

Nontando M. Hadebe University of Free State, Johannesburg, South Africa

Alon Harel Hebrew University of Jerusalem, Jerusalem, Israel

Vanessa Hellmann University of Bielefeld, Bielefeld, Germany

Michael Kolocek ILS - Research Institute for Regional and Urban Development, Dortmund, Germany

Sima Kramer Jerusalem, Israel

Ernst J. Marais University of Johannesburg (and University of the Witwatersrand), Johannesburg, South Africa

Ralf Poscher Max Planck Institute for the Study of Crime, Security and Law, Freiburg, Germany

Caterina Preda University of Bucharest, Bucharest, Romania

Ron Roth Jerusalem, Israel

Marius van Staden University of the Witwatersrand, Johannesburg, South Africa

Roxan Venter University of Johannesburg, Johannesburg, South Africa

Part I
Introduction

Chapter 1
Learning from Dignity

Vanessa Hellmann

Abstract This first chapter serves as an introduction to the topic of human dignity. The chapter follows the endeavors of a group of scholars, including myself, within Phases 1, 2 and 3 of the 2nd Intercontinental Academia on Human Dignity under the rubric of the UBIAS network (network of the University-based Institutes for Advanced Study, http://www.ubias.net/about-the-institute). We produced this volume together as a product of those three phases, and this introduction offers insight into what we discussed during the Academia. We touched upon an enormous variety of aspects, spanning various academic fields such as Philosophy, Religion, Law, Jewish Legal Thought, History, Politics, and Art. This chapter highlights what we discussed, what we learned, and why this academia eventually went far beyond the scope of an academic exchange to become a deeply personal experience. Please note that within this introduction all discussions and events are conveyed by me as I personally recall them. Not everyone mentioned in this chapter was present for all discussions at all times. Additionally, almost all of the time there were additional people present who are not explicitly mentioned in this chapter. Thus, from consulting this introduction only there is no way of telling who has said what and who hasn't. This introduction is about what we learned. It is followed by 16 chapters fostering the academic dialogue we started as being part of this group.

1.1 Introduction

When we, as the fellows of the 2nd Intercontinental Academia on Human Dignity, first came together in Jerusalem, we didn't know each other. We were about 20 strangers from different countries with various academic and personal backgrounds. Originating from Canada, the United States, Brazil, South Africa, the United Kingdom, the Netherlands, Italy, Finland, Romania, Israel, and Germany, spanning eleven countries on four continents, we bring our various countries' backgrounds

V. Hellmann (✉)
University of Bielefeld, Bielefeld, Germany
e-mail: vhellmann@uni-bielefeld.de

S. N. Arel et al. (eds.), *Probing Human Dignity*,
https://doi.org/10.1007/978-3-031-42437-3_1

into conversation. The same breadth emerged from our academic backgrounds. Law, History, Politics, Art, Religion, Philosophy, Spatial Planning, and Anthropology, all featured in the course of our discussions, and, therefore, manifest in this book. We have shared that for each of us the Academia has been a unique endeavor, academically and personally. I share what we learned, not only from our sessions with various senior instructors at the Academia, but also from each other. We worked together; we laughed together, and we cried together, as much of we discussed touched the core of what it means to be human. What we learned deserves to be preserved, if only as I personally recall it. Knowing what we discussed is key to what this book is about, to what is the background for the 16 following chapters.

1.2 Phase 1: Jerusalem, Israel

After a yearlong preparation, the 2nd International Academia on Human Dignity started with Phase 1, hosted by the Israel Institute for Advanced Studies (IIAS) in Jerusalem. Michal Linial, Director of IIAS, and Ulrike Davy, former Director of ZiF, welcomed us to what has become an amazing journey. The two, Michal and Ulrike, gave us an inside on how Ulrike initiated the Academia almost three years before and on how Michal immediately seconded the idea, thus, the evolution of the Academia on Human Dignity and our work together.

1.2.1 Human Dignity: Concepts and Discourses

The first three days of Phase 1 of the Academia in Jerusalem were dedicated to an introduction to human dignity. Marcus Düwell, from Utrecht University, initiated the process by giving us an overview of the contemporary philosophical discourse on human dignity, its concepts and meanings. Following his presentation, we found ourselves in a heated discussion about human dignity as a philosophical and normative concept, as a value, a principle, a right, a source for human rights, and so on. Ambitiously, we immediately approached how to establish a universal definition of "human dignity", or even a definition we could all agree upon. Surprisingly, or perhaps not so surprisingly, we failed. Again and again, and only for the purpose of continuing with the program of the Academia, we agreed to disagree and proceed. We initially intended to circle back to this topic, after we learned more. Indeed, we did circle back briefly to this discussion in Phase 2 of the Academia in Bielefeld and failed again. Finally, we decided to circle back again, but we never did. Thus, agreeing to disagree is what we still do on the matter of a universal definition of "human dignity". As it turned out eventually, the journey was the reward, and the more we learned about "human dignity" the clearer it became that there would never be such a definition.

1.2.2 *Human Dignity, Human Rights and Future Generations*

Our next sessions with Marcus explored the connection between human dignity and human rights. We learned about human dignity as a source for human rights in discussions where moral, legal, and political considerations interconnected. First, we delved into the writings of Immanuel Kant, his "Metaphysics of Morals" and his "categorical imperative" including its interpretation in legal spheres. We examined Kant's understanding of human dignity as it is connected to the rational capacity of human beings and their status as "autonomous beings". Additionally, we learned about Alan Gewirth and his "Principle of Generic Consistency", where human dignity also serves as a foundation for human rights and where human beings are viewed as "autonomous agents". Finally, we discussed a topic which came into view only years later when a young woman we hadn't heard about then refused to go to school on a Monday starting a movement protesting for the rights of future generations on Fridays. "Fridays for Future" had yet to be when we talked about the rights of future generations and on how these rights are connected to human dignity. Among the questions we addressed were justifications for caring about the rights of future generations, the connection between sustainability and human rights, the so called "non-identity problem", the "right to be born", and the idea of "inter-generation rights protection".

1.2.3 *Slavery, Religion and Women's Dignity*

Bernadette Brooten, a Theologian from Brandeis University, followed as an instructor, bringing religion into the discourse. She captivated us with working on ancient text exegeses, something most of the fellows had never done before. The first topic we probed was "Human Dignity and Slavery", where Bernadette took us on a tour through various religious texts, ancient and more recent ones. We read and compared those texts from various angles and discussed questions as to what being a slave means for husbands and wives, for children and parents, for Jews and Non-Jews, for Christians and Non-Christians, and for men and women. Eventually, Bernadette made us aware that ancient religious texts provided a theological justification for slavery for centuries and that, in *Rerum Novarum*, the position of the Roman Catholic Church suddenly changed. Tending to "Slavery, Religion and Women's Dignity", we continued our endeavor with Bernadette and looked, among other things, at the influence of slavery on marriage as an institution, and at the role of women in marriage in Christianity, Islam, and Judaism. Most of us were surprised that questions of slavery as questions of property (law) could be considered by consulting the Bible. Personally, I had never consulted the Bible in order to work on a legal question before. Questions we explored consulting the Bible included the role of men giving their wife and children into slavery and/or being allowed (by law) to give themselves into slavery.

1.2.4 Jewish Sources and Jewish Thought

Another session with Bernadette Brooten focused on the use of human dignity in contemporary Jewish Law (Halakha). In this regard, we learned about a Rabbinical Responsa regarding homosexuality and the use of "kvod habriot" (the dignity of created beings) as an interpretative instrument in coping with the biblical prohibition of homosexual relations. There was a fine line of differentiation regarding homosexual love between men and between women. A mixture of modern religious language, a commitment to ancient traditional sources, and different motivations rooted in modern humanistic values lead to homosexuality's between men and/or women being forbidden, depending on the text. Thus, we also learned about the importance of the use of language—and religious language in particular—in the reconstruction of reality itself, which to me—as a lecturer and teacher in law—seemed to be rather familiar, as law is very much about the use of language in (re-) constructing the reality we live in, as social beings.

Next, Christine Hayes from Yale University taught us about canonical sources of Jewish law and Jewish thought (Bible, Mishnah, and Talmud) attempting to trace the theological foundations of the "idea" of human dignity. She led us through topics such as the divine source of dignity, dignity and the image of God vis a vis dignity and autonomy, dignity and its connectedness to body integrity, and the ways in which persons are stripped from their dignity or excluded from being the owners of such dignity. Questions of restoring dignity after such exclusion are expanded in this book. Both Caterina Preda, in "The Role of Art in Restoring Human Dignity at the Threshold of Forgetting Traumatic Pasts" (Chap. 11) and Stephanie Arel, in "Shame, Trauma, and Guilt: Restoring Dignity through Empathy" (Chap. 12), consider how dignity remains in the aftermath of tragedy and how it can be recovered, or reinhabited.

1.2.5 Human Rights in Israeli Cinematography

In between Bernadette's sessions, Raya Morag from Hebrew University introduced us to the "Representation of Human Rights in Israeli Cinematography during the Intifada". We watched and discussed several scenes from different movies related to this topic. One movie caught our attention: a movie about women serving in the Israeli military. In Israel, military service is mandatory for a certain time for both men and women. The movie displayed women commissioned to the so-called "territories", where Palestinian Arabs live and where they encountered situations where they had to handle dead bodies. Not only the women who were present and had served in the military were deeply touched but everyone was. Eventually, someone made a lengthy comment regarding "necessities", which caused everyone who was present and had served in the military to indicate that especially someone who didn't serve shouldn't form an "easy" opinion.

1.2.6 Human Dignity: The Constitutional Value and the Constitutional Right

Two of our sessions were led by Aharon Barak, former president of the Supreme Court of Israel. Based on his well-known book on human dignity "Human Dignity: The Constitutional Value and the Constitutional Right" we first discussed human dignity as a constitutional value, while emphasizing its normative role. In this regard, human dignity presented itself as a factor that ensures the normative unity of human rights, which is expressed in different ways: first, as a normative basis for constitutional rights in the constitution; second, as an interpretative principle for determining the scope of constitutional rights, including the right to human dignity, and third, as having an important function in determining the proportionality of a statute limiting a constitutional right. To better clarify the status and scope of human dignity as a constitutional right, the next session delved into Aharon Barak's general theory of constitutional rights and the key concept of proportionality.

1.2.7 Human Dignity, Its History and Meaning

Following a "Socratic" approach towards progress of thought, Michael Rosen from Harvard University presented us with several provocative assumptions we heatedly discussed such as: human dignity is humbug; human dignity relies on a notion of universality that renders the concept meaningless; human dignity relies on an "inner transcendental kernel" although there is no such kernel; and human dignity serves as a Trojan horse for inequality, for attacks on liberty and autonomy, human dignity implies a license for undermining democracy. Within the following session, we learned about what Michael called "politics of dignity". Arguing against conceptions of politics proposed by John Rawls (requiring just institutions but no virtuous individuals) and Marxism (requiring total dedication to the cause as an externally given good), he stressed that a whole range of emotions was an intrinsic part of politics. Additionally, Michael introduced us to the "Montgomery bus boycott" as a questions of dignity. According to Michael, the bus boycott was not just about inequality in material terms, but also about rejecting disrespect (and claiming dignity) on a symbolic level through collective action. The slogan was "We rather walk the streets in dignity than ride the bus in humiliation". The Montgomery bus boycott draws, according to Michael, attention to the link between dignity and demeanor.

1.2.8 National Security, Torture, and a Two-State Solution

Michael Rosen's account was followed by a talk with Admiral Ami Ayalon, the former head of Israel's Security Agency "Shin Bet". Admiral Ayalon had been the first head of Shin Bet who had openly admitted the use of torture as a means against terrorism. Within our session, Admiral Ayalon spoke about how his own stance on torture had wavered over time. Afterwards, we discussed his journey to become a strong supporter of a two-state solution between Israelis and Palestinians.

Balancing the (evolving) right to dignity with national security in Israel also lay at the heart of a presentation by Mordechai Kremnitzer from Hebrew University of Jerusalem. We learned again that in Israel torture is an accepted means to an elimination of terrorist threats. Mentioning, in contrast, that in Germany there is an absolute ban of torture, emphasized by the German Federal Constitutional Court, led to a heated debate, which resulted in everyone feeling like a "villain", a villain who was accepting torture in specific circumstances as opposed to a villain who was objecting to torture no matter the excruciating circumstances. An absolute ban on torture was considered by some to be something one could only think of in a country which had never experienced major terrorist threats on their own soil, a sign of western arrogance where the dignity (of the perpetrators) was put above the life of innocents. Questions which arose from this discussion are reflected upon in two chapters of this book. Levi Cooper discusses the issue in "A Sin for the Sake of Heaven: Vigilante Heroes in Law and Culture. An Old-New Paradigm" (in Chap. 2), and Ralf Poscher reflects upon it in "Human Dignity as Taboo, The Hidden Rationality behind the Absolute Legal Prohibition of Torture" (in Chap. 3).

Mordechai Kremnitzer and Bana Shoughry-Badarne, a human rights advocate from Israel, introduced us to a judgement of the Israeli High Court of Justice (HCJ 5100/94 Public Committee Against Torture in Israel et al. v. The State of Israel et al. Judgment, 1999) where the HCJ had found the Israel Security Agency (ISA) was not to be authorized to employ physical means of pressure during an interrogation of a person suspected of violent activity against the state. Additionally, Bana Shoughry-Badarne got deeper into what it could mean to employ physical means of pressure during an interrogation of a person, such as having to sit on a chair in an uncomfortable position during an interrogation. While someone remarked on the knowledge of what torture could mean not being necessary when we would talk in legal and normative terms, there was a strong reminder that at any time it is not wise to only talk in legal and normative terms. Personal impact carries weight: For instance, some present for this session thought about their own children sitting on a chair taking the discussion to heart; and in the following very quiet and considerate discussion eventually some tears were involved.

The future for Palestinian-Arabs and Israelis was also discussed with Sari Nusseibeh, former President of Al-Quds University. Sari Nusseibeh had worked closely with Arafat at one point and gave an impressive historical account of Palestinian-Arabs and Israelis living on one soil. As it happens, Sari Nusseibeh's family has for centuries been the keeper of the key to the Church of the Holy Sepulchre, which is one of Christianity's holiest sites. Supposedly, the Church contains both the site where Jesus was crucified and the location of Jesus's empty tomb where he was buried and resurrected. The keys to this church are being held by a Muslim family because the various dominations of Christianity presented at the Holy Sepulchre wanted someone neutral to open the doors. The Nusseibeh family has done so ever since, although Sari Nusseibeh let us know that actually a cousin of his currently holds the key; he himself has never seen it. During our session with Sari Nusseibeh, some voiced their fear that there is no hope for a future resolution of the conflict between Palestinians and Israelis, and tears were shed again.

Another session by Mordechai Kremnitzer and Michael Karayanni from Hebrew University concerned the dignity of groups and individuals related to the status of Palestinian-Arabs under Israel's Constitutional Definition as a "Jewish and Democratic" State. This session, too, offered deep insight into the situation of Palestinian-Arabs, their role, and their rights.

Finally, fellow Akemi Kamimura from Sao Paulo University picked up on the topic of torture and gave a presentation on "Human (In)dignity in Brazil: Torture and the Situation of Persons Deprived of Liberty", where she drew a dark picture of the situation of persons imprisoned in Brazil.

1.2.9 Human Dignity and Medicine, the Constitutional Charter of Rights

As a former member of the Knesset and Chairman of the Constitution, Law and Justice Committee Menahem Ben-Sasson, who also served as President of Hebrew University of Jerusalem, gave us a first-hand account of his work on "The Constitutional Charter of Rights, the Article on Override and Human Dignity - A Testimony". Phase 1 of the 2nd Intercontinental Academia on Human Dignity concluded with a session on "Challenges to Human Dignity in Health Care" again with Mordechai Kremnitzer, this time together with Mayer Brezis from Hebrew University. The session culminated in an emotional discussion of "Human dignity and Assisted Suicide".

1.2.10 Excursions, Human Dignity Related Sites

Our academic program in Israel was accompanied by several excursions, always with amazing food. On our first day, we toured Jerusalem where we were instructed to pay attention to our surroundings while visiting the Old City. Near the Damascus Gate several incidents involving knife stabbings had recently occurred resulting in injuries to both Palestinians and Israelis. We also learned that the Gaza Strip is fully administered by Palestinian Authority but only parts of the West Bank (including East Jerusalem) are. Indeed, the 1995 Oslo II Accord had established the administrative division of the West Bank into areas A, B, and C as a transitional arrangement. While Area A is administered by Palestinian Authority, Area C is administered by Israel, and Area B is under joint administration. When we left Jerusalem to visit other sights like the Death Sea and the fort of Masada, we came across several barriers and check points where our identification was checked. As we learned, the barriers were initially meant to serve as a temporary security measure at a time of heightened tensions between Israelis and Palestinians and looming terrorist threats. The walls we encountered seemed rather permanent. Visiting the Supreme Court of Israel, we learned more about Israel's Constitution and the status of Palestinians under Israeli Law.

A visit to Yad Vashem was what shook us all to the core. The unspeakable horror of the Holocaust brought us to tears, the Righteous Among the Nations, and shoes, hundreds of shoes and personal items on display representing the millions of items and lives which were taken. Human dignity and the Holocaust lie at the heart of Chap. 13 of this book, where Ron Roth writes about "Standing at the Threshold, Standing on the Edge: Intersections of Human Dignity and the Holocaust". On a personal note, during Phase 1 of the Academia in Jerusalem, several of us, including myself, celebrated Shabbat with a fellow's family. This was the first celebration of Shabbat in my life. It was a sweet and unique experience, and an invitation my grandparents certainly wouldn't have thought possible.

1.3 Phase 2: Bielefeld, Germany

When meeting again for Phase 2 of the 2nd Intercontinental Academia in Bielefeld, Germany, the fellows knew each other, personally and academically, and for everyone it felt like reuniting with their (academic) family. Everyone was thrilled to spend more time together and get to work on "Human Dignity" again. During our time in Jerusalem most of the Israeli fellows stated they wouldn't come to Germany. In the end, almost everyone came.

1.3.1 Human Dignity and the German Constitution

Phase 2 of the Academia opened with a session composed by Gertrude Lübbe-Wolff, former Justice of the German Federal Constitutional Court. Gertrude elaborated on the "untouchability" of human dignity as stated in the German constitution's dignity clause and as interpreted by the German Federal Constitutional Court. The discussion focused on the so called "object-formula" used by the Constitutional Court and on what it means to treat another human being as a "mere object". The topic continued our discussion of torture and the German Aviator Case, touched upon during Phase 1 of the Academia. As mentioned, both topics are also featured in Chap. 2 of this book (written by Levi Cooper) and Chap. 3 (written by Ralf Poscher). Another round of discussion evolved addressing specific restrictions to the freedom of speech in Germany, namely, that the denial of the fact that the Holocaust took place, which in Germany is punishable under criminal law, and whether such a restriction could be justified by giving recourse to human dignity. Freedom of speech/expression is also featured in Chap. 15 of this book, where Roxan Venter writes about "Dignity, Freedom of Expression and the Battle over Hate Speech: A Case Study in Post-Apartheid South Africa".

In a session with Ralf Poscher from Max Planck Institute for the Study of Crime, Security and Law in Germany, we expanded our discussion on the concept of human dignity as put forward by the German Federal Constitutional Court and as presented by German constitutional scholars. In this regard, Ralf put forward two fundamental assumptions; first, that human dignity in the German constitution functions as a narrow principle safeguarding the status of being human (the case of torture can serve as a paradigm example for a violation), and second, that human dignity as a basic feature of mankind cannot be taken away or somehow diminished yet can be disrespected or not sufficiently protected. These assumptions were followed by a heated discussion, where at some point Ralf was surprised to learn that torture is something some of the fellows in their respective countries would not be discussing as an absolute "taboo" (see already above). Ralf's findings on "Human Dignity as Taboo: The Hidden Rationality behind the Absolute Legal Prohibition of Torture" are featured in Chap. 3 of this book. Similar questions are addressed by Levi Cooper with a chapter on "A Sin for the Sake of Heaven: Vigilante Heroes in Law and Culture. An Old-New Paradigm" (Chap. 2).

1.3.2 A History of Human Dignity and Human Rights

Several sessions with Lynn Hunt from the University of California, Los Angeles, addressed why the history of human dignity/human rights matters. According to Lynn, the eighteenth century had been a crucial time for the emergence of human rights. The period generated new cultural attitudes that fostered a new conceptualization of personhood. The new conceptualization of personhood—based on the (equal) moral worth inherent in all human beings—preceded legislation that eventually abolished torture and slavery (for torture and slavery also see already above). Lynn's final session was dedicated to discussing several questions: Is the very idea of seeking universal principles a Western imposition? Is human dignity a notion that is more acceptable across cultures than human rights? What does dignity mean as opposed to the meaning of other terms such as "rights", "honor", or "human image"? How come that certain terms become popular at some point in history, and how does the meaning of those terms change? How is human dignity related to autonomy and equality? On the constitutional protection of rights and human dignity not merely as a right also see Chap. 4 of this book, where Alon Harel writes about "Dignity-Enhancing Constitutionalism".

1.3.3 Human Dignity, Art and Immigration

During Phase 2 of the Academia in Bielefeld video artist Anna Konik introduced us to her new video installation, starting off her exhibition at the ZiF. Under the title "In the same city, under the same sky – interviews with immigrants," the exhibition pointed to the situation of female migrants in various European countries. Her work had already been exhibited in several museums for contemporary art and in the Swedish parliament. The installation raises questions related to "who counts as human?", "whose lives count as lives?", or "what makes a life full of grief?". Together with Anna Konik and Lynn Hunt, the fellows engaged in a discussion on the effects of presenting stories that were first told by refugee woman and then re-told by local women—the idea underpinning Anna's installation. Among other things, Anna explores how the creation and bridging of distance affects the refugee women, the women re-telling the stories, the people listening to the stories, and society at large.

1.3.4 Probing Human Dignity: Fellows Input

In Phase 2 of the Academia in Bielefeld the fellows also gave several presentations themselves. Emily Kidd White presented on the role of human dignity in comparative human rights law, focusing on the role of dignity as a value under the Canadian Charter of Rights and Freedoms. Sima Kramer presented a case where the Knesset sanctioned the privatization of prisons, a legislation eventually declared unconstitutional by the Israeli Supreme Court. The Court held that the transfer of authority with respect to taking peoples' liberty and holding them in prison was in fact a violation of human dignity. Akemi Kamimura and I presented several cases either decided by the German Federal Constitution Court or the Inter-American Court of Human Rights dealing with the conditions prevailing in prison facilities and the treatment of prisoners (or as Akemi would state: "persons deprived of liberty" for Akemi's findings on the treatment of persons deprived of liberty in Brazil also see already above, Phase 1). Guy Carmi presented a critical view of human dignity and the implications of its widespread constitutional use, especially in Israeli Constitutional Law. The concern expressed by Guy related to human dignity as being exploited for not enhancing human rights but rather for curtailing and undermining them, a risky potential mainly for the freedom of speech. Thus, Guy's presentation followed up on our previous discussion with Gertrude Lübbe-Wolff (see above). As we learned over the course of the Academia, freedom of speech is by far Guy's favorite topic of expertise. Johannes Eichenhofer introduced another topic to us when presenting on the relationship between "human dignity and privacy".

Ulrike Davy, not a fellow but one of the founders of the 2nd Intercontinental Academia on Human Dignity, gave a presentation on the rights and protections provided to asylum seekers under German law and raised the question of whether differential treatment permitted under this regime violated the German dignity clause. Asylum Seekers' Dignity is also featured in Ulrike's chapter in this book: "Asylum Seekers' Dignity: Elusive in Europe and Lost in Crisis. At the Threshold of Universality" (Chap. 7). Caterina Drigo presented on social rights under the Italian Constitution, focusing on the rights to social assistance, health, and housing. Caterina's research is featured in Chap. 5 of this book: "Human Dignity, Poverty and Social Exclusion Challenges for Europe". Michael Kolocek introduced a discussion on the right to adequate housing as established by the Universal Declaration of Human Rights. Michael's findings are featured in Chap. 6 of this book: "The Human Right to Housing Through the Lens of Human Dignity as Non-Humiliation".

Lauren Ware's presentation concentrated on if and why "negative" or "painful" emotions (in particular, fear and suffering) play a role when a situation is assessed from the perspective of human dignity. Emotional suffering also lies at the heart of Stephanie Arel's contribution to this book: "Shame, Trauma, and Guilt: Restoring Dignity through Empathy" (Chap. 12). Through an exploration of visual images, Levi Cooper discussed Napoleonic artwork portraying Freedom of Worship, particularly as it applied to Jews. Methodologically, Levi argued for interrogating visual representations when researching legal history and the history of human rights. Sini Kangas' presentation concentrated on special forms of medieval personal rights, addressing the legal status of non-combatants in medieval Christian holy war. Funlola Olojede discussed domestic violence and "wife-battering" as a common practice, even though denied in many cultures, drawing on findings from sociopsychology. Funlola contrasted such practice with readings found in the Old Testament, where, she asserted, "wife-battering" did not appear, and thus, she concluded was not a norm in Biblical culture. The ensuing conversation among the fellows explored the cultural embeddedness of wrongful treatment of women. Following up on this discussion, Akemi Kamimura introduced the topic of "female genital mutilation" as a point of discussion.

Ron Roth sketched a preliminary genealogy of the notion of human dignity in Israeli law from the foundation of the state of Israel until the present day. Ron concentrated on the role of human dignity in Israeli Holocaust discourse and suggested a conceptual differentiation between "dignity"-discourse and "honor"-

discourse. The role of human dignity in Israeli holocaust discourse is also featured in Ron's chapter in this book: "Standing at the Threshold, Standing on the Edge: Intersections of Human Dignity and the Holocaust" (Chap. 13), as was already mentioned. Finally, Stephanie Arel presented different disciplinary perspectives on trauma, its various manifestations, and the structure of the traumatic experience. Stephanie examined the far-reaching consequences of irresponsiveness or delayed response to trauma, the shame that may overwhelm survivors of trauma, and the different modalities of attending to the shattered selves and fragmentary accounts of traumatized victims. As mentioned, Stephanie's work on "Shame, Trauma, and Guilt: Restoring Dignity through Empathy" is featured in Chap. 12 of this book.

1.3.5 *Empathy, Shakespeare's Anthropology and a "Culture of Remembrance"*

Our final sessions in Bielefeld were headed by Aleida Assmann from Konstanz University. Aleida also spoke about empathy (like Stephanie Arel, see above) and the way it has interweaved in different fields and disciplines, spanning the humanities and neurobiology, and reaching from the social sciences to works of art. During her presentation, Aleida differentiated between empathy and other related concepts such as sympathy, pity, compassion, identification, and projection. We discussed the different meanings related to the term and its spectrum of possibilities, and the various levels and stages of emphatic engagement. In her next session, Aleida presented on William Shakespeare's liminal anthropology through a reading of key moments in his plays. She introduced Shakespeare's new articulation of human dignity, shifting its sense as a royal status to a more precarious sense intimately related to human vulnerability, which involves responsiveness and a confirmation of human solidarity. Eventually, this led to a lively discussion on the different roles played by the arts in forerunning and fostering human dignity.

Next, Aleida conducted a session on the "Culture of Remembrance – the German Model" where she gave a chronological account of the social frameworks for collective memory after 1945. While in the first two decades after World War II people in many countries (including Germany and Israel) had embraced a culture of forgetting in order to make room for a brighter future, attitudes and frameworks changed in the late 1960s. According to Aleida, the Eichmann trial opened the door to an "identification mode" (a period when attention turned to the witnesses and the victims of the Holocaust), which was followed by an "ethical mode" (a period stressing the responsibility of the perpetrators) and finalized in an "empathy mode" (a period when suffering was conceived of as a universal predicament accessible through empathy). Both Stephanie's chapter (Chap. 12) focuses on "empathy" and "Restoring Dignity through Empathy" and Caterina Preda's chapter (Chap. 11) trace the restauration of human dignity by asking about "The Role of Art in Restoring Human Dignity at the Threshold of Forgetting Traumatic Pasts". As another part of the "Culture of Remembrance", Aleida's next session focused on what Aleida called "Counter Monuments". Among others, we reflected on the "Memorial to a Memorial" by Horst Hoheisel and Andreas Knitz, where a memorial plate at Buchenwald now serves as a reminder for the 50th anniversary of the liberation of Buchenwald. This session ended with a walk through Bielefeld that traced the local cultures of remembrance, in particular the memorial in front of the main railway station and the "stumbling stones" (Stolpersteine, see below) one can now find in many cities in Germany. For her research on a "Culture of Remembrance," Aleida has won several prestigious awards, including the German Peace Award.

Aleida's last day of sessions began with watching and discussing the documentary "Football under cover", directed by Ayat Najafi and Aleida's son David Assmann. The documentary covers the first and (so far) only meeting of two women soccer teams, one from Berlin and one from Tehran. It touches upon several questions we debated throughout the Academia, one being how human dignity when tightly linked to honor can be questioned and undermined by asserting "dignity" through acts of self-determination or autonomy: "I do what I want even in the face of guards demanding decent behavior in the name of dignity" is one of the key statements by a young Iranian soccer player who was eventually not allowed to take part in the tournament. Finally, Aleida turned our attention to what she called a "spectral turn", a turn in the perception of gross violations of human dignity introduced by "Aftermath Studies". "Aftermath Studies" reflect, for instance, on practices ensuring that human remains found in mass graves many decades after the killings eventually receive a proper burial. These practices may be interpreted as acts aimed at restoring the human dignity of the dead. The aforementioned Stolpersteine (stumbling stones), where people put those "stumbling stones" in front of places where Jewish people had lived, stating their day of birth, day of death and the place and cause of their death, also matches this aim, as the ritual of placing these "stumbling stones" at particular spots in sidewalks brings something from the past to rest in the present.

1.3.6 Extracurricular Activities

Throughout the two weeks of Phase 2 of the Academia, the fellows also embarked on several extracurricular activities, "fluidly" getting to the core of German cultural heritage. The fellows spent the beginning of shabbat together and among other things visited various sites in Berlin and other sites of Germany, including the Buchenwald Memorial.

1.4 Phase 3: Johannesburg, South Africa

Following the success of our meetings in Jerusalem (Phase 1) and Bielefeld (Phase 2), the Johannesburg Institute for Advanced Study (JIAS) with former director Peter Vale extended an invitation to host an additional meeting in Johannesburg, South Africa. Up to this point, our group had already done extensive work on a book project based on Phases 1 and 2 which, after incorporating Phase 3, eventually became the book you are reading right now: "Probing Human Dignity: Exploring Thresholds from an Interdisciplinary Perspective", generously published by Springer Nature and for which we are truly grateful (for a complete thank you see the preface). Phase 3 in Johannesburg provided a unique opportunity to further our book project by discussing the future book chapters among the fellows, while deepening academic our exchange, expanding our horizons and adding another continent to the endeavor. For this purpose, in Johannesburg, the fellows of the first two phases of the Academia were joined by five additional fellows from South Africa, bringing new backgrounds and perspectives to the table. After a warm welcome by JIAS Director Bongani Ngqulunga, each day of Phase 3 of the Academia at JIAS was spent with renown scholars discussing different aspects of Human Dignity considering South Africa's unique history and challenges.

1.4.1 The Negotiation of Human Dignity

The first two days of Phase 3 of the Academia were dedicated to "The Negotiation of Human Dignity" finding common ground in understanding the principle, the value, the right of human dignity, this time with a special focus on the South African scholarly perspective. Ernst Marais from Johannesburg University started out with a presentation on "Human dignity in the post-apartheid eviction context". Ernst's findings in this respect are also featured in Chap. 14 of this book: "Human Dignity and Ubuntu in Eviction Law". Additionally, Marius van Staden from Johannesburg University presented on "The importance of the dignity jurisprudence to Social Protection law". Marius' research is featured in Chap. 9 of this book: "Human Dignity and Labor Protection in South Africa". Mispa Roux from Johannesburg University gave an impressive account on "Restoring the dignity of victims of gross human rights violations through international criminal justice". Roxan Venter, also from Johannesburg University, concluded with a presentation on "Dignity, freedom of expression and democracy: the significance of constitutional values in the South African democratic system". Roxan's findings are featured in Chap. 15 of this book: "Dignity, Freedom of Expression and the Battle over Hate Speech: A Case Study in Post-Apartheid South Africa".

1.4.2 The Struggle for Basic Needs and Rights, Transformative Justice

Another session was dedicated to the "The Struggle for Basic Needs and Rights" in South Africa with presentations by Sasha Stevenson, Head of the Section27 Health Rights Program, on "Health", by Mbongiseni Buthelezi, Director of the Public Affairs Research Institute and Associate Professor of Anthropology and Development Studies at the University of Johannesburg, on "Land and Governance", by Shireen Motala, Professor for Education at Johannesburg University, on "Education in South Africa" and finally, Eddie Webster, Professor at the Southern Centre for Inequality Studies at the University of the Witwatersrand, on "Poverty". Fellows Michael Kolocek and Caterina Drigo added to the discussion with presentations on "Human Dignity and the Human Right to Housing" (Michael) and "Human Dignity and Poverty in Europe" (Caterina). Caterina's findings are featured in Chap. 5 of this book: "Human Dignity, Poverty and Social Exclusion", Michael's conclusions can be found in Chap. 6 of this book: "The Human Right to Housing through the Lens of Human Dignity as Non-Humiliation". In this respect, we will forever be grateful to Michael for introducing the so called "World Happiness Report" to us, which by merely existing (and watching Michael making a speech about it) made us happy. A fond memory for all of us. "Transformative Justice" was a topic of another session, following a judicial but also philosophical strategy for peacemaking after the end of the Apartheid's regime with its inherited conflicts. Among others, Johan Froneman, Justice at the South African Constitutional Court, took it upon him to steer us through the depth of this topic.

1.4.3 Religion and Remembrance, Creativity and Re-Creation

The next sessions were dedicated to "Religion and Remembrance" with presentations by scholars from different religious backgrounds, and to "Creativity and Re-Creation", with presentations by South African artists, writers, and scholars. Nontando Hadebe from St. Augustine College, Johannesburg introduced the topic of "Religion and Remembrance". Her research is featured in Chap. 16 of this book: "Reclaiming African Dignity through Ubuntu and Decolonization as Dangerous Memory". In addition, Maria Frahm-Arp from Johannesburg University presented upon "Pentecostal Charismatic Churches in South Africa" and Barney Pityana spoke from the viewpoint of a human rights lawyer and theologian from the University of South Africa. Rabbi Sa'ar Shanked, Rabbi of the Beit Emanuel Progressive Synagogue in Parktown, Johannesburg, and Moulana Ebrahim Bham, a South African scholar for education, development, advocacy and interfaith, also presented against the background of their unique work experiences. Among the artists, writers, and other scholars who introduced us to the topic of "Creativity and Re-Creation" were Fred Khumalo, Ismail Mohammed, and Michelle Constance. As an award-winning writer and journalist, Fred Khumalo gave a presentation about South African literature and its development over time. Ismail Mohammed, an accomplished playwright, theatre director, and multi-award-winning arts administrator, spoke about arts, culture, and theatre in South Africa. Michelle Constance spoke as the outgoing CEO of Business and Arts South Africa (NPC) giving a fascinating account of the development of the arts scene in South Africa. The topic of "Arts and Dignity" was completed by fellow Caterina Preda from Bucharest University who presented her research findings on "Art and Remembrance", which are featured in Chap. 11 of this book as "The Role of Art in Restoring Human Dignity at the Threshold of Forgetting Traumatic Pasts".

1.4.4 Probing Human Dignity, Furthering our Book Project

During the course of the conference the fellows held several group discussions where they illustrated their prospective contributions to this book. After the new fellows from South Africa presented on their topics which are part of this book, Levi Cooper spoke about human dignity's dilemma where violations of human dignity awarded to a greater good are still violations of human dignity (see Chap. 2: "A Sin for the Sake of Heaven: Vigilante Heroes in Law and Culture. An Old-New Paradigm"). Caterina Drigo taught us about "Human Dignity, Poverty and Social Exclusion" in Europe (see Chap. 5), and Michael Kolocek elaborated on the "The Human Right to Housing" as "Non-Humiliation" (see Chap. 6). Ulrike Davy, one of the founders of the 2nd Intercontinental Academia on Human Dignity, spoke about "Asylum Seekers' Dignity" in Europe" (see Chap. 7), while Sima Kramer elaborated on "Human Dignity and the Law of Work: Between Collectivism and Individualism" (see Chap. 8). Connor M. Ewing introduced us to a decision of the United States Supreme Court regarding same-sex couples and their right to marry, connected to "Equal Dignity" (see Chap. 10). Finally, Caterina Preda and Stephanie N. Arel presented on "Restoring Human Dignity". While Caterina focused on "The Role of Art in Restoring Human Dignity" after dictatorships, especially in Chile's and Romania's past (see Chap. 11), Stephanie elaborated on "Restoring Dignity through Empathy" drawing a connection between "Shame, Trauma, and Guilt" (see Chap. 12).

1.4.5 Human Dignity Related Sites

Complementing our lively academic discourse, we visited several important human dignity-related sites in Johannesburg and the region. First, we went to see Constitutional Hill, which is an area where the Constitutional Court of South Africa is located, visiting the Old Fort Prison complex as well. Within the Prison complex, inmates were held under excruciating circumstances, among them political activists opposing apartheid and striking mine workers. Inmates were separated by skin color, black inmates being treated worse than white ones. There also was a special "Gaol" for women. Known prisoners were Nelson Mandela and Mahatma Gandhi. The Constitutional Court of South Africa in 2004. Its building incorporates bricks and other parts of the former prison, serving as a reminder of how South Africa has overcome the horrors of its past. Outside the court's building one can also visit the "Flame of Democracy" which is an eternal flame lit in the middle of the plaza built into one of the stairwells of the old prison. Visiting parts of the prison, we found an inscription over one of the doorways: "A nation should not be judged by how it treats its highest citizens, but its lowest ones." This struck us as something which relates to a dignified treatment of all human beings, and as something by which not only a nation must be measured.

Further, we drove to Soweto, a township of the City of Johannesburg, which is particularly famous for its resistance during Apartheid. The "Mandela House", where Nelson Mandela lived from 1946 to 1962, is situated in Soweto. The house is now a museum, and you can still see bullet holes and scorch marks from attacks with Molotov cocktails at its façade. We also visited the Apartheid Museum in Johannesburg where an exhibition shows the unbearable pains and horrors imposed by the Apartheid regime, starting with entry tickets that randomly qualify the visitor as "white" or "non-white" and which determine the entrance one may use. Emilia Potenza, the curator at the Museum, gave us a powerful introduction to the museum. Outside of Johannesburg, we visited the Sterkfontein Caves, which are a set of limestone caves of special interest in paleoanthropology. The area in which the caves are located is known as the "Cradle of Humankind", where the beginning of human life on earth supposedly started. Ian McKay from the University of the Witwatersrand took us on a tour there, eventually having all of us crawling on our knees.

The 2nd Intercontinental Academia on Human Dignity has been a unique experience, academically and personally. For that, I will be forever grateful.

For a list of contributors, including the fellows and the full program see: https://scholars.huji.ac.il/iahd. There you may also find a description of our journey including many pictures.

Part II
Solving Dignity: Solutions in Constitutional Law and Jewish Legal Thought

Chapter 2
A Sin for the Sake of Heaven: Vigilante Heroes in Law and Culture. An Old-New Paradigm

Levi Cooper

Abstract A new vista for considering human dignity infringements that claim to be justified is introduced by drawing on a fringe concept in Jewish legal thought. To this end, two German cases are recounted. First, I consider the torture of Gäfgen, orchestrated by deputy police chief Daschner, to reveal the whereabouts of an abductee. Second, I explore the decision to strike the clause in the Luftsicherheitsgesetz (Aviation Security Act) that permitted shooting down airplanes in 9/11 situations. Antinomian critiques of these cases are spotlighted. Aspects of the reactions to the real German cases are compared to vigilante heroes in popular culture, such as Dirty Harry, Batman, Captain America, and *24*'s Jack Bauer. These characters evoke conflicting emotions: human dignity breaches should not be sanctioned, yet audiences want the hero to succeed. Tacitly their actions are approved, though they act outside the law. These cases—real and imagined—are refracted through the prism of "a sin for its own sake" (Hebrew: *aveira lishmah*). According to this notion, a person might be enjoined to commit a crime but is still liable for punishment. This concept is unlike justifications or excuses in criminal law, where the person who commits the act avoids sanction; "righteous transgression" carries the brunt of the legal system. This concept captures the dissonance

This chapter was inspired by the UBIAS Intercontinental Academia on Human Dignity. Research for the chapter was conducted while I had the pleasure and privilege of being a Kreitman Postdoctoral Fellow in Ben-Gurion University of the Negev, Israel. The research was supported in part by the Ludmer International Project on the Jewish Heritage of Galicia and Bukovina at the University of Haifa, Israel and the Jewish Galicia and Bukovina Organization; and in part by a grant from the Israel Science Foundation (no. 672/19) led by Professor Yair Lorberbaum. I had a number of opportunities to present my research and receive valuable and constructive feedback: Buchmann Faculty of Law at Tel Aviv University, Faculty of Law at Hebrew University of Jerusalem, Pardes Institute of Jewish Studies, and Johannesburg Institute of Advanced Studies. I appreciate the feedback and suggestions I received in these forums, and in particular the sage counsel and insightful comments from Arye Edrei, Alon Harel, Ralf Poscher, Shaul Stampfer, and Shira Weiss, and my dear colleagues and mentors of the UBIAS Intercontinental Academia on Human Dignity.

L. Cooper (✉)
Bar-Ilan University, Ramat Gan, Israel
e-mail: Levi.Cooper@biu.ac.il

S. N. Arel et al. (eds.), *Probing Human Dignity*,
https://doi.org/10.1007/978-3-031-42437-3_2

many feel as they personally and perhaps secretly cheer while institutionally they recoil from the vigilante's abuse of human dignity. This interdisciplinary study concludes by considering whether a legal system could use a version of this Jewish law rubric when adjudicating real human dignity cases.

2.1 Introduction

Legal systems that give primacy to human dignity choose between two models. In one model, human dignity is non-derogable; it is an absolute right that is independent of context or circumstance. This is the model enshrined since the 1950s in the European Convention on Human Rights. A similar approach is evident in Germany's constitution, where human dignity is declared *unantastbar*—untouchable and inviolable. In an alternative model, human dignity is a prime but relative value, subject to balancing against other values. This is the model adopted in Israeli law (*Public Committee against Torture v. Prime Minister* 1999).[1]

The two models may provide different legal responses to difficult human dignity cases. For example, cases where authorities consider using torture to extract time-sensitive information; that is, the ticking time-bomb scenario.[2] The untouchable model will immediately disqualify torture on the grounds that it violates human dignity; no consideration will be given to the circumstances or context. In this vein, Article 3 of the Convention for the Protection of Human Rights and Fundamental Freedoms declares:

> **Prohibition of torture**
> No one shall be subjected to torture or to inhuman or degrading treatment or punishment.

This directive has been understood as an absolute right. In contrast, the relative model weighs the particulars of the situation, balancing competing values, before passing judgment as to whether to allow human dignity violations.[3]

Each model (and their various permutations) presents knotty challenges for law-in-action, for the protection of human dignity, and for society at large. Much effort has been invested in comparing, contrasting, and refining the models, and this chapter does not seek to rehash the existing scholarly work. Rather, my aim is to introduce a new paradigm for considering cases like torture to extract time-sensitive

[1] The ruling generated much discussion; see, for example, Rabin and Meydani (2016).

[2] Jeremy Bentham is acknowledged as the first to describe the ticking time-bomb scenario, particularly his unpublished 1804 essay Means of extraction for extraordinary occasions (Davies 2012; Clemens 2017).

[3] Admittedly, it is far from clear that torture is an effective means for extracting information (Schiemann 2016). I acknowledge this important caveat but will set it aside for the purposes of the foregoing discussion.

information. I will discuss real court cases, popular culture, visceral reactions, and a fringe concept in Jewish legal thought known as *aveira lishmah*, possibly translated as "a sin for its own sake." This tapestry of disciplines suggests a new threshold for the contemporary human dignity discourse.

The first part of this study recounts two cases that reached the courts, noting an undercurrent of dissatisfaction with the judgements. The second part links that undercurrent to the vigilante hero movie genre and popular culture. The third part introduces a prism that has yet to be considered in the human dignity discourse: "a sin for its own sake." Despite the allure of this rubric, part four questions whether modern legal systems would find it difficult to adopt a version of the "sin for its own sake" mechanism. Notwithstanding, the rubric furthers our understanding of deep-seated, instinctual responses to some of the most difficult human dignity cases and may even provide direction for courts adjudicating such cases.

2.2 Court Cases

2.2.1 Luftsicherheitsgesetz (2005–2006)

The coordinated terrorist attacks on the United States that occurred on Tuesday morning, September 11, 2001—"9/11"—was a watershed moment in many fields: law, politics, aviation, defense, travel, and more. The attacks involved hijacking passenger airliners and crashing them into significant structures. Two of the hijacked planes were crashed into the North and South Towers of the World Trade Center complex in New York City, and a third plane was crashed into the Pentagon. A fourth plane was steered towards Washington, D.C. but crashed in a field in Pennsylvania after crew and passengers tried to seize control from the hijackers (*The 9/11 Commission Report* 2004).

9/11 was the most fatal airline hijacking in history. Soon after the tragedy, the method of weaponizing a passenger plane was copied, though not with the same destructive results. In January 2002, 15-year-old Charles J. Bishop stole a single-engine Cessna and crashed it into the 28th floor of the 42-story Bank of America building in Tampa, Florida. Bishop was the only fatality. The official report noted Bishop's intention to commit suicide, though his suicide note linked his actions to 9/11 (*National Transportation Safety* 2002).[4]

[4]The suicide note was released a month later: "I have prepared this statement in regards to the acts I am about to commit. First of all, Osama bin Laden is absolutely justified in the terror he has caused on 9-11. He has brought a mighty nation to its knees! God blesses him and the others who helped make September 11th happen. The U.S. will have to face the consequences for its horrific actions against the Palestinian people and Iraqis by its allegiance with the monstrous Israelis--who want nothing short of world domination! You will pay--God help you--and I will make you pay! There will be more coming! Al Qaeda and other organizations have met with me several times to discuss the option of me joining. I didn't. This is an operation done by me only. I had no other help,

A year later, in January 2003, Germany had to deal with the possibility of a 9/11 scenario when Franz Stephan Strambach, a 31-year-old psychology student at the Technical University of Darmstadt, stole a small aircraft in Hessen and threatened to crash it into the European Central Bank in Frankfurt. After causing widespread panic, Strambach landed without any casualties.[5]

9/11 and the copycat incidents raised the question of how to deal with weaponized airplanes carrying innocent civilian passengers. In the aftermath of 9/11, the rules of engagement in the US were reportedly updated (though not published). In October 2003, news outlets reported that US fighter pilots had been training to take down commercial airliners in the event of a 9/11 replay (Schmitt 2003; *US pilots train shooting civilian planes* 2003).

In response to the possibility of 9/11 scenarios, Germany legislated a new aviation security act, the *Luftsicherheitsgesetz*, that went into force in January 2005.[6] Section 14 of the law dealt with a passenger airline turned into a lethal weapon. In the event that a passenger airplane had been hijacked and was now threatening the lives of people who were not on the plane—as in the 9/11 cases—and there was no other viable option, the new law permitted the Bundeswehr (Federal Defense Forces of Germany) to use armed force to neutralize the threat. Thus, the law provided for shooting down the plane, even though this action entailed killing the innocent passengers on board the airplane.

In early 2006, the Bundesverfassungsgericht (Federal Constitutional Court of Germany) declared that this clause was unconstitutional. According to the Court, shooting down a plane in a scenario like this would degrade the passengers who were not perpetrators to the status of an object. As such, downing the plane while objectifying a human being would violate the passengers' inalienable human dignity. In the words of the Court:

> Such a treatment ignores the status of the persons affected as subjects endowed with dignity and inalienable rights. By their killing being used as a means to save others, they are treated as objects and at the same time deprived of their rights; with their lives being disposed of unilaterally by the state, the persons on board the aircraft, who, as victims, are themselves in need of protection, are denied the value which is due to a human being for his or her own sake.[7]

To be sure, such a human dignity infringement would benefit another group: the intended targets of the hijackers. Yet according to German law, human dignity is a right that is untouchable and hence not subject to balancing. There is no room to weigh the lives of the passengers against the lives of the impending victims. The

although, I am acting on their behalf. Osama bin Laden is planning on blowing up the Super Bowl with an antiquated nuclear bomb left over from the 1967 Israeli-Syrian war."

[5]Before landing, Strambach claimed he was trying to draw attention to Judith Resnik, one of the astronauts killed in 1986 when the US space shuttle Challenger exploded. According to Strambach, Resnik was not given appropriate attention probably because she was the first Jewish astronaut (Questions Abound After Wild Ride for Love of Dead Jewish Astronaut 2003).

[6]Bundesgesetzblatt Jahrgang 2005 Teil 1 Nr. 3:83–84 (14 January 2005). English translation: https://germanlawarchive.iuscomp.org/?p=735. Accessed 4 July 2023.

[7]BVerfG, 15.02.2006 - 1 BvR 357/05. http://www.bverfg.de/e/rs20060215_1bvr035705.html. Accessed 4 July 2023.

Court therefore ruled that the law's provision was void (Lepsius 2006).[8] Thus in a 9/11 scenario in Germany, the weaponized passenger airliner would not be shot down in order to preserve the human dignity of the passengers, echoing the Latin maxim: *Fiat justitia et pereat mundus*, let justice be done though the world perishes.

The Court's decision generated judicial, popular, and academic discussion.[9] One controversial point of interest was the response of the then German Minister of Defense, Franz Josef Jung—a lawyer by training—who forthrightly declared that despite the Court's decision, if faced with a 9/11 scenario he would give the order to shoot down the rogue plane. It was also reported that Jung's predecessor, Peter Struck, had taken a similar stance, adding that he would resign immediately after issuing the order (*Breach of Constitution* 2007; Krumrey and Wiegold 2007). Even more surprising was the comment by Dieter Hömig, the very judge who had written the opinion on behalf of the Court, at an event outside the court. Hömig expressed the hope that in such an emergency someone would shoot down the plane and then bear the burden of the legal offense (Janisch 2016).

How should we understand such antinomian—perhaps bold, perhaps brazen—statements? What lies at the root of this strand of critique? Before addressing this question, I turn to a second case.

2.2.2 *Gäfgen (2002–2012)*

In 2002, a 27-year-old law student at Goethe University in Frankfurt, Magnus Gäfgen, abducted and ransomed 11-year-old Jakob von Metzler, the son of a Frankfurt banking family. Gäfgen was arrested after he collected the ransom money but did not reveal the location of the boy. The police believed that young Metzler's life was in imminent danger, with perhaps only hours to live. Gäfgen was in custody, but he was refusing to reveal the whereabouts of the boy. With the clock

[8] Court's decision translated into English: www.bverfg.de/e/rs20060215_1bvr035705en.html; English press release: http://www.bundesverfassungsgericht.de/SharedDocs/Pressemitteilungen/EN/2006/bvg06-011.html; amended German law: https://www.gesetze-im-internet.de/luftsig/index.html. Accessed 4 July 2023.

[9] On the judicial front: the first decision was handed down by the First Senate of the Constitutional Court (BVerfG, 15.02.2006 - 1 BvR 357/05). In another case that reached the court, the Second Senate of the Constitutional Court intended to differ from the First Senate's decision. When one Senate intends to diverge from the decision of another Senate, a plenum of all justices is called upon to decide on the issues in question as outlined by the Senate intending to diverge. In this case, the plenum answered the questions posed by the Second Senate accordingly to the ruling of the First Senate (BVerfG, 3.7.2012 - 2 PBvU 1/11. http://www.bverfg.de/e/up20120703_2pbvu000111.html. Accessed 4 July 2023). Thus, the Second Senate was bound to follow this ruling when ruling on the case before it (BVerfG, 20.3.2013 - 2 BvF 1/05. http://www.bverfg.de/e/fs20130320_2bvf000105.html. Accessed 4 July 2023). English Press release regarding the Second Senate's decision: https://www.bundesverfassungsgericht.de/SharedDocs/Pressemitteilungen/EN/2013/bvg13-027.html; Plenary decision translated into English: https://www.bundesverfassungsgericht.de/SharedDocs/Entscheidungen/EN/2012/07/up20120703_2pbvu000111en.html. Accessed 4 July 2023.

ticking on the boy's life, deputy chief of the Frankfurt police Wolfgang Daschner ordered a subordinate to threaten Gäfgen with torture. The interrogator told Gäfgen that he would be subject to unimaginable pain, that a specialist in interrogation was on his way to interview Gäfgen, that this specialist would inflict more pain than Gäfgen had ever experienced, and that Gäfgen would be raped by fellow prisoners. It was then that Gäfgen confessed and revealed the location of the boy. Jakob von Metzler was found. Sadly, he had already been murdered at the time of Gäfgen's interrogation.

In July 2003, Gäfgen was tried for murder in the Hessen state court. Since Gäfgen's confession had been obtained under illegal duress—that is, the threat of torture—the Court declared the confession inadmissible. During the trial, Gäfgen confessed again, after being notified by the Court that his original confession was inadmissible. The Court allowed evidence that had been procured as a result of the initial confession under duress—Metzler's body, tire tracks, and footprints where the body had been dumped—to support details provided during the second confession. The Court convicted Gäfgen of murder but was critical of the psychological torture employed by the police.[10]

Gäfgen's appeal to the Federal Court of Justice was rejected in May 2004.[11] Then in December 2004, Germany's Federal Constitutional Court refused to examine the case.[12]

Once evidence of the torture came to light, detective Ortwin Ennigkeit and the aforementioned Daschner were temporarily suspended. In December 2004, a Frankfurt court found the two policemen guilty of misconduct. In addition to the criminal conviction which entailed a fine and probation, the policemen were also dismissed from their posts as an administrative measure. The policemen were not, however, given prison sentences (*Police Chief Fined in Torture Case* 2004).[13]

Gäfgen then sued the State of Hessen for damages on account of the torture. Before the case was decided, in June 2005 Gäfgen turned to the European Court of Human Rights (ECtHR) in Strasbourg and filed a complaint against Germany on two grounds relating to the threat of torture: German police had violated his right to a fair trial, and they had impinged on his human dignity. In April 2007, the ECtHR agreed to hear the case. It was first decided in June 2008, and then at Gäfgen's request referred to the Grand Chamber of the ECtHR where the final decision was handed down in June 2010.[14]

---

[10]LG Frankfurt am Main, 28.07.2003 - 5/22 Ks 2/03 3490 Js 230118/02. https://openjur.de/u/168232.html. Accessed 4 July 2023.

[11]BGH, 21.05.2004 - 2 StR 35/04. https://www.hrr-strafrecht.de/hrr/2/04/2-35-04.php. Accessed 4 July 2023. Press release: http://juris.bundesgerichtshof.de/cgi-bin/rechtsprechung/document.py?Gericht=bgh&Art=pm&nr=29251. Accessed 4 July 2023.

[12]BVerfG, 14.12.2004 - 2 BvR 1249/04. http://www.bverfg.de/e/rk20041214_2bvr124904.html. Accessed 4 July 2023. Press release: https://www.bverfg.de/pressemitteilungen/bvg04-114.html. Accessed 4 July 2023.

[13]LG Frankfurt am Main, 20.12.2004 - 5/27 KLs 7570 Js 203814/03 (4/04).

[14]Gäfgen v. Germany. 2008. no. 22978/05, ECHR, 30.06.2008. http://hudoc.echr.coe.int/eng?i=001-87305. Accessed 4 July 2023. Gäfgen v. Germany [GC]. 2010. no. 22978/05, ECHR, 01.06.2010. http://hudoc.echr.coe.int/eng?i=001-99015. Accessed 4 July 2023.

The ECtHR found that German police violated Article 3 of the European Convention on Human Rights. According to the Court, torture can never be justified—even in a ticking time-bomb scenario. Since torture violates human dignity, it is not subject to cost-benefit analysis, nor can it be weighed against other interests such as saving the life of another person. In the words of the Court:

> Torture, inhuman or degrading treatment cannot be inflicted even in circumstances where the life of an individual is at risk.[15]

As far as Gäfgen's claim regarding the right to a fair trial, the Court ruled that unlike human dignity (Article 3 of Convention), the right to a fair trial (Article 6) was not absolute. As the German Constitutional Court had already pointed out, Gäfgen had been convicted on the basis of his subsequent confession, not on the basis of his confession under duress. Thus, the threat of torture and the breach of Article 3, had no bearing on Gäfgen's conviction. Notwithstanding, the Court was critical of the penalties imposed by the German courts on the police—an issue which was not on trial. Thus, the Gäfgen conviction stood, despite the human dignity violation which—in the eyes of the Court—had not been sufficiently dealt with.

Subsequent attempts by Gäfgen to reopen proceedings in German courts were unsuccessful[16]. However, after lengthy proceedings, Gäfgen succeeded in suing the State of Hessen for civil damages on the grounds of the human dignity infringement, and in 2011, the Court awarded him 3000€.[17]

The *Gäfgen* case, like the 2006 *Luftsicherheitsgesetz* decision, triggered much discussion in popular media and in scholarly circles. The conduct of Daschner—the Frankfurt deputy police chief who had given the instruction to threaten Gäfgen with torture—came under particular scrutiny.

During the interrogation, Daschner never sought to conceal his conduct: in a memorandum in the police file, he noted that Gäfgen would be interrogated with the threat of pain, and he notified the public prosecutor of his actions. It later came to light that Daschner had spoken to Norbert Nedela, head of the Hessen Landeskriminalamt (LKA; State Criminal Police Office), who had told him to "show the instruments" to the suspect. On trial, Daschner had testified that he saw the situation as a ticking time-bomb, and that he was driven by a desire and responsibility to save Jakob von Metzler, who he believed was drawing his last breaths.

Despite the rulings in Germany and in Strasbourg, the head of the Gewerkschaft der Polizei (GdP; Trade Union of the Police), issued a statement declaring that the decision should not deter police from using intensive interrogation methods, stopping short of torture (Witthaut 2011). The statement was widely reported in the press (e.g., Connor 2011; *Mörder Gäfgen wird entschädigt* 2011). While the union boss

---

[15] Gäfgen v. Germany [GC]. 2010, § 107.

[16] LG Darmstadt, 09.11.2011 - 1032 Js 60705/10. OLG Frankfurt, 29.06.2012 - 1 Ws 3/12.

[17] LG Frankfurt am Main, 04.08.2011 - Az. 2-04 O 521/05. http://openjur.de/u/168419.html. Accessed 4 July 2023.

was defending the actions of one of his constituents, the statement also had a prospective angle: in the future, police people were encouraged by their union boss to skirt the law. How should we understand the antinomian angle of the statement? Moreover, what was at the root of the forbearing attitude of the German Court in handing down lenient sentences for the convicted torturers?

2.3 Vigilante Heroes

The ethical dilemmas and legal conundrums posed by the *Luftsicherheitsgesetz* decision and the *Gäfgen* case are not confined to courtrooms or scholarly debates. The issues raised by these cases permeate popular culture, where the emotional response to ticking time-bomb scenarios is intuitive: everything must be done to save the victim. The antinomian strands of critique in the two cases tap into this visceral reaction.

When discussing pop culture, I am not just referring to the numerous German television productions that used the *Gäfgen* case as a template. These productions have not been screened with translation or subtitles and are not widely available.[18] Other German productions had a broader reach. Thus, the interactive production entitled *Terror: Ihr Urteil*, presented a German 9/11 scenario before inviting the audience to act as the jury tasked with determining guilt. The audience's verdict would determine which of two endings would be presented. The production was subsequently translated into a host of languages and has been performed in theatres around the world. While there is room for critique (Lübbe-Wolff 2017), the play's popularity and findings tap into the gut reaction I have described. According to the official website, 92% of audience-jurors exonerated the pilot who shot down the hijacked plane with its passengers in order to prevent the plane from crashing into a packed soccer stadium.[19]

Yet the cultural phenomenon of going outside the law to save others is more pervasive than the templates of the two German cases. On the silver screen, the

[18] A crime drama entitled *Eine Frage des Gewissens*, directed by Thomas Bohn, was screened on Arbeitsgemeinschaft der öffentlich-rechtlichen Rundfunkanstalten der Bundesrepublik Deutschland (ARD) in March 2006. A month later, in April 2006, the fourth episode of the crime series *Kommissarin Lucas*, entitled *Das Verhör*, was screened on Zweite Deutsche Fernsehen (ZDF). In December 2008, a documentary entitled *Jakob von Metzler: Tod eines Bankiersohns*, directed by Philipp Engel, was screened as part of *Die großen Kriminalfälle* series (season 7, episode 1). In 2012, a feature film entitled *Der Fall Jakob von Metzler*, written by Jochen Bitzer and directed by Stephan Wagner, was screened on ZDF.

[19] Adapted from a play by Ferdinand von Schirach, the television version was first screened on the German ARD network in 2016. As of June 27, 2023, the official website lists 2786 "trials" in 120 theatres in 31 countries since October 3, 2015. Of 580,272 "jurors," 63.6% of jurors voted not guilty, while 92.5% of audiences returned not guilty verdicts. The raw data invites further research, with the possibility of examining trends over time, according to country, with reference to local and global events, and considering prevailing law. See https://terror.theater. Accessed 4 July 2023.

conundrum is dramatized through the popular cinematic genre of the vigilante hero, as the following examples demonstrate.[20]

2.3.1 *Dirty Harry (1971)*

In 1971, actor Clint Eastwood starred in the title role of rogue police inspector Harry Callahan of the San Francisco Police Department. There is surprising overlap between some of the salient details of *Dirty Harry* and the tragic, real-life murder of Jakob von Metzler.[21]

"Dirty" Harry Callahan tracks the killer known as Scorpio (Andy Robinson) to a stadium where he shoots him in the leg. Fearing for the life of a girl abducted by Scorpio, Callahan tortures the wounded Scorpio, demanding to know where the girl is being held. Scorpio whimpers in pain: "I want a lawyer. ... I have the right for one. ... I have the right for a lawyer! ... I have rights. I want a lawyer." Callahan does not relent, and Scorpio reveals the location. Alas, the girl is found to be dead already. Because Callahan violated Scorpio's rights, he is released from custody. Callahan is disgusted.

In the final scene, Callahan and Scorpio face off, with Scorpio holding a boy at gunpoint. Callahan shoots Scorpio in the shoulder. With his gun aimed at Scorpio, Callahan goads him to reach for his gun, at which point Callahan kills Scorpio. In the film's denouement, Callahan takes out his police badge and throws it into the water before walking away.

Dirty Harry was a commercial success: it was followed by four sequels and other "loose-cannon" police films.[22] In the contemporary American context, *Dirty Harry* tapped into debates over police enforcement and suspects' rights. Early on in the film, a doctor attending a wound on Callahan's leg dismisses Callahan's medical directions ("Just a little tweezers and mercurochrome") by nonchalantly retorting: "Do I come down to the station and tell you how to beat a confession out of a prisoner?" Despite box office success, major reviewing organs were critical of Callahan's violent vigilantism (Kael 1972, 1974; Smith 1993, pp. 90–107).

---

[20] For definitions of vigilantism, see Johnston (1996) and Dumsday (2009).

[21] The link between *Dirty Harry* and *Gäfgen* has already been noted in Poscher (2004, 2006); see also Stümke (2011). *Dirty Harry* drew on an actual case known as the Zodiac Killer, see Graysmith (1986), pp. 179–180; Adams (2005), p. 277.

[22] *Dirty Harry* sequels: *Magnum Force* (1973), *The Enforcer* (1976), *Sudden Impact* (1983), *The Dead Pool* (1988). The first film provided an iconic line that is still quoted today: "I know what you're thinking: 'Did he fire six shots or only five?' Well, to tell you the truth, in all this excitement, I've kinda lost track myself. But being this is a .44 Magnum, the most powerful handgun in the world, and would blow your head clean off, you've got to ask yourself one question: 'Do I feel lucky?' Well, do you, punk?" In 2012, under the US National Film Preservation Act, *Dirty Harry* was selected by the Librarian of Congress for preservation in the National Film Registry (Cannady 2012; Barnes 2012).

Alongside its contemporary American relevance, the issues raised by the film have a timeless quality. Similar debates—in the public square and in academia—arose with the screening of the popular television series *24* (2001–2010, 2014). The series ran for nine seasons and focused on the intrepid Jack Bauer (Kiefer Sutherland) as the protector of the home front in America's global war on terrorism. *24* took the genre of the ticking time-bomb thriller to a new level by using real-time narration mode. The mode was emphasized by the ticking clock that appeared before and after each advertisement, and the title card "events occur in real time" used in the opening sequence of many episodes (Mayer 2007; Lithwick 2008).[23]

24 is just one example of the ubiquitous popularity of the vigilante hero genre, of which *Dirty Harry* can be seen as the paragon. Indeed, 5 years after *Dirty Harry*, on the eve of the release of the third film in the series, Eastwood explained the attraction of his character:

> Nobody does what Harry does. He cuts right down through the bull, tells his boss to shove it, does all the things people would like to do in real life, but can't. . . . Harry thought that if a homicidal maniac could be sent back into the streets because of a technicality, there was something wrong with the law (Flatley 1976).

The "technicality" Eastwood mentions is the law aimed at protecting the rights of the accused. Indeed, the District Attorney (Josef Sommer) reminds Callahan of two landmark US cases that established those rights: *Escobedo* which recognized the right to counsel during interrogation and *Miranda* which required that defendants be made aware of their rights, otherwise statements during interrogation are inadmissible (*Escobedo v. Illinois* 1964; *Miranda v. Arizona* 1966).

At first blush, Callahan's attitude and conduct appear to be an iteration of a recognized Hollywood tropes that were particularly prevalent in "Spaghetti" Westerns in which Eastwood first achieved fame: irreverence and disdain for authority, impotence of law enforcement agencies, and vigilante justice bordering on anarchy. One of the *Dirty Harry* co-writers, John Milius, reflected the blurring of roles when he pointed to "[t]he cop being the same as the killer except he has a badge" (Thompson 1976, p. 12).[24] But *Dirty Harry* goes deeper by tapping into the ticking time-bomb scenario and then having the policeman do what people want to do but they can't because of the constraints of law. Indeed, 1970s San Francisco was not America's Wild West.[25]

Returning for a moment to the film's denouement: *Dirty Harry*'s powerful final sequence recalls the last scene of the 1952 Western, *High Noon*. Callahan holds his police badge, feeling it with his fingers and meditating on it, before tossing it into the sump. In *High Noon*, the town's marshal (Gary Cooper) throws his badge down and

---

[23]For scholarly work on the blurring of the fictional *24* with American legal reality see, inter alia, Kamin (2007), Keslowitz (2008), Van Veeren (2009), Manderson (2011), and Carodine (2011). See also the words of Justice Antonin Scalia cited below.

[24]Eastwood himself would return to explore this tension in *Unforgiven*, his acclaimed 1992 revisionist Western. See Cullen (2013), pp. 17–52; cf. Smith (1993), pp. 263–268.

[25]On the San Francisco context of *Dirty Harry*, see Street (2012).

then rides off with his newly married wife (Grace Kelly), leaving the law's violence behind as he starts his life anew with his partner who is a devout Quaker committed to non-violence.[26] Callahan, however, does not eschew violence; he expresses his disgust for the legal system that he serves, and he realizes that his conduct is unbecoming of an officer of the law. The *Dirty Harry* sequels ensure that we know that Callahan remains within the system. Thus, *Dirty Harry* brings the issue of vigilantism in a democracy into sharp relief, raising the end-justifies-the-means specter.[27]

While there is overlap in the factual patterns of the *Gäfgen* case and the *Dirty Harry* film, the role of the vigilante hero is perhaps best exemplified by comic superheroes that have been celebrated in pop cinema. Two examples—DC Comics' *Batman* and Marvel Comics' *Captain America*—illustrate the trend.

2.3.2 *Batman (2005–2012)*

Since 1939, Batman has been both hero and scourge of Gotham City. He repeatedly battles treacherous villains bent on destroying the city, skirting calls to bring him under police jurisdiction. Batman continues to save Gotham from criminals, though he is perennially hounded as a criminal. Batman is not just a vigilante; he is an outlaw, albeit a revered outlaw. Recent incarnations of the *Batman* franchise—in particular Christopher Nolan's *The Dark Knight Trilogy* (2005–2012)—have brought this aspect to the fore in telling moments.[28]

The first part of the reboot, *Batman Begins* (2005), recounts how Bruce Wayne (Christian Bale) becomes Batman, and this tale turns on the definition of vigilantism. Wayne refuses to join The League of Shadows, accusing them of being vigilantes.[29] Wayne ostensibly chooses a different path, though Gotham's Mayor hardly sees the difference: "No one takes the law into their own hands in my city."

In part two, *The Dark Knight* (2008), Alfred Pennyworth (Michael Caine) tells Wayne that he must not give in to the Joker's demand to remove his mask. Alfred is aware of Batman's place in society: "They'll hate you for it, but that's the point of Batman. He can be the outcast. He can make the choice that no one else can make." Alfred pauses before adding: "The right choice."

---

[26]Regarding the tossing of the badge, see Siegel (1993), pp. 366–367, 375; Eliot (2009), p. 138; cf. Smith (1993), p. 90 calls this "a rather ambiguous gesture." The badge tossing sequence has been used in other films, including *Point Break* (1991), *Shaft* (2000), and *The Dark Knight Rises* (2012).

[27]Burt Lancaster apparently turned down the lead role because he was troubled by the moral of the story; see Buford (2000), p. 269.

[28]Kerstein (2008), p. 138 insightfully identified Batman as "a Clint Eastwood-style vigilante," before cogently arguing for the contemporary relevance of Nolan's rendition.

[29]Originally known as *The League of Assassins* in DC Comics, adapted works renamed the organisation *The League of Shadows* or *Society of Shadows*.

What Alfred sees as the right choice is viewed differently by District Attorney Harvey Dent (Aaron Eckhart) and Police Lieutenant Jim Gordon (Gary Oldman). At a press conference, Dent hears the clamoring that Batman is nothing more than a vigilante. Dent acknowledges the calls: "The Batman is an outlaw," and follows this up with the voice of idealism: "One day, the Batman will have to answer for the laws he's broken."

Complementing Dent's exuberant idealism, Gordon offers the sober voice of law enforcement. He is well-aware of the impossible place of the vigilante superhero in a moral society, saying that Batman is at once "a silent guardian, a watchful protector," but nonetheless, "He's not a hero." When Gordon's son sees Batman flee, he asks, "Why is he running, Dad?" Gordon's answer is insightful: "Because we have to chase him." The film ends with the police launching a manhunt for the fugitive Batman, as Gordon destroys the Bat-signal renouncing his link to the vigilante, perhaps with a heavy heart. It is Gordon's moral integrity that makes him rise above other Gotham City officials, and it is the same virtue that brings him to quietly condemn Batman.

In the final instalment, *The Dark Knight Rises* (2012), Gordon defends his relationship with Batman: "There's a point far out there, when the structures fail you. When the rules aren't weapons anymore, they're shackles, letting the bad guy get ahead . . . One day, you may face such a moment of crisis. And in that moment, I hope you have a friend like I did! To plunge their hands into the filth, so that you can keep yours clean!" John Blake (Joseph Gordon-Levitt), a rookie police officer promoted to detective, is unconvinced as he responds with disgust: "Your hands look plenty filthy to me, Commissioner." Blake represents the voice of the younger Gordon, untainted by steely reality.

In many ways the true hero of Nolan's trilogy is the unflappable Gordon, who is rewarded by successive promotions: Gordon begins the trilogy as a sergeant and is promoted to lieutenant, before being appointed Police Commissioner. Yet Gordon hardly speaks to a broad-cross section of millennial society: no one rushes to the cinema for the next instalment to see what happens to Gordon; no one dresses up as the Police Commissioner.

Writing in *The Wall Street Journal* in 2008, American author Andrew Klavan praised Nolan's iteration of *Batman* as

> a paean of praise to the fortitude and moral courage that has been shown by George W. Bush in this time of terror and war. Like W, Batman is vilified and despised for confronting terrorists in the only terms they understand. Like W, Batman sometimes has to push the boundaries of civil rights to deal with an emergency, certain that he will re-establish those boundaries when the emergency is past (Klavan 2008).[30]

Not all critics subscribed to Klavan's reading of *The Dark Knight*, nor to his assessment of the then-president (Orr 2008). Notwithstanding, Klavan's words are a telling expression of one strand of instinctive response. To be sure, Batman's allure is not his criminality or his antinomianism; rather, people rally around the Caped

[30] See also Smith (1993), pp. 192–194; Wilson (2014).

Crusader *despite* the fact that he breaks the law. It would seem that people innately identify with Batman's moral compass. Gordon is clear: Batman is not our hero; most Batman fans would disagree.

2.3.3 Captain America (2011–2016)

Another reincarnated superhero also foregrounds vigilantism. Following *Captain America: The First Avenger* (2011) and *Captain America: The Winter Soldier* (2014), the following chapter—*Captain America: Civil War* (2016)—addresses America's sense of responsibility for world order, and the idea of United Nations oversight. The plot does not explore the issue with any depth, and the message is clear throughout the film.

The movie pits Captain America/Steve Rogers (Chris Evans) against Iron Man/ Tony Stark (Robert Downey Jr.). Iron Man accepts the idea of UN oversight for The Avengers, because he is cognizant of his own frailty and past errors. Captain America opposes the idea; he is confident in his own judgment of right and wrong, and he is skeptical that a government agency can provide untainted, efficient, and effective oversight. Once the fault line has been determined, there is no room for speculating about the outcome: it is clear that the all-American hero will be justified by the film's conclusion.[31]

America ratifies the accords bringing The Avengers under UN control, and Rogers goes rogue apparently knowing that it is up to him to save the world. One of The Avengers aligned with Stark—War Machine/James Rhodes (Don Cheadle)—calmly issues a line that reflects how incongruous the situation has become: "Congratulations Cap, you're a criminal."

The all-American fighter offers no protest; indeed, he has gone outside the law. Captain America accepts the assertion, seemingly confident that the choice to go outside the law is the correct course. By the film's ending, Stark has realized that Rogers is right. The audience leaves the experience safe in the knowledge that America—Captain and country—will do all that is necessary to protect the world: even if this requires temporarily going outside the law, and certainly not letting an impotent and befouled UN call the shots.

The vigilante who violates human dignity can never be endorsed, yet Dirty Harry, Jack Bauer, and Batman are portrayed as heroes. Viewers want them to succeed, perhaps even seeing them as morally obligated to break the law. Tacitly, the public approves of the vigilante: actions figures and children's costumes, as well as box-office-hit sequels, all celebrate the vigilante. While we may hail vigilantes, the Rule of Law dictates that they must bear the consequences of their decisions to act outside

[31] A similar theme is explored in Miller (1986)—a four-part comic book series—though the juxtaposition of two independent superheros, Batman and Superman, makes the outcome less predictable.

of the law: In *Gäfgen,* the police officer was disciplined; Callahan is never promoted; Batman must continue to live a double life, hiding his existence even from those dear to him, and Captain America is truly a criminal.

The sympathy—perhaps even affinity—for vigilante heroes on the silver screen and in the play *Terror: Ihr Urteil* dovetails with the reaction to the police conduct in *Gäfgen*: The Frankfurt deputy police chief was filling the role of Batman, not of Commissioner Gordon.

2.4 A Sin for Its Own Sake

2.4.1 Talmudic Concept and Its Development

Jewish legal thought has a rubric that can serve as a template for understanding the situations—real and imagined—and reactions that have been considered up to this point, bringing together the trends highlighted thus far and contributing to the discourse.[32] The category is described by the Hebrew term *aveira lishmah*, translatable as "a sin for its own sake." This is a cryptic expression, since it appears in a positive sense but does not spell out what is laudable about committing a sin for the sake of the sin. The Hebrew term has therefore been alternatively rendered as a sin for the sake of Heaven, a sin for the sake of God, holy sin, righteous or idealistic transgression—each term reflecting the paradoxical nature of an act that is both forbidden and applauded.[33]

The term *aveira lishmah* was coined in the *Babylonian Talmud*—the monumental repository of discussion and debate about matters of Jewish law and lore. The exchanges in the Talmud date from the destruction of the Second Temple in the first century until the Muslim conquest at the beginning of the seventh century (Stemberger 1996, pp. 190–224).

The term is seldom invoked, generally appearing in reference to troubling biblical episodes where a sin committed is deemed meritorious. Lauding crime is philosophically and legally problematic. In religious legal systems like Jewish law, applauding sin is also theologically perplexing. Moreover, holy sin blurs the distinction between good and bad, righteous and evil, thereby disrupting social order and flummoxing the quest for meaningful existence. Yet from the perspective of Jewish tradition, this category cannot be dismissed out of hand, since it is mentioned in the Talmud.

---

[32] I am not outlining the approach of Jewish law to ticking time-bomb dilemmas, 9/11 scenarios, or torture; for such an analysis see Bleich (2006).

[33] The lexical problem has been noted: Almoshnino (1563), Eilenburg (1614), and Elimelekh (1787).

The category should not be confused with another category in Jewish law: *mitzvah haba'ah ba'averah*, a righteous act that is achieved through sin (*Babylonian Talmud*, Berakhot 47a and elsewhere). This appellation is used in a negative sense, while holy sin denotes a laudable act. See Mondshine (1996), 315n64, commenting on Scholem (1937). Cf. Kalmanofsky (2002), pp. 11–12.

Consequently, Jewish thinkers have wrestled with the notion and offered different explanations, caveats, and applications.[34]

Aveira lishmah appears in one pericope that appears twice in the Talmud and elsewhere in rabbinic literature, regarding the biblical heroine Jael (*Babylonian Talmud*, Nazir 23b; *Babylonian Talmud*, Horayot 10b; *Yalkut Shimoni* 1521-1527).

According to the Bible, Sisera led the army of King Jabin of Canaan against the Israelites. The Canaanites were defeated, and Sisera fled the battlefield. He reached the tents of Heber the Kenite, and Heber's wife Jael offered him shelter. Jael covered Sisera with a blanket, gave him a jug of milk, and once he fell asleep, she gruesomely killed him (*Judges* 4–5).

The rabbis add a graphic detail drawn from a creative reading of the biblical verses: In order to ensure that Sisera was exhausted so that he would fall into a deep slumber, Jael had intercourse with him multiple times. Thus Jael—who was married to Heber—committed adultery in order to deliver the Israelites.[35]

In the biblical narrative, there is no mention of a sexual encounter. Rather, the story turns on hospitality, allegiance, violence, and female guile (Gottlieb 1981; Fuchs 1985; Bal 1988; Fewell and Gunn 1990). The sages identify the sexual encounter in the repeated verbs in Deborah's song after the event: "At her feet he sunk, he fell, he lay; at her feet he sunk, he fell; where he sunk, there he fell down dead" (*Judges* 5:27). The introduction of sex into the story is an exercise in creative exegesis rooted in intratextual references: Similar turns of phrase are employed elsewhere in sexual contexts, and these references are invoked following the verse's emphasis that Jael is a married woman.[36]

Not only does the Talmud justify Jael's course, but it also ranks her actions together with those of other biblical heroines. Moreover, the Talmud offers a radical rule: a sin for its own sake is greater than—or at least equivalent to—a righteous act performed for ulterior motives.

The notion of righteous transgression has been applied to other biblical stories of sexual impropriety, including Lot's daughters, Tamar and Judah, Ruth and Boaz, Esther and King Ahasuerus. While the category originally had a gender bias, writers refracted other episodes through the lens of holy sin: Abraham in Nimrod's furnace, Jacob stealing the blessings from Esau, dissident leaders in the Korah rebellion, Gideon's night sacrifice outside the Tabernacle, Samson killing himself with the

---

[34] This is not the place to recount the extensive scholarship on holy sin. See Rakover (1992, 2000), Haber (1999), Lichtenstein (2001), Kalmanofsky (2002), Kaniel (2010, 2011, 2013), Klein (2015), Blankovsky (2017), and Magid (2019). A sketch of the landscape will suffice here, since I am interested in one particular strand.

[35] Jael was Kenite, not a Jew, though the rabbis gloss over this point. According to Jewish law, non-Jews are also prohibited from committing adultery. Cf. Kalmanofsky (2002), p. 6 understood Jael's sin to be both adultery and murder.

[36] *Judges* 4:18 drawing on *Genesis* 30:16. Verbs in *Judges* 5:27 appear in sexual contexts in *Genesis* 34:7, *Numbers* 5:13, *Deuteronomy* 22:22, 23, 28, 28:57, *Job* 31:10, *Esther* 7:8. Repeated identification of Jael as Heber's wife in *Judges* 4:17, 21, 5:24.

Philistines, Saul avoiding the slaughter of Amalekite livestock, Elijah sacrificing on Mount Carmel, Jonah's flight, and Mordecai fasting on Passover.

2.4.2 Jewish Law

Commentators grappled with tracing the circumstances that justified holy sin: Does righteous transgression require ex ante authorization? If so, who can authorize such an act—God, a prophet, a court of Jewish law (either actually or constructively), a senior jurist, or individuals for themselves? Does an element of enjoyment automatically disqualify the act from being considered for the sake of Heaven?

Different accounts of the legal logic of *aveira lishmah* have been proffered. These approaches draw on various fields of law in their attempt to categorize, delineate, and explain the notion of holy sin. I will briefly recount three approaches and their drawbacks, before expanding on a fourth approach. This fourth approach is useful for human dignity conundrums, and after presenting the approach I will return to the hard cases discussed earlier.

According to one approach, the realm of law is expanded to include the act under its wing. Thus, this is a case of conflict of norms whereby *lex specialis derogat legi generali*—the specific norm (in this case: the "sin") overrides the general norm (in this case: the prohibition against committing that sin) due to considerations that are internal to the legal system. The specific norm is presumably termed a "sin" because under normal circumstances it would be considered a crime (Trabotto 1519; Isserles 1640). This may echo the mechanism of emergency procedures in modern legal systems (Charlap 2004).

A second approach turns to the field of criminal law. This approach suggests a redefinition of a fundamental aspect of law, giving primacy to intent, attitude, and interiority. Criminality is defined by *mens rea* alone; the act may look like a crime, but pure intent recasts it as righteous conduct. This can be understood as an inverse application of the legal maxim *actus reus non facit reum nisi mens sit rea*—an act does not make a person guilty, unless the mind is guilty. In the case of *aveira lishmah*, since the mind is not guilty, the criminal act is lauded (Albo 1485; Duran 1762; Yosef Hayim 1912).

A third approach moves to jurisprudence, offering a consequentialist account. Where sin affects great salvation, it is deemed to be God's will. The *telos* of the act trumps *nomos*, temporarily suspending law in extraordinary cases. Indeed, the notion of holy sin is rarely evoked, and it mostly appears as a corollary of an end-justifies-the-means approach. This line views righteous transgression as contingent on achieving the *telos* (Kalmanofsky 2002, pp. 5–6). The purest example of this approach would be a case where the action is defined solely by the *telos* with no worthy intent of the actor. A biblical example of such judicial consequentialism might be Judah's intention to sleep with a prostitute who turned out to be Tamar, making the act levirate marriage rather than prostitution (*Genesis* 38).

Each approach has jurisprudential ramifications and/or philosophic challenges (much of which has been considered by scholars). Thus, for example, the first approach designates the act as a "crime"—or in religious terms a "sin"—whereas in other cases of specific laws taking precedence over general laws the act does not carry the same designation.

The second approach veers towards nihilism, as it redefines the notion of criminality, making it solely dependent on the state of mind—a variable that is notoriously difficult to assess. For a legal regime, this approach would provide an untenable conduct rule. Hence, a permutation of this approach views righteous transgression as solely an ex post facto assessment (probably not entrusted in the hands of an earthly court), rather than an ex-ante directive; that is, a heavenly decision rule rather than an earthly conduct rule (Rabinovitch 1984).

The third approach sanctifies *telos* thereby undermining a community's notion of legal meaning or what it means to live in a realm governed by law.[37]

In the present context, I wish to highlight a fourth approach that can be found in the school of Hasidism.[38] According to this approach, the deed has an inherent duality that remains in constant tension. On one hand, the act is indeed a crime; this fact is not mitigated, and for this reason the act is termed "sin." On the other hand, the act is necessary for some higher purpose, and in this sense, it is "for the sake of Heaven." Unlike the other approaches, the inherent paradoxical nature of the act remains unresolved. The person is enjoined to act for the sake of Heaven, yet the act will still be considered a sin; it never becomes normative conduct. As such, the perpetrator must be prosecuted for the crime—either in a spiritual realm or in temporal courts—even though the act was for the sake of Heaven.[39]

In 1825, Rabbi Yekutiel Asher Zalman Enzel Zuzmir (ca. 1790–1858)—a jurist serving in the rabbinate in Stryj, Galicia—wrote:

> In truth, Jael committed a sin when she was adulterous with Sisera, but thus she surmised to take her soul in her hand and to cast her spirit away, and she accepted upon herself to suffer a metaphysical and eternal punishment for her sin, as long as she would save Israel from the hand of its enemy and pursuer (Zuzmir 1825).

According to Zuzmir, the biblical Jael was aware of the criminality of her conduct. She accepted her impending punishment with equanimity and poise, self-assured

---

[37] Hayes (2003), pp. 37–38 suggested that the rabbis went to great efforts to restrict vigilantism through interpretive strategies and legal institutions.

[38] Hasidism refers to the Jewish religious awakening that began in Eastern Europe in the late eighteenth century. The revival coalesced into a movement and flourished in the nineteenth century. Hasidism survived the displacement of the Great War, and then suffered significantly in the Second World War losing some eighty percent of its adherents. Like a phoenix rising from the ashes, Hasidism resurrected itself after the Holocaust. Today, Hasidic communities thrive in America, Australia, Israel, and other centers around the world.

[39] For a similar approach from a philosophical analysis without recourse to this rubric in Jewish law, see Harel and Sharon (2011). It is beyond the present scope to consider the possible link between this legal frame and the philosophical position termed dirty hands deontology (Meisels 2008; Spino and Cummins 2014, pp. 550–551).

that the task of saving Israel required her to commit adultery. The Talmud's celebration of her act does not mitigate her punishment. In some ways, Jael's conduct is even more selfless than it first appeared for she was to suffer the consequences of her conviction.

The duality of holy sin was given prominent expression in the writings of another Jewish law jurist from the school of Hasidism, Rabbi Zvi Elimelekh Shapira (1783–1841). Shapira served in the rabbinate in Munkács, Hungary and then Dynów, Galicia. As scholars have noted, Shapira extensively discussed and developed the concept of holy sin in his philosophical writings (Mondshine 1996; Brown 2013, pp. 359–360; Frankel 2017). Shapira understood that those who commit righteous transgressions are prepared "almost that the soul should go down to Gehenna, and be what may [the soul] sacrifices itself for almost eternal damnation" (Shapira 1868, vol. 1, fol. 50, col. 4). To emphasise the point, Shapira colorfully added:

> And we have already heard of those who love God in our generation who said: 'If we knew well that the recompense for good deeds was Gehenna, and the recompense for sins was the Garden of Eden – nevertheless, it would be more pleasant for our soul to fulfil the commandments that the Creator commanded us' (Ibid).

Shapira repeated his analysis in other contexts, and hasidic writers before and after Shapira adopted similar positions (Shapira 1887, fol. 32, col. 1; Avraham Hayim 1817, pt. 1, fol. 42, col. 2; pt. 3, fol. 28, cols. 1–2; pt. 4, fol. 32, cols. 2–3; Zadok Hakohen 1926).

Lest there be misunderstanding: Shapira did not promote righteous transgressions as a preferred spiritual path; on the contrary, Shapira advocated alternative routes. Inter alia, he noted the dangers of holy sin, as one crime—righteous as it may be—is likely to beget another (Shapira 1850, fol. 55, col. 3; 1868, vol. 2, fol. 7, cols. 3–4).

2.5 Workable Paradigm?

The contradictory nature of holy sin, despite sprouting from a religious legal system, offers a path for understanding the duality of the difficult human dignity cases I have recounted thus far.

The German Minister for Defense who was prepared to shoot down a passenger plane in a 9/11 scenario would have been lauded *and* prosecuted for the very same act—an act that was both righteous *and* criminal. In fact, that was exactly what Justice Hömig had envisaged. The Frankfurt deputy police chief in Gäfgen acted "for the sake of Heaven"—while the court was sympathetic towards him, the criminality of his act was not ignored.

The aforementioned Zuzmir added a pertinent line with a prospective tone:

> Someone who sacrifices his entire soul to suffer eternal pain, for the sake of the love of God and the love of God's holy nation – it is appropriate to count that person of the spiritual pedigree of the Holy of Holies (Zuzmir 1825).

The work of vigilante heroes like Batman and Jack Bauer may be considered righteous and perhaps even holy, but their souls cannot escape the eternal pain that is their lot according to Zuzmir's reading.

To what extent could a version of sinning for the sake of Heaven inform a modern legal system? I say "a version" because unlike religious legal systems, modern legal systems shy from the spiritual realm. The vigilante heroes did not act "for the sake of God" in a manner that could be identified with any particular faith. Indeed, the confessional affiliation of characters discussed in this chapter—fictional and non-fictional—is never spelled out. Yet their conduct reflects deep religiosity: belief in the ultimate value of human life (Frankfurt Police), a higher calling to justice that transcends law-on-the-books (German Minister for Defense, Dirty Harry, Jack Bauer), faith in the essential humanity of a corrupt society (Batman), and devout commitment to a way of life (Captain America).

Even if we copy the holy sin paradigm—*mutatis mutandis*—the transfer of the rubric would not be effective. Since the Enlightenment, legal systems strive for clarity and accessibility. Law attempts to provide people with foresight as to how their conduct will be perceived and received by society. In that way, people are able to choose a course of action, bearing in mind the consequences of their choices.[40] The innate duality of sins for their own sake makes the category an inappropriate tool for a modern legal system. Put simply: it is hypocritical for a legal system to declare—you are obligated to perform this action, *and* you will be punished for it.[41]

The truth is that even ancient Jewish law could not offer this paradigm as a legal possibility. Many writers—like the aforementioned Shapira—acknowledged that the Bible as a legal document could not outline a notion of righteous transgression (Shapira 1868, vol. 1, fol. 50, col. 4; 1887, fol. 32, cols. 1–2). Moreover, the antinomian charm of holy sin was picked up by Sabbateans and Frankists who saw it as medium for hastening redemption by breaking down the existing order (Scholem 1937).[42] Concomitantly, Jewish jurists considered the notion of holy sin anathema to the legal system. It is therefore unsurprising that sinning for the sake of Heaven seldom appears in Jewish legal writing.[43]

---

[40] Gross (2004) advocated an approach along similar lines (without recourse Jewish law), though he left the prosecution question open for ex post facto ratification or rejection. My critique of the holy sin paradigm also applies to Gross' proposal.

[41] It is worthwhile mentioning *The Confession* (1999), a drama film based on the 1966 book *Fertig* by Sol Yurick (1925–2013). Harry Fertig (Ben Kingsley) kills three medical staff who ignored Fertig's son's rising temperature, after which the boy soon died. Fertig confesses and stubbornly refuses to enter a not guilty plea, saying that he acted out of a sense of justice, *and* he must pay for his crimes. Fertig's approach approximates the notion of holy sin under discussion here. Unfortunately, the film's subplots (namely, the lawyer's relationship with Fertig's wife, the crimes of Fertig's employer, and the lawyer's ambition versus his morality) disrupt the storyline's flow and hinder engagement with Fertig's notion of justice.

[42] Sabbateans—people who accepted the messianic claims of Shabbetai Tsevi (1626–ca.1676). Frankists—followers of Jacob Frank (1726–1791), who claimed to be a reincarnation of Shabbetai Tsevi.

[43] To be sure, some scholars overstated the case by arguing that holy sin has no place in the Jewish legal system. Lichtenstein (1975), p. 68 wrote: "As a prescriptive category, the currently popular

When righteous transgression is evoked by jurists, it may be cited as a theoretical construct rather than an operative legal mechanism (Aszod 1880, §61; Sperber 1940). Jurists who discuss applying the doctrine, promptly reject it (Aszod 1880, §140; Sperber 2002). Moreover, the category is not used in prospective rulings, but in ex post facto justifications that may be coupled with censure for comparative conduct in the present or future (Trabotto 1519; Yosef Hayim 1912). The rubric is seldom evoked alone: even where it buttresses a ruling, *aveira lishmah* is cited alongside other interpretive tools (Isserles 1640; Halberstam 2001). In one case, a jurist used the idiom figuratively when advising a colleague to tactically retreat from a public stance (Ibn Adreth 1825).

Admittedly, it is conceivable that jurists used the category in unpublished rulings. Furthermore, we cannot discount the possibility of a gap between law-on-the-books and law-in-action, particularly since holy sin does appear in discursive contexts. Even considering these possibilities, they hardly indicate a mainstream legal mechanism. Thus, the notion of holy sin survived at the edge of law, primarily serving as homiletic clay in the hands of preachers, or as a hermeneutic device for explaining legally problematic episodes of the past.

The paradoxical idiom also offered a subversive myth. It is this form that can serve as a useful totem when considering the intuitive response to 9/11 scenarios or ticking time-bombs.[44]

Vigilantism often reflects dissatisfaction with the justice system, frustration with governance, and moral failure of authority. In a concurring opinion when the United States Supreme Court struck down death penalty schemes on the basis of the Eighth Amendment which prohibits cruel and unusual punishment, Justice Potter Stewart wrote:

> When people begin to believe that organized society is unwilling or unable to impose upon criminal offenders the punishment they "deserve" then there are sown the seeds of anarchy – of self-help, vigilante justice, and lynch law.[45]

Yet even figures who are responsible for administering justice may grapple with outcomes of the legal system. The German Defense Minister, the Constitutional

notion of *averah lishmah* (idealistic transgression) has no halakhic standing whatsoever"; and (1975:85n25): "[T]his apparent priority of telos and motivation over formal law has no prescriptive or prospective implications. At most, it means that, after the fact, we can sometimes see that a nominal violation was superior to a licit or even required act; but it gives no license for making the jump." See also Rabinovitch (1984). Some 25 years later—with the development of computerized databases of Jewish law—Lichtenstein (2001), p. 103 revisited the issue and acknowledged that the category was used in Jewish law. Soon after, on the basis of a similar database search, Kalmanofsky (2002), pp. 12–19 counted 17 responsa that cite the phrase. The criteria for this enumeration are not set out, nor are they self-evident. On one hand, the phrase is more common than that; on the other hand—as I indicate in the following lines—Kalmanofsky seems to overstate its impact.

[44]Regarding the role of theoretical discussions of holy sin, see Brown (2013), pp. 363–364. My foregoing thoughts developed from Meir Dan-Cohen's notion of acoustic separation (1984), and Alon Harel's analysis of why law matters (2013). See also Gross (2004).

[45]Furman v. Georgia. 1972. 408 U.S. 238, 308.

Court judge, the Frankfurt deputy police chief and the German Police Union were not calling for vigilantism; they were wrestling with the outcomes of hard cases. In *Gäfgen*, the justice system only lightly punished the Frankfurt policemen for his human dignity infraction, avoiding the possibility of an unsettling situation whereby the policemen would be severely punished for trying to save a life. In contrast, the ECtHR was able to declare that the Frankfurt policemen deserved harsher punishment, without causing a jarring outcome because the Court ruled that under the circumstances it had no authority to impose such harsh punishment.

In a 2007 law conference in Ottawa, Canada, US Supreme Court Justice Antonin Scalia surprised many when he invoked the achievements of the lead character in *24*, while making an argument in favor of torture:

> Jack Bauer saved Los Angeles ... He saved hundreds of thousands of lives. ... Are you going to convict Jack Bauer? ... Is any jury going to convict Jack Bauer? I don't think so (Lattman 2007).

Scalia seemed to acknowledge the dissonance of Jack Bauer's methods: He would stand trial for torture but having saved lives a jury would not convict him. In contrast, a legal regime that recognized a notion of *aveira lishmah* would be able to laud Jack Bauer while convicting him for human dignity violations.

Modern legal systems may not be suited to adopting a righteous transgression rubric. Yet the notion of *aveira lishmah* may still offer direction when courts grapple with exceptional or particularly difficult human dignity cases. The criminality of the act need not been ignored, though there may be a recognition that the circumstances call for an illegal course of action. This illegal action must be censured. The holy sin paradigm provides for the possibility of contradictory reactions: praise and critique; appreciation and revulsion; endorsement and punishment; responsibility and accountability. In this sense, the ancient Jewish legal paradigm taps into deep-rooted, intuitive, and profound notions of justice and the complexity of human existence.

References

Adams CF (2005) Murder by the Bay: historic homicide in and about the City of San Francisco. Quill Driver Books, Sanger CA, pp 252–278

Albo Y (1485) Sefer ha-'ikkarim. §3:29. I.N. Soncino and Sons, Soncino

Almoshnino M (1563) Tefilla le-moshe. §1:1. Ya'avets, Livorno

Aszod Y (1880) Teshuvot yehuda ya'aleh, vol 2. Löwy & Alkalay, Pressburg

Avraham Hayim of Złoczów (1817) Orei'ah le-hayim. n.p., Berdyczów

Babylonian Talmud

Bal M (1988) Murder and difference: gender, genre and scholarship on Sisera's death (trans: Gumpert M). Indiana University Press, Bloomington

Barnes M (2012) 'Dirty Harry' among films enshrined in National Film Registry. The Hollywood Reporter, December 19. https://www.hollywoodreporter.com/news/national-film-registry-matrix-404536. Accessed 4 July 2023

Blankovsky Y (2017) Sin for the sake of God: a tale of a radical idea in the Talmudic literature. Magnes, Jerusalem
Bleich JD (2006) Torture and the ticking bomb. Tradition 39(4):89–121
Breach of Constitution (2007) Deutsche Welle, September 17. http://p.dw.com/p/BgUe. Accessed 4 July 2023
Brown B (2013) The two faces of religious radicalism: orthodox zealotry and 'Holy Sinning' in nineteenth-century Hasidism in Hungary and Galicia. The Journal of Religion 93(3):341–374. https://doi.org/10.1086/670273
Buford K (2000) Burt Lancaster: an American life. Knopf, New York
Cannady S (2012) 2012 National Film Registry picks in a league of their own. Library of Congress, December 19. https://www.loc.gov/item/prn-12-226/cinematic-firsts-enshrined-in-2012-film-registry/2012-12-19. Accessed 4 July 2023
Carodine MD (2011) Trust is something you've gotta earn, and it takes time. In: Sarat A (ed) Imagining legality: where law meets popular culture. University of Alabama Press, Tuscaloosa, pp 53–64
Charlap YM (2004) Mei marom, vol 16. Beit Zevul, Jerusalem, pp 63–64, 202–206
Clemens J (2017) Bentham, torture, modernity. Cogent Arts & Humanities 4(1). https://doi.org/10.1080/23311983.2017.1390913
Connor R (2011) Killer compensated. Deutsche Welle, August 4. http://p.dw.com/p/12B3B. Accessed 4 July 2023
Cullen T (2013) Sensing the past: Hollywood stars and historical visions. Oxford University Press, Oxford
Dan-Cohen M (1984) Decision rules and conduct rules: on acoustic separation in criminal law. Harvard Law Review 97(3):625–677
Davies J (2012) The fire-raisers: Bentham and Torture. Interdisciplinary Studies in the Long Nineteenth Century 19:15. https://doi.org/10.16995/ntn.643
Dumsday T (2009) On cheering Charles Bronson: the ethics of vigilantism. The Southern Journal of Philosophy 47(1):49–67
Duran SZ (1762) Magen avot. §2:17. M. Attias, Livorno
Eilenburg IB (1614) Be'er sheva. fol. 17, col. 1. Giovanni Cajon, Venice
Elimelekh of Leżajsk (1787) No'am elimelekh. fol. 70, col. 1. J. S. Rapaport, Lwów
Eliot M (2009) American rebel: the life of Clint Eastwood. Three Rivers, New York
Escobedo v. Illinois. 1964. 378 U.S. 478
Fewell DN, Gunn DM (1990) Controlling perspectives: women, men, and the authority of violence in Judges 4&5. Journal of the American Academy of Religion 58(3):389–411
Flatley G (1976) At the movies. New York Times, December 17, p 62. http://www.nytimes.com/1976/12/17/archives/at-the-movies-falk-on-mikey-this-is-no-romp-in-the-park.html. Accessed 4 July 2023
Frankel YY (2017) Ma'amarim mi-torat maran ha-benei yisaskhar.... Agra dekala parashat noah. Y. Y. Frankel, Jerusalem
Fuchs E (1985) Who is hiding the truth? Deceptive women and biblical androcentrism. In: Collins AY (ed) Feminist perspectives on biblical scholarship. Society of Biblical Literature and Scholars Press, Missoula, pp 137–144
Gottlieb F (1981) Three mothers. Judaism 30(2):194–203
Graysmith R (1986) Zodiac. St. Martin's/Marek, New York
Gross O (2004) The prohibition of torture and the limits of the law. In: Levinson S (ed) Torture: a collection. Oxford University Press, Oxford, pp 229–253
Haber Z (1999) 'Aveira leshem shamayim. Mei'aliyot 21:205–228. http://www.daat.ac.il/daat/kitveyet/maaliyot/avera-2.htm, http://www.daat.ac.il/daat/kitveyet/maaliyot/avera1-2.htm. Accessed 4 July 2023
Halberstam YY (2001) She'elot u-teshuvot divrei yatsiv. vol. 6 §81. Shefa Hayim, Netanya
Harel A (2013) Why law matters. Oxford University Press, Oxford

Harel A, Sharon A (2011) 'Necessity knows no law': on extreme cases and uncodifiable necessities. University of Toronto Law Journal 61:845–865
Hayes CE (2003) Palestinian Rabbinic attitudes to intermarriage in historical and cultural context. In: Kalmin R, Schwartz S (eds) Jewish culture and society under the Christian Roman Empire. Peeters, Leuven, pp 11–64
Ibn Adreth S (1825) She'elot u-teshuvot ha-rashba, §238, vol 5. Pietro Meucci, Livorno
Isserles M (1640) She'elot u-teshuvot. §11. M.N. Meisels, Kraków
Janisch W (2016) Der Ricter, der den Abschuss verbot. Süddeutsche Zeitung, 20 October. https://www.sueddeutsche.de/politik/nachruf-der-richter-der-den-abschuss-verbot-1.3215074. Accessed 4 July 2023
Johnston L (1996) What is vigilantism? The British Journal of Criminology 36(2):220–236
Kael P (1972) The current cinema: saint cop. The New Yorker, January 15, pp 78–81
Kael P (1974) The current cinema: killing time. The New Yorker, January 14, pp 84–89
Kalmanofsky J (2002) Sins for the sake of God. Conservative Judaism 54(2):3–24
Kamin S (2007) How the war on terror may affect domestic interrogations: the 24 effect. Chapman Law Review 10:693–712
Kaniel RK-I (2010) Motherhood and seduction in the myth of David's Messianic Dynasty: Hebrew Bible, Rabbinic Literature and the Zoharic Corpus. Ph.D. dissertation, Hebrew University of Jerusalem
Kaniel RK-I (2011) Seed that comes from 'Another Place': the metamorphosis of the Story of Lot's daughters. Jerusalem Studies in Jewish Thought 22:91–119
Kaniel RK-I (2013) "Gedolah Aveirah Lishma": mothers of the Davidic dynasty, feminine seduction and the development of messianic thought, from Rabbinic Literature to R. Moshe Haim Luzzatto. Nashim: A Journal of Jewish Women's Studies & Gender Issues 24:27–52
Kerstein B (2008) Batman's war on terror. Azure 34:136–144
Keslowitz S (2008) The Simpsons, 24, and the law: how Homer Simpson and Jack Bauer influence congressional lawmaking and judicial reasoning. Cardozo Law Review 29(6):2787–2822
Klavan A (2008) What Bush and Batman have in common. The Wall Street Journal, July 25. https://www.wsj.com/articles/SB121694247343482821. Accessed 4 July 2023
Klein A (2015) Gedola 'aveira lishmah. https://tinyurl.com/ybauzmeu. Accessed 4 July 2023
Krumrey H, Wiegold T (2007) Ich würde den Befehl geben. Focus 38:38–39
Lattman P (2007) Justice Scalia Hearts Jack Bauer. The Wall Street Journal, June 20. https://blogs.wsj.com/law/2007/06/20/justice-scalia-hearts-jack-bauer. Accessed 4 July 2023
Lepsius O (2006) Human dignity and the downing of aircraft: the German Federal Constitutional Court strikes down a prominent anti-terrorism provision in the New Air-transport Security Act. German Law Journal 7(9):761–776
Lichtenstein A (1975) Does Jewish tradition recognize an ethic independent of Halacha? In: Fox M (ed) Modern Jewish ethics: theory and practice. Ohio State University Press, Columbus, pp 62–88 [Reprinted in Contemporary Jewish Ethics, ed. Menachem Marc Kellner, 102-123. New York: Sanhedrin Press]
Lichtenstein A (2001) 'Aveira lishmah – hirhurim be-halakha u-ve-mahshava. In: Deutsch H, Ben-Sasson M (eds) Ha-'aher: bein adam le-'atzmo u-le-zulato. Yedioth Aharonoth, Tel Aviv, p 99–125, 481–484
Lithwick D (2008) How Jack Bauer shaped U.S. torture policy. Newsweek, July 25. http://www.newsweek.com/lithwick-how-jack-bauer-shaped-ustorture-policy-93159. Accessed 4 July 2023
Lübbe-Wolff G (2017) "Terror" im Fernsehen, Populismus vor den Toren der Justiz? Deutsche Zeitschrift für europäisches Denken, Merkur, 815:61–69
Magid S (2019) Purim: when the Sin becomes the Mitzvah. Jewish Journal 35(2):14–15
Manderson D (2011) Trust us justice: 24, popular culture and the law. In: Sarat A (ed) Imagining legality: where law meets popular culture. University of Alabama Press, Tuscaloosa, pp 22–52
Mayer J (2007) Whatever it takes: the politics of the man behind "24." The New Yorker, February 19. https://www.newyorker.com/magazine/2007/02/19/whatever-it-takes. Accessed 4 July 2023

Meisels T (2008) Torture and the problem of dirty hands. Canadian Journal of Law & Jurisprudence 21(2):149–173
Miller F (1986) The dark knight returns. DC Comics, New York
Miranda v. Arizona. 1966. 384 U.S. 436
Mondshine Y (1996) The fluidity of categories in Hasidism: Avera lishmah in the teachings of Rabbi Zevi Elimelekh of Dynow. In: Rapoport-Albert A (ed) Hasidism reappraised. Littman Library of Jewish Civilization, London, pp 301–320
Mörder Gäfgen wird entschädigt (2011) August 4. https://www.n-tv.de/panorama/Moerder-Gaefgen-wird-entschaedigt-article3975046.html. Accessed 4 July 2023
National Transportation Safety Board (2002) No. ATL02FA032. https://data.ntsb.gov/Docket/?NTSBNumber=ATL02FA032. Accessed 4 July 2023
Orr C (2008) Batman as Bush, Ctd. The New Republic, July 25. https://newrepublic.com/article/43148/batman-bush-ctd. Accessed 4 July 2023
Police Chief Fined in Torture Case (2004) Deutsche Welle, December 20. http://p.dw.com/p/60xR. Accessed 4 July 2023
Poscher R (2004) Die Würde des Menschen ist unantastbar. JuristenZeitung, 13 August, 15/16: 756–762
Poscher R (2006) Menschenwürde im Staatsnotstand. In: Lenzen W (ed) Ist Foltern (in Ausnahmefällen) erlaubt?. Mentis, Paderborn, pp 48–65 [Also printed in Menschenwürde in der säkularen Verfassungsordnung: Rechtswissenschaftliche und theologische Perspektiven, eds. Petra Bahr and Hans Michael Heinig, 215-231. Tübingen: Mohr Siebeck. And in Schriftenreihe Hofgeismarer Protokolle, Die Wahl der Qual, ed. Michael Goldbach, 53-69. Hofgeismar: Evangelische Akademie Hofgeismar]
Public Committee against Torture v. Prime Minister (1999) HCJ 5100/94, IsrLR 567; originally published in Hebrew: IsrSC 53(4):817
Questions Abound After Wild Ride for Love of Dead Jewish Astronaut (2003) Jewish Telegraphic Agency, January 9. https://www.jta.org/2003/01/09/archive/questions-abound-after-wild-ride-for-love-of-dead-jewish-astronaut. Accessed 4 July 2023
Rabin Y, Meydani A (2016) Public committee against torture in Israel v State of Israel Case. In: Grote R, Lachenmann F, Wolfrum R (eds) Max Planck encyclopedia of comparative constitutional law. Oxford University Press. http://oxcon.ouplaw.com/view/10.1093/law-mpeccol/law-mpeccol-e560. Accessed 4 July 2023
Rabinovitch NE (1984) Yad peshuta, vol 2. Ma'aliyot, Ma'aleh Adummim, p 625
Rakover N (1992) Violation of the law in order to preserve it: 'Gedolah Aveirah Lishmah'. Jewish Law Association Studies 6:107–123
Rakover N (2000) Ends that justify the means. Library of Jewish Law, Jerusalem, pp 15–45
Schiemann JW (2016) Does torture work? Oxford University Press, Oxford
Schmitt E (2003) U.S. practices how to down hijacked jets. New York Times, October 3. http://www.nytimes.com/2003/10/03/us/us-practices-how-to-down-hijacked-jets.html. Accessed 4 July 2023
Scholem G (1937) Mitzvah Haba'ah Ba'averah. Kneset 2:347–392 [English edition: Scholem, Gershom. 1971. Redemption through Sin (trans: Hillel Halkin). The Messianic Idea in Judaism, 78-141. New York: Schocken].
Shapira ZE (1850) Benei yisaskhar. Saul Meyerhoffer, Zolkiew
Shapira ZE (1868) Agra dekala. M. F. Poremba, Lemberg
Shapira ZE (1887) Devarim nehmadim. Żupnik, Knoller u. Hammerschmidt, Przemyśl
Siegel D (1993) A Siegel Film: an autobiography. Farber and Farber, London
Smith P (1993) Clint Eastwood: a cultural production. University of Minnesota Press, Minneapolis
Sperber D (1940) She'elot u-teshuvot afarkasta de'anya, §162. Hirsch M. Ludovic, Satu-Mare
Sperber D (2002) She'elot u-teshuvot afarkasta de'anya, § 180, vol 2. O.G. Pollak, Brooklyn
Spino J, Cummins DD (2014) The ticking time bomb: when the use of torture is and is not endorsed. Review of Philosophy and Psychology 5(4):543–563. https://doi.org/10.1007/s13164-014-0199-y

Stemberger G (1996) Introduction to the Talmud and Midrash (trans: Bockmuehl M), 2nd edn. T&T Clark, Edinburgh, pp 190–224
Street J (2012) Dirty Harry's San Francisco. The sixties: A Journal of History, Politics and Culture 5(1):1–21. https://doi.org/10.1080/17541328.2012.674850
Stümke V (2011) Zwischen gut und böse: Impulse lutherischer Sozialethik. LIT Verlag Münster, Münster, p 287
The 9/11 Commission Report (2004) National Commission on terrorist attacks upon the United States. http://govinfo.library.unt.edu/911. Accessed 4 July 2023
Thompson R (1976) Stoked. Film Comment, July–August, 12(4):10–21
Trabotto J (Giuseppe) Colon ben Solomon (1519) (She'elot u-teshuvot), §167. Daniel Bomberg, Venice
US pilots train shooting civilian planes (2003) BBC News, October 3. http://news.bbc.co.uk/go/pr/fr/-/2/hi/americas/3161354.stm. Accessed 4 July 2023
Van Veeren E (2009) Interrogating 24: making sense of US counter-terrorism in the global war on terrorism. New Political Science 31(3):361–384. https://doi.org/10.1080/07393140903105991
Wilson J (2014) Batman and the problem with vigilante justice. A love story. The Artifice, January 25. https://the-artifice.com/batman-vigilante-justice. Accessed 4 July 2023
Witthaut (2011) Polizei muss intensiv vernehmen dürfen. Gewerkschaft der Polizei. August 4. https://www.gdp.de/gdp/gdp.nsf/id/DE_Witthaut_Polizei_muss_intensiv_vernehmen_duerfen. Accessed 4 July 2023
Yalkut Shimoni (1521-1527) Judges §55. M. Soncino, Salonika
Yosef Hayim of Baghdad (1912) Rav pe'alim, vol 4., OH §2. Y.D. Frumkin, Jerusalem
Zadok Hakohen of Lublin (1926) Takkanat ha-shavin. G. Piment, Warszawa, p 17
Zuzmir YAZE (1825) Hakdama. Arye Leib Hakohen Heller. Avnei milu'im, vol 2., unnumbered pages, 5. Gerson Letteres, Zolkiew

Chapter 3
Human Dignity as Taboo: The Hidden Rationality Behind the Absolute Legal Prohibition of Torture

Ralf Poscher

Abstract From a constitutional point of view, the guarantee of human dignity in the German Basic Law can be understood as a legal taboo categorically ruling out any balancing that would lead to its relativization. It follows that anything we recognize as an infringement on human dignity amounts to a violation thereof. In terms of a paradigm pertaining to the violation of human dignity, this is of particular relevance to the prohibition of torture derived from the guarantee of human dignity. Legally, there is a taboo attached to torture. It is crucial for the guarantee of human dignity that it only postulates a legal taboo. In turn, its "clue" is that it may also be upheld by arguments in the face of a consequentialist approach that would yield a different result when applied to an ethical assessment. The following paper outlines the various aspects of the guarantee of human dignity when viewed as a legal taboo with the aim of demonstrating that its validity extends to and is of particular relevance to extreme threats.

3.1 Introduction

Since the September 11 terrorist attacks (Economist 2003), the inviolability of human dignity no longer seems as self-evident as it once was, even in Western democracies. Indeed, more than 1-year prior to the release of material from Abu

---

The German version of this text was first published in 2006 in the midst of an emerging discussion on preventive torture in Germany, Poscher, Ralf (2006). Menschenwürde als Tabu: Die verdeckte Rationalität eines absoluten Rechtsverbots der Folter. In G. Beestermöller/H. Brunkhorst (Eds.), Rückkehr der Folter: Der Rechtsstaat im Zwielicht? (pp. 75–87). The text has only been updated marginally, since it describes the peculiar state of the debate that has been somewhat overcome by the discussions that have since emerged, but remains telling for the German approach to human dignity. A rather comprehensive documentation of the later German discussion can be found in Manfred Baldus, Kämpfe um die Menschenwürde: Die Debatten seit 1949, 2016.

R. Poscher (✉)
Max Planck Institute for the Study of Crime, Security and Law, Freiburg, Germany
e-mail: r.poscher@csl.mpg.de

S. N. Arel et al. (eds.), *Probing Human Dignity*,
https://doi.org/10.1007/978-3-031-42437-3_3

Ghureib prison, the Economist magazine reported that, based on research conducted by the Washington Post, in the fight against terrorism U.S. intelligence agencies either employed torture methods themselves or let prisoners be interrogated and tortured in third-party countries (Economist 2003). A short time thereafter, the Frankfurt Vice-President of Police relied on the threat of torture to force the kidnapper of Jakob von Metzler to reveal his victim's location. Such events were, and will continue to be, accompanied by deliberations that question the inviolability of human dignity. Moreover, since the September 11 attacks, the use of torture in the U.S. has been openly discussed,[1] while in Germany, the aforementioned actions of the Frankfurt Vice-President of Police led to an abundance of opinions and contributions on the matter. It fits within this picture that Ernst-Wolfgang Böckenförde detected tectonic shifts between Günter Dürig's original commentary on the guarantee of human dignity in Art. 1 para I GG (German Basic Law), which laid the foundation of its doctrinal conceptualization in the 1950s, and the updated version from 2003, which hinted at a relativization of the guarantee's absoluteness (Böckenförde 2003, pp. 33–35).

To follow the irritating, event-driven discussion on the inviolability of human dignity back to a time before the post-9/11 contributions, one can turn to a 1992 lecture that Niklas Luhmann held at the University of Heidelberg in Germany. As a lawyer by training the eminent theorist of an autopoietic system analysis of society always kept an interest in legal issues when they could shed a light on some aspects of his work in sociology. In this lecture, Luhmann discussed the inviolability of human dignity from such an theoretical rather than practical perspective. By posing the question "Do indispensable norms still exist in our society?" (translation RP), Luhmann was interested in the question from his systems theory perspective of societal functional differentiation. In so doing, he asked whether the autonomy of each subsystem can go so far as to ensure that it succeeds in maintaining certain standards at all costs, regardless of irritations that emanate from other subsystems. His interest was not in the self-denial of his own theory. Rather, Luhmann wanted to use the impossibility of "indispensable norms" to show how unlikely and presuppositional functional differentiation is as a societal organization principle (Luhmann 1993, p. 23). Luhmann aimed to demonstrate the limits of system autonomy by taking a norm considered by our society to be indispensable: the inviolability of human dignity as enshrined in the German Basic Law. To refute this apparently irrefutable norm, Luhmann presented a "ticking-bomb scenario" that later transformed into a "ticking-nuclear-bomb scenario," whereby a captured terrorist had left a nuclear bomb on a timer to explode (Luhmann 1993, p. 2). Via these examples, Luhmann demonstrated that a legal system, when confronted with far-reaching threats, can hardly stick to the concept of indispensable norms.

Historically, less-differentiated societies have reacted to the need to make such decisions by simply removing the decision from the auspices of the law. For example, Luhmann pointed to the historical raison d'état of politics in Venice and

[1] For an overview of contemporary American discourse, see Levinson (2004).

to the notion of *ius eminens* espoused by rulers in the eighteenth century (Luhmann 1993, p. 26). Legalized functional equivalents of such maxims can be found in the emergency regulations of modern constitutions.

From a sociological perspective, even though Luhmann was only concerned with an adequate description of the scene, rather than a marginal case of functional differentiation, he recommended the following solutions for the ticking-bomb-example he used: "in spite of all legalistic misgivings . . . the authorization of torture by internationally supervised courts, TV monitoring of the scene in Geneva or Luxembourg, and remote control by telecommunications" (translation RP). While Luhmann saw such ironic suggestions as failing to offer a "satisfying solution to the problem," he noted that "there is also little satisfaction in doing nothing to protect innocents from the fanaticism of terrorists" (Luhmann 1993, p. 27; translation RP).

3.2 The Legal Discourse

The constitutional lawyer Winfried Brugger—who sat in the audience of Luhmann's lecture—remained intrigued by the examples used by the sociologist and their possible impact on the Basic Law (Brugger 2003, p. 11). From a legal standpoint, he saw the solution that Luhmann suggested at the end of his talk confronted with an unambiguous constitutional provision. At the very beginning of the Basic Law (Art. 1 para I GG) it states that "Human dignity shall be inviolable": a simple, unconditional guarantee. While lawyers have, at times, experienced difficulties with this guarantee—due to its abstract nature, borderline cases (e.g., genetic engineering) are sometimes difficult to classify—at the time of Luhmann's lecture, uniform consensus existed that the guarantee prohibited torture and humiliating punishment (Kloepfer 1976, pp. 405, 418 f.). In this matter, no leeway existed: all actions that violate human dignity are forbidden. Thus, in legal discourse, the guarantee of human dignity was considered to be inviolable and, historically, has not been open for discussion.

Stimulated by Luhmann's lecture, Brugger began to develop a doctrinal justification of torture for the cases constructed by Luhmann (Brugger 1995, pp. 414–416, 446–455). He spared no methodical effort to justify the use of torture in the scenarios mentioned and, in so doing, sought to not only overcome the unequivocal wording of Art. 1 para I GG, but almost a dozen other constitutional, European, and international regulations. Ultimately, he relied on constitutional balancing to find a compromise, a method commonly used when fundamental rights conflict, except for the guarantee of human dignity (Brugger 1995, p. 450; Brugger 1996, pp. 165, 169). Brugger concluded that if the torture—limited and controllable suffering—of a single terrorist, who has implicated herself and is able to stop the torture at any time, is appropriate and necessary to prevent the deaths and unforeseeable suffering of a large number of people, then the guarantee of the terrorist's human dignity is subordinate. This accords with the balancing doctrine that is already applied in the context of the right to life of terrorists and the admissibility of a final rescue shot (Brugger 1995, p. 448).

Brugger's theses befell an awkward fate: despite the well-researched methodological and fundamental arguments laid out by Brugger, his theses found no attention in the literature and even less acceptance. Even though Brugger tried to insert his theses into the discussion multiple times, his suggestions were never expressly rejected. Rather, any attempt to discuss them was simply ignored.[2] The guild of constitutional lawyers refused to support his rationalizing view of the guarantee of human dignity. When it came to the absolute protection of human dignity, it would appear that the German discussion wanted to avoid discussions and arguments.

Yet it is not only the hostility to discourse that is conspicuous, but also its "irrationality." Our general constitutional proportionality and balancing approach, which Brugger uses to solve the conflict, corresponds to the pattern of purposive rationality. Indeed, it resembles Max Weber's classic definition: "Whoever acts in a purposively rational manner orients their action to the purpose, means and associated consequences of an act, and so rationally weighs the relation of means to ends" (Weber 2019, pp. 102, 103). In the case of the guarantee of human dignity, however, we avoid the use of any such balancing and stick, instead, to a value rationality approach. The result of this is strikingly described by Weber: "From the perspective of purposive rationality, however, value rationality must always be irrational, the more so when action is governed by values. For the more that action elevates such absolute values, the less it reflects on the consequences of such action, and the more unconditional do considerations of inner disposition [...] become" (Weber 2019, p. 103). By refusing to balance the human dignity of a terrorist with the suffering and death of innocent victims—regardless of the consequences—we are, according to Weber, acting irrationally.

What might explain this unusual reaction to the challenges posited by Luhmann? Do we actually lose our purposive rationality when we interpret Art. 1 para I GG literally and protect human dignity absolutely? Or is Luhmann correct in proposing that, ultimately, there are no such things as indispensable norms in our legal system?

3.3 Human Dignity as Taboo

An answer to these questions can be obtained by looking at how we deal with human dignity: not from the doctrinal, internal perspective of the law, but instead from an external sociologically-oriented point of view that assesses the different forms that behavioral prohibitions can take. This approach demonstrates that the Basic Law's

[2] As to the perception of Brugger, see Brugger (2003), 5. II.

guarantee of human dignity does not have the structure of a simple prohibition, but rather that of a taboo.[3]

3.3.1 Terminology

The linguistic indication given by the term "inviolable"—which is not used elsewhere in the Basic Law—provides a first hint of support that the guarantee of human dignity is a taboo and not just a prohibition. As to the term "taboo" itself, this is one of the few widely-used terms borrowed from an indigenous language. Captain James Cook first encountered the Tongan term *ta pu* during his South Sea expeditions (Schröder 1994–1995, pp. 127, 128). The term is considered the opposite of *noa* (the ordinary) and is invariably translated as the extraordinary, the sacred, the characterized, or the "untouchable" (Schröder 1995, p. 15).

What makes the concept of taboo interesting from a theoretical standpoint is that despite a subtle variation in meaning, there is agreement that taboos are special qualified norms that can be best connotated by the archaic concept (Marschall 1976, p. 877; Reimann 1985, p. 421; Schröder 1995, p. 5; Balle 1990, p. 17) without it being necessary to determine how closely this sociological adaptation conforms with the original Polynesian concept (Seibel 1990, p. 75). In any case, it is clear that a sufficiently large vacuum for the designation of special qualified prohibitions existed in our everyday language and that, consequently, the term taboo was adopted because it best captures the connotations that come along with this kind of norm (Seibel 1990, pp. 84 f.). To understand the inviolability of human dignity as a taboo also means that any legal dealings with it, or discussions about it, are also strongly associated with the specific features of taboos.

3.3.2 Refusal to Discuss

The first observation that calls for explanation is the very refusal to enter into a purposively rational discussion on the absoluteness of the guarantee of human dignity. Taboos—such as incest or pedophilia—are often associated with further taboos concerning their thematization. Even raising such topics is considered taboo. Accordingly, contributions which thematize the guarantee of human dignity are not regarded as a contribution to discussion, but as a taboo. Consequently, such contributions are ostracized: as exemplified by the longstanding refusal to discuss Brugger's theses.

[3]On the general relationship between taboo and law, see Depenheuer (2003); on the protection of taboos in criminal law, see Hörnle (2003), paras 106 ff.

3.3.3 Prohibition to Act

The informal thematization taboo is further underscored by the fact that the guarantee of human dignity is protected from legal intervention. Among indigenous peoples, classic taboos of this sort mostly concern something relevant to the identity of the indigenous community that is absolute and unquestionable.

3.3.4 Identity Through Taboo

The classical taboos of indigenous peoples were constitutive to the identity of their communities. These taboos were often incorporated into totem animals to distinguish a community and its honored and cherished rules of behavior—particularly concerning death and food taboos—from other communities. The identity-forming content of these taboos corresponds with the guarantee of human dignity insofar as the latter is fundamental to the identity of post-war German society. This is evident not only by the fact that it is the very first provision of the Basic Law, but also from a constitutional-historical perspective. It is precisely with the inviolable nature of human dignity that the Basic Law seeks to distance the Federal Republic of Germany from National Socialism. [4] Like the totem animals of indigenous communities, post-war German society places a taboo on the value that is most relevant to its identity. By placing a taboo around the notion of human dignity, post-war Germany is legally securing its most fundamental value by relying on an archaic form of regulation. Durkheim would thus feel affirmed, for taboos belong to the constitutive elements that allow for fundamental differentiation between the sacred and the profane, in not only archaic but also modern societies (Durkheim 1969, p. 62).

3.3.5 Absoluteness

Taboos correspond with unconditional and absolute protection. Nothing can justify breaking a taboo. Taboos cannot be balanced against other values, they can only be broken. This logic also applies to the Basic Law's guarantee of human dignity. According to our traditional doctrinal understanding, nothing—not even the scenarios posited by Luhmann and Brugger—can legitimize an exception to the guarantee. Neither legal reservations nor the emergency provisions of the Basic Law—or any other provisions for that matter—can limit the guarantee. Moreover, Art. 79 para 3 GG, expressly prohibits amendments to the guarantee of human dignity. Thus, deviation away from the absolute protection of human dignity lies outside the conceivable scope of the German legal system.

---

[4] E.g. Decision of the German Federal Constitutional Court, BVerfGE 39, 1/67.

3.3.6 Irrationality

The tabooing further explains why our society not only places absoluteness on the guarantee of human dignity but also why we refuse to entertain any discourse on the matter, including discussions about its justification. For taboos, no justification is required to explain their existence. For example, indigenous peoples neither had any reason nor any interest in justifications for their far-reaching incest taboos. Our legal system's treatment of the guarantee of human dignity is structurally similar. Of course, we have many good reasons to protect human dignity: it is not only fundamental to our personality,[5] but for our sociality. However, within our otherwise purposively rational system of fundamental rights, no other doctrinal justification for the absolute inviolability of human dignity can be given that corresponds to the instrumental rationality otherwise observed in our legal system.

3.4 Rationality of the Taboo

The fact that taboos do not need to be justified does not, however, mean that reasons cannot be provided for their existence. For instance, today we have a variety of biological and sociological explanations for the incest taboo, such as the avoidance of hereditary defects (Hirsch 1990, pp. 5 ff.) or (in its interpretation as a social imperative) to force family communities into social openness (Schelsky 1955, pp. 88 ff.). However, in most traditional societies that viewed incest as taboo, such explanations where neither obvious nor asked for. From an external perspective, such explanations are, however, visible, even if they were concealed from the societies at the time.

If the guarantee of human dignity is a legal taboo, then the question arises whether, as with other taboos, a concealed rationality exists for the absoluteness of the guarantee, which, although not visible within the internal framework of the legal system, can be perceived from an external legal-sociological perspective? Is there a concealed purposive rationality to explain the taboo, which is simply not accessible to the legal system, just as the biological and sociological explanations for the incest taboo were not accessible to indigenous societies?

From the perspective of the law concealed the purposive rationality of the absolute guarantee of human dignity comes to the fore when the consequences of the inviolability of human dignity in the face of a ticking-bomb scenario are imagined. Legally, the requisite "tragic choice" can only be made at the expense of the innocent victims (and in Luhmann's nuclear scenario, at the expense of the entire world). The legal principle *Fiat lex, et pereat mundus* prevails. Thus, the world cannot be saved in compliance with the law: it can only be saved by someone who is

[5] E.g. Decision of the German Federal Constitutional Court, BVerfGE 30, 173/214.

ready and willing to transcend the legal framework and bear the full legal consequences of their actions.

The police officer who resorts to the use of torture in the ticking-bomb scenario clearly violates Art. 1 GG. Moreover, the officer also abuses her position of authority and commits the criminal offenses of assault and battery. A reliance on the defense of emergency assistance would, in all likelihood, be rejected: due either to the fact that the application of emergency assistance rules to official acts is generally rejected (Haas 1978, pp. 319 ff.; Jakobs 1991, margin no 42) or because special restrictions are placed on how police officers are to conduct their official duties (Roxin 1997, margin no 95). Without such protections, it would be possible to violate the guarantee of human dignity without consequences (Jeßberger 2003, pp. 711, 713 f.); Hilgendorf 2004, pp. 331, 339). The exclusion of emergency assistance as a legal defense by an officeholder to justify a criminal offense is in conformity with international law, with international prohibitions on torture explicitly excluding any justifications for torture based on emergency or war scenarios[6] and requiring that violations be sanctioned.[7] In all likelihood, these requirements also apply even when the person who relies on the emergency assistance justification has a close relationship to the potential victims. Regardless, a person who violates the human dignity taboo runs the risk of being severely sanctioned. Thus, in the ticking-bomb scenario, the world can only be saved by someone who is willing to go to prison for it.

The purposively rational approach to such "tragic choices" lies in the fact that the presumed readiness of an individual to sacrifice herself to save the world is, of itself, an effective protection against the usurpation of a "tragic choice" situation. For the hero of the tragedy is cemented by the inescapable link between rescue and sanction. This ensures—as far as legally possible—that the claim of a "tragic choice" will only occur under the most extreme, almost theoretical,[8] circumstances. And it is only under such circumstances that restrictions on human dignity are proposed with purposively rational arguments. In contrast to the creation of legal exemptions, this approach does not run the risk of extensive interpretation, unauthorized use, reliance on exculpatory factual errors, or procedural undermining.

The case of the "U.S. Army Field Manual on Interrogation" [9] in Iraq succinctly illustrates the fact that efforts to legally quantify violations of human dignity can easily derail. This is, by all means, not the only such example. In Israel, the 1987 "Landau Commission,"[10] chaired by the former president of the Supreme Court of

[6]Compare with Art. 2 Abs. 2 Übereinkommen gegen Folter und andere grausame unmenschliche oder erniedrigende Behandlung oder Strafe, BGBI. 1990 II, p. 246.

[7]Compare with Art. 4 Abs. I Übereinkommen gegen Folter und andere grausame unmenschliche oder erniedrigende Behandlung oder Strafe, BGBI. 1990 II, p. 246.

[8]The theoretical character of the examples is emphasized by Schlink (2002), p. 6.

[9]For more, see e.g., FAZ, 14 May 2004, pp. 1 f.

[10]On the report of the Landau Commission and its reception, Gur-Arye and Jessberger (2011), pp. 238–241.

Israel, reacted to terrorism interrogation practices of the General Security Service (Shin Bet) which regularly resulted in the physical abuse of Palestinians. As the Commission was convinced that the use of physical force during terrorism interrogations could not be renounced without endangering the existence of the State of Israel. It developed a set of rules to define circumstances when the use of "moderate measures of physical pressure" would be considered permissible. This was done in an attempt to make interrogations more orderly and less secret (Imseis 2001, pp. 328, 333 ff.). The government implemented the recommendations of the Landau Commission in the same year: this express permission quickly resulted in a dramatic increase in the use of "moderate measures of physical pressure" during the interrogation of Palestinians. In light of this, in 1999, the Supreme Court of Israel ruled the use of "moderate measures of physical pressure" unconstitutional (Imseis 2001, pp. 328/339 ff.; Economist 2003, p. 21).[11]

Because the law sanctions violations of human dignity in all cases, i.e., by demanding a sacrifice for any violation of the taboo, the usurpation of "tragic choice" is made unattractive: violations are not rewarded, and there will always be a price to pay—especially in cases of factual error. While the police officer who actually saves many innocent lives—or even the world—may hope for a pardon or a lenient verdict, the individual who senselessly breaks the taboo—or tortures an innocent victim—can expect neither. This logic corresponds to what is known about archaic taboos: breaking a taboo will always results in the taboo breaker (Freud 1913, pp. 35, 43) suffering, as taboos do not know exculpatory error-doctrines. In "Totem and Taboo," Freud reports on indigenous warriors who, in defending their village from attackers, broke their society's killing taboo. Due to this violation, they were often excluded from the community for months (Freud 1913, pp. 48 ff.). In other indigenous cultures, eating the king's food—even unwittingly—would break a taboo and result in death (Freud 1913, p. 55).

Given innumerable experiences with the socially-disintegrating effects of human dignity violations, particularly through torture, and given that the law has not been able to contain such excesses, society has adopted to no longer leave the management of "tragic choices" solely to the legal system. In the everyday fight against terrorism and criminality—for which additional information is of course always useful, but for which no one has yet questioned the ban on torture—the absolute legal prohibition on violations of human dignity results in the *de facto* implementation of far-reaching protections. On the one hand, due to the sanctions associated with the breaking of the taboo, it is not to be expected that a police officer—in day-to-day investigative work or even in cases of terrorism and serious crime—will sacrifice her career, profession, and freedom in order to obtain information that only potentially, through long and possibly uncertain causal chains, may lead to the aversion of a still abstract danger. On the other hand, in extreme cases that justify exceptions from the prohibition of torture—such as the immediate and concrete danger to a large number of people—society relies on the fact that, in such

[11] The decision leaves a possible justification of force used by an agent in a state emergency.

exceptional circumstances, someone will be found to make an individual ethical decision, which no law or regulation could make her do anyway (Schlink 2002, p. 6), in order to take the necessary actions, even when this will be at her own expense. It is the interplay between legal taboos and individual, ethically answerable taboo breakages that enables the appropriate handling of theoretical and actual "tragic choice" situations. The case of the Frankfurt Vice-President of Police followed this pattern. In part, it is true that his actions were met with ethical understanding (e.g. Mackenroth 2003, p. 6). However, this did not hinder the appropriate institutions from pursuing the crime: the Vice-President of Police was transferred to another post, accused in a criminal court, and—albeit mildly and conditionally—sentenced. [12]

The handling of ticking-bomb scenarios is deeply rooted in our popular culture. An abundance of books and films exist that take up the "Dirty Harry" theme (also see Cooper, in this volume, Chap. 2): a cop who uses all means available, up to and including torture, to save innocent victims from terrorists, organized criminals, and madmen. The figure of the police officer who is willing to make personal sacrifices when it comes to breaking the law is an integral component of the genre. "Go on out and get some air, fatso," says Dirty Harry to his trailing partner as he is about to drive the heel of his boot into the gunshot wound of the kidnapper he has hunted down, in order to get information about the whereabouts of the abducted schoolgirl whom he believes is still alive. Yet, just like the real-world case of Jakob von Metzler, the schoolgirl is already dead at the time of the forced testimony. And just like the Frankfurt Vice-President of Police, Dirty Harry will never become the police commissioner; instead, he spends his time fighting (mostly in vain) against his transfer and suspension. But it is precisely because he makes an individual, ethically-responsible decision—and bears the brunt of the sanctions it brings—that he is the hero of the genre.

3.5 Conclusion

How can these considerations be summarized? Firstly, it can now be understood why doctrinal relativizations of the guarantee of human dignity are not viable under the German Basic Law. Attempts to subjugate the absoluteness of the guarantee of human dignity to a balancing approach otherwise practiced in fundamental rights doctrine misjudge the special socio-legal status of the prohibition contained in Art. 1 GG. The guarantee of human dignity does not contain a simple restraint, like the Basic Law's other fundamental rights, that is open to purposively rational

[12] In a way the taboo was later even reinforced in ECtHR, application no. 22978/05, 1 June 2010, par. 124, which found the punishment of the officers too lenient with respect to the violation of Art. 3 ECHR.

deliberations, but rather a taboo, the absolute validity of which is neither subject to any dogmatic balancing act nor as a regulatory type in need of it.

Secondly, while not perceptible to the legal system itself, socio-legal considerations can reveal the purposive rationality of the taboo. Legal efforts to "soften" the guarantee of human dignity have proven vulnerable to usurpation and inflation. Only an absolute legal prohibition can prevent human dignity violations. By demanding a personal sacrifice from anyone who breaks the taboo—even if it is done to save the world—the guarantee ensures, insofar as the law can, that "tragic choices" are only taken when exceptional conditions, such as the ones discussed by Luhmann, really occur. In these cases, the legal taboo of human dignity relies on the ethically responsible decision of the individual, the seriousness of which is secured by the personal sacrifice the breaking of the taboo requires. As opposed to other societal problems, the law does not contribute to a solution by legalizing the behavior it deems necessary, but rather by threatening to sanction behavior that is, in exceptional cases, deemed necessary. From a legal perspective, this solution is paradoxical. However, in a socio-legal perspective, the purposive rationality of the absolute inviolability of human dignity—even in extreme and exceptional cases—becomes apparent. In the discussed tragic choice scenarios, the rationality of the absolute guarantee of human dignity only emerges through the contrasting interplay between law and ethics.

Finally, Luhmann's question on the indispensability of norms can now be answered. Contrary to Luhmann's assumption, the law can—even in the extreme cases suggested by him—declare human dignity inviolable. It is not only due to its dogmatic claim to absoluteness but also due to its instrumentalization of the difference between law and ethics, that the guarantee of human dignity is *ta pu* as opposed to *noa*—extraordinary as opposed to ordinary.

References

Balle C (1990) Tabus in der Sprache. Lang, Frankfurt/Main

Böckenförde E-W (2003) Die Würde des Menschen war unantastbar. FAZ, September 3, pp 33–35

Brugger W (1995) Würde gegen Würde. Verwaltungsblätter für Baden-Württemberg 16:414–416, 446–455

Brugger W (1996) Darf der Staat ausnahmsweise foltern. Der Staat 35:67–97

Brugger W (2003) Darf der Staat foltern? Eine Podiumsdiskussion. para 11. https://www.rewi.hu-berlin.de/de/lf/oe/hfr/deutsch/2002-04.pdf. Accessed 30 June 2023

Depenheuer O (ed) (2003) Recht und Tabu. VS Verlag für Sozialwissenschaften, Wiesbaden

Durkheim E (1969) Journal Sociologique, p 62 (previously l'année soziologique, vol. I, 1896/97)

Freud S (1913 [1999]) Totem und Tabu. In: Freud A, Bibring E, Krist E (eds) Gesammelte Werke, vol 9. Fischer, Frankfurt/Main, pp 35, 43

Gur-Arye, Miriam/Jessberger, Florian. 2011. The protection of human dignity in interrogations: may interrogative torture ever be tolerated? Reflections in the light of recent German and Israeli experiences Israel Law Rev 44: 229-262.

Haas R (1978) Notwehr und Nothilfe. Lang, Frankfurt/Main. pp. 319 ff.

Hilgendorf E (2004) Folter im Rechtsstaat? JuristenZeitung 7:331–339

Hirsch M (1990) Realer Inzest, 2nd edn. Psychosozialverlag, Gießen, pp 5 ff.
Hörnle T (2003) Grob anstößiges Verhalten. Klostermann, Frankfurt/Main
Imseis A (2001) "Moderate" torture on trial: critical reflections on the Israeli Supreme Court Judgment concerning the legality of general security service interrogation methods. Berkeley J Int Law 19(2):328–349
Jakobs G (1991) Strafrecht Allgemeiner Teil, 2nd edn. de Gruyter, Berlin
Jeßberger F (2003) Wenn du nicht redest, füge ich Dir große Schmerzen zu, JURA, pp 711–715
Kloepfer M (1976) The exception that makes the rule: Grundrechtstatbestand und Grundrechtsschranken in der Rechtsprechung des Bundesverfassungsgerichtes. In: Starck C (ed) Bundesverfassungsgericht und Grundgesetz, vol 2. Mohr Siebeck, Tübingen. pp. 405 ff.
Levinson S (ed) (2004) Torture. Oxford University Press, Oxford
Luhmann N (1993) Gibt es in unserer Gesellschaft noch unverzichtbare Normen? C.F. Müller, Heidelberg
Mackenroth G (2003) Richter Mackenroth zieht Folter-Äußerungen zurück, Associated Press. Süddeutsche Zeitung, February 25, p 6
Marschall W (1976) Tabu. In: Ritter J, Gründer K (eds) Historisches Wörterbuch der Philosophie, vol I. Schwabe, Basel
Reimann H (1985) Tabu. In: Görres-Gesellschaft (ed) Staatslexikon, vol 5, 7th edn. Herder, Freiburg
Roxin C (1997) Strafrecht Allgemeiner Teil, vol I, 3rd edn. Beck, München, § 15, Rn. 95
Schelsky H (1955) Soziologie der Sexualität. Rowohlt, Hamburg. pp 88 ff.
Schlink B (2002) Darf der Staat foltern? Eine Podiumsdiskussion, p 6. https://www.rewi.hu-berlin.de/de/lf/oe/hfr/deutsch/2002-04.pdf. Accessed 30 June 2023
Schröder H (1994–1995) Tabu. Antrittsvorlesungen Wintersemester 1994/95. Europa-Universität Viadrina, Frankfurt/Oder
Schröder H (1995) Tabuforschung als Aufgabe interkultureller Germanistik. In: Jahrbuch Deutsch als Fremdsprache, vol 21. iudicium, München, p 15
Seibel K (1990) Zum Begriff des Tabus. Eine soziologische Perspektive. Johann Wolfgang Goethe-Universität, Frankfurt/Main, p 75
The Economist (2003) Is torture ever justified? 9 January 2003. https://www.economist.com/leaders/2003/01/09/is-torture-ever-justified. Accessed 30 June 2023
Weber M (2019) Economy and society: a new translation [ed and transl: Tribe K]. Harvard University Press, Cambridge, pp 102/103

Chapter 4
Dignity-Enhancing Constitutionalism

Alon Harel

Abstract Human dignity is often perceived as an independent right. However, in this chapter, I provide a different account of human dignity. Particularly, I argue that the constitutional entrenchment of rights (as opposed to the mere protection of rights by statutes) is required by dignity-based concerns. Specifically, I maintain that *constitutional* protection of rights indicates that rights impose duties on the state; they are not a byproduct of its will or inclinations, and therefore, *constitutional* protection of rights is dignity-enhancing. More specifically, a constitutional bill of rights transforms and restructures the relationship between the citizens and the state in various ways. It is a form of acknowledgment that rights are not mere privileges granted to citizens; their protection is not contingent on the preferences or the judgments of the people. In the absence of constitutional entrenchment of rights, rights can be understood to be protected merely because the legislature prefers to protect them or judges them to be justified or even because judges hold them to exist. The constitutional entrenchment of rights is, therefore, qualitatively different from mere legislative protection of such rights, and such protection is required by dignity-based considerations.

4.1 Introduction

Article 1 of the German Constitution protects the right to dignity.[1] It asserts that "human dignity shall be inviolable. To respect and protect it shall be the duty of all state authority." The South-African Constitution makes a similar assertion entrenching the value of dignity with the right to dignity.[2] Therefore, human dignity

[1] Article 1, Basic Law for the Federal Republic of Germany.

[2] Article 1 of the South African Constitution entrenches the value of dignity and article 10 protects the right to dignity.

A. Harel (✉)
Hebrew University of Jerusalem, Jerusalem, Israel
e-mail: alon.harel@mail.huji.ac.il

S. N. Arel et al. (eds.), *Probing Human Dignity*,
https://doi.org/10.1007/978-3-031-42437-3_4

in various jurisdictions has become a constitutionally-entrenched norm, and vast literature has explored what dignity means or ought to mean.

This chapter does not discuss the constitutionally-entrenched right to dignity. Instead, I defend the claim that a constitutional bill of rights is required for the maintenance of dignity in a liberal state. It is thus the dignity-enhancing effects of the *form* of constitutionally entrenching rights that I am interested in rather than the constitutional right to dignity. More particularly, I argue that *constitutionally* entrenched rights are fundamentally different from rights that are protected by legislation as only the former provide a recognition that the state is morally or politically obliged to protect such rights and that such rights are moral rights that pre-exist their legal recognition.

I assume that there are fundamental rights that ought to be protected in every state independently of the question of whether people want these rights to be protected, judge them to be desirable, or provide a legal recognition to these rights.[3] Those rights can be legally protected in different ways e.g. by the executive, through legislation, or by constitutionally entrenching these rights. Last, I argue that dignity dictates that those rights be constitutionally protected.[4] A constitutional bill of rights transforms and restructures the relationship between the citizens and the state in various ways. It is a form of acknowledgment that rights are not mere privileges granted to citizens; their protection is not contingent on the preferences or the judgments of the people. In the absence of constitutional entrenchment of rights, rights can be understood to be protected merely because the legislature prefers to protect them or judges them to be justified or even because judges hold them to exist. The constitutional entrenchment of liberties is, therefore, qualitatively different from mere legislative protection of such liberties. It indicates that the protection of these rights is a duty on the part of the state rather than a choice made by it.

To establish this claim, I start by defining what I mean by a constitution. A constitution is not a document or a text; it is a set of norms that guide the behavior of public officials, politicians, judges, etc. I distinguish between two types of constitutional norms: first, constitutional norms which create new duties, and second, constitutional norms which replicate pre-existing moral or political obligations. I focus my attention on the latter category. Last, I maintain that the value of liberty-protecting binding constitutional norms is not based only or primarily on their effectiveness but on their *binding* nature. Constitutional entrenchment of rights is a form of recognition that the protection of rights is a duty imposed on the state—a duty that exists independently of its entrenchment in the legal system. A constitution is, therefore, not merely an instrument to effectively protect rights; in fact, the

[3]This assumption is accepted by all including the opponents of constitutionalism. For a discussion see also Harel (2003), p. 247.

[4]Note that by using the term constitutionally protected, I do not presuppose that they need to specifically appear in the Constitution. It is enough that they are recognized as constitutional by the courts or by other officials.

constitutional entrenchment of rights transforms these rights in ways that are conducive to human dignity.

Most importantly, this chapter rejects what I in the past labeled constitutional instrumentalism, namely the view that constitutions are mere instruments designed to bring about desirable outcomes (Harel 2014, part III). Instead, I suggest that binding constitutional norms are justified not by the prospect of thereby securing just or correct outcomes but by the way they convey publicly the status of rights and the grounds for protecting them (Harel 2014, Chap. 5).

4.2 The Nature of Constitutional Norms

The term constitution and the term constitutional norms is used in different contexts in different ways. In the US, the Constitution is a document which includes provisions that override regular statutes, and the courts are in charge of enforcing it; in the UK, a constitution consists of an uncodified set of rules, conventions, and precedents which govern the relations between the branches of power, in particular between the monarch and the Parliament. For my purposes, a constitutional norm is a norm that is grounded in practices, conventions, and shared understandings of legislators, lawyers, and public officials and guides their behavior (Harel 2014, pp. 152–158). Thus constitutional norms are nothing but norms that are recognized as constitutional or foundational and treated as such.

This definition has important implications: A constitutional norm is not necessarily written as the case of the English constitutional conventions testifies (Dicey 1959, p. 24). It also need not be enforceable by the courts.[5] Some constitutions are enforceable, while others are not or are only partly enforceable.

Constitutional norms are simply norms that guide behavior, and, in order to guide behavior, they need not be either written or even enforceable. What is, however, unique in constitutional norms as defined here is that constitutional norms guide not only public officials but also the legislature itself. Constitutional norms are the supreme norms of the legal system and consequently guide all branches of power.

A constitution may contain two types of constitutional norms: binding and non-binding. The binding constitutional norms impose duties (that are typically grounded in rights), while the non-binding may dictate that certain norms are 'constitutionally worthy." To the extent that a constitution consists of non-binding norms, these norms can have symbolic value (Corbin 1936), or they may serve to solidify or unify the political community (Grimm 2008). This chapter focuses its attention on binding constitutional norms.

[5] Some written constitutions include specific provisions of unenforceability of some of the provisions. See e.g. part IV of the Indian Constitution entitled: directive principles. Yet, even the non-enforceable provisions are binding. See Sect. 37 of the Indian Constitution.

Constitutional norms are positive legal norms; they form part of the legal system. Hence, to interpret a constitutional norm, it is not enough to use logic or reason; in addition, one has to resort to the way the norm has been interpreted or used in the past, to the conventionally accepted articulation of the norm and the ways it was understood and applied in the past. Conformity with the constitutional norm presupposes an ongoing framework of practices with participants immersing themselves in formulating, articulating, and shaping the meanings of constitutional norms. The constitutional discourse is, therefore, a practice-oriented discourse that is grounded in the way decision-makers understand, interpret, and apply the constitution.

The guidance of decision-makers by constitutional norms is an intentional guidance; the participants subject themselves to the guidance of the norms and, when they are not guided (or believed not to be guided) by it, they are typically criticized by other participants for failing to do so. Most typically, their response to such criticisms is not that the constitutional provisions are not binding but that they have a different understanding or interpretation of these norms. It is agreed, therefore, by most or all prominent decision-makers, that the constitutional provisions are binding, and disputes among them are not the byproduct of a controversy as to whether the constitution binds but a byproduct of a controversy as to what the constitution means or entails. Note that under this characterization, written documents that are not efficacious, such as the Constitution of the Soviet Union, are not genuinely constitutions as they do not serve to guide decision-makers. What constitutes a constitution are the ultimate practices of decision-makers, not written documents or solemn (inefficacious) declarations.

There are two types of binding constitutional directives: There are norms that *create* obligations that did not pre-exist their constitutional entrenchment, and there are norms that replicate pre-existing moral or political obligations.[6] Thus, for instance, the US Constitution establishes a constitutional federal republic and determines the structure of government, Congress, and other institutions. Those institutions are created by the Constitution. Perhaps there were pragmatic reasons that justify entrenching these institutions (rather than others), but they are certainly not morally mandatory institutions. The constitutional framers could have established other mechanisms of decision-making. But, in addition, the US Constitution replicates pre-existing moral (or political) rights; for instance, it protects freedom of speech, freedom of religion, equality, etc. Those rights have been understood by the founders of the Constitution to bind all public authority, and their constitutional entrenchment was designed to give effect to the pre-existing duties of the state.[7] Let us label this category of constitutional norms morally-replicated constitutional norms and explore in greater detail the nature of morally-replicated rights.

Some constitutional provisions hinge primarily or exclusively on the will of the polity. For instance, the polity ought to settle disagreements with respect to the

[6] For this distinction, see Alexander (2009), p. 229.

[7] Here the term state refers to the US federation and not to the states composing it.

procedures required to bequeath property. The resulting settlement reflects preferences and judgments. Once the society selected a constitutional provision of this type, it created a duty which did not exist before the constitutional entrenchment of this provision. Once the duty is created, this duty provides reasons to comply with it simply because this duty has been created and became salient. Legally or constitutionally entrenching such a duty created expectations and guided individuals to act in certain ways. Consequently, often one has reasons to honor the expectations created by the legal duty. But note that the moral reasons to be guided by these duties are the byproduct of constitutional entrenchment; the moral reasons did not pre-exist the constitutional entrenchment. In contrast, other constitutional norms incorporate premoral rights into the legal system. In such cases, the polity incorporates pre-existing moral and political rights and makes them legally (or constitutionally) binding (and, often, also enforceable by the judiciary). In doing so, the polity ought to identify what the content of the moral rights is—a content which does not depend on its will. The former category is the category of created legal rights, while the latter category can be labeled replicated, or incorporated moral rights. In this chapter, I focus exclusively on the latter category—the category of pre-existing moral rights which were entrenched in the constitution—morally-replicated constitutional rights.

The entrenchment of morally-replicated constitutional rights transforms the content of the pre-existing moral norms. Once the pre-existing moral rights are entrenched, they are also transformed; in particular, they become more determinate. There are three features which differentiate morally-replicated rights from pre-existing moral rights. First, in contrast to the pre-existing moral rights, binding replicated constitutional rights are *positive* legal rights. Second, they are determinate rights, in other words their content is typically more determinate and clear than the pre-existing moral rights and third their identification typically requires legal expertise. In these three respects, the morally-replicated constitutional rights differ from the pre-existing moral rights

4.2.1 Constitutional Rights Are Positive Legal Norms

Unlike moral or political rights, morally-replicated constitutional rights are rooted in practices and conventions of certain communities. To establish the existence of such a right, it is not sufficient to deliberate abstractly; in addition, it is necessary to examine practices, investigate existing conventions, explore the past behavior of public officials, and interpret previous decisions.

4.2.2 Determinacy and Specificity

The moral rights underlying morally-replicated constitutional rights are highly abstract and indeterminate. There are typically numerous ways of interpreting or applying these rights. To illustrate, both the US and European countries protect freedom of expression vigorously. In both cases, this right can be characterized as a morally-replicated constitutional right because citizens have a pre-existing political right to free expression independently of whether it is constitutionally (or even legally) entrenched. But, the norm of protecting speech took different forms in the US and in European jurisdictions. The constitutionally entrenched replicated moral rights are not, therefore, a mere replica of the underlying moral right. Instead, such rights are the byproduct of a choice on the part of the polity as to which among the morally feasible moral duties would eventually govern the polity. Further, the specific determination of the constitutionally-entrenched right changes and develops with the practices used by officials to implement the norm. New conventions are created, and often old ones are abandoned. To employ the phrase used by some US constitutional theorists, *the constitution is a living tree; it adapts itself to new times.*

Also note, that often by entrenching the right in the constitution and acting in accordance with it, the determinate entrenched right itself gains normative strength as a result of its being entrenched and practiced. In other words, the political community has reasons to conform to the new more determinate right simply because it was constitutionally entrenched and, thereby, created expectations which merit respect.

4.2.3 Expertise

Given that the content of the morally-replicated constitutional right is contingent upon existing practices and conventions, these rights are typically accompanied by interpretative privileges of public officials: judges, lawyers, politicians, etc. While no one has any special privileges in reasoning about morality, constitutional provisions are typically interpreted and applied by experts. Yet, given the fact that such rights must satisfy the requirements of the pre-existing moral rights, non-experts also have a role in their interpretation. In fact, in making certain judgments about how to behave, every citizen needs to interpret constitutional provisions. Replicated binding constitutional rights are not technical norms whose interpretation is exclusively granted to experts, but they are also not moral norms whose identification does not presuppose expertise.

4.2.4 Summary

Let us sum up the discussion so far: Constitutional rights are grounded in practices that bind the legislature. We distinguished between binding and non-binding constitutional rights. We also distinguished between created and morally-replicated binding constitutional rights, and we analyzed the differences between morally-replicated constitutional rights and the underlying moral rights. The next section will identify the moral significance of this category and, in particular, will establish that morally-replicated constitutional rights are dignity-enhancing. In their absence, the protection of fundamental rights is defective even when it is effective.

4.3 Dignity-Based Constitutionalism and Morally Replicated Constitutional Rights

Why, if at all, should pre-existing moral or political rights be constitutionally entrenched? Why should they not merely be honored by the state? What can explain the urge to constitutionalize such liberties?

One natural answer is instrumental: constitutionally entrenched moral or political rights-based duties (either enforceable or unenforceable) prompt legislatures (and other branches of government) to conform to their moral duties. There are several reasons why constitutional duties are more likely to be effective than other means of protecting rights. Constitutional rights are often entrenched, and changing them is often costly. Further, typically they are also publicly salient and therefore serve to educate the public. Hence, it could be argued that constitutionally entrenched rights have deeper roots than other rights: they are stable, difficult to change, and they are, as a rule, better rooted in the belief system of the citizens.

To the extent that constitutional entrenchment serves to "improve" the decision-making of the legislatures and other decision-makers, bills of rights play an important *instrumental* role in facilitating effective protection of rights. This view is the one that guides the writings of Joseph Raz, who believes that the only difference law, in general, and constitutions, in particular, make in a moral space is one of providing better guidance concerning the demands of right reason than direct (or independent) deliberation on the part of citizens as to what these demands are and how to pursue them (Raz 1986, p. 53). To put it simply, when a person obeys the law, she is more likely to make better decisions than she would have made otherwise. Hence, law in general and constitutions, in particular, are desirable if and to the extent that they are likely to bring about more (or better) convergence between behavior and the demands of right reason than would have been brought about without the law. Raz is the best and the most articulate advocate of instrumental constitutionalism, namely of the view that constitutions can be contingently desirable to the extent that they improve decision-making (Raz 1998).

While Raz provided a general framework, constitutional theorists often develop more specific theories, and, in particular, such theorists provide a detailed description of what they believe the demands of right reason that ought to be brought about by the constitutional directives are. They often argue that the constitutional provisions are conducive to the protection of rights, democracy, consistency, etc. Let me provide a few examples: In discussing the US Constitution, Ronald Dworkin maintained that:

> I see no alternative but to use result-driven rather than a procedure-driven standard for deciding them [institutional questions]. The best institutional structure is the one best calculated to produce the best answers to the essentially moral questions of what the democratic conditions actually are, and to secure stable compliance with those conditions (Dworkin 1996).

Dworkin believed that the constitution is designed to protect fundamental rights. In contrast, John Hart Ely believed that the constitution is a procedural document and that the goals of the Constitution should favor a "participation-oriented representation." (Hart Ely 1980). It is, therefore, effective representation that should be the aim of constitutional design. Alexander and Schauer prefer to regard the law in general and the constitution in particular as an instrument for the authoritative settlement of disagreements. In their view:

> [o]ne of the chief functions of law in general, and constitutional law in particular, is to provide a degree of coordinated settlement for settlement's sake of what is to be done (Alexander and Schauer 2000).

Bruce Ackerman regarded the Constitution as a means of protecting his dualist structure consisting of constitutional politics on the one hand and normal politics on the other hand (Ackerman 2007). In his view, the Constitution is designed to protect constitutional politics that is the byproduct of deliberative long-term effort from the risks of being controlled by the forces of normal politics. As a matter of fact, constitutional theory can be regarded as a long series of attempts to explain why constitutions bring about, as a contingent matter, better decisions than would have been made in their absence. These theories are all guided by Raz's instrumentalist framework; the constitution is valuable on the grounds that it is likely to bring about better convergence between reason on one hand and behavior on the other.

In the past, I have criticized the instrumentalist approach to law in general and to constitutions in particular (Harel 2014, pp. 1–7): Constitutional directives are not merely means to protect rights, democracy, settle disagreements or protect constitutional politics. As a matter of fact, constitutionalizing rights are not a means or an instrument of protecting rights (although constitutional rights may *also* serve this purpose). Constitutional norms that protect rights are not an instrument; they are the form of acknowledgment that such rights are binding upon public authorities and pre-exist their constitutional entrenchment. Before I explain why, let me first reiterate two arguments I made against legal instrumentalism.

Legal instrumentalism is the view that law in general and constitutions, in particular, serve to improve political decisions. However, there are two difficulties regarding this view. First, it is hard and most typically impossible to establish the causal relationship between the legal norms and the desirable decisions likely to result from them. In our context, it is difficult to maintain that constitutional entrenchment of rights brought about morally better decisions than would have been brought about in its absence. The US Constitution is perhaps a good example. Although some highly important rights-protecting decisions have been made on its basis, it also provided a basis for protecting the rights of slave owners (*Dred Scott v. Sandford* (60 US 393, 1856) and depriving workers' rights (*Lochner v. New York*

(198 U.S. 45, 1905). Hence, it is unclear whether constitutional rights bring about better or more morally worthy decisions than those that would have been brought about in their absence. The question of whether constitutions are indeed conducive to justice in the long run hinges on so many contingencies that it cannot be determined by social science methods. As a matter of fact, social scientists have even argued that constitutions have little, if any, effect on the degree to which rights are protected (Chilton and Versteeg 2020).

Further, instrumental arguments often lead us astray as they try to provide a quasi-scientific instrumental justification to sentiments which are grounded in other non-contingent considerations. In the past, I have illustrated this claim by using an analogy based on utilitarian reasoning. Utilitarianism aims to justify the prohibition of slavery by arguing that slavery is detrimental to utility. The claim that slavery is detrimental to utility may be correct or false, but it is definitely beside the point: slavery is wrong for other reasons. There is, therefore an incongruity between the utilitarian explanation and the underlying reasons that motivate the struggle against slavery. To apply it to our context, instrumental justifications used to justify the constitutional provisions are incongruent with the underlying sentiments and passions that sustain the public concern for constitutions. Simply put, we want constitutions not only or primarily because they bring about morally better results (as a contingent matter) than governments without constitutions. We want them because they transform our status in the state from being mere beneficiaries of the preferences and judgments of the state to being the beneficiaries of duties owed to us by the state.

Constitutional norms which entrench pre-existing moral duties are dignity-enhancing. What constitutional entrenchment of pre-existing moral rights contributes is the public recognition that basic moral rights are owed to citizens, and consequently, they impose duties on the government. They are not given to them as a gesture of the legislature, as a gift, or even as a merely considered judgment on the part of the legislature. The constitutional bill of rights is a public declaration that is grounded in practices and conventions that rights matter and that their protection on the part of the state is a rights-based moral duty.

Take the recognition of gay marriage. There are at least two ways of granting gay people the right to marry. One is based on standard majoritarian sentiments. To facilitate gay marriages, one may change the law and recognize such marriages. This decision on the part of the legislature can be done for many reasons. It can be done because we believe that marriage is about love and intimacy, and those can exist independently of the genders of the parties. It can be done because it is conducive to the economy, as gay couples may be more productive if their intimacy is officially recognized. Thus, the decision to recognize gay marriage on the part of the legislature can be understood and interpreted in different ways. Further, citizens living in a state where their rights are protected in this way are at the mercy of the legislature. This does not imply that their rights are not *effectively* protected. It implies, however (as I will show below) that their protection does not honor their status as rights-bearers.

Compare it to a case where a court has declared that gay marriage is required by the equal protection clause of the constitution[8] or the dignity-based provision (for this also see Ewing in this volume). A decision of this type on the part of the Court can only be grounded in the conviction that the state has a duty to recognize gay marriage, namely that it is a fundamental right of same-sex couples. This duty does not hinge upon the goodwill of the legislature, and therefore, same-sex couples cannot be described as being at the mercy of the legislature. Hence, although in both of these cases, same-sex couples can marry, the public meaning of their right to marriage is fundamentally different. In such a case, the Court does not create the right; it merely announces that it is entrenched in the Constitution.

More generally, constitutionally-entrenched rights are fundamentally different from rights created by legislation. Prior to constitutional entrenchment, the right-protecting decisions of the legislature can be plausibly interpreted as grounded in the inclinations, or perhaps, in the judgments of the legislature concerning the public good. Even if the legislature, in its deliberations, declares its conviction that the rights it protects are ones that are grounded in pre-existing moral rights, such a declaration on its part can always be challenged. What turns such norms into dignity-based rights is the constitutional entrenchment of these norms which conveys the shared understanding that these norms bind the legislature and that the legislature cannot act otherwise without violating its duties.

This observation can be rephrased in terms of dignity. A constitutional bill of rights honors dignity not because the bill contains a provision protecting dignity, and also not because dignity is more likely to be protected when rights are constitutionally entrenched, as constitutional instrumentalists argue. Instead, as I argued earlier, it is the constitutional *form* of entrenching rights that is a prerequisite for the full recognition of individuals as rights-bearers. Hence, the relation between constitutions and the protection of dignity is not a contingent feature of constitutions—one that hinges upon their content or effectiveness. Instead, it is a necessary feature of constitutions. The constitutional entrenchment in itself rather than merely its contingent effects is dignity-enhancing.

This analysis also explains the specific role that courts have in maintaining constitutional provisions. Legislatures are typically perceived to be a vehicle for giving effect to the will of the people or, at times, to their judgments concerning what is good or bad. Courts, in contrast, are (at least ideally) bastions of reason. The standard account given to these institutions is an instrumental account. Under this standard account, institutions are mere means to the realization of the right decisions, and the question of what counts as a right decision does not hinge upon who makes it. To determine, therefore, what the role of courts or legislatures is, one has to determine which among these institutions is more likely to reach the right decisions.

I believe this account is misguided. Institutions are not mere instruments for the production of decisions. The choice to assign a particular role to an institution does

[8] For the US decision along these lines, see *Obergefell v. Hodges* 576 US 644 (2015); for the South African decision, see *Minister of Home Affairs v. Fourie* 2006 (1) SA 524 (CC).

not rest merely on its competence. It is often the case that the agent assigned to make a certain decision plays an important role in publicly signifying what the decision is about. By assigning decisions concerning the scope of rights to courts, the polity indicates that it perceives such decisions to be grounded in reason rather than in will. Courts are called upon to make such decisions not because they are moral experts or experts on what reason dictates, but because by granting them the power to make constitutional decisions, these decisions are publicly recognized as reason-based rather than will-based decisions.

4.4 Conclusion

Dignity is an elusive concept. It is often difficult to assert that a particular right is grounded in dignity. The vagueness of dignity also explains why often opposing views are justified in terms of dignity (see Hellmann in this volume). These concerns led some theorists to conclude that dignity ought to be eradicated from the dictionary of clear-headed minds (Baragic and Allan 2006; Pinker 2008). This chapter indicates that there is a way to salvage dignity from its enemies. What characterizes dignity is not what it protects but how it protects it (Harel 2014, p. 60). This chapter suggests that dignity dictates the form of protection of basic liberties; more particularly, it dictates that basic liberties should be constitutionally protected as only constitutional protection acknowledges that basic rights bind not because they were created by the state but they were created by the state because they bind it.

References

Ackerman B (2007) The living constitution. Harvard Law Rev 120:1737

Alexander L (2009) Of living trees and dead hands: the interpretation of constitutions and constitutional rights. Can J Law Jurisprud 22(2):229

Alexander L, Schauer F (2000) Defending judicial review: a reply. Const Comment 177:455

Baragic M, Allan J (2006) The vacuous concept of dignity. J Hum Rights 5:257

Chilton A, Versteeg M (2020) How constitutional rights matter. Oxford University Press

Corbin ES (1936) The constitution as an instrument and as a symbol. Am Polit Sci Rev 30:1071

Dicey AV (1959) Introduction to the study of the law of the constitution, 10th edn. Macmillan Education Ltd, p 24

Dworkin R (1996) Freedom's law: the moral reading of the American Constitution. Harvard University Press, Cambridge

Grimm D (2008) Integration by constitution. Int J Constit Law 3:193

Harel A (2003) Rights-based judicial review. Law Philos 22:247

Harel A (2014) Why law matters. Oxford University Press

Hart Ely J (1980) Democracy and distrust: a theory of judicial review. Harvard University Press, p 74

Pinker S (2008) The stupidity of dignity. The New Republic

Raz J (1986) The morality of freedom. Oxford University Press

Raz J (1998) On the authority and interpretation of constitutions. In: Alexander L (ed) Constitutionalism: philosophical foundations

Part III
Fields of Dignity as Threshold Spaces

Chapter 5
Human Dignity, Poverty and Social Exclusion Challenges for Europe

Caterina Drigo

Abstract In a world in which inequalities often seem to prevail over fundamental human rights, particularly in traditionally wealthy contexts, such as the European one, poverty, social exclusion, and cultural barriers push entire sectors of the population to the margins of society placing them in conditions of enormous strain. These populations are thus not able to fully enjoy the fundamental rights recognized by the legal order. Starting from an empirical analysis of the European regulatory framework on measures to combat poverty and social exclusion, the aim of this chapter is to investigate whether the human dignity protection should imply that there are some fundamental rights that should not be negatively affected by poverty and social exclusion. In other words, how can theoretical and conceptual distinctions of the term "dignity" be drawn to inform new perspectives that probe its ambiguity, seek to offer clarity, and push past thresholds to develop new paradigms that cross disciplinary lines while speaking to mutual goals and needs of post-modern societies and individuals? From the set of social rights and fundamental duties provided at the level of the European Union and emerging in several Constitutions, this chapter questions if it is possible to derive a formal duty for public authorities in the struggle against poverty. Furthermore, I probe whether the principle of human dignity can be considered the basis of various measures to combat poverty and explore whether human dignity can be conceived in a deontic perspective.

5.1 Introduction

In a world in which inequalities often seem to prevail over fundamental human rights, particularly in traditionally wealthy contexts, such as the EU one, more and more segments of the population find themselves in enormous financial difficulty. Because of poverty, they are socially pushed to the margins of the society, and their rights are often not properly guaranteed.

C. Drigo (✉)
University of Bologna, Bologna, Italy
e-mail: caterina.drigo@unibo.it

S. N. Arel et al. (eds.), *Probing Human Dignity*,
https://doi.org/10.1007/978-3-031-42437-3_5

Poverty, social exclusion, invisible—but thick—cultural barriers, push entire sectors of the population to the margins of society and place them in conditions of significant difficulty so that they are not able to fully enjoy the fundamental rights recognized by the legal order they belong to.

This impinges heavily on the fullness of the concept of citizenship and even on the democratic nature of the European legal systems in view of the fact that a "democratic state must be realized around the idea of inclusion and encourage the effective participation of its citizens in political, social, economic and cultural life" (Pérez Miras 2018, p. 1).

But this also deeply affects the processes of inclusion and integration of migrants—the "latest arrived", the "others", who very often coincide with the poorest [1]—and requires to rethink the notion of citizenship, configuring it as a social citizenship in those legal contexts that define themselves as democratic and based on respect for substantial equality, human dignity, and solidarity. [2]

It can be argued that poverty relates to, and is linked to, power. The needy often remain "voiceless" in contemporary representative democracies: "the rich are powerful, they often influence political decisions in their favor and they are also able to *manage* political power" (Petrella 2006, p. 61). Consequently, the sense of *res publica* and that of culture, solidarity and sense of sharing, which should characterize it, are lost.

Starting from an empirical analysis of the European regulatory framework on measures to combat poverty and social exclusion, the aim of this chapter is to find out if human dignity can be considered foundational for combating poverty, and if so, if human dignity can be conceived as a constitutional, and European, duty to fight against poverty.

The European Union, the States, and even their local authorities play an important role in the implementation of the principle of substantial equality, and even of human dignity, conceived of as right to a dignified and decent life.

In my research, I seek to investigate whether human dignity protection should imply that there are some fundamental rights that should not be negatively affected by poverty and social exclusion. In other words, how can theoretical and conceptual distinctions of the term "dignity" be drawn to inform new perspectives that probe its ambiguity, seek to offer clarity, and push past thresholds to develop new paradigms that cross disciplinary lines while speaking to mutual goals and needs of post-modern societies and individuals?

From the set of social rights and fundamental duties provided at the level of the European Union and emerging in several Constitutions, this chapter questions if it is possible to derive a formal duty for public authorities in the struggle against poverty?

[1] For example, according to ISTAT, in Italy one third o migrants family are living below the poverty rate, and that data is increasing. Data published in June 2022, https://www.istat.it/it/files/2022/06/Report_Povertà_2021_14-06. See also the considerations of the Italian Constitutional Court, dec. n. 44 of 2020 and n. 19 of 2022, in www.giurcost.org.

[2] On the evolution of the notion of citizenship in societies where significant factors of cultural diversity are present: Benhabib (2006) and Taylor-Gooby (2008).

Furthermore, I probe whether the principle of human dignity can be considered the basis of various measures to combat poverty and explore whether human dignity can be conceived in a deontic perspective.

5.2 Poverty and Social Exclusion Through the Prism of Dignity

5.2.1 Poverty and Social Exclusion: A Matter of Dignity?

5.2.1.1 The Protean Dimension of Human Dignity

Any study that involves human dignity, poverty, and social exclusion requires a preliminary consideration of the definition of the essential features of these concepts and to the drawing attention to of the various problematic aspects inherent in this activity.

As known, human dignity has been the object of deep studies from a philosophical, moral and juridical point of view. [3] The connection between human dignity and fundamental human rights is widely recognized among scholars, who conceive of dignity as a precondition and justification for such rights. In theoretical reconstructions, human dignity has often been associated with the hendiadys freedom– equality. [4] It is from this sense of equality that it is essential to start. Furthermore, poverty, dignity, equality and fundamental human rights are inseparably interrelated concepts. [5]

States have the duty to remove the inequalities that exist from a substantive point of view, striving to put individuals in a position to effectively enjoy and exercise constitutional fundamental rights and to be able to express one's personality. However, the methods of action and the constraints provided for by the state constitutions are manifold. [6] Similarly, the European Union builds the Charter of Fundamental Rights around three "pillars", dignity, equality and solidarity, welded in an inseparable *unicum* which finds significant expansive potential in the EU Treaties.

Establish merely formally the duty to work to remove inequalities and poverty as precipitated by the legal recognition of human dignity is obviously not in itself sufficient to guarantee effective protection. On one hand, scholars and judges commonly acknowledge the fact that the hard core of human rights (conceived as

---

[3] *Ex multis,* recently, we can recall: Bedfor et al. (2022); Grimm et al. (2018); Sangiovanni (2017); Barak (2015); Düwell (2014); McCrudden (2014); Kateb (2014).

[4] *Ex multis,* see: Krienke (2020); Leher (2018); McCrudden (2014); Kwan and Bowpitt (2005).

[5] As constantly reaffirmed also in the United Nations' context. See, for example: Braveman and Gruskin (2003), p. 543.

[6] With regard to Italian Consitution see Tripodina (2015), pp. 1 ff.; Tripodina (2013). The author explores the theme of the reconstruction of the constitutional foundations of the *ius existentiae* in the Italian legal order.

negative rights) resists any limitation and *vulnera* because of their deep connection with the over-arching principle of human dignity, although the substance of some of these rights express a distinct cultural framing that might resist attempts of assimilation and might require specific consideration (i.e. freedom of religion).

On the other hand, the connection between fundamental social rights and the principle of human dignity is less clear, and "in at least two respects, social rights seem to contradict human dignity's universality" because of the relativity of their contents and the relativity of their applicability (Huster 2018, p. 416).

This relativity implies, in concrete terms, that the mere formal recognition and guarantee of "the inviolable rights of those who are marginalized or socially excluded is simply and hypocritically a *flatus vocis*" (Modugno 2008, p. 1392).

Those who are in a deep state of poverty, suffering from social exclusion or suffering of form of marginalization, are not able to effectively enjoy several fundamental human rights, both negative and social rights.

Those who are in need are often not able to provide for themselves and to enjoy a dignified life as proclaimed in the *Universal Declaration of Human Rights* (UDHR, spec art. 22, 23, 25) and several other international documents, such as the CFREU and individual, national Constitutions.

Those who are in need are not able to be part of the community they belong to: so, day by day, their dignity is denied.

Significant, to this purpose, appears to be the African concept of *Ubuntu* [7] where the very essence of any human being is determined by its being part of a community, harmoniously interrelating with that community and its members. Human dignity is sustained through practice of Ubuntu, and when conditions, such as poverty and social exclusion, that prevent an effective participation and relationship with the community exist, both *Ubuntu* and dignity are denied. Consequently, "a human rights framework based on a notion of dignity as including a respect for the humanity in others contains within it an understanding of our inescapable interconnectedness as members of multiple communities and societies" (Yamin 2015, p. 31). This social dimension of human dignity implies that tools to fight against poverty "[encompass] both the physical existence of a human being as well as the possibility to maintain interpersonal relationships and a minimal degree of participation in social, cultural and political life" (BVerfG but also 1 BvL 10/10 - 1 BvL 2/11 of 2012 [8] and 125,175).

5.2.1.2 Conceptualizing Poverty and Social Exclusion

According to what precedes, we may affirm that exist a duty of the public authorities to work in the fight against poverty and social exclusion, but to understand the

[7] On the concept of *Ubuntu*, recently, Ogude (2019).

[8] Bundesverfassungsgericht, judgements in https://www.bundesverfassungsgericht.de/SharedDocs/Entscheidungen/EN/2012/07/ls20120718_1bvl001010en.html. Accessed 4 June 2019.

concreteness and extension of such duty, it is appropriate to provide the essential coordinates to define those concepts, however, with the awareness that "the *object poverty* draws [...] the limits of a field of transformations, tensions, variable compositions" (Coccoli 2017, p. 73). [9]

One element unites the various evolutionary stages and possible definitions of poverty: it is "the evidence of a lack", the evidence "of a deficit in accessing dignified living standards" (Faur 2008, p. 178).

Moving from a diachronic perspective, evoking the Christian tradition (Tarello 1964; Lambertini 2000) and even the Buddhist one, those who are to be considered poor are those who do not possess the goods necessary to live, those that do not have on them "that power which manifests itself in an activity corresponding to the exercise of property or of other real right" (Ruotolo 2012, p. 210). However the mere absence of *dominium* on essential good, "is not a necessary condition for having poverty, although a sufficient one" (we may think of the poor who have a piece of land but do not have the economic means to exploit it—Ruotolo 2012, p. 213).

Poverty emerges as an existential condition of impotence: as a "fundamental incapacitation" (Sen 2000, p. 92), linked to a plurality of factors and not exclusively translatable into the state of extreme indigence determined by the total or almost total absence of *dominium* on essential goods.

Poverty impairs human dignity whenever its consequences debase people, or reduces them to a mere object.

Therefore, poverty is not to be defined just with reference to income distribution, but to "the social concept of the minimal conditions of existence". These minimal conditions are "connected to the social conception of what is needed for living human life", they reflect "the concept of humanity prevalent in each society" and also "the idea of a threshold for economic citizenship in the society" (Margalit 1998, p. 229).

Poverty shows us, therefore, two complementary aspects: on the one hand the insufficiency of economic resources that precludes a dignified life for oneself and one's family; on the other hand, the difficulty of participating in public life, that is to say the difficulty of assuring the community to which one belongs of one's proper contribution for the realization of the common good.

Poverty can be considered, therefore, not only as a shortage of material goods but also as a shortage of "human and social" goods, which implies a "lack of autonomy of the person and inability to exercise his status as a citizen" (Susín Bertán 2011, p. 243; Beca-Frei 2018, pp. 101 ff.). In this sense "poverty appears as the denial of human dignity" where human dignity implies that individuals be recognized as citizens "and, consequently, poverty expresses the denial of citizenship" (Petrella 2010, p. 1).

---

[9] For an effective diachronic analysis of the changes in the concept of poverty from the ancient age to the contemporary age, see Sassier (1990).

As far as sociological/economic studies are concerned, different levels of poverty must be distinguished according of their measurability and according to the level of severity they assume. Scholars usually distinguish between *absolute poverty* and *relative poverty*. The former corresponds to the absolute inability to obtain supplies of goods and services that are essential for one's own existence (Mendola 2002, pp. 11 ff.), while the latter is linked to the spending capacity for consumption, having as a point of comparison the standards of the reference community (Daly 2002; Dierckx 2010; Ruotolo 2012; Halvorsen and Hviden 2016).

There is also the notion of *almost poverty* applied to those individuals or families who have a consumption expenditure that is very close to, but slightly exceeds, the poverty threshold. The notion of *almost poverty*, as well as that of *relative poverty*, depends on the contexts in which a person lives, and vary from state to state and even from region to region.

The so-called *transient poverty* should also be considered. Linked to the strong precarization of the job market and to the instability of family relationships, the *transient poverty* has a significant impact on the European context. In fact, over a five-year period, about a third of the European population at least once, and for shorter or longer periods of time, fell below the poverty line, according to more or less burdensome dynamics, depending on the welfare regime existing in the various States (Ranci and Pavolini 2015, pp. 113 ff.; Fourage and Layte 2005, pp. 407 ff.).

Drafting the range of possible policies to tackle poverty issues requires awareness about how the concept of poverty has evolved over the decades: first an individual problem, poverty has become both a political issue and a matter of active social inclusion. Contemporary societies are facing new challenges due to the significant exclusion and disqualification of large part of population, both citizens and migrants, that are being denied the enjoyment of fundamental rights and a proper place in the society (see, *infra*, par. 2.3—For a diachronic perspective of economic-political theories on the point: Santoro 2012, pp. 21 ff.; Bonelli 2012, pp. 59 ff).

Therefore, any contemporary discussion on poverty shall take into account social exclusion issues.

In an age of globalization, given the deep crisis of traditional economic and political models, we can trace a direct (and constantly evolving) link between unequal distribution of resources (economic, cultural, social) which impair poor, problematic relations with the public dimension and other groups or social players (Bonelli 2012, pp. 59 ff.).

Poverty might imply social stigmatization and marginalization, expressing what has been defined as "the new face of apartheid" (Despouy 1996, p. 37). In this context, poverty is deeply connected both with "incapacitation" (Sen 2000, see *supra*) and with the concept of *social exclusion*. Leaving aside the economic (in)-availability and the data relating to consumption, the concept of social exclusion involves those who are in a state of neglect or who are homeless, as well as those who experience social deprivation and incomplete participation in the main social institutions because they lack the fundamental tools (especially cultural) that allow inclusion in a specific social context (AAVV 2001, pp. 14 ff.; Ruotolo 2012, pp. 210 ff.; Roman 2012, pp. 83 ff.; Bilchitz 2007).

Marginalization and poverty are phenomena deeply interrelated with discrimination and violation of the equality principle: "people experiencing poverty or social exclusion are more likely to be victims of discrimination, and people who, in one form or another, suffer discrimination are more likely to be socially excluded" (Roman 2012, p. 90; Fresno 2005, p. 62).

Social exclusion emphasizes the essence and the quality of the relationship among individuals and the society, expressing the impossibility that they enjoy substantial freedom to live a worthy life, the type of life to which they give value.

Social safety provisions and minimum income policies prevent people from falling into absolute or relative poverty. However, tackling the problem of the weakening of social ties associated with the identarian, economic and cultural fragmentation of society remains a significant challenge.

Unfortunately, the tendential discrepancy between official data on poverty and the real condition of a State is well known. Moreover, it is reductive to think of people living in poverty only in terms of a lack of availability of economic resources, neglecting the countless other kinds of deprivation which negatively condition a precarious state and prevent it from being overcome. Poverty must also be conceived as connected to the effective enjoyment of rights such as food, health, housing, work, family, education, participation in public life, which are the first to be questioned and denied.

In light of the above, poverty shall be measured according to a kaleidoscope of indicators that do not take into consideration only the elements of material deprivation and the characteristics of the work activity performed (i.e. precariousness, irregularity and underpayment of the job).

We must consider all those conditions of fragility and social exclusion that do not find room for expression in the statistics of relative poverty. Poverty and social exclusion, conceived in this way, pose "problems of justice" and directly involve the State and public institutions (including the EU) as actors who have "the task, the duty and the power to guarantee the rights, to realize justice" (Benvegnù-Pasini et al. 2011, p. 16, but see also Nussbaum 2013; Rawls 2017; Dworkin 2011; Waldron 2010). Currently, in Europe, more than 21.6% is at risk of poverty and social exclusion. [10] This percentage has decreased since 2008, but is still enormous: roughly one in five people in the EU experienced at least one of the following three forms of poverty: monetary poverty, severe material deprivation, or living in a household with very low work intensity (see, *infra,* para 3). Their condition is a matter of justice *and* a matter of dignity.[11]

[10]Latest available data (updated at June 2023. Accessed September 2023. Source, Eurostat).

[11]Leher (2018, p. 39), recalling McCrudden and A. Barak thoughts, conceives "human dignity as a realization of justice".

5.2.2 Dignified Life and Welfare Systems

Stressing the importance of human dignity, and specifically the concept of a *dignified life,* is essential in order to evaluate welfare systems and policies to combat poverty and social exclusion implemented at European, national, and local levels.

In other words, the action of public authorities can, and even must, be assessed in relation to the extent to which the dignity of the poorest and most vulnerable people is protected.

Furthermore, the concept of dignity, the elements taken as a parameter in qualifying life as "dignified", can be used as a classification frame for welfare systems that, at least traditionally, were evaluated and considered in light of some limited parameters (Kwan and Bowpitt 2005, p. 11; Ranci and Pavolini 2015, pp. 113 ff.; Carrozza 2010, pp. 207 ff.). Over the years scholars have tried to overcome the traditional classification schemes by evaluating "the goodness" of welfare systems in light of factors such as gender, belonging to ethnic minorities, or being in conditions of vulnerability (such as minors or women). Therefore, the objects of evaluation are the social and psychological conditions of people involved, the level of interpersonal relationships, and the higher or lower rate of social exclusion or participation in social and public life: all are elements considered in connection with human dignity and the fullness of a truly dignified life. It follows that, according to scholars, "the dignity of welfare recipients will be assessed from an economic, social and psychological perspective, while the performance of a welfare system will be evaluated by the impact of its provisions on key elements of human dignity" (Kwan and Bowpitt 2005, p. 10).

As known, the development of the welfare state was driven by the goal to eradicate, or reduce, inequalities and poverty (Saunders 2010, pp. 526 ff.), or at least some of their humiliating features. Poverty and social exclusion "corrode human dignity" through "exposure, lack of shelter... vulnerability and helplessness; abandonment to failure", in one word, humiliation (Margalit 1998, p. 227).

Several models of welfare states' regimes have been proposed, and the main criticism they have to face is due to the fact that the measures adopted could led to impair the autonomy of the needy, often not encouraged to overcome their impairment and turned into "parasites drugged by public funds who are no longer able to rely themselves" (Margalit 1998, p. 237).

The challenge of modern welfare states is to tackle poverty and social exclusion in the framework of both a real "social state of law" and the fundamental principles of equality, solidarity and dignity which represent pillars of the CFREU and Constitutions of European States.

Individuals, whether they are citizens or migrants, will be able to exercises their liberties and rights freely or participate actively and fully in the society only within a framework based on real equality in distribution of resources and opportunities.

5.2.3 *Poverty and Social Exclusion as Obstacles to Active Citizenship: Hints of Reflection*

As anticipated in the premises, the concepts of poverty, equality and human rights are interconnected, and poverty must be considered a "violation of human rights" (Faur 2008, p. 165)[12] insofar as it, especially if extreme, negatively affects development human and the "fullness of human rights" (Dulitzky 2008, p. 107).

It is important to grasp the two complementary aspects of poverty: on the one hand the insufficiency of economic resources, which hinders the enjoyment of a dignified life, and on the other, the correlative difficulty of actively participating in public life, assuring to the community of belonging (or of welcome) the necessary contribution to ensure the common good (Benvegnù-Pasini et al. 2011, p. 15).

We must bear in mind the strong connection between social inclusion and eradication of poverty as a way to enjoy an effective active citizenship and contribute to democracy (Marshall 1992; Huster 2018, p. 419; Stephens 2010, p. 511; Ippolito 2010, pp. 71 ff.—see *infra*, para 5.4). A democratic State realizes itself around the idea of inclusion and implementation of an effective participation of citizens in political, social, economic and cultural life. So we have to consider poverty in a broad sense which "includes a lack of material, human and social goods that determines the lack of autonomy of the person and his inability to exercise his condition as a citizen" (Susín Bertán 2011, p. 244; Pérez Miras 2018). So "for people living in poverty, being a citizen means being free to make one's own choices: not so much being 'free to do whatever you like' but, above all, to be free to exercise your rights and responsibilities, having control over your life and your future. Situations of poverty, like the lack of a decent income, makes it necessary to choose among basic needs which is a priority (healthy food, housing, school costs, healthcare costs, etc.). At the same time, the possibilities of making choices are considerably reduced so only forced choices remain (Combat poverty, insecurity and social exclusion service 2017, p. 16). Poverty is, then, not only "a constituent factor in the violation of social rights" (Roman 2012, p. 98) but also an impairment to "social citizenship" (Daly 2002, p. 17).

But the economic crisis that affected and still affects Europe, combined with migration flows, "the spread of cosmopolitan norms and transformations of sovereignty" (Benhabib 2011, p. 96) forces us to investigate new theoretical paradigms of citizenship and enjoyment of social rights in the European "confuse panorama" (Benhabib 2006, p. 122; Kymlicka and Norman 2000; Ippolito 2010, pp. 71 ff.).

---

[12] On this point is very clear: Comisión Interamericana de Derechos Humanos (CIDH), Tercer Informe sobre la situación de los Derechos Humanos en Paraguay, 2001, in http://www.cidh.org/countryrep/paraguay01sp/indice.htm. See also: Comisión Interamericana de Derechos Humanos (CIDH), Pobreza Y Derechos Humanos, 2017, at http://www.oas.org/es/cidh/informes/pdfs/pobrezaddhh2017.pdf; Commissioner for Human Rights, Eradicate poverty through human rights-based fiscal policies, 14.10.2022, at https://www.coe.int/en/web/commissioner/-/eradicate-poverty-through-human-rights-based-fiscal-policies.

5.3 Dignified Life and Fight Against Poverty: The Supranational Dimension

5.3.1 The International Dimension

The twentieth century narrative on human rights showed the overcome of the traditional bipartition among individual and negative freedoms and positive ones, emphasizing the social and psychological needs of human beings and the indivisibility and interdependence of human rights.

In this context, the role of human dignity is crucial and should be conceived as a unifying factor in a framework in which "civil and political rights protect individual's autonomy against arbitrary action by the authorities" and "economic, social and cultural rights protect this autonomy against social insecurity" (Roman 2012, p. 84; but see also Meyer-Bish 2004, p. 48).

International law shows sensitivity for the value/principle of human dignity both axiologically understood and conceived of as concrete declinations such as the right to a dignified life and to a standard of living adequate, including food, clothing, housing, etc (see art. 1 and 25 UDHR).

In addition to the UDHR, several International Charters or Conventions of regional importance reproduce the same protection, although not always according to explicit coordinates.

The definition of precariousness (lack of basic security) as promoted by the United Nations is particularly significant. It reads as follows: "[t]he lack of basic security connotes the absence of one or more factors enabling individuals and families to assume basic responsibilities and to enjoy fundamental rights. The situation may become widespread and result in more serious and permanent consequences. The lack of basic security leads to chronic poverty when it simultaneously affects several aspects of people's lives, when it is prolonged and when it severely compromises people's chances of regaining their rights and of reassuming their responsibilities in the foreseeable future" (Despouy 1996, p. 63. But see also UN Human rights council 2010).

The stressed connection between poverty and violation of human rights implies a shift of institutional authorities' action and the responsibility of the whole society from a ethical and economic sphere to a legal one, implying a concrete legal effort to fight against these. This is well known at international level, where it is stressed that "anti-poverty policies are more likely to be effective, sustainable, inclusive, equitable and meaningful to those living in poverty if they are based upon international human rights. For this to occur, human rights need to be taken into account in all relevant policy-making processes" (UN Committee on Economic, Social and Cultural Rights 2010: para 137). Therefore, fighting poverty is not only a social, economic and political issue but also a legal one: it is an issue relating human rights under the principle of their indivisibility and interdependence.

5.3.2 The European Dimension: The Council of Europe System

Considering the European landscape, human dignity plays a central role in the Council of Europe system, although it is not explicitly mentioned by the ECHR.

And the same ECHR appears to be permeable to the social dimension thanks to the ECtHR's evolutive jurisprudence according to which "[e]liminating what are judged to be social injustices is an example of the functions of a democratic legislature" (*James et al. v. the United Kingdom,* Appl. n. 8793/79, 1986, para 47; *Berger-Krall et al. v. Slovenia,* Appl. n. 14717/04, 2014—on the connection between the fight against poverty, human dignity and democracy see, infra, para 5.4).

The Court is aware that "[t]he combat against extreme poverty has become a fundamental development issue". Indeed, "[e]conomic development and the increase of wealth have paradoxically drawn attention to the most underprivileged, who have been left out of this phenomenon. The considerable discrepancy in living standards, sometimes within a single society, has given rise to a real awareness at the international level" (ECtHR, *Gabrid v. The Nederlands*, App. n. 43494/09, 2017).

In parallel, the European committee of Social Rights states that "[h]uman dignity is the fundamental value and indeed the core of positive European human rights law – whether under the European Social Charter or under the European Convention of Human Rights," and social rights such as "health care" are a "prerequisite for the preservation of human dignity" (in *International Federation of Human Rights Leagues (FIDH) v. France,* Complaint No.14/2003, 2004, para 31).

The field of protection shall also be extended to migrants in an irregular situation. They cannot be deprived of their "most basic rights enshrined in the Charter, nor to impair their fundamental rights, such as the right to life or to physical integrity or human dignity" (ESCR, *Defence for Children International (DCI) v. Belgium,* Complaint n. 69/2011, 2012, para 28).

The ECtHR tries to provide concrete protection especially when it finds violations of human dignity in the exposition of people, whether they are citizens, or belong to minority groups, such as Roma, or asylum seekers, to a situation of extreme material poverty. Moreover, ECtHR's outcomes are often the same of the ECJEU (see, for example, the so called *Dublin cases*, on Dublin system regulation and conditions of migrants and asylum seekers). [13]

However, with regard to the impact that a State's lack of economic resources can exert on some rights of a social nature and, more generally, in the balance between

[13] About citizens, see, recently, *Gabrid v. The Nederlands,* App. n. 43494/09, 2017. About asylum seekers, *H.F. et al v. France*, Appl. nn. 24384/19 and 44234/20, 2022; *M.S.S. v. Belgium and Greece* [GC], app. n. 30696/09, 2011. In the same terms, the CJEU, see recently, *Abubacarr Jawo v. Bundesrepublik Deutschland,* C-163/17, 2019; *Staatssecretaris van Veiligheid en Justitie – Y.Z. and Others/e.a.,* C-557/17, 2019 on Dublin III regulation. With reference to Roma people see *Moldovan et al. v. Romania,* app. n. 41138/98 and 64320/01, 2005.

domestic financials availability and human rights impaired by poverty, the ECtHR at times shows an oscillating jurisprudence.

As far as the negative effects of the economic crisis and their impact are concerned, over the past ten years the ECtHR's jurisprudence aimed at recognizing a significant margin of appreciation to the States,[14] especially when social benefits arise, such as the right to housing. [15]

In some cases, however, the Court limits the state's margin of appreciation and is also inclined to identify some positive obligations if the applicants belong to particularly vulnerable categories (such as minors) [16] or are members of minorities subject to hateful discrimination (such as the Roma). [17]

Furthermore, in relation to absolute rights, such as art. 3, the ECtHR is constant in reiterating that the lack of state economic resources cannot justify a violation of the Convention, finding that "a situation of serious deprivation", a significant *vulnus* to essential needs, in the indifference of the public authorities, "is incompatible with human dignity". [18]

5.3.3 The European Union System

5.3.3.1 Legal Framework

In the European Union system, we find several legal provisions dedicated both to human dignity, and to the principle of solidarity, which represents the normative basis for provisions and policies aimed at eradicating poverty and social exclusion, guaranteeing a dignified life that can be met both in the founding treaties and in derivative EU law, as well as in policies and practices related to the soft law area. [19] However, as is widely seen among scholars, "the theme of the relationship between fundamental rights and social policies in the fight against poverty invests ... a particularly sensitive side" being still partially "controversial which is the space of

[14]ECtHR: *Koufaki and Adedy v. Greece,* App. n. 57665/12 and. 57657/12, 2013, but, partially contra, *N.K.M. v. Hungary,* App. n. 66529/11, 2013.

[15]Recently, ECtHR: *Hudorovič et al v.. Solvenia,* App. n. 24816/14 and 25140/14, 2020.

[16]So, for example, in ECtHR, *Nencheva et al. c. Bulgaria,* App. n. no. 48609/06. 2013, the Strasbourg's judges found a violation of the right to life "in a situation of economic crisis where 15 disabled children and young adults placed in care had died, during the winter of 1996-1997, for lack of food, heating and basic care" (§ 117).

[17]ECtHR: *Hudorovič et al c. Solvenia,* cit. § 139.

[18]So, for example, in assessing the conditions of detention, the ECtHR also took into consideration the difficult socio-economic conditions of the States involved (*M.S.S. v. Belgium and Greece [GC],* cit., § 253; *Budina v. Russia,* App. 45603/05, 2009).

[19]See, for example, art. 3, par 5 TEU or artt. nn. 9, 10, 19, 45–48, 145–150 e 151–161 del TFEU or artt. nn. 1 and 34 CFREU.

the social dimension of the European Union", [20] at least in terms of its relevance and concrete impact.

The fight against poverty and social exclusion is part of the system of promoting social justice and fundamental rights that characterizes the action of the European Union which was, from its very beginning, inspired by, and founded on, the values of respect for human dignity and solidarity. The EU system, then, legitimates and requires the adoption of measures to support incomes and contrast social exclusion. Such measures may be conceived as (at least partially) released from the execution of a work activity.

According to Art. 34, para 2,3, CFREU, "[e]veryone residing and moving legally within the European Union is entitled to social security benefits and social advantages in accordance with Community law and national laws and practices" and this is "[i]n order to combat social exclusion and poverty" so that the EU may recognize and respect "the right to social and housing assistance so as to ensure a decent existence for all those who lack sufficient resources" (for a comment: Orlandini and Chiaromonte 2017, pp. 643 ff.). The provision in article 34, last paragraph, highlights the existence of the right to a final or basic protection network. A "buffer" to be activated if the social security system provided by the previous paragraphs fails.

In any case, it remains to be proven whether legal effects derive directly from article 34 CFREU. According to scholars (Ziller 2017, pp. 1042 ff.), State implementation is necessary and in its absence there can be no regulatory constraints for the member States, without prejudice to the possibility of adopting the CFREU as an interpretative parameter of internal law, including the constitutional one.

Moving the investigation lens towards the TFEU, in the first place there is a sort of parallelism between social and employment policies and economic policies: in both cases, the competence to define these policies belongs to the Union, while the States are called to coordinate the corresponding internal policies according to procedures provided for the TFEU (art. 2, par. 3 TFEU).

The European Union has shared competence in matters of social policy (albeit limited to the aspects defined in the TFEU) and of economic, social and territorial cohesion (art. 4, par. 2, TFEU), in addition, art. 5 TFEU requires that the EU "shall take measures to ensure the coordination of the employment policies of the Member states" and establishes that it "may take initiatives to ensure the coordination of Member states's social policies . . .".

In addition, the proper functioning of the internal market presupposes the harmonization of social systems (art. 151, par. 3, TFEU), the achievement of a high employment level and the fight against marginalization. Objectives that can only be achieved if the EU works in adequate synergy and coordination with its Member states, in consideration of the significant impact of its policies on state's budgets and domestic organization (art. 153, par. 1, TFEU).

Moreover, in the TFEU social security and social protection are one of the subjects that can be harmonized in accordance with the principle of subsidiarity,

[20] (our translation) Mattone (2013), p. 208. See also Reichlin (2013), pp. 215 ff.

even with directives, after unanimous deliberation by the EU Council (art. 21, par. 3, TFEU). Consequently, because of the burdensomeness of the expected quorum, some measures to combat poverty and social exclusion, (such as, for example, basic income or emergency income) can also be traced back to the subject of "the integration of persons excluded from the labor market" (art. 153, par. 1, lett. *h*) to be combined with lett. *c*) or *j*) of art. 153, par. 1, TFEU respectively aimed at "social security and social protection of workers" and the "combating of social exclusion," whose implementation follows the ordinary regulatory procedure.

To introduce incisive anti-poverty rules such as, for example, the minimum guaranteed income, the Union has not resorted to the tools indicated by the aforementioned regulations (Somma 2019, p. 442).

Nonetheless, since the 1980s in the last century, European political narrative on measures to combat poverty showed a certain sensitivity for the issue of poverty and social exclusion,[21] although it only gained more relevance in more recent times, in the wake of the economic crisis of the second half of the 2000s. [22]

5.3.3.2 The Fight Against Poverty

Regardless of the theoretical foundation of measures to support poverty such as basic income, and despite the institutional difficulties, it is praiseworthy that the *Europe 2020 Strategy* European institutions, and in particular the Commission, have placed the fight against poverty at the center of the economic, social and employment agenda (European Commission 2010a, b; Sabato et al. 2018, pp. 14 ff.; Ferrera and Jessoula 2016, pp. 62 ff.; Peña-Casas 2012, pp. 159 ff.).

This strategy replaced the previous Lisbon strategy with a less ambitious but more realistic quantitative target. The aim is to reduce the number of poor people by about 20 million (compared to 2008), working to fight social exclusion and promoting the adoption of synergistic and complementary strategies for all member States (European Commission 2010b).

Today, concretely, the European Union contrasts poverty and social exclusion in the realization of social policy through different tools: (a) implementing non-legislative cooperation—c.d. OMC—open method of coordination; [23]

[21] See Resolution on combating poverty in the European Community, 16 September 1988, A2-171/88; Council Recommendation of 24 June 1992, 92/441/EEC, on common criteria concerning sufficient resources and social assistance in social protection systems; Council Recommendation of 27 July 1992, 92/442/EEC, on the convergence of social protection objectives and policies.

[22] For example, Commission Recommendation on the active inclusion of people excluded from the labour market [2008/867/EC]; European Parliament. 2010. (2010/2039(INI)) Resolution on the Role of minimum income in combating poverty and promoting an inclusive society in Europe; European and Economic Social Committee. 2019. (2019/C 190/01). Opinion on For a European Framework Directive on a Minimum Income.

[23] Open Method of Coordination (OMC). See: [COM(2008) 418def.] see also: Larocque and Noël (2014), pp. 333 ff.

(b) intervening with Anti-discrimination legislation;[24] (c) preparing specific legal protections for potential victims; (d) implementing incentive measures for specific groups or categories (Article 19 TFEU); [25] (e) working, in general, in order to facilitate the relaunch of economic growth and, in parallel, implementing the employment rate, both qualitatively and quantitatively.

In addition to this, especially in terms of the measures to be implemented within by the Member States, a very significant role is played by the *European Social Fund* (ESF). The ESF makes EU funding available to co-finance actions aimed at combating discrimination and helping the most disadvantaged to access the labor market.

Since 2014, as a reaction to the observed increase in poverty levels, a specific Fund of European Aid was created, *The Fund for European Aid to the Most Deprived* (FEAD) with the task of supporting EU countries' actions to provide material assistance (providing food and/or basic material assistance to the most deprived) together with social inclusion measures. [26]

5.3.3.3 Recent Developments

More recently, in 2017, in order to implement the levels of equity and the propensity for the social sphere of the Union and the convergence towards better living and working conditions in increasingly flexible labor markets, the Inter-Institutional Proclamation on the European Pillar of Social Rights was introduced. [27] This document builds upon 20 key principles and sets social protection and inclusion as one of three channels of intervention. The Pillar, indeed, aims at favoring (a) equal opportunities and access to the labor market; (b) fair working conditions; (c) social protection and inclusion.

As far as social protection and inclusion are concerned, the *Pillar* proclaims some rights in favor of "weak" people or those in need, or in a state of poverty: (1) childcare and support to children, with particular reference to specific measures to enhance equal opportunities; (2) adequate social protection for all kind of workers, regardless of the type of contract; (3) adequate measures to support unemployment, support that implies the activation "from public employment services to (re)integrate in the labor market and adequate unemployment benefits of reasonable duration, in line with their contributions and national eligibility rules" (art. 13); (4) provision of an adequate minimum income for "everyone lacking sufficient resources" in order to ensure "a life in dignity at all stages of life, and effective access to enabling goods

[24] See: Kennedy and Danesi (2022), The fight against poverty, social exclusion and discrimination.

[25] Such as disable people (see. European strategy on disability 2010–2020 (COM(2010)0636), or women or young people in search for a job.

[26] Regulation (EU) No 223/2014 of the European Parliament and of the Council of 11 March 2014 on the Fund for European Aid to the Most Deprived.

[27] The European Pillar of Social Rights (2017/C 428/09) has been jointly signed by the European Parliament, the Council and the Commission on 17 November 2017, at the Social Summit for Fair Jobs and Growth in Gothenburg.

and services"; (5) provision of the right "to resources that ensure living in dignity" or of the right "to a pension commensurate to .... contributions and ensuring an adequate income" (art. 15).

However, for those who can work "minimum income benefits should be combined with incentives to (re)integrate into the labor market" (art. 14). As far as this last point is concerned, it seems that, at the moment, from a regulatory point of view, the European institutions have limited themselves to "call on all Member States to introduce adequate minimum income schemes, accompanied by back-to-work support measures for those who can work and education and training programs adapted to the personal and family situation of the beneficiary, in order to support households with inadequate income and enable them to have a decent standard of living" and to call on, in parallel, "on the Commission and the Member States to ensure the full participation of all stakeholders, in particular social partners and civil society organizations, in the design, implementation and monitoring of minimum income policies and programs" (par. 61 of the European Parliament resolution of 24 October 2017 on minimum income policies as a tool for fighting poverty (2016/2270 (INI)).

Moreover, the aforementioned *Pillar* proclaims the right to timely access to quality healthcare at affordable costs; the right to income support measures that guarantee a dignified life for people with disabilities; the right to long-term care services of a good quality and affordable cost; as well as specific rights for those who are deprived of housing or in a state of vulnerability, are also provided by the Pillar of social rights (artt. 15–18). In addition, those who are in need shall have the right to "access to social housing or housing assistance of good quality"; vulnerable people shall "have the right to appropriate assistance and protection against forced eviction," and homeless shall be provided of "adequate shelter and services" in order to "promote their social inclusion" (art. 19). Finally, not only must the right to have access to essential quality services (such as access to water, sanitation, energy, transport, financial services and digital communications) be established but specific support measures must also be envisaged for those who are in need (art. 20).

Despite the effort of the European institutions to be praiseworthy, the practical realization of the rights proclaimed above and the actual possible enjoyment by those in need seems to be largely unsatisfactory. In fact, the document cited lastly does not have binding regulatory value and furthermore, aspires to give protection to legal situations or interests that need not only the intervention of EU Member States, but also the intervention of their territorial entities and local authorities. Institutional authorities and territorial entities, that, especially where they are holders of autonomous legislative powers—whether they are entities belonging to federated states (Germany, Austria or Belgium) or expressing different contexts for the valorization of autonomies (Spain, Italy, UK)—exercise many skills related to the social assistance and social inclusion policies, giving various expression to the principle of subsidiarity, conceived both in a vertical and horizontal sense.

Then, in May 2018, the Commission issued its proposal for an ESF+ (2021–2027) to incorporate the FEAD and other programs.[28] The European Social Fund Plus (ESF+) has now become the main funding instrument, as it provides EU funding to co-finance measures to fight poverty and exclusion, combat discrimination and help the most disadvantaged to access the labor market.[29]

However it must be stressed that the recent economic crisis, which emerged following the health emergency caused by the diffusion of the Sars-CoV2 pandemic and the consequences of Ukraine war, are forcing European institutions and States to reconsider their interventions also due to the high number of new unemployed and people in need and the wide category of working poor.[30]

Moreover, since its assignment, the new President of the European Commission had expressed the Commission's intention to implement and develop the European pillar of social rights and had presented a proposal for a Council decision on guidelines for Member States' policies in favor of the occupation.[31]

The impact of the epidemiological emergency from Codiv19 on the economies of the European States and on employment levels has prompted the Commission to propose a further proposal to amend the FEAD [32] and on 24 April 2020 the Regulation (EU) 2020/559, amending the previous Regulation (EU) 223/2014,[33] was published in the OJEU. The goal is to make operational a series of exceptional and particularly flexible measures in order to protect the most vulnerable categories and satisfy their immediate needs (e.g. in the form of food aid, supply of protective

[28] Proposal for a Regulation of the European Parliament and of the Council laying down common provisions on the European Regional Development Fund, the European Social Fund Plus, the Cohesion Fund, and the European Maritime and Fisheries Fund and financial rules for those and for the Asylum and Migration Fund, the Internal Security Fund and the Border Management and Visa Instrument. During the 2014–2020 period, the Union's contribution to the Fund was over 3.8 billion euros. The member states of the Union also co-finance the fund by guaranteeing coverage of at least 15% of the costs of their programs.

[29] The ESF+ brings together four previous funding instruments: the European Social Fund, the European Fund for the Most Deprived, the Youth Employment Initiative and the European Program for Employment and Social Innovation (EaSI). From 2021 to 2027 the ESF+ has a total budget of almost 99.3 billion of euros. The Regulation (EU) 2021/1057 also sets out the criteria for allocating resources and expenditure.

[30] According to Eurostat, In-work at-risk-of-poverty rate, in 2021, 8.9% of workers were at risk of poverty (data increasing from 8.5% of 2010). Eurostat data updated in 01.02.2023. And there are high differences from country to country. In Italy, for example, the percentage rises to 12.3, in Romania to 17.1.

[31] European Commission. 2020. (COM(2020) 70) Proposal for a Council Decision on guidelines for the employment policies of the Member States.

[32] European Commission. 2020. COM(2020) 141 final 2020/0058 (COD). Proposal for a regulation of the European Parliament and of the Council amending Regulation (EU) No 223/2014 as regards the introduction of specific measures for addressing the COVID-19 crisis.

[33] European Parliament and Council. 2020. Regulation (EU) 2020/559 amending Regulation (EU) No 223/2014 as regards the introduction of specific measures for addressing the outbreak of COVID-19.

devices or support to categories in difficulty).[34] In parallel, the European Parliament adopted a series of resolutions aimed at drawing attention to the harmful consequences of the pandemic for certain categories of vulnerable people, urging the adoption of a comprehensive anti-poverty strategy and calling on Member States to take strong responsibility in fighting poverty and social exclusion. In particular, the European Parliament approved: (a) the Resolution of 17 April 2020 on EU coordinated action to combat the COVID-19 pandemic and its consequences (2020/2616 (RSP); (b) the Resolution of 8 July 2020 on the rights of persons with intellectual disabilities and their families in the COVID-19 crisis (2020/2680(RSP)); (c) the Resolution of 17 September 2020 on the implementation of National Roma Integration Strategies: combating negative attitudes towards people with Romani background in Europe (2020/2011(INI)); (d) the Resolution of 24 November 2020 on tackling homelessness rates in the EU (2020/2802(RSP)); (e) the Resolution of 21 January 2021 on access to decent and affordable housing for all (2019/2187 (INI)); and, finally, (f) the Resolution of 5 July 2022 on women's poverty in Europe (2021/2170(INI)).

More recently, thanks to a proposal of the European Commission of October 2020, Directive (EU) 2022/2041 of the European Parliament and of the Council of 19 October 2022 on adequate minimum wages in the European Union was adopted: a regulatory instrument aimed at providing EU workers with adequate minimum wages and decent living and working conditions.

Also on the initiative of the European Commission (Proposal for a Council Recommendation COM(2022) 490 final of 20.09.2022), the Council adopted on 30 January 2023 a Recommendation on minimum income (2023/C 41/01). The Council's objective is to ensure a life in dignity at all stages of life, with the aim of combating poverty and social exclusion and promoting a high level of employment by promoting adequate income support, in particular through minimum income, and effective access to basic and essential services for those who lack sufficient resources, and by promoting the integration into the labour market of those who are able to work, in line with the active inclusion approach (para. 1, Recommendation 2023/C 41/01).

5.3.3.4 A Partial Evaluation

Concluding this examination, it appears significant to point out that—especially since the entry into force of the Lisbon Treaty and despite the European policies activated in this area and the coordinated action carried out by the European institution, the years show that there isn't a tendency towards harmonization, towards a promotion of integrated anti-poverty policies, based on the notion of "active inclusion" (Clegg 2016, pp. 77 ff.). In practice, as anticipated, the Member

[34] For an overview see. https://www.europarl.europa.eu/news/en/headlines/society/20200323STO75625/coronavirus-eu-countries-to-get-help-from-solidarity-fund. Accessed 30 June 2023.

States of the Union do not seem to be equally sensitive to European policies to combat poverty. Wide A margin is left to the States and to their territorial entities.

According to somc scholars, the German case is paradigmatic. Germany shows a singular paradox: although it has a strong influence in Europe, especially in European economic policy and in decision-making processes, Germany appears not be very sensitive to European social policies. It does not seem capable of giving impetus to domestic correspondent policies, preferring to pursue its own actions according to an articulation that intersects various federal competences, Länder competences and local competences (especially after the 2006–2009 constitutional reforms—Zimmermann and Petzold 2018, p. 94).

Therefore, the political contexts or the national pressures/sensitivities are articulated, so that there are many approaches to "anti-poverty policies", to a large extent also dependent on the level of financial autonomy enjoyed by the competent bodies and the availability of resources. With reference to this last profile, the set of measures approved at European level in the last decade has conditioned and still conditions the methods of action of the Member States.[35]

It is crucial, as European constitutional judges well know, to enhance, where possible, the efforts of all branches of government involved to cooperate in an attempt to operate a reasonable and proportionate balance between economic and financial equilibrium and fundamental social rights (to be recognized both to citizens and aliens legally resident in a certain territory and, to a certain extent and with reference to their essential core, also to "irregular" migrants).

In this respect, the recourse to the principle of solidarity assumes a central role. From a different point of view, it is nevertheless appropriate to conceive a new model of protection of social rights, inscribed in a process (multidimensional and multi-temporal) of constitutionalization of the EU that endorses both the role of human dignity in the determination of rights' intangible core and in the conception of social rights that does not respond to a merely egalitarian vision, but takes into account the specificities of each situation in order not to aggravate (if not to solve) problems regarding the sustainability of welfare states systems. [36]

5.4 Final Thoughts

The analysis of the national and European regulatory framework, as well as the studies of economists and sociologists, shows that, in the fight against poverty, instruments of a merely economic and financial nature are not sufficient. The possible situations or conditions of poverty are variegated and the dynamics of

[35] See, for example, Spain, Italy or Portugal. Pérez Miras (2018); Drigo (2017), pp. 273 ff.

[36] It seems proper to quote Holmes, according to witch "taking rights seriously means taking scarcity seriously", to remember that in these areas is the politics, more than the courts, to decide on the concrete allocation of economic resources: Holmes and Sunstein (1999), p. 94.

possible social exclusion that affect the dignified existence of those who are in need are articulated.

Therefore, the tools to which the States can resort to—and where competent, also their territorial entities—must be necessarily diversified, in order to achieve that equality, solidarity and dignity, which are pillars of the European Union and of the Constitutions of its member States.

The analysis of the European context shows clearly how the issue of welfare and the ensemble of those services of a welfare nature, of income support and, more generally, of combating poverty and social exclusion, is organized according to a highly variable geometrical panorama.

A highly variable geometrical view exists both in the comparison between Member States of the European Union, and, within certain limits, in the comparison between the different territorial entities which are part of the same State.

If, traditionally, the Scandinavian countries show a greater propensity towards the implementation of welfare systems and the adoption of mechanisms to support income and fight poverty compared to the countries of southern Europe, the increase in migration has placed new challenges on the maintenance of such "virtuous" legal orders.

Moreover, systems like the Spanish, Italian, Portuguese and even Greek ones present a historical background, a system of values and institutional characteristics not so different from each other. And these elements have contributed to the definition of a welfare system distinct from the Anglo-Saxon model, from the continental model and from that of Northern Europe (on this last point see: Arriba and Moreno 2005, pp. 140 ff.; Castles et al. 2010; Johansson and Panican 2016).

Many of the differences that emerge—in terms of attention to the fight against poverty and social exclusion—are attributable both to the "financial health" of European countries (and of their territorial entities) and to the need or not for plans and programs to reduce public spending, in order to meet EU requirements.

The problems that many countries in continental Europe and northern Europe are facing, although significant, are however distant from the problems some southern European states, such as Greece, Spain, Portugal and Italy faced, and to a large extent continue to face. In these systems, although to varying degrees, European policies to reduce public spending have had a greater impact, determining, as a logical consequence, a reduction in spending for social and welfare benefits. Consequently, situations of crisis and difficulties emerged and continue to emerge as a result of the economic crisis and the increase in unemployment; precariousness and the rates of socio-economic inequality existing have worsened.

Recently, the health and economic crisis that has afflicted and is still afflicting Europe has hit hardest those countries that have already been through a severe economic and financial crisis in recent decades, and a further worsening of critical situations is now on the horizon, especially in certain regions.

Wanting to try to carry out a provisional assessment of the "efficiency" of European instruments to combat poverty, we must express a partial frustration.

Surely, the Europe 2020 Strategy shows a greater sensitivity of the European institutions to the social dimension. However, many authors point out that the set of instruments deployed at European level to combat poverty and social exclusion are not so effective (*Ex multis*: Peña-Casas 2012, pp. 159 ff.; Roman 2012, pp. 83 ff.), especially for the category of the working-poor. And this, both because the objectives to be achieved seem, in fact, unreachable (because of the non-binding force of many of the tools and policies put in place) and because domestic policies remain central, crucial, and often unsatisfactory.

Recent Eurostat analysis shows that in 2022 (data available in February 2023) almost 94.1 million Europeans will be at risk of poverty and social exclusion, representing more than 21% of the total European population. Although this represents a significant reduction from the peak of 123 million people in 2012, it is still far from the target set by the EU2020 strategy.

The challenges posed by the fight against poverty, particularly in the context of an economic crisis that appears to have become systemic rather than cyclical; the consequences of the covidien pandemic and the war in Ukraine; the profound changes in the labor market that often lead to the proliferation of poor and precarious workers (often *working-poor*) unable to access the loan system banking, to enjoy adequate and decent housing or to have full access to health-care; and the migratory phenomenon that strikes us daily in all its drama with regard to consequences, are all factors that stimulate the study of the fight against poverty and social exclusion according to a multifaceted perspective, using an integrated system of tools that place the human being and dignity at the center.

EU and European States shall intervene by involving all levels of government, in a synergistic way, to try to maximize the value of synergies and virtuous social inclusion circuits: for example, by encouraging access to quality work, professional training, education, access to quality care at affordable prices and decent housing, access to "ethical" funding channels, and micro-credit to be allocated to projects that allow the acquisition of autonomy for people excluded from traditional channels. The mere donation of sums of money, declined as a measure from the merely welfarist nature, far from eradicating the phenomena of exclusion and exploitation, or from stimulating entrepreneurship and micro-entrepreneurship, also have a series of negative effects that the legislators must necessarily take into account.

Responding to the questions posed at the first paragraph of this work: the normative framework analyzed shows clearly that the respect of human dignity protection implies that there are fundamental human rights that should not be negatively affected by poverty and social exclusion, even despite the concrete problems of justiciability of social rights. [37] Human dignity can and shall be conceived in a deontic perspective implying the need of intervention and the duty for public authorities, whether they are supranational and domestic, to struggle against poverty. But we all are also aware of the existence of a significant gap between the formal regulatory data and the substantial one.

The economic crisis that has been affecting Europe for years, together with the instrumentalization of the migration phenomenon, have become a constant in the

[37] On justiciability problems, ex multis: Boyle (2020) and King (2012).

political debate in many European states, fueling populism and sovranism which undermine European stability and cohesion.

In this context, the fight against poverty and social exclusion might represent an instrument of cohesion and a fundamental tile to preserve the essential conditions to guarantee European level of democracy, in a perspective of real subsidiarity and inclusive activating citizenship.

And this seems especially true in recent times, when we witness worrying symptoms from many European countries. Recently, for example, the Hungarian Constitutional Court has modified some of its own precedents, asserting the constitutionality of a law that criminalizes homeless (Chronowski and Halmai 2019[38]).

This decision appears to be a very serious *vulnus* to the value of human dignity and the stigmatization of those who are different, the poor, and those who are socially marginalized; it reflects the betrayal of principles enshrined both internationally and at European level.

We can trace a direct connection between poverty and democracy, although their relationship may be conflictual, as stressed by scholars. The presence of a high level of development is considered a "requisite for the transition and to the sustainability of contemporary democracies" (Berg-Schlosser 2012, p. 217). Among the various patterns and pathway of democratization and democracy, a *fil rouge* can be found in the under-representation and exclusion of those groups of people considered socially weak, and who are pushed to the margins of society. The relational dimension of poverty (Dierckx 2010), especially extreme poverty, opens to equality and discrimination issues. As it is well expressed by a scholar: "the crucial test for judging a democracy or any other system of government is the extent to which its decision processes favor the protection and expansion of human rights, or the expansion of the freedom of those strata that at a given time are at least free – whether their chains are made by economic or cultural impoverishment, political disfranchisement or lack of equality" (Bay 1970, p. 351).

Populist and excluding narrative and politics are mobilized against minority groups, poor and those who are different or not corresponding to an assumed proper "identity", and this put democracy in danger.

In this worrying context, the empowerment of those left of the margins, the implementation of pluralistic channels, and a reconfiguration of citizenship along more inclusive and substantial lines might be an effective defense for democracy. The respect of fundamental human rights, inscribed in the rule of law, is the very essence of democracy.

[38] According to the authors "[t]he Constitutional Court declares that the criminalization and imprisonment of homeless people is not unconstitutional. According to the majority people living in need or at streets shall not be protected by the right to human dignity nor do they share the value of equal dignity".

References

AAVV (2001) Promoting the policy debate on social exclusion from a comparative perspective. Coe Publishing, Strasbourg

Arriba A, Moreno L (2005) Spain – poverty, social exclusion and "safety nets". In: Ferrera M (ed) Welfare state reform in southern Europe. Fighting poverty and social exclusion in Italy, Spain, Portugal and Greece. Routledge, NY, p 141 ff

Barak A (2015) Human dignity. The constitutional value and the constitutional right. Cambridge University Press, Cambridge

Bay C (1970) Behavioral research and the theory of democracy. In: Kariel HS (ed) Frontiers of democratic theory. Random House, NY, p 327 ff

Beca-Frei JP (2018) Pobreza: un problema de derechos humanos. ¿Qué hacer cuando la legislación profundiza la pobreza? Dikaion 1:101 ff

Bedfor D, Dupré C, Halmai G, Kapotas P (eds) (2022) Human dignity and democracy in Europe: synergies, tensions and crises. Elgar, U.S.

Benhabib S (2006) I diritti degli altri. Raffaello cortina editore, Milano

Benhabib S (2011) Dignity in adversity. Human rights in troubled times. Polity Books, U.S. – U.K.

Benvegnù-Pasini G, Bezze M, Vecchiato T (2011) Diritti, senza doveri e risorse male utilizzate. In: Caritas Italiana – Fondazione "E. Zancan", Poveri di diritti. Rapporto 2011 su povertà ed esclusione sociale in Italia, AAVV. il Mulino, Bologna, p 15 ff

Berg-Schlosser D (2012) Poverty and democracy – chances and conflicts. In: Redefining and combating poverty. Human rights, democracy and common goods in today's Europe. AAVV. COE Publishing Editions, Strasbourg, p 217 ff

Bilchitz D (2007) Poverty and fundamental rights: the justification and enforcement of socio-economic rights. OUP, Oxford

Bonelli L (2018) Examining the relationship of poverty. In: Redefining and combating poverty. Human rights, democracy and common goods in today's Europe. COE Publishing ed, 2012, Strasbourg, p 59 ff

Boyle K (2020) Economic and social rights law: incorporation, justiciability and principles of adjudication. Taylor & Francis

Braveman P, Gruskin S (2003) Poverty, equity, human rights and health. Bull World Health Organ 81(7):539 ff

Carrozza P (2010) Riforme istituzionali e sistemi di welfare. In: Campedelli M, Carrozza P, Pepino L (eds) Diritto di Welfare. il Mulino, Bologna, p 207 ff

Castles FG et al (eds) (2010) The Oxford handbook of welfare state. OUP, U.S.

Chronowski N, Halmai G (2019/6/11) Human Dignity for Good Hungarians Only: The Constitutional Court's Decision on the Criminalization of Homelessness. In: VerfBlog, 2019/6/11. https://verfassungsblog.de/human-dignity-for-good-hungarians-only/

Clegg D (2016) Combating poverty through "active inclusion"? The European and national context. In: Johansson H, Panican A (eds) Combating poverty in local welfare systems. Active inclusion strategies in European cities, in combating poverty in local welfare system. Palgrave Macmillan, UK, p 77 ff

Coccoli L (2017) Il Governo dei poveri all'inizio dell'età moderna. Jouvence, Milan

Combat poverty, insecurity and social exclusion service (2017) Citizenship and poverty. Contribution to political debate and action. Biennial report 2016-2017, 16, in http://www.combatpoverty.be/publications/combatpoverty2017_summary.pdf. Accessed 30 June 2023

Comisión Interamericana de Derechos Humanos (CIDH) (2017) Pobreza Y Derechos Humanos, at http://www.oas.org/es/cidh/informes/pdfs/pobrezaddhh2017.pdf

Commissioner for Human Rights (2022) Eradicate poverty through human rights-based fiscal policies, 14.10.2022, at https://www.coe.int/en/web/commissioner/-/eradicate-poverty-through-human-rights-based-fiscal-policies

Council of the European Union (2023) Council Recommendation of 30 January 2023 on adequate minimum income ensuring active inclusion 2023/C 41/01

Daly M (2002) Access to social rights in Europe. Adopted by the European Committee for Social Cohesion. Council of Europe Publishing, Strasbourg

Despouy L (1996) Final report on human rights and extreme poverty/submitted by the Special Rapporteur. (E/CN.4/Sub.2/1996/13), in https://digitallibrary.un.org/record/236619

Dierckx D (2010) Empowerment of people experiencing extreme poverty. In: Strengthening social cohesion. Council of Europe Publishing, Strasbourg, p 51 ff

Drigo C (2017) La grammatica giurisprudenziale dei diritti ai tempi della crisi. Le Corti costituzionali nel gorgo della politica. Legittima ingerenza o influenza sulla forma di governo? Alcune riflessioni sui casi portoghese e italiano. In: Teruel Lozano GM, Pérez Miras A, Raffiotta EC (eds) Constitución e Integración Europea Derechos fundamentales y sus garantías jurisdiccionales. Dykinson, Spain, p 273 ff

Dulitzky AE (2008) Pobreza y derechos humanos en el sistema interamericano Algunas aproximaciones particulares. Revista IIDH 48:107 ff

Düwell M (2014) Human dignity: concepts, discussions, philosophical perspectives. In: Düwell M, Braarvig J, Brownsword R, Mieth D (eds) The Cambridge handbook of human dignity. Cambridge University Press, Cambridge, pp 23–49

Dworkin R (2011) Giustizia per i ricci. Feltrinelli, Milano

European and Economic Social Committee (2019a) (2019/C 190/01). Opinion on For a European Framework Directive on a Minimum Income

European and Economic Social Committee (2019b) (2019/C 190/01). Opinion on For a European Framework Directive on a Minimum Income, in https://eur-lex.europa.eu/legal-content/EN/TXT/?uri=uriserv:OJ.C_.2019.190.01.0001.01.ENG&toc=OJ:C:2019:190:FULL. Accessed 30 June 2023

European Commission (2008a) Recommendation on the active inclusion of people excluded from the labour market [2008/867/EC]

European Commission (2008b) COM(2008) 418def. Comunicazione della Commissione al Parlamento europeo, al Consiglio, al Comitato economico e sociale europeo e al Comitato delle regioni, del 2 luglio 2008, intitolata "Un rinnovato impegno a favore dell'Europa sociale: rafforzamento del metodo di coordinamento aperto per la protezione sociale e l'integrazione sociale". In https://eur-lex.europa.eu/legal-content/IT/TXT/HTML/?uri=LEGISSUM:em0011&from=EN

European Commission (2010a) COM(2010) 2020 final, Communication from the Commission Europe 2020, in https://eur-lex.europa.eu/legal-content/EN/TXT/PDF/?uri=CELEX:52010DC2020&from=it

European Commission (2010b) COM(2010) 758 final, Communication: The European Platform against Poverty and Social Exclusion: A European framework for social and territorial cohesion EC(2010) 1564 final, COM(2010) 758 final, December 2010, https://eur-lex.europa.eu/LexUriServ/LexUriServ.do?uri=COM%3A2010%3A0758%3AFIN%3AEN%3APDF

European Commission (2018) COM(2018) 375 final. Proposal for a Regulation of the European Parliament and of the Council laying down common provisions on the European Regional Development Fund, the European Social Fund Plus, the Cohesion Fund, and the European Maritime and Fisheries Fund and financial rules for those and for the Asylum and Migration Fund, the Internal Security Fund and the Border Management and Visa Instrument. In https://eur-lex.europa.eu/resource.html?uri=cellar:26b02a36-6376-11e8-ab9c-01aa75ed71a1.0003.02/DOC_1&format=PDF. Accessed 30 June 2023

European Commission (2020a) COM(2020) 141 final 2020/0058 (COD). Proposal for a regulation of the European Parliament and of the Council amending Regulation (EU) No 223/2014 as regards the introduction of specific measures for addressing the COVID-19 crisis in https://ec.europa.eu/transparency/regdoc/rep/1/2020/EN/COM-2020-141-F1-EN-MAIN-PART-1.PDF

European Commission (2020b) (COM(2020) 70) Proposal for a Council Decision on guidelines for the employment policies of the Member States in https://eur-lex.europa.eu/legal-content/EN/TXT/?qid=1595362601190&uri=CELEX:52020PC0070. Accessed 30 June 2023

European Commission (2022) Proposal for a Council Recommendation on adequate minimum income ensuring active inclusion COM/2022/490 final
European Parliament (2010) (2010/2039(INI)) Resolution on the Role of minimum income in combating poverty and promoting an inclusive society in Europe in https://eur-lex.europa.eu/legal-content/EN/TXT/PDF/?uri=CELEX:52010IP0375&from=EN. Accessed 30 June 2023
European Parliament (2017) Resolution of 24 October 2017 on minimum income policies as a tool for fighting poverty (2016/2270(INI)). In http://www.europarl.europa.eu/doceo/document/TA-8-2017-0403_EN.pdf. Accessed 30 June 2023
European Parliament (2020a) Resolution of 24 November 2020 on tackling homelessness rates in the EU (2020/2802(RSP)) at https://www.europarl.europa.eu/doceo/document/TA-9-2020-0314_EN.html. Accessed 30 June 2023
European Parliament (2020b) Resolution of 17 September 2020 on the implementation of National Roma Integration Strategies: combating negative attitudes towards people with Romani background in Europe (2020/2011(INI)) at https://www.europarl.europa.eu/doceo/document/TA-9-2020-0229_EN.html. Accessed 30 June 2023
European Parliament (2020c) Resolution of 8 July 2020 on the rights of persons with intellectual disabilities and their families in the COVID-19 crisis (2020/2680(RSP)) at https://eur-lex.europa.eu/legal-content/EN/TXT/?uri=CELEX:52020IP0183. Accessed 30 June 2023
European Parliament (2020d) Resolution of 17 April 2020 on EU coordinated action to combat the COVID-19 pandemic and its consequences (2020/2616(RSP) at https://www.europarl.europa.eu/doceo/document/TA-9-2020-0054_EN.html
European Parliament (2021) Resolution of 21 January 2021 on access to decent and affordable housing for all (2019/2187(INI)) at https://www.europarl.europa.eu/doceo/document/TA-9-2021-0020_EN.html. Accessed 30 June 2023
European Parliament (2022) Resolution of 5 July 2022 on women's poverty in Europe (2021/2170 (INI)) at https://eur-lex.europa.eu/legal-content/EN/TXT/?uri=CELEX:52022IP0274. Accessed 30 June 2023
European Parliament and Council (2020) Regulation (EU) 2020/559 amending Regulation (EU) No 223/2014 as regards the introduction of specific measures for addressing the outbreak of COVID-19. In https://eur-lex.europa.eu/legal-content/EN/TXT/PDF/?uri=CELEX:32020R0559&from=EN
European Parliament and Council (2022) Directive (EU) 2022/2041 of the European Parliament and of the Council of 19 October 2022 on adequate minimum wages in the European Union at https://eur-lex.europa.eu/legal-content/EN/TXT/?uri=CELEX%3A32022L2041. Accessed 30 June 2023
European Parliament, Council and Commission (2017) (2017/C 428/09). European Pillar of Social Rights in https://eur-lex.europa.eu/legal-content/IT/TXT/PDF/?uri=CELEX:32017C1213(01)&from=IT. Accessed 30 June 2023
Faur E (2008) La pobreza como problema de derechos humanos. Nuevas orientaciones para históricas privaciones. Revista IIDH 47:165 ff
Ferrera M, Jessoula M (2016) Poverty and social inclusion as emerging policy arenas in the EU. In: Halvorsen R, Hvinden B (eds) Combating poverty in Europe. Elgar, Northampton, p 62 ff
Fourage D, Layte R (2005) Welfare regimes and poverty dynamics: the duration and recurrence of poverty spells in Europe. J Soc Policy 3:407 ss
Fresno JM (2005) Addressing the interface between discrimination and poverty. In: The EU we want: views from those fighting poverty and social exclusion of future development of the EU. European Anti-Poverty Network, p 61 ff. in https://www.eapn.eu/wp-content/uploads/2006/02/theeuwe%20want_en.pdf. Accessed 30 June 2023
Grimm D, Alexadra K, Christoph MC (eds) (2018) Human dignity in context. Exploration of a contested concept. Nomos, Baden Baden
Halvorsen R, Hviden B (2016) Combating poverty in Europe. Elgar, Northampton
Holmes S, Sunstein CR (1999) The cost of rights: why liberty depends on taxes. W.W. Norton & co, NY-London

Huster S (2018) The universality of human dignity and the relativity of social rights. In: Grimm D, Kemmerer A, Mollers C (eds) Human dignity in context. Exploration of a contested concept. Nomos, Baden Baden, p 415 ff
Ippolito F (2010) Cittadinanza e cittadinanze. Tra inclusione ed esclusione. In: Campedelli M, Carrozza P, Pepino L (eds) Diritto di Welfare. il Mulino, Bologna, p 71 ff
Johansson H, Panican A (eds) (2016) Combating poverty in local welfare system. Palgrave Macmillan
Kateb G (2014) Human dignity. Harvard University Press, U.S.
Kennedy A, Danesi S (2022) The fight against poverty, social exclusion and discrimination, at https://www.europarl.europa.eu/factsheets/en/sheet/60/the-fight-against-poverty-social-exclusion-and-discrimination
King J (2012) Judging social rights. Cambridge University Press, U.K.
Krienke M (ed) (2020) Ripensare il diritto naturale e la dignità umana: tradizione e attualità di due topoi etico-giuridici. Giappichelli, Torino
Kwan CC, Bowpitt G (2005) Human dignity and welfare systems. The Policy Press, Bristol
Kymlicka W, Norman W (2000) Citizenship in diverse societies. OUP, Oxford
Lambertini R (2000) La povertà pensata. Evoluzione storica della definizione dell'identità minoritica da Bonaventura ad Ockam. Mucchi, Modena
Larocque F, Noël A (2014) The politics of poverty in the European Union: how states respond in the open method of coordination on social inclusion. Policy Polit 42(3):333 ff
Leher SP (2018) Dignity and human rights. Routledge, NY and London
Margalit A (1998) The decent society. Harvard University Press, Cambridge, London
Marshall TH (1992) Citizenship and social class. In: Marshall TH, Bottomore T (eds) Citizenship and social class. Pluto Press, London, p 3 ff
Mattone S (2013) Diritti fondamentali e politiche sociali nell'anno europeo di lotta alla povertà. In: Civitarese Matteucci S, Guarriello F, Puoti P (eds) Diritti Fondamentali e politiche dell'Unione europea dopo Lisbona. Maggioli Editore, Rimini, p 208 ff
McCrudden C (ed) (2014) Understanding human dignity. OUP, Oxford
Mendola D (2002) Approcci, metodologie e dati per le analisi di povertà. In: Carbonaro G (ed) Studi sulla povertà. Problemi di misura e analisi comparative. Franco Angeli, Milano, p 11 ff
Meyer-Bish P (2004) Méthodologie pour une présentation systémique des droits humains. In: Birbosia E, Hennebel L (eds) Classer les droits de l'homme. Bruylant, Bruxelles, p 47 ff
Modugno F (2008) I diritti del consumatore: una nuova "generazione"di diritti? In: Scritti in onore di Michele Scudiero, II. Jovene, Napoli, p 1363 ff
Nussbaum M (2013) Creating capabilities. The human development approach. Belknap Press of Harvard University Press, Cambridge
Ogude J (ed) (2019) Ubuntu and the reconstitution of community. Indiana University Press, U.S.
Orlandini G, Chiaromonte W (2017) Art. 34. In: Mastroianni R, Pollicino O, Allegrezza S, Pappalardo F, Razzolini O (eds) Carta dei diritti fondamentali dell'Unione europea. Giuffrè, Milano, p 643 ff
Peña-Casas R (2012) Europe 2020 and fight against poverty and social exclusion: fooled into marriage? In: Natali D, Vanhercke B (eds) Social development in European Union 2011. OSE, ETUI, Bruxelles, p 159 ff
Pérez Miras A (2018) Exclusión Social y Declaraciones de derechos estatutarios in España. Italian papers on Federalism, 2, in http://italianpapersonfederalism.issirfa.cnr.it/homepage.html
Petrella R (2006) El Derecho a soñar. Propuestas para una sociedad más humana, Fundación Intermón Oxfam
Petrella R (2010) Estrategias para acabar con la pobreza, 2010, in http://www.fdacomin.org/media/20100322163911_RiccardoPetrella.pdf. Accessed 30 June 2023
Ranci C, Pavolini E (2015) Le politiche di welfare. il Mulino, Bologna
Rawls J (2017) Una teoria della giustizia. Feltrinelli, Milano

Reichlin P (2013) La sfida al modello sociale europeo. In: Civitarese Matteucci S, Guarriello F, Puoti P (eds) Diritti Fondamentali e politiche dell'Unione europea dopo Lisbona. Maggioli Editore, Rimini, p 215 ff

Roman D (2012) Guaranteeing human rights in situations of poverty. In: AAVV (ed) Redefining and combating poverty. Human rights, democracy and common goods in today's Europe. COE Publishing Editions, Strasbourg, p 83 ff

Ruotolo M (2012) Sicurezza, Dignità e lotta alla povertà. Editoriale scientifica, Napoli

Sabato S et al (2018) Europe 2020 and the fight against poverty: from target to governance. In: Jessoula M, Madama I (eds) Fighting poverty and social exclusion in the EU. Routledge, London & NY, p 14 ff

Sangiovanni A (2017) Humanity without dignity. Moral equality, respect, and human rights. Harvard University Press, Cambridge & London

Santoro E (2012) A historical perspective: from social inclusion to excluding democracy in redefining and combating poverty. Human rights, democracy and common goods in today's Europe. COE Publishing, Strasbourg, p 21 ff

Sassier P (1990) Du bon usage de pauvres. Histoire d'un thème politique (XVIe – XXe siècle). Fayard, Paris

Saunders P (2010) Inequality and poverty. In: Castles FG, Leibfried S, Lewis J, Obinger H, Pierson CP (eds) The Oxford handbook of the welfare state. OUP, U.S, p 527 ff

Sen A (2000) Lo sviluppo è libertà. Perché non c'è crescita senza democrazia. Mondadori, Milano

Somma A (2019) Contrasto alla povertà e politiche attive del lavoro: reddito di cittadinanza, reddito minimo garantito e regime delle condizionalità. DPCE 2:433 ff

Stephens JD (2010) The social rights of citizenship. In: Castles FG, Leibfried S, Lewis J, Obinger H, Pierson CP (eds) The Oxford handbook of the welfare state. OUP, U.S., p 512 ff

Susín Bertán R (2011) La regulación de la pobreza: el tratamiento jurídico-político de la pobreza: los ingresos mínimos de inserción. Universidad de La Rioja, Servicio de Publicaciones, Spain

Tarello G (1964) Profili giuridici della povertà nel francescanesimo prima di Ockham in Scritti in memoria di Antonio Falchi, Annali della Facoltà dell'Università di Genova III. Giuffrè, Milano, p 5 ff

Taylor-Gooby P (2008) Reframing social citizenship. UOP, U.S.

Tripodina C (2013) Il diritto ad un'esistenza libera e dignitosa. Giappichelli, Torino

Tripodina C (2015) Reddito di cittadinanza come "risarcimento per mancato procurato lavoro". Il dovere della Repubblica di garantire il diritto al lavoro o assicurare altrimenti il diritto all'esistenza. Costituzionalismo.it 1:1 ff

UN Committee on Economic, Social and Cultural Rights, Poverty and the International Covenant on Economic, Social and Cultural Rights: statement adopted on 4 May 2001, E/C.12/2001/10, para 13, in https://digitallibrary.un.org/record/452397

UN Human rights council (2010) [A/HRC/14/31]. Report of the independent expert on the question of human rights and extreme poverty, 31 March 2010 in https://www.refworld.org/docid/4c061e242.html. Accessed 30 June 2023

Waldron J (2010) Socioeconomic rights and theories of justice. New York University Public Law and Legal Theory Working Papers. Paper 245. http://lsr.nellco.org/nyu_plltwp/245

World Bank (2013) Poverty prospects in Europe: assessing progress towards the Europe 2020 poverty and social exclusion targets in New European Union Member States in http://documents.worldbank.org. Accessed 30 June 2023

Yamin AE (2015) Power, suffering, and the struggle for dignity: human rights frameworks for health and why they matter. University of Pennsylvania Press, U.S.

Ziller J (2017) Sub. art. 51. In: Mastroianni R, Pollicino O, Allegrezza S, Pappalardo F, Razzolini O (eds) Carta dei diritti fondamentali dell'Unione europea. Giuffrè, Milano, p 1042 ff

Zimmermann K, Petzold N (2018) The German way: reaffirming sovereignty, while accommodating the EU anti-poverty strategy. In: Jessoula M, Madama I (eds) Fighting poverty and social exclusion in the EU. Routledge, London and NY, p 78 ff

Chapter 6
The Human Right to Housing Through the Lens of Human Dignity as Non-humiliation

Michael Kolocek

Abstract Housing is a human right (Article 25 UDHR; Article 11 ICESCR). Human dignity is sometimes seen as a right in itself and sometimes as a basis for rights. For the most part, national as well as international jurisprudence evaluates the right to housing without referring to human dignity. This chapter considers certain violations of the human right to housing through the lens of human dignity defined as non-humiliation. The chapter is based on the assumption that the human right to housing cannot be fully implemented in the future. I focus on examples of the human right to housing at the threshold of autonomy and humiliation, where a person's choice to live in poor housing conditions constitutes an avoidance of other human rights violations. I present a concept of human dignity that does not necessarily help to fulfill the human right to housing, but which stands for alleviating situations in which affected people experience being humiliated.

6.1 The Human Right to Housing

Worldwide, a large number of people consider access to adequate housing as obvious. They think about the most suitable location to live, or ask, which tenure form (homeownership vs. renting) fits best for them and their family. They do not think about housing as a human right, and they unlikely ask what that means. However, housing is a human right under Article 25 of the Universal Declaration on Human Rights (UDHR).

In the following, I show that the view on the right to housing by governments and other global actors has changed during the last decades. Therefore, I look at discourses that have their roots in the UDHR. The UDHR is not a binding document but considered a global consensus (Davy 2015) of almost all countries worldwide and a point of departure for several human rights treaties. One of these treaties is the

M. Kolocek (✉)
Research Institute for Regional and Urban Development, Dortmund, Germany
e-mail: michael.kolocek@ils-forschung.de

S. N. Arel et al. (eds.), *Probing Human Dignity*,
https://doi.org/10.1007/978-3-031-42437-3_6

International Covenant on Economic, Social and Cultural Rights (1966, hereafter ICESCR).

> The States Parties to the present Covenant recognize the right of everyone to an adequate standard of living for himself and his family, including adequate food, clothing and housing, and to the continuous improvement of living conditions. The States Parties will take appropriate steps to ensure the realization of this right, recognizing to this effect the essential importance of international cooperation based on free consent. (Article 11, para 1, ICESCR)

The term "rights" might indicate that people can claim violations of their rights before a court. The implementation system of the ICESCR works slightly differently. The rights of the ICESCR (hereafter also: ESC rights) are obligations of the states that ratified the Covenant (Henkin 1979). Article 2 para 1 ICESCR reads that "[e]ach State Party to the present Covenant undertakes to take steps [...] to the maximum of its available resources, with a view to achieving progressively the full realization of the rights recognized in the present Covenant." The member states of the ICESCR submit States Parties reports on the progress they make in achieving the observance of the ESC rights (Article 16, para 1 ICESCR). This reporting is accompanied by the UN Committee on Economic, Social and Cultural Rights (CESCR, hereafter also: the Committee) with Concluding Observations to the States Parties reports, General Comments on the content of certain rights, and other documents. Since 1977, when the first State Party report was submitted, a huge data base has emerged that allows full exploration of the changing view on ESC rights, including the right to housing, by the member states of the ICESCR and the Committee.

In 1991, the Committee on Economic, Social and Cultural Rights published a General Comment on the right to housing in order "to identify some of the principal issues which the Committee considers to be important in relation to this right" (CESCR 1991: para 5). This General Comment is a reference point not only for the more than 160 states who submit reports under the ICESCR, but also for several publications on the right to housing (Kenna 2008; Kolocek 2013; Moons 2018). The Committee states that the right to housing "should be seen as the right to live somewhere in security, peace and dignity" (CESCR 1991: para 7). The Committee does not present any further explanations regarding what security, peace, or dignity mean. Instead, the Committee focuses on adequacy and lists seven aspects of adequate housing that should be taken into account: legal security of tenure; availability of services, materials, facilities and infrastructure; affordability; habitability; accessibility; location; and cultural adequacy (CESCR 1991: para 8). The Committee's list offers an orientation to the main aspects of adequate housing—no more, no less. Each of the aspects might be deepened, and each situation must be considered individually. If one of these aspects is not fulfilled, the housing situation is inadequate; in other words, if any of these aspects is not met, the right to housing is not fully realized and is, therefore, violated. However, the list already implies that not every housing rights violation is per se a human dignity issue and, of course, vice versa. If you have to pay a disproportionately large amount of your income for housing, for instance, the aspects of affordability might be violated. In this example, the right to housing is not fully fulfilled, but, as I will show, this violation does not constitute a violation of human dignity.

As all other human rights, the human right to housing is a "living instrument" (Davy 2013, p. 23); its contents and meaning have changed during the past decades. The discourse between the ICESCR member states and the Committee on the right to housing has proven this change of meaning (Kolocek 2015, 2017). When states reported on their obligations under the human right to housing in the 1970s and 1980s, the discussion was dominated by numbers. Affected or vulnerable people were mostly considered an anonymous mass to whom states responded with mass construction programs: "Between 1971 and 1977, 922,000 flats were built or modernized, which improved housing conditions for 3 million citizens" (German Democratic Republic 1979, p. 8). From about 2000 onward, the tone of discourse changed. Instead of praising themselves for mass construction programs, the states began to report several individual measures that responded to the individual needs of the affected persons. People affected by or vulnerable to inadequate housing were regarded differently, as autonomous persons. The states moreover differentiated between certain groups that faced inadequate housing; for example, the states differentiated between Sinti and Roma, refugees, indigenous people, single mothers, and asylum seekers. They talked about housing in the context of other rights and needs such as the right to food or the right to health. For instance, by reporting its housing policy, Poland talks about state-supported organizations that

> run night shelters, shelters, homes for single mothers, food banks, treatment and nursing establishments, hospitals and hospices, homes for refugees, vocational workshops, hostels for violence victims, communities, re-adaptation and protected housing establishments, Mediation Centres. Emergency assistance centres have been also organized, and they include: warming shelters, eating-houses, kitchens for the poor, points of medical and sanitary aid, points offering assistance in kind, daily shelters, clubs, legal, psychological and family assistance points. (Poland 2007: para 577)

People satisfy several needs at home (such as privacy, eating, drinking, or sleeping). It is obvious that inadequate housing has enormous consequences for the everyday life of the affected people when these needs cannot be satisfied. By mentioning warming shelters, eating-houses, or kitchens for the poor, Poland illustrates that the country recognizes other rights and needs of the affected persons. Moreover, Poland differentiates between certain groups such as families, single mothers, or refugees. There are, however, aspects of inadequate housing that are not as visible at first glance, tenure security for instance. The Committee regards tenure security as one of seven aspects of adequate housing:

> [A]ll persons should possess a degree of security of tenure which guarantees legal protection against forced eviction, harassment and other threats. States parties should consequently take immediate measures aimed at conferring legal security of tenure upon those persons and households currently lacking such protection, in genuine consultation with affected persons and groups. (CESCR 1991: para 8a)

As long as people do not have tenure security, their right to housing is not fully fulfilled. At the moment, a lot of governments and other actors have to deal with non-formal housing situations, such as housing on land that has been occupied without permission. Tenure security is closely connected to property rights. However, tenure security does not necessarily mean a person's having a formal land title. It could also be understood as being safe not to be arbitrarily evicted. The ICESR discourse shows that states and other governmental actors began to accept that millions of people live outside of formal housing markets, and they regard them more and more as full members of the society.

Sometimes, tenure security begins with recognition of the people by authorities, and recognition starts with language. Consider someone living in a non-formal settlement on the edge of a mega city in the Global South. From the perspective of recognition, there is a significant difference between calling such a settlement *illegal* or *informal*. The term *illegal* is closely connected to a violation of law, while the term *informal* stands for something that is neither illegal nor formal. When a state or another actor calls a settlement *informal* rather than *illegal*, it does not automatically mean that the people living there enjoy full tenure security. However, by choosing the term *informal* instead of the term *illegal*, the state recognizes that it considers the inhabitants of this settlement more likely right holders rather than right violators. The reporting of the member states in the ICESCR discourse shows that housing conditions formerly considered *illegal* were increasingly called *informal* (Kolocek 2017, p. 146).

This rising recognition of people affected by inadequate housing also emerges at other levels of discourse, for instance, the jurisdiction of the European Court of Human Rights (ECtHR). The European Court of Human Rights decides on the grounds of the rights stated in the European Convention on Human Rights, which has been signified by 47 members states, including states that geographically only partially pertain to Europe. In 2004, the European Court of Human Rights (ECtHR 2004: Öneryıldız vs. Turkey) had to decide whether the owner of a house built without permission could claim a violation of the right to the peaceful enjoyment of his possessions, protected by Article 1 Protocol 1 of the European Convention on Human Rights (ECHR). The case is remarkable because the house was built in a non-formal neighborhood in Istanbul without any formal permission from the local council—in other words, it could be considered an example of illegal or informal housing.

In 1993, the house had been damaged as a result of a methane explosion in a disused garbage tip. The applicant claimed for compensation for the damage of his home. He argued that the domestic authorities failed to protect his proprietary interest because they failed to inform the inhabitants of the danger posed by the tip in the settlement. The Court found that the domestic authorities had not complied with their positive obligations under Article 1 Protocol No. 1. The Court argued that the dwelling, while built illegally on land that belonged to the state, had been tolerated by the Turkish planning authorities for many decades and therefore had to be regarded as the applicant's property. The authorities failed to do everything within their power to protect the applicant's proprietary interest in the light of a risk they knew or ought to have known about (see also ECtHR 2018: para 158).

The case was neither explicitly about the right to housing, nor was human dignity at stake. The case was primarily about the right to property and therefore about tenure security. However, the case indicates the changing view of how the law considers people living in illegal or informal housing settings (Davy and Pellissery 2013; Ploeger and Groetelaers 2007). For a long time, people living in illegal or informal housing were more likely to be regarded as people who violated (planning) law—as criminals, so to speak. In the best case, such individuals were ignored by planning authorities and only received the attention of NGOs and scholars (Deininger 2003; de Soto 2000; Dey Biswas 2014; Kolocek 2012; Neuwirth 2006, 2011; Payne 2001; Roy 2005). Now, people living in non-formal housing settings are considered members of the society, as citizens so to speak.

Despite the rising recognition on the right to housing and people living in non-formal settings by states and other global actors, the number of people living in inadequate housing continues to be on the rise (Kothari and Chaudhry 2012; Human Rights Council 2020). The realization of the right to housing for all in the near future remains elusive; it is unlikely that all aspects of adequate housing will be met for all human beings worldwide. The rising numbers might represent a failed progressive realization of the human right to housing. The global community will never completely fulfill the human right to housing, no matter how hard it tries. In the next section of the chapter, I explore the relationship between the human right to housing and human dignity.

6.2 Human Dignity in Discourses on the Human Right to Housing

Scholarship around "human dignity" reveals the difficulty in defining the term (e.g., Barak 2015; Düwell 2014; Gewirth 1992; Rosen 2012); as Waldron (2015, p. 121) asserts: "our understanding of its meaning is a work-in-progress." Human dignity is sometimes seen as a right in itself, sometimes as a basis for rights. Article 1 UDHR states that "All human beings are born free and equal in dignity and rights." Careful readers recognize the term "and" in the quotation. The UDHR states that there is human dignity, *and* there are rights. This can be interpreted in the way that human dignity is not a right, but something else, or at least more than a right, for instance, a "framework right" (Barak 2015, pp. 156–160). Beitz (2013) shows that human dignity, absent from pre-war efforts to promote human rights, achieved a certain currency by the end of World War II. He concluded that "we cannot say from the record that the framers of either document had any articulate or agreed conception of human dignity or that their views of the nature and substance of human rights were much influenced by it" (Beitz 2013, p. 268). The preambles of the UDHR and both treaties ICCPR and the ICESCR state that rights derived from the inherent dignity of the human person. In such a reading, human dignity is "the origin of rights which [...] we conceive [...] as an extralegal authority whose instructions the international community obeys by drafting and ratifying human rights treaties" (Davy 2017, p. 16). Waldron was skeptical, stating that it might be "a mistake to put too much weight on the logic and detail of any of these preambular formulations" (Waldron 2015, p. 118). Nevertheless, on the international level, human dignity is a reference point to greater or lesser degrees (Beitz 2013).

Usually, national as well as international jurisprudence evaluates the content of the right to housing without referencing human dignity. Human dignity seems to come up only in "hard cases" (Barroso 2012, p. 380) on subjects such as abortion, same-sex marriage, or assisted suicide (Barroso 2012, pp. 380–391). From a juridical point of view, housing does not seem to be a "hard case", and as far as I know, there are only a few exceptions.

The Committee on ESC rights uses human dignity vaguely as one of three concepts when trying to come closer to an understanding of what adequate housing means (see above). The media, to mention another example, sometimes use human dignity to raise public awareness, for example when describing the living conditions of homeless people (Meert et al. 2004). Housing NGOs mention the term dignity in debates on housing rights violations or use dignity as part of their names (e.g., dignityhousing.org; projectdignity.org), but only seldom explain in detail their concept of human dignity.

Human dignity is likely to be considered offended when not simply one human right is violated but more than one or, as the following example shows, when more than one aspect of inadequate housing is affected. In a well-known South African case, the Constitutional Court of South Africa (SACC) had to decide whether the occupier might improve her housing conditions on her own expense, but without the owner's permission (Daniel v Sribante and Another 2017; see also Marais and Muller 2018). The owner tried to prohibit the applicant's housing improvement to make her dwelling habitable. The Court ruled that this prohibition of improvement would infringe the applicant's right to human dignity:

> If you deny an occupier the right to make improvements to the dwelling, you take away its habitability. And if you take away habitability, that may lead to her or his departure. [...] Take away the home that is the fulcrum of security of tenure, the way of life of an occupier will be dislocated. And that will offend her or his human dignity. (Daniel v Sribante and Another 2017: para 33–34)

In this case, human dignity was explicitly considered a right. Sometimes, human dignity serves as a trump card that helps to raise the strength of an argument, to highlight the meaning of certain human rights, or to stress the damage human rights violations might cause.

Occasionally, the violation of the right to housing might cause no damage at all, as the following example demonstrates. Imagine the housing situations of people living in villages in very rural areas of less developed countries, often without having a legal title, access to energy, or basic sanitation. Of course, taking the aspects of inadequate housing into consideration, one might call this a non-fulfilled human right to housing. However, I would argue that this living situation does not necessarily offend human dignity. It is also conceivable that people have strong ancestral ties to the land they inhabit, pride in their heritage, and feel content with their living arrangements. No concrete line here separates rights from dignity, but a number of living situations might raise housing rights issues that nevertheless not violate human dignity of those affected.

In order to accurately interpret housing rights violations in relationship to human dignity, I propose a framework in which human dignity is understood in terms of humiliation (Lindner et al. 2011; Margalit 1996). But what does humiliation mean in the context of housing and human rights? Davy (2014a, b, 2017) introduces human dignity and humiliation into the scholarly discussion on spatial planning issues that particularly address housing. He adopts Margalit's (1996) concept of dignity as non-humiliation. In the book *The Decent Society*, Margalit (1996) evaluates the relationship between dignity, humiliation, and self-respect (and other concepts). For Margalit, a society is decent when the political, religious, or private institutions do not humiliate people. Institutions humiliate people when they give them a sound reason to see their self-respect injured (Margalit 1996, p. 9). Margalit discusses humiliation in the context of certain situations such as unemployment, privacy, or punishment, but does not focus on housing issues. B. Davy takes Margalit's book an advice for policy makers and planners not only to focus on efficiency and concepts of justice, but also to focus on different levels of humiliation (2014a, b, 2017).

Connecting Margalit's and Davy's contributions on humiliation to the right to housing, one has to ask: Does a society that does not fully realize the human right to housing humiliate people? Yes and no. A challenging example for a humiliating violation of the right to housing is discussed by Waldron (1991), who examines homelessness from the perspective of freedom. Waldron reflects on the everyday life of homeless people. As Waldron (1991, p. 296) states, "[e]verything that is done has to be done somewhere. No one is free to perform an action unless there is somewhere he is free to perform it. Since we are embodied beings, we always have a location". He mentions the need to urinate as an example that shows the spatial dimension of humiliations: "If someone needs to urinate, what he needs above all as a dignified person is the freedom to do so in privacy and relative independence of the arbitrary will of anyone else" (Waldron 1991, p. 320). Waldron impressively explains why homelessness is both a violation of the right to housing, and a violation of human dignity: homlessness people have many reasons to see their self-respect injured. This is the main difference to the above-mentioned example of the people living in villages in very rural areas. But what does "having a sound reason" mean? B. Davy discusses—but does not solve—a central conceptual problem: "A person's dignity results from how she or he think about themselves. Dignity is the most personal manifestation of the self. [A] person's self-respect can hardly be questioned in public deliberation without submitting this person to humiliation" (Davy 2014b, p. 9). People decide on their own whether they have a sound reason to consider themselves humiliated or not (Davy 2014b, p. 11). This "ability to make your own decisions without being controlled by anyone else" (Cambridge Online Dictionary 2018) is autonomy, the next concept that I shall bring into discussion.

6.3 The Human Right to Housing at the Threshold of Autonomy and Non-humiliation

From a historical point of view, the increasing recognition of autonomy, among other concepts such as empathy or equality, is one precondition for an understanding of human dignity and human rights: "To have human rights, people had to be perceived as individuals who were capable of exercising moral judgment" (Hunt 2007, p. 27). Autonomy is "the ethical element of human dignity. It is the foundation of the free will of individuals [. . .]. An autonomous person establishes the rules that will govern his or her life" (Barroso 2012, pp. 367–368). Barroso differentiates between three ideas of autonomy: private autonomy, public autonomy, and the existential minimum. The last idea emphasizes that people cannot be autonomous without adequate living conditions that are protected by minimal social rights (Barroso 2012, p. 371). Autonomy can lead to housing rights violations and sometimes even to humiliating situations. In the following, I would like to take inadequate housing in Hong Kong as an example, while stressing that the Hong Kong case is not unique. Consider a person who lives in a rural area in China. As a peasant, this person does not earn enough in the rural area and can barely afford good health care and education for his or her children. This is why the person decides to work in Hong Kong, a place with a reputation for strong economic growth, efficient planning, impressive skyscrapers, but which has extreme housing costs and horrible housing conditions. Due to high housing costs and availability issues on the formal housing markets, some people have no choice but to live in a "cage-home," a space not much larger than a mattress, usually surrounded by a cage in which the resident can lock him or herself. Marsh (2016) uses the term to include cubicle-flats, bed-space apartments, roof-top slums, and minuscule subdivided units; he states that these places "are not homes at all. They are the embodiment of squalor—cramped, dank, dimly lit dwellings averaging 15 square feet in size" (Marsh 2016, p. 159). Considering cage homes, the Committee on Economic, Social and Cultural Rights responded to a State Party report of the People's Republic of China and criticized, "[T]he Committee remains deeply concerned that the right to housing of many people in Hong Kong remains unfulfilled. In the Committee's view, bed-space apartments, or cage homes, are an affront to human dignity" (CESCR 2001: para 25). Here is how China answered to the critics:

> [W]e believe that our approach is the right one. The people who live in bed-space apartments do so largely out of choice for convenience, economic and other personal reasons. There is ample provision in government hostels—which are clean, safe and well managed—to accommodate the relatively small numbers involved. Yet they remain underutilized, probably because their targeted occupants place a higher value on location and convenience than on the standard of their living environment. (People's Republic of China 2003: para 592)

If, as China maintains, some people really do place a higher value on location than on their dignity, the right to housing is situated at the threshold of autonomy and humiliation. The cage home case illustrates a main housing rights problem that is difficult to solve. What should policy makers do, when people bring themselves into housing rights violating situations that give them sound reasons to consider themselves humiliated? From the Committee's point of view, China had to stop people living in cage homes because they violate the right to housing, and (!) they are an affront to human dignity.

From the perspective of autonomy, the cage home example is not that different from a Syrian migrant, now living in a refugee camp in Paris, or a person from Eastern Europe working in a German slaughterhouse and sharing a small and overcrowded apartment with other workers near his workplace. All these people have brought themselves into situations of inadequate housing that additionally might give them sound reasons to consider themselves humiliated. Of course, one can question how autonomous their decisions really were. Very likely these people placed themselves into such a situation to escape from other problems. These problems also could be framed as other human rights violations such as escape from armed conflicts or the experience of extreme levels of poverty.

6.4 Conclusion

In the future, states and other policy makers around the world will not be able to fully realize the human right to housing, which would mean that not all aspects of adequate housing will be met for all people worldwide. By considering the human right to housing through the lens of autonomy and human dignity as non-humiliation, I propose to differentiate between certain types of housing rights violations. I presented different examples for non-fulfilled housing rights. Some are likely to be considered a violation of human dignity because the affected people might have sound reasons to consider themselves humiliated—others are not. I presented a list of seven aspects of inadequate housing, which is a very often mentioned reference point in discourses on the right to housing. The right to housing is not fully fulfilled when one of the seven aspects of adequate housing is not met. However, sometimes only one aspect is lacking, and sometimes almost all aspects are lacking, as in cases of homelessness. I argue, the progressive realization of the right shall not start with satisfying the aspects of inadequate housing but with asking if and when the affected people have sound reasons to consider themselves humiliated. When assessing violations of the human right to housing, I suggest the following steps:

The first step is a step backwards: question if and how autonomous the affected person's decision really was. Two cases are conceivable here. In Case 1, the housing conditions have always been inadequate, but for some reasons the affected people do not care. Moreover, they deny considering themselves humiliated. Typical examples might be the non-formalized housing conditions of travelers, nomads, or indigenous people. I assume that there might be some housing aspects, the affected persons would like to have improved. However, a large-scale relocation or improvement program could cause additional damage, because the people affected might start feeling humiliated by the government's paternalistic attitude. The United Nations

Declaration on the Rights of Indigenous Peoples (UNDRIP 2007) explicitly states that indigenous people, "in exercising their right to self-determination, have the right to autonomy or self-government in matters relating to their internal and local affairs, as well as ways and means for financing their autonomous functions" (Article 4 UNDRIP). This includes "the right to be actively involved in developing and determining health, housing and other economic and social programs affecting them and, as far as possible, to administer such programs through their own institutions" (Article 23 UNDRIP). So, if indigenous people accept living in a situation that does not fully meet all aspects of adequate housing, no human dignity problem applies in their case. In other words, autonomy trumps the human right to housing, as long as the violation of the right to housing is not humiliating. Perhaps, recognizing peoples' autonomy to live in non-formal housing settings starts with calling the settlements *informal* rather than *illegal*.

In Case 2, the person's decision to live in inadequate housing is based on desperation. Recalling my example of the cage home dweller, he or she chose to live in inadequate housing because the person could not fulfill other rights, the right to work, to health, or the right to education for his or her children, for instance. What might first look like an autonomous decision appears less autonomous if we take the concept of autonomy seriously. A person in this scenario merely has the "autonomy" to decide which human rights violations they prefer, and they often prefer a violation of their right to housing. Policymakers can respond to Case 2 by trying to eliminate the causes of "voluntary inadequate housing", whether they lie in the education system, the health care sector, the job market, or elsewhere. In fact, responding to Case 2 requires specific information (in other words: research) on the motives of people who "choose" to live in inadequate housing. While some causes might be obvious (such as armed conflicts, debts, family violence, or poverty and lack of prospects in rural areas), others may still be unexplored. I do not anticipate that such a policy can abolish inadequate housing entirely—which brings me to the second step.

The second step is, literally speaking, a step forward and is based on the conclusion that, in the future, fulfilling the human right to housing is impossible. In the second step, policymakers focus on the everyday life of the affected persons. They have to ask precisely why and when the affected people have sound reasons to feel humiliated in their everyday life. Therefore, it is necessary to differentiate between the different forms and places of inadequate housing. In the second step, one has to be aware that the right to housing encompasses the enjoyment of other human rights, such as the right to health care, the right to food, the right to privacy, or the right to security. Sometimes, it starts with asking simple questions such as Waldron (see above) did, when he brought up the need to use a toilet for homeless people.

In this chapter, I first explained the content of the human right to housing. I showed examples for violations of the right to housing and argued that not every violation is a human dignity issue. I explained why it is unlikely that the progressive realization of this right will completely succeed. From time to time, autonomy is the reason why the progressive realization of the human right to housing does not fully succeed. This is acceptable as long as the affected people do not have a sound reason to consider themselves humiliated.

References

Barak A (2015) Human dignity. The constitutional value and the constitutional right. Cambridge University Press, Cambridge

Barroso LR (2012) Here, there, and everywhere: human dignity in contemporary law and in the transnational discourse. Boston Coll Int Comp Law Rev 35(2):331–393

Beitz CR (2013) Human dignity in the theory of human rights: nothing but a phrase? Philos Public Aff 41(3):259–290

Cambridge Online Dictionary (2018). https://dictionary.cambridge.org. Accessed 30 June 2023

CESCR (2001) Consideration of reports submitted by states parties under articles 16 and 17 of the Covenant. Concluding Observations of the Committee on Economic, Social and Cultural Rights. China: Hong Kong Special Administrative Region. E/C.12/1/Add.58

CESCR (Committee on Economic, Social and Cultural Rights) (1991) General Comment No. 4. The right to adequate housing (Art. 11, para 1, of the Covenant). E/C.12/1991/1

Constitutional Court of South Africa. *Daniel v Sribante and Another*. 11 May 2017. (CCT50/16) [2017] cultural ZACC 13; 2017 (4) SA 341 (CC); 2017 (8) BCLR 949 (CC)

Davy U (2013) Social citizenship going international: changes in the reading of UN-sponsored economic and social rights. In: Davy B, Davy U, Leisering L (eds) Exploring global social citizenship: human rights perspectives, vol vol 22, supplement 1. International Journal of Social Welfare, pp S15–S31

Davy B (2014a) Raumplanung und die Politik der Würde. In: Blaas W, Bröthaler J, Getzner M, Gutheil-Knopp-Kirchwald G (eds) Perspektiven der staatlichen Aufgabenerfüllung: Zwischen budgetärer Knappheit und integrativem Anspruch: Für Wilfried Schönbäck zum 70. Geburtstag. Verlag Österreich, Wien, pp 51–76

Davy B (2014b) Non-humiliating plans! A human rights approach. Working paper no. 15. https://www.researchgate.net/publication/338267375_Non-humiliating_plans_a_human_rights_approach. Accessed 30 June 2023

Davy U (2015) Der 'Universalismus' in der Allgemeinen Erklärung der Menschenrechte: Die Arbeit am Konsens, 1946-1948. In: Heintz B (ed) Menschenrechte in der Weltgesellschaft. Campus-Verlag, Frankfurt, M., pp 198–235

Davy B (2017) Human dignity and property in land - a human rights approach. In: Pellissery S, Davy B, Jacobs HM (eds) Land policies in India: promises, practices and challenges. Springer, Singapore, pp 1–33

Davy B, Pellissery S (2013) The citizenship promise (un)fulfilled: the right to housing in informal settings. In: Davy B, Davy U, Leisering L (eds) Exploring global social citizenship: human rights perspectives, vol vol 22, supplement 1. International Journal of Social Welfare, pp S68–S84

de Soto H (2000) The mystery of capital. Why capitalism triumphs in the west and fails everywhere else. Basic Books, New York

Deininger K (2003) Land policies for growth and poverty reduction. World Bank and Oxford University Press, Washington, DC

Dey Biswas S (2014) Land rights formalization in India. Examining de Soto through the lens of Rawls' theory of justice. Working paper no. 18. https://www.researchgate.net/publication/275965306_Land_rights_formalization_in_India_Examining_de_Soto_through_the_lens_of_Rawls%27_theory_of_justice. Accessed 30 June 2023

Düwell M (2014) Human dignity: concepts, discussions, philosophical perspectives. In: Düwell M, Braarvig J, Brownsword R, Mieth D (eds) The Cambridge handbook of human dignity. Cambridge University Press, Cambridge, pp 23–49
ECtHR (European Court of Human Rights) (2018) Guide on Article 1 of Protocol No. 1 to the European Convention on Human Rights. Protection of property
German Democratic Republic (1979) Reports submitted in accordance with council resolution 1988 (LX) by states parties to the covenant concerning rights covered by articles 10 to 12. E/1980/6/Add.6
Gewirth A (1992) Human dignity as the basis of rights. In: Meyer MJ, Parent WA (eds) The constitution of rights: human dignity and American values. Cornell University Press, Ithaca, pp 10–28
Henkin L (1979) International human rights as 'rights'. Cardozo Law Rev 1:425–447
Human Rights Council (2020) Guidelines for the implementation of the right to adequate housing. Report of the Special Rapporteur on adequate housing as a component of the right to an adequate standard of living, and on the right to non-discrimination in this context. A/HRC/43/43
Hunt L (2007) Inventing human rights. A history. W.W. Norton & Company, New York and London
Kenna P (2008) Globalization and housing rights. Indiana J Global Leg Stud 15(2):396–469
Kolocek M (2012) Land policy and the social floor to housing. The case of Latin America and Africa. Working paper no. 15. https://bbv.raumplanung.tu-dortmund.de/storages/bbv-raumplanung/r/Downloads/Publications/2012_Kolocek_Housing_LA_Africa.pdf. Accessed 30 June 2023
Kolocek M (2013) The human right to housing in the 27 member states of the European Union. Eur J Homelessness 7(1):135–154
Kolocek M (2015) Das Menschenrecht auf Wohnen. Interpretationen im globalen Kontext. RaumPlanung 182(6):10–15
Kolocek M (2017) The human right to housing in the face of land policy and social citizenship. A global discourse analysis. Palgrave Macmillan, Basingstoke and New York
Kothari M, Chaudhry S (2012) Housing, land and sustainable development. In: Social Watch Report. The right to a future, pp 38–41. https://www.socialwatch.org/node/13960. Accessed 30 June 2023
Lindner EG, Harting LM, Spalthoff U (2011) Human dignity and humiliation studies: a global network advancing dignity through dialogue. Policy Futures Educ 9:66–73
Marais EJ, Muller G (2018) The right of an ESTA occupier to make improvements without an owner's permission after Daniels: Quo vadis statury interpretations and development of the common law? S Afr Law J 135(4):766–798
Margalit A (1996) The decent society. Harvard University Press, Cambridge
Marsh L (2016) The strategic use of human rights treaties in Hong Kong's cage-home crisis: no way out? Asian J Law Soc 3(1):159–188. https://doi.org/10.1017/als.2015.23
Meert H, Cabrera P, Christensen I, Koch-Nielsen I, Maas R, Maurel E (2004) The changing profiles of homeless people: homelessness in the written press: a discourse analysis. https://www.feantsaresearch.org/download/2004_homelessness_in_the_written_press456255587918371547 9.pdf. Accessed 30 June 2023
Moons N (2018) The right to housing in law and society. Routledge, New York and London
Neuwirth R (2006) Shadow cities. A billion squatters, a new urban world. Routledge, New York
Neuwirth R (2011) Stealth of nations. The global rise of informal economy. Pantheon Books, New York
Payne G (2001) Urban land tenure policy options: title or rights? Habitat Int 25:415–429
People's Republic of China (2003) Initial reports submitted by states parties under articles 16 and 17 of the Covenant. E/1990/5/Add.59
Ploeger HD, Groetelaers DA (2007) The importance of the fundamental right to property for the practice of planning: an introduction to the case law of the European Court of Human Rights on Article 1, Protocol 1. Eur Plan Stud 15(10):1424–1438

Poland (2007) Fifth periodic reports submitted by states parties under articles 16 and 17 of the Covenant. E/C.12/POL/5

Rosen M (2012) Dignity. Its history and meaning. Harvard University Press, Cambridge and London

Roy A (2005) Urban informality: toward an epistemology of planning. J Am Plan Assoc 71(2): 147–158

Waldron J (1991) Homelessness and the issue of freedom. UCLA Law Rev 39(1):295–324

Waldron J (2015) Is dignity the foundation of human rights? In: Rowan Cruft S, Liao M, Renzo M (eds) Philosophical foundations of human rights. Oxford University Press, Oxford, pp 117–137

Chapter 7
Asylum Seekers' Dignity: Elusive in Europe and Lost in Crisis. At the Threshold of Universality

Ulrike Davy

Abstract Asylum seekers are often not welcome when they ask for international protection, in particular, if the countries they turn to are rich and the asylum seekers destitute. States are reluctant to shoulder the additional burden. Does that reluctance affect the respect due under an embedded norm declaring that human dignity is inviolable? Is showing less respect to asylum seekers legitimate? My contribution deals with that question from the perspective of law and the perspective of state-led

My contribution builds on knowledge and skills acquired in various venues of collaborative and interdisciplinary research. First ideas on asylum seekers' dignity were presented at the Intercontinental Academia on Human Dignity, hosted by the Israel Institute for Advanced Studies (IIAS) in March 2016 and the Zentrum für interdisziplinäre Forschung (ZiF) in Bielefeld in August 2016, under the aegis of the global network of University-Based Institutes for Advanced Study (UBIAS). My gratitude extends to Michal Linial, then director of the IIAS, who became a dear friend during my terms in Jerusalem; to Nadiv Mordechay, the IIAS coordinator whose wisdom was invaluable for composing the program; to the ZiF Board of Directors who strongly believed in the benefits of international cooperation; to my fellow instructors Aleida Assmann, Aharon Barak, Bernadette J. Brooten, Marcus Düwell, Moshe Halbertal, Christine Hayes, Lynn A. Hunt, Mordechai Kremnitzer, Gertrude Lübbe-Wolff, Ralf Poscher and Michael Rosen; and to the fellows of the Intercontinental Academia on Human Dignity, Stephanie N. Arel, Guy E. Carmi, Levi Cooper, Caterina Drigo, Dascha Düring, Johannes Eichenhofer, Connor M. Ewing, Vanessa Hellmann, Akemi Kamimura, Sini Kangas, Michael Kolocek, Sima Kramer, Tamar Megiddo, Omer Michaelis, Funlola Olojede, Anita von Poser, Caterina Preda, Ron Roth, Talia Schwartz-Maor, Lauren Ware, and Emily Kidd White. The time we spent together is a cherished memory. The Collaborative Research Center in Bielefeld on Practices of Comparing (SFB 1288) funded by the German Research Foundation (DFG) provided an ideal environment for reflecting on notions of equality and universality. The NRW Forschungskolleg FlüGe – Herausforderungen und Chancen globaler Flüchtlingsmigration für die Gesundheitsversorgung in Deutschland was a most welcome platform for gaining insights into some very practical aspects of the refugee crisis 2015/2016. Yüsra Şimşek helped with cite checking. Thank you all!. The contribution was finalized in March 2023.

U. Davy (✉)
University of Bielefeld, Bielefeld, Germany

University of Johannesburg, Johannesburg, South Africa
e-mail: ulrike.davy@uni-bielefeld.de

S. N. Arel et al. (eds.), *Probing Human Dignity*,
https://doi.org/10.1007/978-3-031-42437-3_7

welfare. In Germany, the constitutional right to respect of human dignity implicates the individual right to be granted a subsistence minimum, irrespective of nationality. Is there a similar right at the level of the European Union? My contribution explores the role of human dignity in European politics (focusing on politics during and in wake of the refugee crisis 2015/16), European law (focusing on the directives regarding the reception of asylum seekers), and European adjudication (focusing on pertinent case law of the European Court of Justice and the European Court of Human Rights). Based on an analysis of policy documents, the legal histories of relevant directives and case law, I argue that, at the Union level, human dignity is at best at the periphery of values that actors have in mind when they define or grant a subsistence minimum to asylum seekers. However, I also argue that there are arguments that could move 'dignity' to the center of political and legal debates.

7.1 Introduction

In 2015 and 2016, Germany was at the center of what was quickly termed a "refugee crisis" by German media and politics. In 2015, 480,000 applications for asylum were lodged with the Bundesamt für Migration und Flüchtlinge, the (only and central) German authority responsible for deciding upon requests for international protection (Bundesamt 2016). In 2016, the number of applications lodged was 746,000 (Bundesamt 2017). Both in 2015 and 2016, most of the applicants were Syrian nationals. All in all the number of their applications reached 433,000. But the characteristics of the crisis were not only rising numbers of applications and rising numbers of non-nationals crossing Germany's Southern borders following the decision of Federal Chancellor Angela Merkel to relinquish border controls in September 2015. Germany was also the site of highly publicized crimes, such as the sexual assaults on women orchestrated by groups of young men, alleged asylum seekers from the Maghreb, on New Year's Eve 2015, the ax-attack committed by an asylum seeker from Afghanistan or Pakistan on passengers in a train close to Würzburg, a suicide bomb initiated by a young Syrian at the Ansbach music festival in July 2016, the rape and murder of a 19-year-old medical student volunteering for a private aid organization, and the truck-attack targeting the visitors of a well-known Berlin Christmas market in December 2016, perpetrated by a rejected asylum seeker from Tunisia. And, last but not least, Germany was the site of a new right-wing political movement, which fed on and instilled fear, hatred and xenophobia.

As the crisis reached its climax in late 2015, early 2016, German lawmakers responded with amendments to the criminal code, to the law regarding entry and residence, to the asylum law and to the law granting a subsistence minimum to asylum seekers (Davy 2019; on the influence of right-wing politics Davy 2018). Many of these amendments tightened existing rules regarding expulsion and social benefits. Some of the amendments were met with scholarly critique (Brings and Oehl 2016; Janda 2017, 2018; Davy 2018, 2019; von Harbou 2016; but see also Di Fabio 2016; Thym 2016). The starting point for criticizing the cut-down on social benefits for asylum seekers was a judgment by the German Federal Constitutional Court

(Bundesverfassungsgericht, in the following, BVerfG), released in July 2012. [1] The July 2012 judgment stated in no uncertain terms that asylum seekers could, on an equal footing with citizens, rely on the right to respect of human dignity, enshrined in Article 1(1) Grundgesetz. That broadly conceived right, so the court held, included a more specific right for people in need, nationals and non-nationals alike as long as they resided on German territory (paras 62, 63), namely a right to a subsistence minimum. The court was quite elaborate regarding the standard underpinning the right to a subsistence minimum:

> The . . . guarantee of a dignified minimum existence does not only cover those means that are absolutely necessary to maintain a dignified life. It guarantees the entire minimum existence as a comprehensive fundamental rights guarantee, that encompasses both humans' physical existence, that is food, clothing, household items, housing, heating, hygiene and health, and guarantees the possibility to maintain interpersonal relationships and a minimal degree of participation in social, cultural and political life, since a human as a person necessarily exists in social context (para 64).

And, addressing lawmakers in parliament who were, by the court, asked to redress certain shortcomings of the then existing law on asylum seekers' benefits, the court added:

> If the legislature wishes to consider the particular characteristics of specific groups of individuals when determining the dignified minimum existence . . . , it may not . . . differentiate across the board in light of the recipients' residence status. Such differentiation is only possible if their need for existential benefits significantly deviates from that of other persons in need (para 73).

Even if some aspects of the BVerfG's propositions might be open to differing interpretations or contestation (e.g. Eichenhofer 2012; Rothkegel 2012; Deibel 2013; Baer 2014; Frerichs 2014; Lenze 2014; Petersen 2014; Dietz 2015; Rixen 2015; Janda 2016; Oppermann 2017), two things are not. For one, human dignity as enshrined in Article 1(1) Grundgesetz is conceived of as universal. All human beings present in German territory are right holders. For another, differing benefits—in particular, lower benefits for asylum seekers—must reflect differing needs. Otherwise, differences in benefits are illegitimate. In other words, the making of such differences, e.g. by lawmakers, violates the dignity clause of the Grundgesetz.

Surely, in 2015 and 2016, the whole of Europe was affected by the crisis, the exceptional position of Germany among European countries notwithstanding. In 2015, about 1.8 million illegal border crossings were detected at the EU external borders, compared to a bit more than 200,000 in 2014 (European Commission 2018a, p. 2). Migratory movements peaked in particular on the Eastern Mediterranean route, leading from Turkey to Greece, then through the Balkan countries to Western European countries, primarily to Germany as the "most wanted" among the European countries. In September, October, and November 2015, the number of illegal crossings from Turkey to Greece was about 150,000 per month; most of those migrants were Syrians, Afghanis, and Iraqis (European Commission 2016b Annex

[1] Bundesverfassungsgericht, judgment of the First Senate of 18 July 2012, 1 BvL 10/10.

1, p. 4). In 2016, the illegal border crossings were still around 500,000 (European Commission 2018a, p. 2). Yet, after the implementation of the EU-Turkey Statement,[2] migratory movements had again turned to the more dangerous crossing-overs along the Central Mediterranean route leading to the shores of Italy (European Commission 2017a, p. 11). For these migrants, the main point of departure was Libya. The main nationalities were Eritrean, Tunisian, Nigerian, Guinean, and Ivorian. In 2015 and 2016, the number of applications lodged in the EU exceeded 1.2 million (European Commission 2018b, p. 4).

During the crisis, scholarly interest in Germany focused primarily on the Schengen acquis and the Dublin system, the former securing free movement and the absence of border controls within the Schengen area, the latter identifying the (one and only) Member State responsible for processing asylum applications lodged within the EU. Obviously, both regimes did not function properly in 2015 and 2016 (Hailbronner and Thym 2016; Peukert et al. 2016; Kluth 2016). The plight of asylum seekers (in Greece, in Italy, in Hungary) was a constant theme in the daily news. Yet, 'human dignity,' a value and right laid down by the EU Charter of Fundamental Rights[3] was absent from all debates. Article 1 of the Charter reads: "Human dignity is inviolable. It must be respected and protected." The silence provokes the question I want to deal with: Does the dignity clause of the Charter also encapsulate an individual right to be provided with a subsistence minimum, similarly to Article 1(1) German Grundgesetz? If so, what does this right mean for people seeking international protection in the EU? The questions relate tightly to how Europeans conceptualize the 'solidarity' they owe to people in peril and in need: Does the concept involve a threshold dividing people in two groups: in one group of people that are considered close and familiar and, hence, deserving of solidarity, and in one group considered alien and unrelated, and, hence, not deserving of solidarity? More technically, does EU law conceptualize 'human dignity' as a universal value that rejects the drawing of thresholds?

I shall answer these questions in steps. Section 7.2 of my contribution deals with politics. Section 7.2 seeks to identify the values underpinning EU migration policies as they were fleshed out in certain arenas in 2015 and 2016. I concentrate, on the one hand, on the conclusions of the European Council, i.e. the quarterly statements of the heads of state or governments of all Member States of the EU defining the general political direction and the priorities of the EU. On the other hand, I concentrate on selected communications issued by the European Commission, meant to prepare the meetings of the European Council and to implement the conclusions drawn by the European Council, such as the European Agenda on Migration and various connected progress reports. The timeline for the analysis presented in Sect. 7.2 starts in late 2013, when a boat carrying around 500 migrants sank off the coast of

[2]EU-Turkey Statement, 18 March 2016. http://www.consilium.europa.eu/en/press/press-releases/2016/03/18/eu-turkey-statement/. Accessed 31 January 2023.

[3]Charter of Fundamental Rights of the European Union, OJ 2016 C 202/393 (in the following, Charter).

Lampedusa, an Italian island, and almost 400 people drowned. That incident triggered the first clear value statements at the Union level. The timeline of the analysis ends at the end of 2019. The analysis comprises 32 statements by the European Council (conclusions summarizing ordinary and extraordinary meetings; the 2015 Valetta Action Plan; the 2017 Malta Declaration) and 72 papers issued by the European Commission. The analysis relies on ATLAS.ti, a tool for the qualitative analysis of large bodies of texts. The codes I used aimed to explore 'values' and 'measures': What were the values the European Council and the Commission took resort to when they framed their policies and measures responding to the crisis? How were values and measures related to one another? What was the role of 'human dignity?' Section 7.3 turns to EU law, concentrating on the directives supposed to guide the Member States when they define the kind of livelihood they want to provide for asylum seekers who arrive destitute in their territories (reception conditions).[4] Based on an analysis of the legal histories of the pertinent directives (proposals of the Commission, records of the debates in the Council and in the European Parliament), this part tracks the meaning of 'human dignity' in the context of providing a subsistence minimum: What are the dignity standards the directives intend to prescribe?[5] Section 7.4 focuses on the case law of the European Court of Justice (in the following, ECJ): Is there an elaborate proposition to be found in the case law sketching what the Member States owe to asylum seekers when they define and then implement reception conditions? I shall argue that, even if we have a closer look at the politics of the EU (Sect. 7.2), the law regarding reception conditions (Sect. 7.3) and the case law of the ECJ (Sect. 7.4), we are pretty much left in the dark when we seek to systematize how EU politics and EU law conceptualize asylum seekers' dignity. There is, so far, little guidance by case law. That is why Sect. 7.5 offers a critique, in particular a critique aiming to explore the meaning of the dignity clause enshrined in Article 1 of the Charter. In Sect. 7.5, I shall pinpoint where the ECJ could give relevance to the dignity clause of the Charter. Drawing on the case law of the European Court of Human Rights (in the following, ECtHR), I shall present some arguments that might bolster a more robust stance. Section 7.6 summarizes my findings.

[4]Directive 2003/9 laying down minimum standards for the reception of asylum seekers, OJ 2003 L 31/18 (in the following, Directive 2003/9); Directive 2013/33 laying down standards for the reception of applicants for international protection (recast), OJ 2013 L 180/96 (in the following, Directive 2013/33).

[5]I shall not deal with the particular regime established by the EU for people leaving the Ukraine following the military invasion by Russian forces on or after 24 February 2022. For details of the regime see Council Implementing Decision establishing the existence of a mass influx of displaced persons from Ukraine within the meaning of Article 5 of Directive 2001/55/EC, and having the effect of introducing temporary protection, OJ 2022 L 71/1.

7.2 Politics: From Protecting Lives to Protecting Borders

7.2.1 European Council

When framing and describing the incident off shore of Lampedusa and, later, the so-called crisis occurring in 2015 and 2016, the European Council did not once make a reference to human dignity.

Humanitarian Sentiment. Before and during the crisis, the European Council certainly expressed feelings of shock, pity, sympathy, and compassion. But when doing so, 'human dignity' was apparently not in the mind of the European Council. The European Council preferred to talk about "its deep sadness at the recent tragic events in the Mediterranean in which hundreds of people lost their lives" (European Council 2013a, preamble). "Protecting and saving lives at the EU's external borders" was singled out as a priority matter in migration policies (European Council 2013a, para 47). Yet, protecting and saving lives did not necessarily imply giving access to EU territory. The European Council rather envisioned stepping up external border controls and increasing the engagement with third countries in order to make sure that migrants would not embark on their "hazardous journeys" (European Council 2013b: para 41). The European Council also identified the parties bearing the main responsibility for the tragedies, namely the "organized people smugglers and human traffickers" (European Council 2015a: para 16) and the illegal migrants who ought to be discouraged "from risking their lives" (European Council 2015b: para 5). At the end of 2015, when events came closer to the European heartland and people literally began to march to EU territories on foot, humanitarian sentiment shifted to the situation in countries along the Eastern Mediterranean or Balkan route. In February 2016, the European Council announced: "the humanitarian situation of migrants along the Western Balkan route calls for urgent action using all available EU and national means to alleviate it" (European Council 2016a: para 8). And again, that call did not imply giving access to EU territory. It simply meant providing "humanitarian assistance internally" (ibid), hence in the region. When agreement was eventually reached with Turkey in the spring of 2016—published as EU-Turkey Statement in a press release—and the borders along the Balkan route were sealed off again, the "humanitarian crisis" moved back to the Central Mediterranean route, exposing Italy again as the main frontline state. In June 2017, the European Council stated: "Loss of life and continuing migratory flows of primarily economic migrants on the Central Mediterranean route is a structural challenge and remains an issue of urgent and serious concern" (European Council 2017: para 21). Regionalism, i.e. aid delivered in the region affected, continued to inspire the measures the European Council envisioned. In the summer of 2018 and in the geographical context of the Mediterranean route, politics favored the idea of "regional disembarkation platforms" in order to prevent the tragic loss of life (European Council 2018: para 5).

Solidarity and Responsibility. Apart from humanitarian sentiment, policy statements released by the European Council drew on the notions of 'solidarity' and 'responsibility.' These two values appeared regularly as a pair, and the statements were always brief. To give but one example from the conclusions of the European Council reached in the summer of 2015: In June 2015, the European Council held very generally that: "Europe needs a balanced and geographically comprehensive approach to migration, based on solidarity and responsibility" (European Council 2015b: para 1). Obviously, such statements reflected the values enshrined in Article 80 of the Treaty on the Functioning of the European Union,[6] an article that concludes the treaty's chapter on "policies on border checks, asylum and immigration."[7] However, the meaning attached to those principles by the European Council is all but clear. Was the European Council talking about moral or legal responsibilities? If the European Council was referring to legal responsibilities, where is their basis? Who is responsible? And, who are the beneficiaries of solidarity? With 'responsibility' in mind, the European Council sometimes referred vaguely to "a common obligation" (European Council 2015c: para 1), a reference that seemingly addresses Member States, but leaves everything else open.[8] Sometimes, the European Council referred, even more vaguely, to a "global responsibility," for instance, with regard to humanitarian assistance to be provided to Syrian refugees (European Council 2016a: para 8) or, in the context of combatting human trafficking, reference was made to a "shared responsibility between countries of transit, origin and destination" (European Council 2014a: para 34). The sources of these responsibilities were generally not mentioned. References to the "Union's commitment to international protection" (European Council 2014b: para 7) or "the right to seek asylum" (European Council 2015c: para 3) can be found in the texts adopted by the European Council, but those references are rare exceptions. 'Solidarity,' that much can be drawn from the context and the usage of the word, is conceptualized as a value that is supposed to guide the Member States' conduct vis-à-vis other Member States. Mostly, references to solidarity were made when the European Council talked about the principles underlying the Common European Asylum System or its reform.[9] In October 2016, for instance, the European Council called "for work to

---

[6]Consolidated Version of the Treaty on the Functioning of the European Union, OJ 2016 C 202/47 (in the following, TFEU).

[7]Article 80 TFEU reads: "The policies of the Union set out in this Chapter and their implementation shall be governed by the principle of solidarity and fair sharing of responsibility, including its financial implications, between the Member States. Whenever necessary, the Union acts adopted pursuant to this Chapter shall contain appropriate measures to give effect to this principle."

[8]The conclusions adopted on 15 October 2015 (European Council 2015c: para 1) read: "Tackling the migration and refugee crisis is a common obligation which requires a comprehensive strategy and a determined effort over time in a spirit of solidarity and responsibility."

[9]The Common European Asylum System was initiated in 1999 (European Commission 2000). The term covers several legal acts adopted by the Union that aim to introduce common standards for the granting of asylum (international protection). The Common European Asylum Systems comprises directives proscribing procedural safeguards, standards for the reception of asylum seekers, and standards with regard to the grounds for granting international protection. The system also comprises a regulation defining the Member State which is responsible for examining an application for asylum (Dublin regulation) and a regulation establishing a database of the fingerprints of asylum seekers (EURODAC).

be continued on the reform of the Common European Asylum System, including on how to apply the principles of responsibility and solidarity in the future" (European Council 2016b: para 9). The Common European Asylum System links and binds Member States only.

7.2.2 European Commission

The policy papers of the Commission were more elaborate, in many ways. That is true for the conceptualizing of the crisis, the framing of values—generally and with regard to responsibility and solidarity specifically, and the remedies the Commission proposed in order to cope with the crisis. Furthermore, the policy papers document a dramatic change in the perception of what should be the guiding principles. The Commission moved from issuing strong value statements in 2015 to more pragmatic and EU-centered positions in 2017. And clearly, some values got lost along the way, 'human dignity' being among the values lost.

Conceptualizing the Crisis. The word "crisis" appeared for the first time in May 2015, in a communication on "A European Agenda on Migration," where the Commission, after having referred to "the human tragedy in the whole of the Mediterranean," asserted: "The migration crisis in the Mediterranean has put the spotlight on immediate needs" (European Commission 2015a, pp. 3, 6). Having said so, the Commission turned to self-criticism. The Commission spoke of "structural limitations" of the EU migration policy and of the (neglected) "need to strike the right balance in its migration policy" (Ibid 6). The Commission's political answer to the crisis comprised several elements, including a "robust fight against irregular migration, traffickers and smugglers" and a "strong common asylum policy," combined with a "new European policy on legal migration" (Ibid).

According to the Commission's May 2015 communication, the fight against irregular migration implicated enhanced border management, criminal law addressing trafficking, but also the introduction of legal pathways to the European countries. The call for a strong common asylum policy signaled, foremost, the Commission's discontent with the situation prevailing in 2015. With regard to the state of affairs in early 2015, the Commission diagnosed a "lack of mutual trust between the Member States" and that, so the Commission concluded, had "a direct impact on asylum seekers who seek to 'asylum shop,' but also on EU public opinion: it encourages a sense that the current system is fundamentally unfair" (Ibid 12). The May 2015 communication certainly disapproved of asylum shopping, like many policy papers before. But the Commission was not (yet) willing to admit that something was fundamentally wrong with the Common European Asylum System. The Commission still thought that existing rules provided "the basis for mutual confidence" (Ibid). Its criticism rather targeted slow and incoherent implementation, and that is why the Commission considered initiating a number of infringement procedures (Ibid).[10]

A bit later, things changed. In September 2015, when irregular migration started to peak, the Commission conceded that orderly border management was no longer feasible. The Commission stated: "In the current refugee crisis, the EU is confronted with situations where the sheer number of persons crossing the external border of a Member State exceeds the capacity to manage the arrival of migrants in an orderly manner" (European Commission 2015c, Annex 2, p. 2). Indeed, the number of irregular border crossings stood at 1.8 million, and all States affected by the movements had decided to resort to a "wave-through" policy, including the EU frontline states Greece and Italy. Migrants were free to walk to Germany. Member States along the route introduced border controls, a doubtful move from the perspective of the Schengen acquis. And the Commission's reproach came swiftly. In February 2016, the Commission demanded: "[All] Member States must commit to ending the 'wave-through' approach to those who indicate an interest in applying for asylum elsewhere" (European Commission 2016a, p. 3). Equally swiftly came a change in policies, against the backdrop of some somber remarks dating from March 2016: "[In] recent months the system has been shaken to its core by the scale of the challenge of facing up to the largest refugee crisis since the Second World War" (European Commission 2016c, p. 2). In 2016, the crisis was expressly described as "global," triggered by a variety of causes, such as conflicts, natural disasters, climate change, poverty, globalization in transport and communication, deception by traffickers, lack of opportunities, or demographics, and, most importantly, as lasting (European Commission 2016a, p. 2; European Commission 2016i, p. 2). Hence, the (mere) introduction of temporary emergency measures was no longer deemed adequate. Instead, the global lens prompted calls for a more radical strengthening of the Common European Asylum System (European Commission 2016a, p. 2), as the whole system seemed to be put in question in the wake of the crisis. For the Commission, the re-introduction of permanent (internal) border controls was not a political option. The costs were deemed too high (European Commission 2016c, p. 3).[11] In 2017 and 2018, attention was almost exclusively on the management of the external borders of the EU, such as the tightening of controls and the breaking of the business of smugglers and human traffickers, and on partnership agreements with

[10] The idea of launching infringement procedures was put into practice in the fall of 2015, when the Commission initiated 37 infringement procedures against 19 Member States, continued infringement procedures in one case, and sent out requests of information to Member States in eight cases (European Commission 2015b, Annex 7). The implementation of Directive 2013/33 (reception conditions) proved particularly slow. By February 2016, the number of pending infringement procedures had grown to 58 (European Commission 2016a, p. 21). These numbers were unprecedented.

[11] The Commission contended: "The reintroduction of internal border controls on a sustained basis within the EU would not solve the challenges of the migration crisis, yet it would entail huge economic, political and social costs for the EU and the individual Member States. It would also risk putting in jeopardy the judicial and police cooperation that has become one of the key elements of added-value arising from the Schengen system." European Commission (2016c), p. 3.

relevant countries of origin or transit, intended to resolve the root causes of migration or to win partners willing to help stopping migratory flows (European Commission 2017b).[12] Making (potential) migrants stay outside the realm of the Union or securing their return to a country of transit or the country of origin had become an overriding goal, also for the sake of the Schengen regime.

Values. In early statements, the Commission expressed sympathies for migrants, similar to the responses given by the European Council. The Commission spoke of "tragic events," "a tragic milestone" (European Commission 2014, p. 2) and of the "plight of thousands of migrants putting their lives in peril" (European Commission 2015a, p. 2). Yet, the Commission also used much stronger wording, implicating, at first glance, weighty duties on the side of the EU. In May 2015, the Commission remarked: "Europe should continue to be a safe haven for those fleeing persecution," and then added: "Europe cannot stand by whilst lives are being lost" (Ibid 3). When numbers of border-crossings soared in September 2015, the Commission gave no disparaging signals. On the contrary, the Commission announced: "Together we must show the world that the Union is capable of managing this crisis" (European Commission 2015b, p. 2). Critics were pacified or silenced: "Migrants who have been legally admitted by Member States should not be faced with reluctance or obstruction. They should be given every assistance . . . This should be seen as central to the values Europeans should be proud of" (European Commission 2015a, p. 7).

These strong words, however, were not backed by strong arguments or by proposals that challenged the Member States' opposing attitudes or policies. Whenever the Commission came to stressing values that had already been translated into legal duties (such as the duty to protect deriving from international law), the Commission appended qualifiers making the duties seem less strict or burdensome. Some documents, for instance, conceded that the rights of migrants needed to be balanced against certain State interests, such as securing the borders, Europe's economic prosperity, social cohesion, or the wish to avoid pull factors (e.g. European Commission 2015a, p. 2). The duty to protect was just one value in a basket of values. In

[12] For a sketch of the new external dimension of the European migration policies see European Commission (2016i). Among the countries that were of interest because they were significant countries of origin were Afghanistan, Pakistan, Bangladesh, Ethiopia, and Nigeria. The most relevant countries of transit were Jordan and Lebanon on the one hand (because these countries hosted large numbers of Syrian refugees) and Libya on the other hand (because Libya was the main starting point for the dangerous crossing-overs along the Central Mediterranean route). Since Libya was politically unstable, the five African priority countries chosen after the Valetta Summit in November 2015 included Niger, Nigeria, Senegal, Mali, and Ethiopia. Libya was not among them (European Commission 2016n, p. 4). The role of Turkey (as a country of transit) was special. The willingness of Turkey, in the wake of the EU-Turkey statement of 18 March 2016, to introduce tight border controls and to re-admit irregular migrants from Greece was crucial for the drying-out of the Eastern Mediterranean route in the spring of 2016. As the Commission stated in June 2016, the impact of the arrangement with Turkey "was immediate" (European Commission 2016i, p. 2). For its support, Turkey received a total of EUR 3 billion in 2016–2017 (earmarked for assistance for refugees) (Ibid 4). In 2018, Turkey hosted 3.5 million registered Syrian refugees. With the funding provided by the EU, over 1.3 million refugees received assistance, including monthly cash transfers, education, and health care (European Commission 2018b, p. 7).

other documents, references to migrants' rights simply served the interests of the EU or of the Member States, not the interests of the migrants. Time and again, the Commission emphasized that certain proposed measures—such as forced returns or the cooperation with Turkey—would not undermine the rights of migrants (European Commission 2015a, p. 10; European Commission 2015d, p. 2; European Commission 2016d, p. 2). In either case, individual rights provided no shield against the measures envisaged in the particular context. The few references to human dignity were no exception. In most instances, the context of these references was forced return, with the Commission giving the reassurance that forced returns would, in any case, respect the dignity of the returnees (e.g. European Commission 2015a, p. 10). To sum up, the Commission's strong words did not entail strong measures aimed to overcome the unwillingness of Member States to shoulder a share of the burden. The overall message to the world was that the EU was not willing to generously offer a sanctuary. Against that background, it comes as no surprise that the humanitarian 'success' in managing migratory flows was measured in numbers of lives saved, without contemplating the quality of the lives that had been saved, through rescue operations at sea or through preventing people from embarking vessels unfit for crossing over the Mediterranean sea (e.g. European Commission 2017c, p. 3).

Responsibility and Solidarity. In the usage of the Commission, the terms "responsibility" and "solidarity" gained distinct and concrete meanings, and these meanings were perfectly attuned to how the Commission conceived of the (international) duty to protect, namely as a duty conditioned by European law.

For the Commission, 'responsibility' was primarily defined by EU law, in particular, the Common European Asylum System, and no other order, legal or otherwise. In a December 2013 communication, the Commission stated: "Member States have the responsibility to invest and build up capacity to ensure a flexible and effective national system of asylum, migration and reception in accordance with the EU acquis" (European Commission 2013b, p. 19). Under the EU acquis, the duty to protect lay with one Member State only, i.e. the Member State identified by the rules laid down by the 2013 Dublin Regulation.[13] And the Dublin system necessarily created (and creates) so-called frontline states in the case of massive migratory flows. In EU parlance, a "frontline state" is a Member State where people seeking protection enter EU territory first, and the country of first entry is, if the entry is illegal, identified by the Dublin rules as being the country responsible for the processing of the applications. In 2015 and 2016, Greece and Italy were frontline states created by the Dublin system. Greece and Italy were the main points of illegal entry, all responsibilities were theirs. That imbalance inherent in the Dublin system was the reason why the Commission did not just mention "responsibility," but also "solidarity," declaring that "[r]esponsibility and solidarity go hand in hand" (Ibid). Frontline

[13] Regulation 604/2013 establishing the criteria and mechanisms for determining the Member State responsible for examining an application for international protection lodged in one of the Member States by a third-country national or a stateless person (recast), OJ 2013 L 180/31.

states ought not to be left alone, that was the message of the Commission. In a later statement, the Commission was even more outspoken: "In such situations, the Union must support a Member State which faces disproportionate migratory pressure at its external border. This is an imperative in a Union that is governed by the principle of solidarity" (European Commission 2015c, Annex 2, p. 2). And because other Member States were considered duty-bound to also shoulder a part of the burden, the responsibilities under the Common European Asylum System were perceived as, ultimately, shared responsibilities. In the best-case scenario, the responsibilities were "shared evenly amongst Member States" (European Commission 2016a, p. 22). Member States willing to shoulder their share were deemed to act rationally, even to act in their own interests. Because, as the Commission claimed in March 2016, the difficulties faced by frontline states in the protection of the external border "have an impact on the European Union as a whole" (European Commission 2016c, p. 7). People would move on to other Member States, an experience several Member States had to go through during the crisis of 2015 and 2016. That is why the Commission championed tirelessly for the introduction of measures based on shared responsibilities, such as hotspots in Greece and Italy, the establishment of a European Border and Coast Guard, common search and rescue operations in the Mediterranean sea, or the relocation to other Member States of asylum seekers stranded in Greece and Italy.[14]

Values Lost. In 2014 and 2015, at the very start of the crisis, the duty to protect—based on either moral or legal grounds—was undoubtedly in the forefront of political thinking. In the spring of 2015, public statements were unconditional. "The immediate imperative is the duty to those in need," the Commission asserted in May 2015 (European Commission 2015a, p. 2). In September 2015, when the crisis peaked, the promise of protection became linked to strict policies of return. The Commission announced: "Increasing the rate of return of irregular migrants needs to go hand in hand with the EU's renewed efforts to protect those in need" (European Commission

[14] At the height of the crisis, the Council of the EU decided in September 2015, by a majority vote, to support Greece and Italy through establishing a legal framework for the relocation of 120,000 applicants present in Greece or Italy to other Member States of the EU according to a quota system announced in the annex of the decision. The relocation of applicants was to be put into practice and coordinated by a network of (national) liaison officers and the European Asylum Support Office. See Council Decision 2015/1601 establishing provisional measures in the area of international protection for the benefit of Italy and Greece, OJ 2015 L 248/80. The Czech Republic, Hungary, Romania and Slovakia voted against the plan and, thereafter, abstained from making relocation commitments unlike other Member States. The Council's decision was taken to court by Slovakia and Hungary. In September 2017, the ECJ ruled that the Council's decision was legitimate and valid under the powers conferred upon the Union under Article 78(3) TFEU. See ECJ, judgment of 6 September 2017, cases C-643/15 and C-647/15, Slovak Republic and Hungary v Council of the European Union. In December 2017, the Commission brought action against the Czech Republic, Hungary and Poland, seeking the ECJ to declare that the three countries had failed to fulfil their obligations under Council Decision 2015/1601. In April 2020, the ECJ rejected all pleas in defense of their policies tabled by the Czech Republic, Hungary and Poland. See ECJ, judgment of 2 April 2020, cases C-715/17, C-718/17 and C-719/17, Commission v Poland, Hungary and Czech Republic (Temporary mechanism for the relocation of applicants for international protection).

2015d, p. 2). Linking protection (of the deserving) tightly to return (of the undeserving) was quite obviously a concession to critics whose voices could be heard loud already in the fall of 2015, also in Council meetings. Enhancing return, so the Commission explained at that point in time, was "essential for maintaining public trust in the EU's asylum system and support for helping persons in need of international protection" (Ibid).

In the spring of 2016 and after reaching agreement with Turkey, 'restoring order' and 'stemming the flows' became the most prominent values, overriding all other values. The Commission left no doubt in early 2016: "Restoring orderly management of borders on the Eastern Mediterranean/Western Balkans route is the most pressing priority for the European Union today. . . . This will require tough decisions, determined action, responsibility and solidarity by all Member States" (European Commission 2016a, p. 3). That newly proclaimed value had an impact on what protection was supposed to mean. 'Restoring order' implied that entry was now to be granted only to those who were willing to lodge their application in the Member State responsible under the Dublin system (Ibid 12, 13). And that had, for one, implications for the Member States, in particular the frontline states. In the words of the Commission: "When a person crosses the border irregularly, they should be given the opportunity to apply for international protection: if they do, the Member State of first entry must grant access to national asylum procedures . . . If they do not apply for asylum, the Member State of first entry . . . should refuse entry" (Ibid 12). 'Restoring order' had, for another, implications for migrants. Migrants were now not only seen as right-holders, but also as duty-bearers. To use once more the words of the Commission: "[The] responsibility of border control is the mirror image of the obligations of migrants at the border – the basis of 'no registration, no rights'" (Ibid). As the new value (restoring order) gained strength, the value of protecting lives did not totally vanish from the Commission's statements. Yet, protecting lives became conditioned, it meant protecting lives according to the EU rules on state responsibilities. It was, under no circumstances, deemed acceptable that asylum seekers tried to choose their country of asylum. Also, protection in one of the Member States became to be seen as the second-best solution only. The preferred and best solution was now what was called "regional protection" (i.e. protection in the region of or close to the conflict triggering migratory movements). Regional protection seemed a prerequisite for orderly (external) border management, at least in the long run. As the Commission put it in May 2016: "Protection in the region and resettlement from there to the EU should become the model for the future, and best serves the interests and safety of refugees" (European Commission 2016f, p. 2). International protection provided by the Member States of the EU had, in political thinking, become a matter of choosing applicants, instead of being a matter of being chosen.[15]

---

[15]In the light of recent ECJ case law, some of the Commission's premises did not reflect existing EU law. That is particularly true for the Commission's assumption that people seeking international protection ought to turn to the Member State of first entry first. No such obligation could be derived from the Dublin system in force at the material time. See ECJ, judgment of 14 January 2021, cases C-322/19 and C-385/19, KS and MHK v The International Protection Appeals Tribunal, paras

7.3 Law: Dignity Without Standards

7.3.1 Background

Serious talk about reforming the Common European Asylum System began, a bit tentatively, in May 2015, when the Commission released its "European Agenda on Migration" (European Commission 2015a). In an effort rather to stabilize the existing system, the Commission proposed to reflect upon a "completion" of the Common European Asylum System, such as a common Asylum Code and the mutual recognition of asylum decisions (Ibid 17). The proposal might have been motivated by the sense that, in order to restore confidence in the fairness of the system, a "more European approach" was in order (Ibid 2). However, discontent with the existing system became more pronounced in the fall of 2015 (European Commission 2015b). In the early days of September 2015 and against the background of the wave-through policies prevailing in the Southern part of the Union, the Commission became convinced of "the need to review the Dublin Regulation" (Ibid 12). A few months later, in the summer of 2016, a completely reformed Common European Asylum System was deemed necessary to remedy a "system which was unable to cope with people effectively ignoring the rules and travelling to the country of their choice" (European Commission 2016i, p. 5). The Commission launched a first package of proposals in May 2016 aimed at a recast of the Dublin Regulation and the Eurodac Regulation as well as the establishment of the European Union Agency for Asylum (European Commission 2016f, g, h). A second package of proposals was launched in July 2016, suggesting a recast of the Reception Directive 2013/33, a Qualification Regulation, a Regulation establishing a common asylum procedure in the EU, and a Regulation establishing a Union Resettlement Framework (European Commission 2016j, k, l, m).

Of all proposals launched in the spring and summer of 2016, the proposal to recast the Reception Directive 2013/33 is the most pertinent in my context. Debates on the introduction of harmonized reception conditions for asylum seekers (pending their applications) throughout the European Union dates back to early 2001. So far, and hence for about 20 years, various attempts to reach a substantive consensus across Member States on (minimum) reception conditions—and the substance of asylum seekers' dignity—have been made. None of them was very successful.

82–84. See also ECJ, judgment of 30 June 2022, case C-72/22 PPU, MA v Valstybes sienos apsaugos tarnyba, paras 58–75, ruling that Member States may not refuse to grant the status of asylum seeker to third-country nationals who have crossed the border into the country in an illegal manner, even in the event of a declaration of martial law or of a state of emergency.

7.3.2 *Directive 2003/9*

In May 2001, the Commission proposed for the first time to lay down minimum standards for the reception of applicants for asylum (European Commission 2001). The Commission had two reasons for doing so. One related to the dignity clause in Article 1 of the Charter; the other was more pragmatic. The Commission intended, for one, to introduce minimum standards for the reception of applicants for asylum that "will normally suffice to ensure them a dignified standard of living" (Ibid 6th recital). For another, the Commission intended to thwart "secondary movements of applicants for asylum influenced by the variety of conditions for their reception" (Ibid 7th recital). The provision sketching the material reception conditions (the Member States were expected to grant) was supposed to be brief, leaving it to the Member States to concretize a very vague standard. The draft provision read: "Member States shall make provisions on material reception conditions to ensure a standard of living adequate for the health and the well-being of applicants and their accompanying family members as well as the protection of the fundamental rights" (Ibid Draft Article 15[2]). The Council, who was the next EU organ to carry on with the proposal, was willing to accept the proposed provision, yet made it even shorter by deleting the reference to fundamental rights. Also, the reference to "well-being" was not welcome in the Council. The Council preferred "subsistence" instead. Article 13(2) of the Directive 2003/9 thus stated: "Member States shall make provision on material reception conditions to ensure a standard of living adequate for the health of the applicants and capable of ensuring their subsistence." Member States were given complete leeway with respect to the form of the material reception conditions (in kind, financial allowances, vouchers).[16]

When evaluating the regime introduced by Directive 2003/9 in 2007, the Commission was highly critical (European Commission 2007). Regarding the provision on material reception conditions, the Commission took primarily issue with the wide margin of discretion left to the Member States, with respect to form as well as with respect to sufficiency. The wide range of discretion, so the Commission asserted, would undermine the very objective of the Directive, namely to create a level playing field throughout the Union and to dampen secondary movements by applicants. In the opinion of the Commission, varying reception conditions worked as a pull factor, and pull factors ought to be avoided.

[16] The term "material reception conditions" was defined by the Directive 2003/9 so as to include housing, food and clothing, provided in kind, or as financial allowances or in vouchers, and a daily expenses allowance, Article 2(j).

7.3.3 Directive 2013/33

The Commission's next proposal was indeed quite ambitious. Late in 2008, the Commission proposed to recast Directive 2003/9 with the explicit aim to ensure a higher degree of harmonization and better standards of protection for the Common European Asylum System, in particular regarding material reception conditions (European Commission 2008). Regarding the then existing Directive 2003/9, the Commission saw deficiencies from the perspective of guaranteeing a dignified standard of living and from the perspective of limiting secondary movements. To overcome these deficiencies, the Commission proposed to oblige Member States, when providing material reception conditions, to ensure that the total value of these conditions was equivalent to the amount of social assistance granted to the nationals of the Member State hosting the asylum seekers (Ibid 25). The proposal left the (ultimate) defining of the material reception conditions in the hands of the Member States. However, the Commission intended to establish a standard, binding for the Member States when they adopted their laws, namely equal treatment with nationals. Neither the Council nor the European Parliament were prepared to discuss the Commission's proposal in great depth (Davy 2019). Treating nationals and asylum seekers equally was politically beyond imagination. The Commission withdrew the proposal.

The follow-up proposal of the Commission was more cautious (European Commission 2011). The Commission insisted on the view that reception conditions "should ensure a dignified standard of living and be comparable throughout the Union" (Ibid 2). The right to respect of human dignity remained explicitly a parameter for the Commission's stance (Ibid 5). But the Commission conceded that Member States should be given more flexibility for lawmaking and standard-setting at the national level. Thus, the 2011 proposal no longer included a reference to equal treatment with nationals. Instead, the proposal suggested introducing "points of reference" or "benchmarks" (Ibid 7). The idea was to leave the power of defining the points of reference or benchmarks with the Member States, yet oblige each Member State to establish quantifiable standards that would, for the Commission, then facilitate the monitoring of the level of support provided to applicants throughout the Union. Standards valid for nationals were deemed relevant in the context; however, the Member States were given the power to deviate from those standards if such deviation was justified.[17]

The follow-up proposal of the Commission was still not the kind of compromise the Council and the European Parliament were willing to accept (European

---

[17] The proposed provision was supposed to read: "Where Member States provide material reception conditions in the form of financial allowances or vouchers, the amount thereof shall be determined on the basis of the point(s) of reference established by the Member States concerned either by law or practice to ensure adequate standards of living for nationals, such as the minimum level of social welfare assistance. Member States may grant less favourable treatment to asylum applicants compared to nationals in this respect, where it is duly justified." European Commission (2011): draft Article 17(5).

Commission 2013a). While agreeing to making a reference to nationally defined minimum standards, the Council and the European Parliament opted for a very broad draw-back clause that rendered the reference to national minima basically meaningless. The first sentence of the draft article that became Article 17(5) of the Directive 2013/33 says: "Where Member States provide material reception conditions in the form of financial allowances or vouchers, the amount thereof shall be determined on the basis of level(s) established by the Member States ... to ensure adequate standards of living for nationals." Under sentence 1, national benchmarks delineating the subsistence minima accorded to nationals are declared relevant. Yet, the second sentence reads: "Member States may grant less favourable treatment to applicants compared with nationals ... where those level(s) aim to ensure a standard of living higher than that prescribed for applicants under this Directive". The second sentence of Article 17(5) of the Directive 2013/33 creates a dilemma. In an attempt to clarify the dignity standard under the directive, the first sentence refers to dignity standards used for nationals at the national level. The second sentence says that these national dignity standards are of no relevance if they are higher than the directive's standards. The problem is, the directive does not define what its dignity standard is, apart from referring to national standards in sentence 1. How can anyone determine whether those national standards are more (or less) favorable than the standards laid down by the directive? A yardstick is needed for answering that question. And the directive is silent regarding that yardstick. Given that silence, Member States may rely on sentence 2 as they think fit. The Commission's attempt to clarify the dignity standard underlying the Directive 2013/33 has failed.

7.3.4 COM(2016) 465 final/2

When the Commission announced its intention to reform the whole Common European Asylum System (European Commission 2016e), it did so with a view to remedying "significant structural weaknesses and shortcomings ... of European asylum and migration policy" (Ibid 2). In the summer of 2016, the Commission prepared seven legislative initiatives, including a proposal to recast the Directive 2013/33 (European Commission 2016j).[18] In 2019, all proposals were still pending before the Council and the European Parliament (Council of the European Union 2019). Little was known about the debates taking place at EU level. Still, I have reasons for assuming that the Commission's 2016 proposal to recast the Directive 2013/33 does indeed foreshadow the political trend prevailing in the Member States, even beyond 2019. The 2016 proposal was clearly more willing to accommodate the interests of Member States than past ones. Any future legislative proposal will most likely start from there, even though the 2016 proposal was eventually shelved because of the new legislative term starting with the 2019 elections to the

[18] See supra Sect. 7.3.1.

European Parliament. In the fall of 2020, the newly installed Commission promised to draw on the political consensus already achieved and to ensure a quick adoption of a revised Reception Directive (European Commission 2020, pp. 3, 10; Lehner 2022).

Against this background, a (future) Reception Directive is likely to continue to serve a dual purpose. One purpose might still relate to human dignity. As a value and individual right, human dignity ranked high in the Commission's 2016 proposal. The proposal contained 25 references to 'dignity.' That was an unprecedented number of references. Stressing 'dignity' so often was obviously the Commission's response to some Member States' policies during the crisis. The proposal admitted quite openly that, during the crisis, "some Member States" had "persistent problems in ensuring adherence to the reception standards required for a dignified treatment" of asylum seekers (European Commission 2016j, p. 3). Stressing dignity was thus a reminder of one of the fundamental European values that had, in the eye of the Commission, been neglected in 2015 and 2016. The second purpose of a (future) Reception Directive is most likely to flank the (future) Dublin Regulation. Like the current Dublin Regulation, the 2016 draft Dublin Regulation proposed to concentrate all responsibilities regarding the processing of asylum applications in the hands of one Member State only (European Commission 2016f). There were no dramatic changes in that regard. But the draft Reception Directive paid more attention (than the current Directive 2013/33) to the fact that differing reception conditions throughout the Union may thwart the intended outcome of the Dublin regime. In the words of the Commission: The "divergences contribute to secondary movements and asylum shopping, create pull factors, and ultimately lead to an uneven distribution among the Member States of the responsibility to offer protection to those in need" (European Commission 2016j, p. 1).

Two sets of rules fleshed out in the 2016 draft Reception Directive are relevant in my context: the (draft) provisions linking the reception conditions more closely to the Dublin system and the (draft) provisions defining the reception condition standards. The first set of provisions conceptualized the benefits accorded under the new Reception Directive as a social welfare add-on to the new Dublin system. The second set of provisions defined the reception standards and, indirectly, 'human dignity.'

Linking Reception Conditions and the Dublin System. The 2016 reform package was quite uncompromising regarding secondary movements of asylum seekers. The 2016 draft Dublin Regulation set the stage. The 2016 draft Dublin Regulation suggested introducing an individual obligation to lodge the application for international protection in the Member State of first entry, if that country was entered in an irregular manner, or, if a Member State has allowed entry, in that Member State (European Commission 2016f: draft Article 4). Draft Article 4 thus aimed to legalize a maxim that the Commission had often stressed in 2016, namely that an applicant had neither "the right to choose the Member State of application nor the Member State responsible for examining the application" (Ibid 15). Failure to comply with the obligation was supposed to entail consequences. Some were procedural, facilitating a quick return to the Member State responsible. I leave those consequences aside. Some consequences related to material reception conditions, and this was where the 2016 draft Reception Directive stepped in. The Commission's proposal suggested, first, to adopt a provision saying that applicants shall not be entitled to the reception conditions set out by the directive (for compliant applicants) in any Member State other than the one in which they are requested to be present, and that was the country of first entry or the country of legal entry (European Commission 2016j: draft Article 17a). When adopted, a provision like this would drastically limit the scope of the directive. Only one Member State would be fully duty-bound by the future directive. Secondly, and with respect to returnees (i.e. asylum seekers who had left the responsible Member State and were subsequently returned to that State), the draft suggested enhancing the discretionary powers of the Member State (European Commission 2016j: draft Article 19). According to draft Article 19, the responsible Member State was then free to opt for providing benefits in kind only and for reducing or, in exceptional cases, for withdrawing the daily allowances in cash. Thirdly, applicants who had left the responsible Member State were supposed to face consequences with respect to their freedom of movement (Ibid draft Article 7). Under draft Article 7, Member States were then allowed to assign a certain place where the applicants were required to stay and Member States were allowed to introduce reporting duties. In those cases, the Member States' duty to provide material reception conditions were subject to the actual residence by the applicant in that specific place.

Setting Reception Standards and Human Dignity. The high number of references to 'dignity' notwithstanding, the 2016 draft Reception Directive gave up on the idea of introducing a common European standard determining, in quantifiable terms, the 'dignified' subsistence minimum in cash. The realities on the ground were apparently the main reason for abandoning the idea of having some sort of benchmark. The Commission's 2016 draft conceded that the actual transfers provided by Member States were "in most cases well below all the possible benchmarks or thresholds examined" (European Commission 2016j, p. 8). Demands implicating a raise in benefit levels were expected to fail (again), in the European Parliament as well as in the Council of the EU. Also, and more importantly, the meaning of the term "human dignity"—as used by the 2016 draft Reception Directive—seemed to vary according to context. I detect at least four different contexts and, per implication, four groups of applicants whose dignity was conceptualized in a differing manner.

For one, the Commission's 2016 proposal was still striving to institute what was called "standard conditions for the reception of applicants that will suffice to ensure them a dignified standard" (Ibid recital 10). But the (standard) reception conditions were meant to accommodate only the dignity of applicants adhering to the obligation (introduced by the draft Dublin Regulation) to seek protection in the responsible Member State (Ibid draft Article 17). The second group comprised applicants who were, in violation of the duty under the draft Dublin Regulation, present in a Member State that was not responsible for examining their application. In those cases, the 2016 draft Reception Directive proposed applying a rather opaque rule (Ibid draft Article 17a). Under draft Article 17a(1), such an "applicant shall not be entitled to the [standard] reception conditions." Yet, draft Article 17a(2) added that "Member States shall ensure a dignified standard of living for all applicants." What standard was this compared to the 'standard' standard referred to in draft Article 17(1)? The draft gave no answer. The third group encompassed applicants who were present in the responsible Member State, but had, prior to that, failed to comply with the obligation under the draft Dublin Regulation (e.g., returnees). With regard to the third group, the Member State was allowed to resort to sanctions, such as to providing benefits in kind only or to reducing (or withdrawing) the daily allowances (Ibid draft Article 19[1]–[2]). Again, the 2016 draft reminded Member States that, "under all circumstances" they were supposed to "ensure a dignified standard of living for all applicants" (Ibid draft Article 19[3]). Finally, the fourth group comprised applicants who were present in the Member State responsible for examining their application, but who were also subject to restrictions with regard to their freedom of movement, because—for example—they were returnees and there were reasons to believe that they would re-try to abscond (Ibid draft Article 7 [1]–[2]). For that group, access to (curtailed) reception conditions could be additionally restricted. Under draft Article 7(2)(d), the provision of reception conditions "shall be subject to the actual residence by the applicant in that specific place." If the applicants had left that place without prior permission, Member States were, under the 2016 draft, no longer bound by any rule.

Even if the standards were not spelled out in detail by the 2016 draft Reception Directive, it seems clear that the draft proposed higher standards of receptions conditions and lower standards according to the willingness of asylum seekers to comply with the duties laid down by the envisaged Dublin regime. The variation of standards (and, accordingly, the grouping of asylum applicants) underlying the 2016 draft Reception Directive begs the question: Is it legitimate to introduce varying dignity standards for varying groups of applicants? The prospect of varying standards will certainly outlast the 2014–2019 legislative term. I shall be back to that question in my critique.

7.4 Adjudication: Dignity Under Construction

The number of ECJ judgments that deal with the reception conditions accorded to asylum seekers is very limited. The handful of cases that prompted the court to interpret the dignity clause under Article 1 of the Charter reveal just a few robust propositions. The Charter's notion of human dignity is still underdeveloped in the ECJ's case law.

Case of Cimade and GISTI. In Cimade & GISTI,[19] the referring court was called upon to decide on the validity of a French circular dealing with subsistence benefits for asylum seekers. Under the circular, asylum seekers were excluded from the

[19]ECJ, judgment of 27 September 2012, case C-179/11, Cimade & Groupe d'information et de soutien des immigrés (GISTI) v Ministre de l'Intérieur, de l'Outre-mer, des Collectivités territoriales et de l'Immigration.

entitlement to the benefit in cases where—according to the Dublin regime—another Member State was responsible for processing the application. The referring court asked the ECJ whether the Directive 2003/9 also extended to Dublin cases and when exactly the responsibilities of the transferring Member State (here, France) would cease to apply. Was there a moment in time, when the applicants were still present in French territories, but France was no longer bound by its duties under the Directive 2003/9? Drawing on the definition of the term "asylum seeker" given in Directive 2003/9, the ECJ held that only the actual transfer of the asylum seeker by the requesting Member State would bring to an end its responsibilities for granting minimum reception conditions (para 55). Pointing to the dignity clause of Article 1 of the Charter, the ECJ added that the "asylum seeker may not ... be deprived – even for a temporary period of time ... – of the protection of the minimum standards laid down by that directive." What we learn from Cimade & GISTI is that providing the subsistence minimum to asylum seekers present in the territory is required under all circumstances. We learn nothing about pertinent standards.

Case of Saciri and Others. In Saciri and others,[20] the ECJ moved a bit more to the point. In October 2010, the Saciri family had lodged an application for asylum with the office responsible in Belgium for asylum cases. The family also requested, again turning to the responsible agency (Fedasil), to be accommodated and provided with other necessities of life. However, Fedasil sent the Saciri family away, because the reception facilities were deemed overrun by great numbers of asylum seekers. The Saciri family was, following that, not able to find a place willing to accept them, and there was no law that guaranteed accommodation and livelihood if and when Fedasil's capacities were stressed out. Fedasil was prepared to provide a cash benefit, but the amount of the benefit did not suffice for the family to be able to rent a flat on the (private) market. The legal dispute before the national courts was about the amount of money Member States were obliged to provide under the Directive 2003/9 when they decided to grant the minimum reception conditions in cash rather than in kind. One of the courts referred to the ECJ: Were Member States, when acting under Article 13(5) of the Directive 2003/9, obliged to make sure that the amount of the cash benefit enabled asylum seekers to obtain accommodation on their own, relying on what was on offer on the private housing market? The ECJ reiterated that compliance by Member States with the dignity clause in Article 1 of the Charter required that asylum seekers were, as long as they remained in the territory, granted the minimum standards laid down by the Directive 2003/9 (para 35). Regarding the question of adequacy of standards, the ECJ first rephrased what was said in Article 13(2) of the directive and in recital 7 of the preamble[21] and then concluded

[20] ECJ, judgment of 27 February 2014, case C-79/13, Federaal agentschap voor de opvang van asielzoekers v Selver Saciri et al.

[21] Article 13(2) of Directive 2003/9 read: "Member States shall make provisions on material reception conditions to ensure a standard of living adequate for the health of applicants and capable of ensuring their subsistence." Recital 7 of the directive read: "Minimum standards for the reception of asylum seekers that will normally suffice to ensure them a dignified standard of living and comparable living conditions in all Member States should be laid down."

succinctly: "Consequently, ... allowances must be sufficient to ensure a dignified standard of living and adequate for the health of applicants and capable of ensuring their subsistence by enabling them to obtain housing, if necessary, on the private rental market" (para 42). Clearly, the last part of the court's conclusions moved beyond simply repeating the language of the directive: If asylum seekers had, because of a Member State's choice, to turn to the market in order to get accommodation, then States had to make sure that the amount of the benefits in cash was attuned to the prices landlords would expect them to pay. Accommodation is part and parcel of a 'dignified standard of living.'[22] But what is the relevant standard for the accommodation due under 'human dignity,' and what else is due? There is no answer to be found in Saciri and others.

Case of Abdida. In Abdida,[23] the content and the validity of a provision laid down in Directive 2008/115 was at stake.[24] Although the case did not relate to the minimum reception conditions defined under Directive 2003/9 or Directive 2013/33, the case is important in my context. Both the Directive 2003/9 and the Directive 2013/33 deal with non-nationals who are, as long as they have the status of asylum seekers, legal residents, precarious as their status may be. Directive 2008/115 addresses state responsibilities with regard to third-country nationals who are illegal aliens. The illegal aliens may be rejected asylum seekers, but that is not necessarily the case. In Abdida, the ECJ reminded Member States (and the Union lawmakers) that illegal aliens were not exempt from the right to respect of human dignity under Article 1 of the Charter and the corresponding state duties:

In 2009, Abdida, a Nigerian national, requested that he be granted an exceptional leave to remain in Belgium, due to his suffering from a particularly serious illness. As his application was deemed admissible, Abdida received social assistance. In 2011, his application for an exceptional leave to remain was rejected. The Belgian authority held that Abdida's country of origin was able to provide the medical treatment the applicant was in need of. Following the rejection of his application, Abdida lost his social assistance and was left to his own devices. The questions brought before the ECJ were: Was Belgium's course of action in line with Union law, in particular the Directive 2008/115? How was Article 14(1) of Directive 2008/115 to be interpreted? Article 14(1) required that, pending the return of illegally staying third-country nationals, Member States were required to provide "emergency health care and essential treatment of illness." Did that imply that, apart from emergency health care and essential treatment, the Member States had no obligations regarding livelihood (food, clothing, housing)? The ECJ rejected such assumptions in clear yet brief terms. The ECJ ruled: "The requirement to provide emergency

[22] See also ECJ, judgment of 14 May 2020, FMS v Országos Idegenrendészeti Föigazgatóság, paras 245, 295, emphasizing that under no circumstances Member States are allowed to detain applicants simply in order to provide a livelihood.

[23] ECJ, judgment of 18 December 2014, case C-562/13, Centre public d'action sociale d'Ottignies-Louvain-la-Neuve v Moussa Abdida.

[24] Directive 2008/115 on common standards and procedures in Member States for returning illegally staying third-country nationals, OJ 2008 L 348/98 (in the following, Directive 2008/115).

health care and essential treatment of illness under Article 14(1)(b) of Directive 2008/115 may"—in a situation where the person concerned lacked the means—"be rendered meaningless if there were not also a concomitant requirement to make provision for the basic needs of the third country national concerned" (para 60). Against the backdrop of "the fundamental rights and dignity of the persons concerned" (para 42), Member States may not opt out of their duty to provide a subsistence minimum to people present in their territories, even if those people happen to be illegal aliens.[25] Again, we learn that, as in the previous cases, 'human dignity' serves as a pivotal yardstick for defining state responsibilities with respect to the subsistence minimum. And again, we do not learn what 'human dignity' implies regarding standards.

Case of Haqbin. In Haqbin,[26] an Afghan national who was still a minor at the relevant time, was, for fifteen days, excluded from material reception conditions by the Belgian Federal Agency for the reception of asylum seekers (Fedasil), following his being involved in a brawl between some residents of a reception center. When excluding Mr. Haqbin, the agency relied on Article 20(4) of Directive 2013/33.[27] Mr. Haqbin slept rough for some nights in Brussels' parks and stayed with friends and acquaintances for other nights. After the expiry of the period set for the exclusion from the benefits, Mr. Haqcin was transferred to another reception center and continued to receive benefits. Following the events, Mr. Haqbin suit for compensation (for the damages suffered) before a labour court, and the labour court referred to the ECJ. The Belgian labour court asked, inter alia, whether the Member States were, even in the case of a reduction or a withdrawal of material reception conditions, obliged to ensure a dignified standard of living during the period of exclusion or whether the Member States could, in this case, simply rely on the prospective that private institutions, such as charities, might jump in?

When answering the Belgian labour court's question, the ECJ did not address the more general question as to whether the reduction or the outright withdrawal of material reception conditions might, per se, constitute a violation of the State's duty under Article 1 of the Charter regarding human dignity. The ECJ concentrated on the

[25] See also ECJ, judgment of 19 June 2018, case C-181/16, Sadikou Gnandi v État belge, para 63; ECJ, judgment of 30 September 2020, case C-402/19, LM v Centre public d'action sociale de Seraing, paras 50–55.

[26] ECJ, judgment of 12 November 2019, case C-233/18, Zubair Haqbin v Federaal Agentschap voor de opvang van asielzoekers.

[27] Article 20(4) of the Directive 2013/33 reads: "Member States may determine sanctions applicable to serious breaches of the rules of the accommodation centres as well as to seriously violent behaviour." The provision is part of an article with the heading "Reduction or withdrawal of material reception conditions." Article 20(5) specifies the considerations that ought to be taken into account in the course of decision-making. According to the first sentence, decisions for reduction or withdrawal of material reception conditions or sanctions shall be taken individually, objectively and impartially. Also, decisions shall be based on the particular situation of the person concerned, taking into account the principle of proportionality. According to the second sentence, Member States "shall under all circumstances ensure access to health care ... and shall ensure a dignified standard of living for all applicants."

"sanctions" under Article 20(4), holding that this provision envisaged a broad range of responses to serious breaches of the rules of accommodation, including the assigning of a different part of the reception center, the prohibiting of getting in touch with specified residents, or the transfer to another center (para 52). For the court, the withdrawal of benefits seemed not the only, and not even the preferred response under Article 20(4). Against that background, the court's eventual finding is of little surprise. The court held that a Member State cannot, under Article 20(4), provide for a sanction consisting in the withdrawal, even temporarily, of material reception conditions relating to housing, food or clothing, in so far as this would have the effect of depriving an applicant of the possibility of meeting his or her most basic needs (para 56). The court also held that the obligations under the Directive 2013/33 were obligations to be fulfilled by the Member States. It was on the Member States to guarantee a dignified standard "continuously and without interruption" (para 50). States must not rely on the jumping-in of private charities.

Still, in order to reach its findings, the ECJ drew on arguments that puzzle. On the one hand, the court insisted that Article 1 of the Charter required that applicants would not find themselves in a situation of extreme material poverty, i.e. a situation that would not allow them to meet their most basic needs (a place to live, food, clothing, personal hygiene, physical and mental health) (para 46). Ensuring the most basic needs of the applicants is, undeniably, the very aim of the Directive 2013/33. On the other hand, the court clearly accepted that the benefits guaranteed under the Directive 2013/33 might, under certain circumstances, be withdrawn according to Article 20.[28] At the same time, the court insisted (again) that—even then—a dignified standard of living was to be guaranteed (paras 48, 50). It is difficult to reconcile these arguments with logic. The first argument says, in short, human dignity demands A. The second argument says, you can take away A, but you still have to respect human dignity. From the perspective of logic, both arguments cannot be true: If human dignity demands A, Member States cannot take away A without violating their duties under Article 1 of the Charter. If, however, A can be taken away without Member States violating their duties under Article 1 of the Charter (duty to respect human dignity), Article 1 does not unconditionally demand A. It seems that in Haqbin, the ECJ had reservations with respect to the unconditionality of Article 1, yet was not prepared to elaborate on the conditions underlying Article 1 of the Charter. We are, once more, left in the dark.[29]

---

[28]Under Article 20(1) of Directive 2013/33 Member States may reduce or withdraw material reception conditions in cased where the applicant has abandoned the assigned place of residence, the applicant did not comploy with reporting duties, or the applicant has lodged a subsequent application. Under Article 24(2) of Directive 2013/33, Member States may reduce material reception conditions if an applicant has, for no justifiable reason, not lodged the applicant as soon as reasonably practicable after arrival in that Member State.

[29]See also ECJ, judgment of 1 August 2022, case C-422/21, Ministero dell'Interno v TO, paras 36–47, where the emphasis of the court's ruling is more on the obligation of the Member States to ensure a dignified standard of living for the applicants for international protection. From the perspective of the dignity clause under Article 1(1) of the German Grundgesetz see BVerfG,

7.5 Critique: Dignity Relative, Fragmented and Conditioned?

To build up stronger arguments for criticizing EU politics and EU law, I turn to the case law of the European Court of Human Rights (in the following, ECtHR). The case law of the ECtHR has some bearing in the context of Union law. Under the Treaty on European Union,[30] the Member States declare their attachment to the principles of liberty, democracy and "respect for human rights and fundamental freedoms," and the rule of law (recital 4). Article 2 TEU re-asserts that the Union is founded on a number of values, inter alia, the respect for human rights. Article 6 TEU is even more specific with respect to the rights enshrined in the European Convention for the Protection of Human Rights and Fundamental Freedoms.[31] The rights, as guaranteed by the ECHR and as resulting from the constitutional traditions common to the Member States, are meant to constitute general principles of the Union's law.[32] In a similar vein, the Charter affirms that, in so far as the Charter rights correspond to the rights guaranteed under the ECHR, "the meaning and scope of those rights shall be the same" as those laid down by the ECHR.[33] Although not binding, the case law of the ECtHR thus serves as a valuable and valued guidance for the ECJ, in particular in the context of interpreting the Charter.[34]

From the perspective of the ECHR, EU politics and EU lawmaking on the standards for the reception of asylum seekers—in each instance, politics and lawmaking are linked to 'human dignity'—pose three important questions. For one, EU politics seems to proceed on the assumption that human dignity is (but) one value among other important values the Union strives to achieve. Against the backdrop of the ECHR, is human dignity relative and subject to balancing? Secondly, EU lawmakers seemingly proceed on the assumption that human dignity comes in grades. For asylum seekers, the notion of dignity seems to imply a lesser standard than that applicable to nationals. Against the backdrop of the ECHR, is human dignity fragmented, i.e. differing, according to the status of the people concerned? Thirdly, in the aftermath of the refugee crisis, EU lawmakers seemed to assume that benefits meant to secure a dignified livelihood for asylum seekers can legitimately be lowered for asylum seekers who fail to comply with duties aimed at implementing the (new) Dublin regime. Under the draft Reception Directive, the 'dignified'

---

judgment of 5 November 2019, 1 BvL 7/16, adjudicating on the legitimacy of sanctions that can and may be imposed under a German regime designed to provide for a subsistence minimum covering the basic needs of job seekers.

[30]Consolidated Version of the Treaty on European Union, OJ 2016 C 202/13 (in the following, TEU).

[31]European Treaty Series No. 5 (in the following, ECHR).

[32]Article 6(3) TEU.

[33]Article 52(3) Charter.

[34]See e.g. ECJ, judgment of 24 April 2018, case C-353/16, MP v Secretary of State for the Home Department, para 38.

reception conditions accorded to applicants who fail to adhere to EU rules are less favorable than the 'dignified' reception conditions accorded to law-abiding applicants. Against the backdrop of the ECHR, may States, when making provision for providing the subsistence minimum, introduce conditions that asylum seekers need to comply with if they want to raise a valid claim to the 'standard' benefits? My answers to the three questions are supposed to move 'human dignity' from the periphery of the ECJ's adjudication to its center, at least in cases relating to the reception conditions designed to accommodate the needs of asylum seekers.

Yet, prior to dealing with the three questions, I must establish a link between 'human dignity' and the rights guaranteed by the ECHR.

7.5.1 Dignity and Degrading Treatment

Of all the rights enshrined in the ECHR, the rights laid down by Article 3 are closest to 'human dignity.' Article 3 reads "No one shall be subjected to torture or to inhuman or degrading treatment or punishment." While the text of the article does not explicitly mention human dignity, the link is firmly established by ECtHR case law. When elaborating on the general principles underlying Article 3, the ECtHR usually starts with stressing that the article "enshrines one of the most fundamental values of democratic societies."[35] Recent judgments further stress that the prohibition contained in the article "is a value of civilization closely bound up with respect for human dignity."[36] The prohibition is even deemed "part of the very essence of the Convention."[37] Still, the court has so far not explained exactly how 'torture,' the 'inhuman' and the 'degrading' relate to 'human dignity.' When it comes to defining 'torture,' 'inhuman' treatment (punishment), or 'degrading' treatment (punishment), the ECtHR usually stresses intense pain and suffering as the main characteristics of torture or inhuman treatment (punishment), without making any connection to human dignity.[38] Degrading treatment (punishment), however, always was and still is primarily defined by the court as an assault on human dignity. According to

[35] See e.g. ECtHR, judgment of 28 July 1999, Selmouni v. France, para 95 (the applicant claimed to have been ill-treated while being held in police custody); ECtHR, judgment of 1 June 2010, Gäfgen v Germany, para 87 (the applicant was threatened with considerable physical pain should he fail to release vital information about the whereabouts of a victim).

[36] ECtHR, judgment of 28 September 2015, Bouyid v Belgium, para 81 (the applicants were slapped in the face during interrogation at a police station).

[37] ECtHR, judgment of 15 December 2016, Khlaifia v Italy, para 158 (the applicants complained about the reception conditions prevailing on the island of Lampedusa).

[38] According to ECtHR case law, treatment is to be considered 'inhuman' if it is inflicted premeditated, causing actual bodily injury or intense physical or mental suffering. In order to qualify as 'torture', the infliction of pain or suffering must involve a purposive element. The threshold of 'torture' is deemed to be reached where intense pain or suffering is inflicted, for instance, with the aim of obtaining information. See e.g. Gäfgen (fn 35) paras 89–90.

long-standing case law, degrading treatment is treatment that "humiliates or debases an individual, showing a lack of respect for, or diminishing, his or her human dignity, or arouses feelings of fear, anguish or inferiority, capable of breaking an individual's moral or physical resistance."[39] The prohibition of degrading treatment is the link between Article 3 ECHR and human dignity I want to build upon.

Another starting point for my critique is the recent case law of the ECtHR that connects the prohibition of degrading treatment to welfare rights. That case law came as a bit of a surprise. For decades, the ECtHR had been reluctant to accept that the ECHR had implications regarding individual welfare. When the ECtHR was called upon to decide whether the deportation of an illegal immigrant who was seriously ill was legitimate under Article 3, the court was not inclined to interfere: "Article 3 does not place an obligation [on Member States to provide] free and unlimited health care to all aliens without a right to stay within" their jurisdictions.[40] In a case relating to Article 8 ECHR, the court held reassuringly: "While it is clearly desirable that every human being have a place where he or she can live in dignity and which he or she can call home, there are unfortunately in the Contracting States many persons who have no home. Whether the State provides funds to enable everyone to have a home is a matter for political not judicial decision."[41] And yet, once the ECtHR had accepted that Article 3 implied positive obligations for the Member States, for instance in the case of detention, given the particular vulnerability of the detainees,[42] other vulnerable groups entered the picture and the scope of applicability of Article 3. When a pensioner complained before the ECtHR that the amount of pension she was entitled to in Russia would not suffice for her to make a living, the court did not find that the applicant's situation constituted degrading treatment in the sense of Article 3.[43] But the court also remarked obiter that "a wholly insufficient amount of pension and social benefits may raise an issue under Article 3."[44] Such state responsibilities might be involved where "an applicant, in circumstances wholly dependent on State support, found herself faced with official indifference when in a situation of serious deprivation or want incompatible with human dignity."[45] Five other cases, all questioning the reception conditions prevailing in Greece, Italy, Belgium and France, drew on the concept of vulnerability and dependency on State aid, this time with respect to asylum seekers present in Member States' territories.[46] In each case, the court found that the respondent State

[39] ECtHR, decision of 18 June 2009, Budina v. Russia, p. 6. See already ECtHR, judgment of 25 April 1978, Tyrer v United Kingdom, para 33.

[40] ECtHR, judgment of 27 May 2008, N v United Kingdom, para 44.

[41] ECtHR, judgment of 18 January 2001, Chapman v United Kingdom, para 99.

[42] See e.g. ECtHR, judgment of 26 October 2000, Kudla v Poland, para 94.

[43] Budina (fn 39).

[44] Budina (fn 39), p. 5.

[45] Budina (fn 39), p. 6.

[46] ECtHR, judgment of 21 January 2011, MSS v Belgium and Greece, paras 250, 263; ECtHR, judgment of 4 November 2014, Tarakhel v Switzerland, paras 119–120; ECtHR, judgment of 7 July

was liable under Article 3. There can be no doubt any longer that, under Article 3 ECHR, asylum seekers have a right to be provided with a subsistence minimum that guarantees a livelihood in dignity (Aranguiz 2021, p. 611; Slingenberg 2022, p. 106). The corresponding duty lies with the State in whose territories the asylum seekers are being present, all responsibilities (of other States) for the examination of applications for asylum notwithstanding.

7.5.2 *Dignity: Relative or Absolute?*

Arguments used by EU organs or the Member States in their dealings with migration issues that assume that duties deriving from 'human dignity' (Article 1 of the Charter) could be out-balanced by counter-weighing interests of States are deeply flawed, whatever these interests of the States are, the wish to avoid a financial burden; a preference for nation-first politics; the wish to pay tribute to voters' preferences; or the prevention of criminal acts committed by asylum seekers. The ECtHR has held many times that the duties under Article 3—and the same applies to the Member States' duties under Article 1 of the Charter (Aranguiz 2021, p. 603; Slingenberg 2022, p. 108)—are of an "absolute character."[47] The court said so in cases involving so-called negative duties only[48] as well as in cases involving positive duties, i.e. State duties aiming to protect individuals from harm inflicted by other private parties or duties aiming to ensure the availability of medical care or dignified living conditions.[49] The "most fundamental value" laid down in Article 3 must be respected irrespective of circumstances, no matter what the applicant is guilty of, no matter how difficult and exceptional the refugee crisis is the State has to cope with, and no matter what the local political preferences are. The obligations under Article 3 ECHR and Article 1 of the Charter stand steady.[50]

2015, VM v Belgium; ECtHR, judgment of 28 February 2019, Khan v. France, paras 76–95; ECtHR, judgment of 2 July 2020, NH v. France, paras 155–188.

[47] See e.g. ECtHR, judgment of 2 May 1997, D v United Kingdom, para 47.

[48] Tyrer (fn 39) para 30.

[49] See e.g. ECtHR, judgment of 29 April 1997, HLR v. France, para 40; MSS (fn 46) para 218.

[50] See also ECJ, judgment of 5 April 2016, case C-404/15, Aranyosi, paras 85, 86; ECJ, judgment of 19 March 2019, case C-163/17, Jawo, para 78. There is but one case decided by the ECtHR holding that "inherent in the whole Convention is a search for a fair balance between the demands of the general interest of the community and the requirements of the protection of the individual's fundamental rights" (N v United Kingdom, fn 40, para 44). The dissenting justices Tulkens, Bonello and Spielmann immediately protested fiercely, and the idea of weighing and searching for a fair balance vanished from case law dealing with Article 3.

7.5.3 Dignity: Fragmented or Universal?

At the time of writing, there are four EU directives in place making provision for the securing of a subsistence minimum in the context of third country migratory movements. All except one does so with an explicit reference to 'human dignity' in the preamble. The first to be adopted (and the one that is silent on human dignity) was the Directive 2003/109 defining the status of long-term resident third-country nationals.[51] Next in line was Directive 2008/115 on the status of illegal third-country nationals pending removal. The third was Directive 2011/95 defining the prerequisites for according refugee status or subsidiary protection status.[52] And the fourth and last one was Directive 2013/33 on the status of third-country nationals seeking international protection (reception standards).

From the point of view of providing the subsistence minimum, these directives create four different statuses, and these statuses can be ranked according to range of rights attached: The worst status is accorded to illegal third-country nationals. Directive 2008/115 only grants access to "emergency health care and essential treatment of illness" (Article 14[1][b]). Other needs are not explicitly to be covered. The second to worst status is the status designed for asylum seekers pending their application. Under Directive 2013/33, asylum seekers are promised subsistence, but Member States are free to treat asylum seekers less favorably than their own nationals; the directive falls short of fixing a minimum standard.[53] Third-country nationals who have been granted subsidiary protection are granted a more favorable and more reliable status with regard to the subsistence minimum. Directive 2011/95 promises social protection, including the necessary social assistance, on an equal footing with nationals of the Member State concerned (Article 29[1]). But the directive allows for a derogation from that promise. Member States may limit social assistance to "core benefits" (Article 29[2]). Yet, the core benefits must be provided at the same level and under the conditions as the (core) benefits provided for the nationals. Third-country nationals have a similar status under Directive 2003/109 (Article 11[4]). Finally, the best status is granted to third-country nationals who have acquired refugee status. Under Directive 2011/95, refugees must be given access to social assistance on an equal footing with nationals (Article 29[1]). Member States are not allowed to make exceptions.

EU lawmakers seemingly think that 'human dignity'—understood as standard—is different for different groups of third-country nationals. Ranked according to status and the benefits accorded, these groups comprise (from worst to best

[51] Directive 2003/109 concerning the status of third-country nationals who are long-term residents, OJ 2004 L 16/44 (in the following, Directive 2003/109).

[52] Directive 2011/95 on standards for the qualification of third-country nationals or stateless persons as beneficiaries of international protection, for a uniform status for refugees or for persons eligible for subsidiary protection, and for the content of the protection granted (recast), OJ 2011 L 337/9 (in the following, Directive 2011/95).

[53] See supra Sect. 7.3.3.

treatment): illegal third-country nationals, asylum seekers, third-country nationals who are long-term residents or enjoy subsidiary protection, and refugees. The ranking seemingly resonates the idea that 'humanity' or 'mankind' may be divided in sub-sections and that the members of these sub-sections may be conceived of as differing in their needs, simply because of their belonging to different sub-sections. Ideas like that—some of them racist in outlook—have been rejected by post-war human rights thinking and human rights law. Post-World War II human rights are founded on the assumption that there is only one humanity encompassing all human beings (Davy 2015). The assumption also affects the understanding of 'human dignity.' 'Dignity' is equally conceived of as universal, as being the same for everyone at all times, and everywhere. That does not imply that the universalistic concept of human dignity underlying post-war human rights law is universally accepted and implemented. But non-acceptance and non-implementation do not affect the idea underpinning human rights. Also, the idea of human dignity being universal does not imply that, regarding the subsistence minimum, everyone ought to receive the same benefit. 'Universality' of dignity means that the standards are the same, in other words, that for everyone, and everywhere, 'degrading' treatment involves fear and anguish, humiliation, and the feeling of being inferior in worth. Also, if we follow the case law of the ECtHR, 'universality' means that for everyone, and everywhere, these feelings must reach a certain level of severity,[54] an assumption that obviously reflects the stigma that the ECHR seeks to attach to treatment or punishment prohibited by Article 3. Finally, deciding whether or not the threshold of the 'degrading' treatment has been reached, is not left to the applicants (and their subjectivities). The court employs a set of (objective) indicators, such as the duration of the treatment, its effects, or—regarding living conditions—the degree of deprivation. Again, the indicators apply to everyone, and everywhere.[55] Yet, when it comes to assessing individual cases and when the standards are applied, differing results may ensue. This is where the ECtHR rightly relies on the concept of vulnerability: The level of severity may, in (imagined) absolute terms, be different for little children, healthy young men, pregnant women, or 90-year-old men. And it seems self-understood that what is required for having a dignified livelihood is not the same for children, young men, pregnant women, or the elderly. Benefits tailored to secure the subsistence minimum may and must differ. What is outlawed by the notion of universal dignity is a difference in standards. It goes against the grain of universality if the standard applicable to group A pays attention to acute illness only whereas the standard for group B is more comprehensive. It goes against the grain of universality of human dignity if the standard applicable to group C is confined to

[54] See e.g. Budina (fn 39), p. 6.

[55] The subtleties of the ECtHR case law were overlooked by ECJ in Jawo (fn 50). In Jawo, the ECJ seems to suggest that Article 3 ECHR required a "particularly high level of severity" (para 91) when applicants raise objections regarding the living conditions they would face when transferred to the EU Member State responsible for the examination of their asylum application. The ECtHR has never said so when interpreting Article 3 ECHR.

"core benefits" whereas group D receives a whole range of benefits, for no other reason than their varying rights to remain in the country defined by immigration law.

Directives 2003/109, 2008/115, 2011/95 and 2013/33 violate the dignity clause under Article 1 of the Charter.

7.5.4 Dignity: Conditioned or Unconditioned?

The Commission's 2016 legislative draft regarding the recasting of Directive 2013/33 (European Commission 2016j) proposed introducing conditions (originating in a future Dublin system) that asylum seekers need to fulfil if they want to have access to the standard reception conditions under a revised Reception Directive, inferior as these benefits may be compared to the subsistence benefits accorded to nationals.[56] Access to the standard reception conditions was supposed to require that the asylum seekers lodge their application in the Member State which is, under the Dublin system, responsible for processing their claims. If adopted, such a concept would establish a new and additional hierarchy of beneficiaries, namely a hierarchy among the group of asylum seekers who rank (as a group) second to last anyway.[57] The benefits designed to accommodate the needs of asylum seekers who fail to comply with the conditions deriving from the Dublin system would be even less favorable than the benefits granted under the standard reception conditions. Clearly, the 2016 draft Reception Directive paid tribute to the ECJ's position in Abdida.[58] With a view to asylum seekers who were, under the proposal, to be treated the worst (the ones who ignore EU rules on responsible Member States), the draft reminded Member States that they "shall ensure a dignified standard of living for all applicants" (Ibid draft Article 17a[2]; draft Article 19[3]). That was, translated into a draft directive, the message the ECJ had given in Abdida. Still, even if that reminder had been more than a lip service, the regime suggested by the 2016 draft was open to criticism, and I concentrate on the conditions proposed, not the new hierarchies. The hierarchies would, for reasons already given,[59] incompatible with the notion of 'universal' human dignity.

The rights under Article 3 ECHR that relate to living conditions are, as a matter of principle, not unconditional. The ECtHR's emphasis on "vulnerability" as a decisive factor for determining the positive obligations, and the required "level of severity" of treatment certainly introduces (sufficient, not necessary) conditions for considering a claim to be valid. And it seems no coincidence that early references to "vulnerability" relate to cases where the applicants have been held in detention.[60] Detainees are

[56] See supra Sect. 7.3.4.

[57] See supra Sect. 7.3.4.

[58] See supra Sect. 7.4.

[59] See supra Sect. 7.5.3.

[60] Kudla (fn 42) para 94.

confined to certain spaces and cut off from public attentiveness. Detainees are literally in the hands of the state. Detainees wholly depend on the state when they are in need of medical assistance or certain diets. Generally, the ECtHR case law indicates that "vulnerability" may be created by certain (spatial) circumstances, such as being detained in prison, being confined to living in camps, being placed in a state-led social home, or being present and questioned in a police station.[61] It is also quite obvious that "vulnerability" might be prompted by personal characteristics. In that regard, the ECtHR refers sometimes "to an applicant's ability to cater for his most basic needs, such as food, hygiene and shelter."[62] When it comes to assessing individual abilities, the court pays attention to (individual) behavior, such as the failure to accept the offer of temporary accommodation and the individual will and choice to remain on the streets for several months, or the failure to contribute to solving a dire situation, for instance, through reporting to or cooperating with the authorities.[63] More specifically, age is surely a factor that is of relevance. For the ECtHR, children are to be given special attention and special protection.[64] The same goes for the elderly or people who are ill.[65] Finally, and this is important for my argument, the ECtHR is paying attention to (legal) status. Asylum seekers are consistently classified by the court as a population group that is to be considered particularly underprivileged and vulnerable.[66] Further conditions—for example, conditions relating to the willingness to generally abide by the law—are absent from the court's case law under Article 3 ECHR. One could even argue that States violate the absolute character of Article 3 ECHR when they make the providing of the subsistence minimum dependent on the willingness of asylum seekers to comply with legal duties that have no bearing on their being in need of aid. Against the background of existing case law, non-compliance with respect to duties that do not relate to overcoming the situation that triggers the rights under Article 3 is irrelevant.[67] Conditions like the ones envisioned by the 2016 draft Reception Directive will violate Article 3 ECHR.

---

[61] See e.g. ECtHR, judgment of 23 March 2016, Blokhin v Russia, para 136; ECtHR, judgment of 28 June 2011, Sufi and Elmi v United Kingdom, paras 291–292; ECtHR, judgment of 17 January 2012, Stanev v Bulgaria, paras 206–213; Bouyid (fn 36) paras 100–104.

[62] Sufi and Elmi (fn 61) para 283.

[63] ECtHR, decision of 26 June 2001, O'Rourke v United Kingdom, p. 6; Budina (fn 39), pp. 6–7; MSS (fn 46) para 259; VM (fn 46) para 151.

[64] See e.g. ECtHR, judgment of 12 October 2006, Mubilanzla Mayeka and Kaniki Mitunga v Belgium, para 50 (detention of an unaccompanied five-year-old in the same conditions as adults).

[65] See e.g. Stanev (fn 61).

[66] MSS (fn 46) paras 232, 233, 251; Tarakhel (fn 46) paras 97, 118; VM (fn 46) para 136. The position of the ECtHR is not uncontested, though. See the dissenting opinion of Judge Ranzoni, joined by Judges López Guerra, Sicilianos and Lemmens in VM (fn 46), p. 10; for an empirically grounded concept Leboeuf (2022).

[67] See supra Sect. 7.5.2. When assessing the validity of Section 1a of the Asylbewerberleistungsgesetz, German courts face similar questions under Article 1 Grundgesetz. Section 1a allows for a reduction of social benefits if rejected asylum seekers continue to stay in the country or decline to cooperate with the authorities that seek to remove them from German territory. Many courts hold

7.6 Conclusion

The main thrust of my contribution is about directing scholarly and practical attention to the 'dignity' of the migrants who are among the most neglected in Europe and by EU law, i.e. asylum seekers reaching European territories. I argue that, even in the crisis of 2015 and 2016, their 'dignity' was basically a non-issue when the European Council drew its quarterly conclusions aimed to give a broad outline of the policies of the EU, including asylum policies. In the policy papers of the Commission, 'dignity' was just one among other values EU policies were supposed to achieve. I also demonstrate that 'dignity' remains on the periphery of EU lawmaking. The directives defining the reception conditions of asylum seekers—past, present, possibly future—shy away from prescribing standards that would substantially limit the Member States' discretion when they move to determine the subsistence minimum. Moreover, EU law introduces hierarchies among the beneficiaries of the subsistence minimum, between nationals and third country nationals, among third country nationals, and, maybe soon, among asylum seekers. The ECJ upholds 'dignity' as a right and value that is of relevance for lawmaking and the implementation of law. However, the ECJ refrains from putting Member States under pressure. The ECJ gives a hint here and there, but the hints do not add up to a coherent and detailed concept. I argue that the ECJ has, given the more elaborate case law of the ECtHR, good reasons for being more straightforward and more demanding. When confronting the idea that 'human dignity' might be less weighty than certain state interests, the ECJ could affirm the absolute character of Article 1 of the Charter. When confronting a legislative act that allows for treating asylum seekers less favorably than nationals or other asylum seekers, the ECJ could assert the universal character of Article 1 of the Charter. And when confronting a legislative act that ties the access to social benefits to conditions that are not needs-related, the ECJ could advance the argument that the right under Article 1 of the Charter is not subject to other conditions than need and dependency and their alleviation.

References

Aranguiz A (2021) Bringing the EU up to speed in the protection of living standards through fundamental social rights: drawing positive lessons from the experience of the Council of Europe. Maastricht Journal of European and Comparative Law 28:601–625

Baer S (2014) Das Soziale und die Grundrechte. Neue Zeitschrift für Sozialrecht 23:1–5

that the reduction of social benefits—a sanction responding to the violation of individual duties—is legitimate under the dignity clause laid down by Article 1 Grundgesetz, even if the subsistence minimum is undercut. See e.g. Bundessozialgericht, judgment of 12 May 2017, B 7 AY 1/16 R; Sozialgericht Lüneburg, decision of 12 September 2017, S 26 AY 35/17 ER; Sozialgericht Osnabrück, decision of 25 September 2017, S 44 AY 13/17 ER; Bayerisches Landessozialgericht, decision of 17 September 2018, L 8 AY 13/18 B ER.

Brings T, Oehl M (2016) Verfassungswidrige Kürzungen und nachgeschobene Berechnungen. Zeitschrift für Ausländerrecht und Ausländerpolitik 36:22–31
Bundesamt für Migration und Flüchtlinge (2016) Asylgeschäftsstatistik für den Monat Dezember 2015
Bundesamt für Migration und Flüchtlinge (2017) Asylgeschäftsstatistik für den Monat Dezember 2016
Council of the European Union (2019) Progress Report on the Reform of the Common European Asylum System and Resettlement. Council Document 6600/19, 26 February 2019
Davy U (2015) Der "Universalismus" der Allgemeinen Erklärung der Menschenrechte: Die Arbeit am Konsens, 1946–1948. In: Heintz B, Leisering B (eds) Menschenrechte in der Weltgesellschaft. Deutungswandel und Wirkungsweise eines globalen Leitwerts. Campus Verlag, Frankfurt/New York, pp 198–235
Davy U (2018) Sozialleistungen für Nicht-Deutsche: Zugang durch globale Gleichheitsrechte. In: Rolfs C (ed) Migration und Sozialstaat. Sozialrechtslehrertagung 2018. Erich Schmidt Verlag, Berlin, pp 9–38
Davy U (2019) Refugee crisis in Germany and the right to a subsistence minimum: differences that ought not be. Georgia Journal of International and Comparative Law 47(2):367–450
Deibel K (2013) Leistungseinschränkungen im Asylbewerberleistungsrecht. Zeitschrift für Sozialhilfe/Sozialgesetzbuch 52:249–255
Di Fabio U (2016) Migrationskrise als föderales Verfassungsproblem. https://www.jura.uni-bonn.de/fileadmin/Fachbereich_Rechtswissenschaft/Einrichtungen/Lehrstuehle/Di_Fabio/Gutachten_Bay_DiFabio_formatiert.pdf. Accessed 30 June 2023
Dietz A (2015) Leistungseinschränkungen nach § 1a AsylbLG für Asylbewerber aus sicheren Herkunftsstaaten. Die Öffentliche Verwaltung 68:727–734
Eichenhofer E (2012) Menschenwürde durch den Sozialstaat – für alle Menschen? Die Sozialgerichtsbarkeit 59:565–568
European Commission (2000) On a Community immigration policy. COM(2000) 757 final
European Commission (2001) Proposal for a Council Directive laying down minimum standards on the reception of applicants for asylum in Member States. COM(2001) 181 final
European Commission (2007) Report on the application of Directive 2003/9/EC of 27 January 2003 laying down minimum standards for the reception of asylum seekers. COM(2007) 745 final
European Commission (2008) Proposal for a Directive laying down minimum standards for the reception of asylum seekers (recast). COM(2008) 815 final
European Commission (2011) Amended proposal for a Directive laying down standards for the reception of asylum seekers (recast). COM(2011) 320 final
European Commission (2013a) Communication pursuant to Article 294(6) of the Treaty on the Functioning of the European Union concerning the Position of the Council on the adoption of a Directive of the European Parliament and of the Council laying down standards for the reception of asylum seekers. COM(2013) 415 final
European Commission (2013b) On the work of the Task Force Mediterranean. COM(2013) 869 final
European Commission (2014) 5th Annual Report on Immigration and Asylum (2013). COM(2014) 288 final
European Commission (2015a) A European Agenda on Migration. COM(2015) 240 final
European Commission (2015b) Managing the refugee crisis: immediate operational, budgetary and legal measures under the European Agenda on Migration. COM(2015) 490 final/2
European Commission (2015c) Annex 2. COM(2015) 490 final/2 Annex 2
European Commission (2015d) EU Action Plan on return. COM(2015) 453 final
European Commission (2016a) On the State of Play of Implementation of the Priority Actions under the European Agenda on Migration. COM(2016) 85 final
European Commission (2016b) Annex 1. EU-Turkey Joint Action Plan – Implementation Report. COM(2016) 85 final Annex 1
European Commission (2016c) Back to Schengen. A Roadmap. COM(2016) 120 final

European Commission (2016d) Next operational steps in EU-Turkey cooperation in the field of migration. COM(2016) 166 final
European Commission (2016e) Towards a reform of the Common European Asylum System and enhancing legal avenues to Europe. COM(2016) 197 final
European Commission (2016f) Proposal for a Regulation establishing the criteria and mechanisms for determining the Member State responsible for examining an application for international protection lodged in one of the Member States by a third-country national or a stateless person (recast). COM(2016) 270 final/2
European Commission (2016g) Proposal for a Regulation on the European Union Agency for Asylum and repealing Regulation (EU) No 439/2010. COM(2016) 271 final
European Commission (2016h) Proposal for a Regulation on the establishment of 'Eurodac' for the comparison of fingerprints for the effective application of [Regulation (EU) No 604/2013 establishing the criteria and mechanisms for determining the Member State responsible for examining an application for international protection lodged in one of the Member States by a third-country national or a stateless person], for identifying an illegally staying third-country national or stateless person and on requests for the comparison with Eurodac data by Member States' law enforcement authorities and Europol for law enforcement purposes (recast). COM (2016) 272 final/2
European Commission (2016i) On establishing a new Partnership Framework with third countries under the European Agenda on Migration. COM(2016) 385 final
European Commission (2016j) Proposal for a Directive laying down standards for the reception of applicants for international protection (recast). COM(2016) 465 final/2
European Commission (2016k) Proposal for a Regulation on standards for the qualification of third-country nationals or stateless persons as beneficiaries of international protection, for a uniform status for refugees or for persons eligible for subsidiary protection and for the content of the protection granted and amending Council Directive 2003/109/EC of 25 November 2003 concerning the status of third-country nationals who are long-term residents. COM(2016) 466 final
European Commission (2016l) Proposal for a Regulation establishing a common procedure for international protection in the Union and repealing Directive 2013/32/EU. COM(2016) 467 final
European Commission (2016m) Proposal for a Regulation establishing a Union Resettlement Framework and amending Regulation (EU) No 516/2014 of the European Parliament and the Council. COM(2016) 468 final
European Commission (2016n) First Progress Report on the Partnership Framework with third countries under the European Agenda on Migration. COM(2016) 700 final
European Commission (2017a) Third Progress Report on the Partnership Framework with third countries under the European Agenda on Migration. COM(2017) 205 final/2
European Commission (2017b) On the Delivery of the European Agenda on Migration. COM (2017) 558 final
European Commission (2017c) Progress report on the European Agenda on Migration. COM(2017) 669 final
European Commission (2018a) Progress report on the Implementation of the European Agenda on Migration. COM(2018) 250 final
European Commission (2018b) Progress report on the Implementation of the European Agenda on Migration. COM(2018) 301 final
European Commission (2020) On a New Pact on Migration and Asylum. COM(2020) 609 final
European Council (2013a) European Council 24/25 October 2013. Conclusions
European Council (2013b) European Council 19/20 December 2013. Conclusions
European Council (2014a) European Council 20/21 March 2014. Conclusions
European Council (2014b) European Council 26/27 June 2014. Conclusions
European Council (2015a) European Council meeting (19 and 20 March 2015). Conclusions
European Council (2015b) European Council meeting (25 and 26 June 2015). Conclusions
European Council (2015c) European Council meeting (15 October 2015). Conclusions

European Council (2016a) European Council meeting (18 and 19 February 2016). Conclusions
European Council (2016b) European Council meeting (20 and 21 October 2016). Conclusions
European Council (2017) European Council meeting (22 and 23 June 2017). Conclusions
European Council (2018) European Council meeting (28 June 2018). Conclusions
Frerichs K (2014) Verfassungsrechtliche Spielräume des Gesetzgebers bei der Verhinderung sozialleistungsmotivierter Wanderbewegungen. Zeitschrift für europäisches Sozial- und Arbeitsrecht 13:279–288
Hailbronner K, Thym D (2016) Grenzenloses Asylrecht? Die Flüchtlingskrise als Problem europäischer Rechtsintegration. Juristen Zeitung 71:753–763
Janda C (2016) Das Recht auf Existenzsicherung – eine Frage der Kostenersparnis? Zeitschrift für Rechtspolitik:152–154
Janda C (2017) Migrationssteuerung durch Recht? Die Abschreckung von armen Zuwanderern am Beispiel von Asylsuchenden aus sicheren Herkunftsstaaten. In Jahrbuch für Recht und Ethik. Annual Review of Law and Ethics 25:239–255
Janda C (2018) Gesetzgebung in der "Flüchtlingskrise". In: Hill H, Wieland J (eds) Zukunft der Parlamente – Speyer Konvent in Berlin. Beiträge zur Tagung der Deutschen Universität für Verwaltungswissenschaften in Zusammenarbeit mit dem Innenausschuss des Deutschen Bundestages, pp 83–91
Kluth W (2016) Begrenzung der Schutzgewährung versus alternative Formen der Migrationssteuerung. Zeitschrift für Ausländerrecht und Ausländerpolitik 36:1–8
Leboeuf L (2022) Lost in translation? The promises and challenges of integrating empirical knowledge on migrants' vulnerabilities into legal reasoning. German Law Journal 23:976–991
Lehner R (2022) Das neue EU-Asylpaket: Reformgesetzgebung in der Krise. Zeitschrift für Gesetzgebung:191–199
Lenze A (2014) Ist die Debatte um die Gewährleistung eines menschenwürdigen Existenzminimums beendet? Zeitschrift für Sozialhilfe/Sozialgesetzbuch 53:745–752
Oppermann D (2017) Leistungseinschränkungen und Sanktionen als Mittel zur Bewältigung der Flüchtlingswelle. Zeitschrift für europäisches Sozial- und Arbeitsrecht 16:55–62
Petersen V (2014) Das unabweisbar Gebotene im Sinne des § 1a AsylbLG – neu justiert. Zeitschrift für Sozialhilfe/Sozialgesetzbuch 53:669–680
Peukert A, Hillgruber C, Foerste U, Putzke H (2016) Die Flüchtlingskrise rechtsstaatlich bewältigen. Juristen Zeitung 71:347–350
Rixen S (2015) Zwischen Hilfe, Abschreckung und Pragmatismus. Gesundheitsrecht der Flüchtlingskrise. Neue Zeitschrift für Verwaltungsrecht 34:1640–1644
Rothkegel R (2012) Das Gericht wird's richten – das AsylbLG-Urteil des Bundesverfassungsgerichts und seine Ausstrahlungswirkungen. Zeitschrift für Ausländerrecht und Ausländerpolitik 32:357–369
Slingenberg L (2022) European case law on migrants' social and mobility rights: the need for a comparative approach in assessing 'human rights overreach'. Netherlands Quarterly of Human Rights 40:98–117
Thym D (2016) Integration kraft Gesetzes? Grenzen und Inhalte des "Integrationsgesetzes" des Bundes. Zeitschrift für Ausländerrecht und Ausländerpolitik 36:241–251
von Harbou F (2016) Unterstützen und Strafen: Das Integrationsgesetz. Neue Juristische Wochenschrift 70:2700–2704

Chapter 8
Human Dignity and the Law of Work: Between Collectivism and Individualism

Sima Kramer

Abstract Human Dignity is one of the central ideas behind the law of work. One of the main changes to the law of work in the last few decades has been the move from collectivism to individualism. This has affected the way that the human dignity of workers is expressed. This chapter examines conceptual changes to the idea of human dignity and argues that while the commitment to human dignity remains unwavering in some of the countries discussed in this chapter, the fall in collectivism has led to the silencing of employee voice and the reduction of worker participation, which has left workers at the threshold of a comprehensive concept of human dignity.

8.1 Introduction

Workers have long suffered from various forms of exploitation, and the law of work[1] evolved with the aim of providing basic protections for them as a group inherently at risk. Historically, these protections began with collective labor law i.e., the law of unions and collective agreements. Later, work law evolved to include individual employment law, that is, legislation, case law, and contracts, that applies irrespective of union membership. In this chapter, "collectivism" refers to collective labor law and its related ideas, while "individualism" refers to individual employment law and its related ideas.

Some jurisdictions have seen a marked shift away from collectivism in the last few decades, so that the individualist approach has come to cover a greater portion of workers.[2] This chapter analyzes what this shift means for the concept of human

[1] Or work law—I use these terms interchangeably to refer to all forms of legal norms regarding worker's rights, both collective and individual, whether legislation or case law.

[2] This development has mainly been evinced in common law jurisdictions and this chapter focuses on Israel as a case study, citing additional jurisdictions where relevant.

S. Kramer (✉)
Jerusalem, Israel
e-mail: sima_kramer@yahoo.co.uk

S. N. Arel et al. (eds.), *Probing Human Dignity*,
https://doi.org/10.1007/978-3-031-42437-3_8

dignity at the crossroads of these two legal approaches. The chapter begins by describing the goals of work law related to human dignity and reflected in theoretical literature, international instruments, and positive law. Then I describe the tectonic shift from collectivism to individualism in work law. The following section examines what this shift means for the competing concepts of human dignity that emerge. The chapter concludes by suggesting that while a multifaceted approach to work law is welcome and captures the tensions of the current world of work, without strengthening the self-governance aspect, workers may be left at the threshold of a comprehensive concept of human dignity, vulnerable to opportunistic encroachments on the ground.

8.2 Human Dignity and the Law of Work

Commitment to human dignity[3] lies at the heart of work law, and the protection of this idea, whether through legislation or collective agreements, is one of the main goals of work law (Dukes 2008). Human dignity emerges from one of the central tenets of work law that has stated, in various formulations, from as early as 1914 that "labour is not a commodity" (US Clayton Act of 1914), meaning that the reduction of the power to work to a material commodity is a violation of the dignity of mankind (Bellace 2011). As such, this commitment is in line with core assumptions about dignity according to which all individuals are autonomous, unique, and entitled to be treated with respect, bearing a right to be free of harm to one's person or property (Ehrenreich 1999; Yamada 2007).

The connection between work law and human dignity is reflected in a number of international instruments. The Universal Declaration of Human Rights, for example, which establishes that "All human beings are born free and equal in dignity and rights", lists a number of work related rights in article 23 and connects human dignity to "just and favourable remuneration" in subsection 3. Similarly, the Charter of Fundamental Rights of the European Union states explicitly that "every worker has the right to working conditions which respect his or her health, safety and dignity (Toth 2008), thus emphasizing the connection between human dignity and the conditions in which work is carried out. This connection is also evident in the ILO's "decent work" ideal (Blackett 2007). So too the constitution of the International Labour Organization recognizes that "all human beings, irrespective of race, creed or sex, have the right to pursue both their material well-being and their spiritual development in conditions of freedom and dignity, of economic security and equal opportunity" (annex, art. II, § (a), Oct. 9, 1946, 15 U.N.T.S 40, 106).

A stronger sense of this connection emerges when dignity is viewed as the foundation for work rights (Yamada 2009). According to this view, respect for

[3]This chapter intentionally avoids a strict definition of human dignity, but rather focuses on the essence of the term and how it has changed over time for workers.

human dignity justifies many, if not all, of the common protections work law provides such as a right to minimum wage (Davidov 2009), protection from unfair dismissal (Collins 1992), and the prohibition on workplace discrimination (Fredman 2001). This is a result of the importance of work to the individual in terms of economic, social, and psychological wellbeing, which reveals how human dignity is tied up in the way the individual is treated at work (Radin 1996).

8.3 Collectivism and Individualism in the Law of Work

The aim of this part of the chapter is to describe the impact on work law resulting from the shift from collectivism, as evinced by collective labor law, to individualism, as evinced by individual employment law.

Collectivism in work law is characterized by centralized collective bargaining, high union density,[4] and pacts between the social parties or partners.[5] Under these conditions, industrial relations are left to management and unions with limited state or legal intervention. The collective bargaining model effectively functions as a system of self-governance, determining the substantive rights and duties of the social partners (Cox 1958). It requires extensive negotiations between well-organized groups representing labor on the one hand and capital, or the employers, on the other hand, to produce collective agreements formulated at the industry level, if not the regional or even state level, typically having a mandatory effect (Teulings and Hartog 1998). The notion of collective labour law has been described as being "to construct law that minimizes the role of law itself" and the social partners as "agencies of regulated self-regulation" (Mundlak 2007).

While this chapter focuses on Israel as a case study, the move away from unionization has been seen in additional common law jurisdictions such as the United States and England. In the United States for example, the peak of union membership in the private sector was in 1953 when unions represented 35.7% of workers whereas in 2006 union membership declined to 12% (Hirsch and Macpherson 2003). In the United Kingdom, union density fell from over one-half to under one-third during the last two decades of the twentieth century while the first decade of the twenty-first century saw it drop to below one-quarter of the workforce (Davies 2009). So too in Israel, union membership began to fall, from the peak in 1959 when membership was at 85%, until 2004 when membership was at about 35% (Mundlak 2007). The Israeli Central Bureau of Statistics reported that in 2012 this figure had dropped to 25%; that is, only a quarter of Israel's employees were members of a union (Israeli Central Bureau of Statistics (2023)).

---

[4] "Union density" refers to the proportion of paid workers who are union members.

[5] The term "social parties" is used to refer to representatives of employers and representatives of the employees, in other words, parties capable of signing a collective agreement.

The next section will discuss how these changes in union density impacted the priorities of work law, at the threshold of human dignity for workers. First, however, it is important to understand the inroads of the liberal rights discourse into work law. If collectivism was characterized by centralized collective bargaining, high union density and a high degree of self-governance and autonomy for the social parties, individualism in work law developed in three main ways: The entrance of NGOs into the field of work law, a rise in individual rights-based legislation, and a rise in litigation.

8.3.1 The Entry of Interest-Based Organizations

Israel of the 1980s reflected a growing sense of multiculturalism (Shafir and Peled 1998). At the same time, collective labor law was notorious for not actively advancing the interests of minorities or women. To this day, collective labor law is criticized for not representing the weakest workers in the market (Lurie 2014). During the 1960s and 1970s, in the United Kingdom too, people began to question the fairness of the collective labor system for much the same reason (Kirton and Healy 2013). For example, in 1951, only 27% of women workers were union members compared to 56% of men, which led unions to ignore or attack women's claims for better treatment at work and demands for equal pay (Davies and Freedland 1993). This was one of the triggers for promotion of worker's rights through legislation, as will be discussed below.

The decline in organized labor's macrosocial role led to the entry of new associations from civil society stepping into the representational gap that emerged and further diluting the exclusive influence of the social partners (Freeman et al. 2005). NGOs were not a new phenomenon in Israel; however, their number and the range of fields in which they were active increased significantly from the end of the 1980s and onwards. Through active lobbying for changes in legislation and drives for precedential adjudication, the influence of NGOs spread from typical civil society functions, to include the representation of interests traditionally connected to the structure of the labor market and the welfare state.

One example of the involvement of NGOs in legislation is the first amendment to the 1988 Equal Opportunity at Work Act. Extensive work carried out by the *Aguda*—the Israeli National LGBT Task Force—brought about the inclusion of a prohibition on discrimination on the basis of sexual orientation in 1992 (Yonai 1998). Other examples include NGOs representing women, which brought about the legislation of the 1987 Equal Retirement Age for Women and Men Act, as well as extensions of privileges for women and parents in the 1954 Employment of Women Law and a revised version of the 1996 Equal Pay for Women and Men Act. So too, Bizchut—the Israeli Human Rights Center for People with Disabilities—effected the legislation of the 1998 Equal Rights of People with Disabilities Act (Ziv 1998).

NGOs also initiated several high-profile cases in the field of workplace equality. Some examples include a case for equal rights for a gay employee and his partner (HCJ 721/94 El-Al v. Danilevitz 48(5) PD 749 [1994] (Isr.)), a lawsuit on discrimination in hiring filed by the Women's Lobby (National Labour Court 56/3-129 Plotkin – Eisenberg Brothers 33 PDL 481 (Isr.)), affirmative action cases filed by the Women's Lobby (HCJ 456/94 Women's Lobby v. Government of Israel 48(5) PD 401 (Isr.); HCJ 2671/98 Women's Lobby v. Minister of Labour and Welfare, 52(3) PD 630 [1998] (Isr.))' and the first law suit over comparable worth which was initiated by the Association for Civil Rights in Israel (Regional Labour Court (BS) 001576/99 Nidam – Rali Electronics [2003] (Isr.) (2000) Nevo Legal Database (by Subscription) (Isr.)). NGOs were instrumental in advancing worker's rights in the field of civil rights as well, including the freedom of occupation, the right to privacy, and freedom of speech (National Labour Court 90/08 Isakov v. State of Israel – Commission of Employment of Women Law (Feb. 2, 2011) Nevo Legal Database (by Subscription) (Isr.)).

8.3.2 *The Rise of Individual Rights Legislation*

With the weakening of the collective labor law regime as described above, work law had to be rewritten to replace the old system, which led to a rise in regulatory solutions. Interestingly, the focus of many of these laws was on rights on dismissal—protection from termination motivated by discriminatory treatment or dismissals that are discriminatory in their impact (Estlund 2005). For example, section 9 of the 1954 Employment of Women Law was amended repeatedly during the 1990s to expand the protection of women against dismissal during pregnancy and after giving birth. Section 2 of the 1988 Equal Opportunity at Work Act, section 8 of the 1998 Equal Rights of People with Disabilities Act and section 41 A of the 1949 Discharged Soldiers (Reinstatement in Employment) Act were amended in that period, to prohibit discriminatory dismissals. So too, 1996 saw the passing of the Protection of Workers Law (Exposure of Offense of Unethical Conduct and Improper Administration) granting protection from dismissal to whistleblowers, and the 1998 Prevention of Sexual Harassment Act prohibited the dismissal of a person making a complaint about experiencing sexual harassment.

Not all the laws addressing individual employee's rights were concerned with the end of the employment relationship. For example, section 29 of the 2000 Genetic Information Act not only expanded the prohibited bases for discrimination but also established the conditions in which an employer may demand that an employee take genetic tests. Similarly, the 1951 Women's Equal Rights Law was significantly amended in 2000; section 15 of the 1959 Civil Service (Appointments) Act was amended in 2004 to require affirmative action, and the 1964 Equal Pay for Women and Men Act was rewritten in 1996.

A similar development has been described in the United Kingdom, most notably following the election of the Labour government in 1997, which introduced several new rights for workers (Giddens 1998). Coming after a decade long strategy of restricting collective action and set against declining union membership as described above, this development contributed significantly to shifting the center of gravity of UK work law towards a more individualist direction (Davies 2009).

One example is the introduction of the national minimum wage (DTI, Fairness at Work (1998) (Cm 3968) para 3.2) and more generally, the reduced hostility to European directives in work law, which effectively increased individual worker's rights. After signing the Protocol and Agreement on Social Policy of the Maastricht Treaty, directives such as the Parental Leave Directive and the Part-Time Worker's Directive, were extended to the UK and implemented (Directive 96/34/EC (extended to the UK by Directive 97/75/EC) and Directive 97/81/EC (extended to the UK by Directive 98/23/EC) respectively). The EU has also been a significant source of new legislation requiring employers to consult workers on major business decisions for example on collective redundancies, health and safety, and transfers of ownership of business. The Labour government was also responsible for the for the enactment of the Human Rights Act 1998 (HRA), which came into force in 2000, giving effect in English law to most of the rights in the European Convention on Human Rights.

8.3.3 Individualized Justice in the Courts

The courts' tendency to promote individual rights at the expense of collective interests is exhibited in the case law regarding individual bargaining in workplaces governed by collective agreements. The National Labour Court increasingly took an "all or nothing" approach, so that employees who had bargained individually for rights that improve on the collective agreement were denied other rights rooted in the collective agreement (National Labour Court 57/4-4 General Histadrut – Moriah Hotels (Dec. 26, 1996)). This served to weaken the significance of collective labor law by introducing a judge-made exception to the broad principle of the supremacy of the collective norm over individual norms, as espoused by section 22 of the 1957 Collective Agreements Law.

The courts' interventionist strategy stood in stark contrast to its approach during the corporatist era as a multitude of opportunities to scrutinize collective bargaining and collective agreements were brought before them. Whereas in the past such claims would have been thrown out at earlier stages, the courts now actively produced decisions applying the liberal rights discourse to these previously autonomous fields. For example, in National Labour Court 52/4-12 General Histadrut and Sea Officer's Union – Zim 26 PD 23 (Isr.), the court rejected the principle established in a collective agreement that the employer must reject job applicants who are not union members.

As regards collective agreements, the National Labour Court and Supreme Court expressed an unprecedented willingness to place these under judicial review, repeatedly finding these to be discriminatory. The case of Naomi Nevo is a good example (HCJ 104/87 Dr. Naomi Nevo v. National Labour Court 44(4) PD 749 [1990] (Isr.)).

Nevo was employed by the Jewish Agency as a researcher. The conditions of her employment were determined by a collective agreement signed between the *Histadrut* and her employer. According to these, she had to retire at the age of 60 unlike her male colleagues who had to retire at the age of 65. She initiated proceedings arguing that the different retirement ages set by the collective agreement were discriminatory and that she had a right to equality in this respect; however, her arguments were rejected by the National Labour Court. On the other hand, her petition to the Supreme Court, sitting as a High Court of Justice, was accepted, and the term in the collective agreement was rendered void.

The significance of the Naomi Nevo case was in its recognition of the individual rights of employees in an area that had, until then, been accorded to the full autonomy of the social parties. Furthermore, the decision advanced the principle of equality instead of preferring the primacy of the collectively bargained norm. This reflected the preference of individual rights over collective concerns.

This section has described the move from collectivism to individualism in work law. We now turn to analyze the way in which the idea of human dignity evolved at the juncture of this dramatic change.

8.4 Shifting Concepts of Human Dignity in the Law of Work

8.4.1 Human Dignity in Collectivism

The rights to unionize and bargain collectively, central to collectivism in work law, have been recognized as derived from the right to human dignity (Davidov 2004, 2010). Unpacking the idea of the self-governance reflected in collectivism reveals that it advances the human dignity of workers on a number of dimensions.

Outwardly, self-governance is evident in the relations between the national legal system and the industrial relations system, which have been described as "collective laissez-faire" (Kahn-Freund 1954): the national legal system minimizes intervention in industrial relations and promotes rules maintaining their legal autonomy, thus reinforcing the human dignity of the workers (Spector 2006).

Another dimension on which the self-governance of collectivism advances human dignity can be described as inward-facing and reflects relations between workers. In general, the self-governance of the collective bargaining system begins with the unions, which are formed voluntarily by employees, engendering democratic participation through institutions such as elections and voting, typical examples of inward self-governance. Unions provide, among other things, an institutional context in which workers can formulate and express their aims and ambitions, collect their voices, and experience the dignity that comes with having the opportunity to affect the decisions governing their lives (Klare 2014).

Aside from the democratic principles involved in the formation of the unions, their routine maintenance and their duties of representation of the workers, the inward dimension of self-governance is evident also in the interactions and negotiations between the union and employer representatives, as well as in the result, the collective agreement. Thus, collective agreements advance human dignity by setting out fair wage scales, working hours, training, health and safety, overtime, pension rights, termination procedures, disciplinary rules, grievance mechanisms, and rights to participate in workplace or company affairs. The concept of human dignity conveyed here encompasses the ability of the individual, the worker, to make decisions about what life, or work life, to pursue, in the absence of undue constraints on this ability; dignity, in this framework, also includes the idea of correcting all "unchosen disadvantages" to ensure equality of opportunity (Freedland and Kountouris 2011).

8.4.2 *Human Dignity in Individualism*

In contrast to the idea of human dignity evinced by collective labor law, the concept of human dignity reflected in individual employment law was characterized by an increased reliance on litigation to resolve workplace conflicts. The increase in rights-based legislation described previously required court-centered enforcement, whether initiated by individuals or by NGOs (Hepple 2005). Those involved in work law turned increasingly to the courts, and the courts in turn, produced decisions aimed at advancing individualized justice, rooted in specific rights, instead of collective justice, increasingly at its expense (Collins 2011; Raday 1996). This section reviews the content given to the idea of human dignity of workers through individualism in work law, focusing on Israeli case law.

The labor court, troubled by the crisis of collective labor law, turned to constitutional values and human rights, specifically the right to human dignity, as a tool in redesigning work law (Mundlak 2007). Effectively, the labor court set about deriving new standards for workers, from the right to human dignity, and there are many examples.

One group of individual rights relating to the workplace, evolving out of the idea of human dignity, includes the right to work[6] and the right to a dignified income[7] (Schultz 2000; Beatty 1980), as well as the right to fulfilling work, as opposed to monotonous and repetitive work.[8]

Another example can be found in the courts' discussion of covenants not to compete. The court protected the employee's right to freedom of occupation, under the umbrella of a constitutional debate which included the right to human dignity,

[6]National Labour Court 722-09-11 State of Israel – Israeli Medical Association (4.9.11) (Isr).

[7]National Labour Court 359/99 Levy – Israel Broadcasting Authority 36 PDL 400 (Isr), 407–408.

[8]National Labour Court 51/4-21 General Histadrut – Israeli Water Industries (Tahal), 23 PDL 3.

significantly limiting the employer's ability to control her employee's career choices, post-employment.[9] In a similar approach, the labor court recognized the employee's freedom of speech for journalists, with respect to the publisher's right to manage his paper, also citing human dignity as a rationale.[10]

Recognition of the employee's right to privacy, through the right to human dignity, has led to limitations on the use of psychological testing at work,[11] the employer's access to employee's emails,[12] health checks, surveillance, and the right to freedom of movement.[13] The reasoning behind many of these decisions relied upon the employee's right to property in their workplace. A more controversial right, which quickly gained ground in the decisions of the labor courts,[14] the employee's right to property in their workplace, was derived from the constitutional right to human dignity, which is expressly formulated as including the right to own property. Putting forward a form of worker's right to property in the workplace was used as a tool to advance the workers' human dignity interests against the employer's property interests, in the constitutional-style balancing of interests analysis (Deakin and Morris 2012; Njoya 2007). A final category of rights to be discussed as emerging from the right to human dignity in individual employment law can be described as "relational rights". These are rights to be treated in a dignified way at the workplace, without bullying or harassment of any kind.[15] While many countries belonging to the continental law tradition legislated specific laws on these matters, in countries like Israel and the United States, these issues have been advanced through the courts, using human dignity reasoning.[16]

Viewed altogether, these cases reflect a marked departure from the collectivist approach of the 1970s and 1980s and a move in the direction of an awareness of the individual employee as bearing a right to human dignity in the workplace.

---

[9]National Labour Court 164/99 Frummer and Checkpoint Technologies Ltd. Redguard Ltd. 34 PDL 294 [1999] (Isr.) (which was endorsed by the Supreme Court in CA 6601/96 AES Systems Ltd. – Sa'ar, 54(3) PDI 850 [2000] (Isr.).

[10]National Labour Court 93/3-223 Palestine Post –Yechiel 27 PDL 436 (Isr.).

[11]National Labour Court 97/4-70 Tel Aviv University – General Histadrut 30 PDL 385 (Isr.).

[12]National Labour Court 90/08 Isakov v. State of Israel – Commission of Employment of Women Law (Feb. 2, 2011) Nevo Legal Database (by Subscription) (Isr.)).

[13]National Labour Court 1459/02 Buchiman – Best Entrepreneurs Ltd. 38 PDL 824 [2003] (Isr.).

[14]See for example National Labour Court 98/3-7 Moa'adim – State of Israel 31 PD 441(Isr.); National Labour Court 375/99 Israeli Company for the Development of Kfar Manda (1977) – Gaber 35 PDA 245 [2000] (Isr.); National Labour Court 40000058/98 General Histadrut and National Committee of Administration Workers in State-Owned Hospitals – State of Israel 35 PD 103 (Isr.); National Labour Court 1008/00 Horn and Leibovitz Ltd., – the General Histadrut 35 PD 145 [2000] (Isr.); National Labour Court 400024/98 General Histadrut and Sea Officers Union – Zim, 36 PD 392 [2000] (Isr.); National Labour Court 1189/00 Levinger – State of Israel (Sep. 20th, 2000) Nevo Legal Databade (by Subscription) (Isr.).

[15]National Labour Court 56/293-3 Jane Doe – Unidentified Company (14.10.97).

[16]District Labour Court (Jer) 38335-03-14 Naftali - State of Israel (10.2.16), District Labour Court (TA) 25725-05-14 Kaffer – Scan Doc Ltd (29.5.16), District Labour Court (Jer) 16100-04-12 Marchkovski – Ahava (29.11.14).

8.5 Discussion

The first part of this chapter focused on the concern for the human dignity of workers that characterizes work law, as it emerged from international instruments and theoretical legal literature, as well as from positive law. The second part of this chapter described the dramatic shift that occurred from a collectivist idea of work law as embodied by collective labor law, to a more individualist idea of work law, as embodied by individual employment law. The third part of this chapter characterized the way in which human dignity is advanced by both collective labor law and individual employment law. Given the unwavering work law commitment to human dignity, this part of the chapter compares the idea of human dignity emerging from the respective approaches to work law.

The collective labor law idea of human dignity is closely tied up with self-governance. This was expressed in a clear and succinct way by the Supreme Court of Canada in 2007:

> The right to bargain collectively with an employer enhances the human dignity, liberty and autonomy of workers by giving them the opportunity to influence the establishment of workplace rules and thereby gain some control over a major aspect of their lives, namely their work. Collective bargaining is not simply an instrument for pursuing external ends. . .rather [it] is intrinsically valuable as an experience in self-government. . .Collective bargaining permits workers to achieve a form of workplace democracy and to ensure the rule of law in the workplace. Workers gain a voice to influence the establishment of rules that control a major aspect of their lives.[17]

The decision, which established that the right to collective bargaining, is protected by the Canadian Charter of Rights and describes how the mechanics of the protection of human dignity under collective labor law goes through voice and self-governance: the *ratio* of the decision contributed to outward self-governance, and the rhetoric addressed inward self-governance, as discussed in the previous section.

Indeed, unions, much like legislation in individual employment law, aim to provide workers with the dignity of a living wage and the ability to pay for life's necessities. However, they do this by facilitating voice, which in itself and more directly reinforces human dignity by allowing individual workers to express themselves with regard to their fate as workers. The union role in organizing, advocacy, and representation reinforces the essential (Kirton and Healy 2013) freedom and value of humans even as they work for others, which underpins the widespread ideas of human dignity.

By contrast, the concept of human dignity emerging from the above description of individual employment law emphasizes the role of the individual worker demanding specific rights from the employer, most often after-the-fact, that is, post-dismissal or post-rights violation. The tools applied in this context—legislation, litigation, or NGO representation—reaffirm the workers' autonomy vis-à-vis the employer, thereby reinforcing their human dignity; however, the emphasis is on the results,

---

[17] Facilities Subsector Bargaining Association v. British Columbia, SCC, 2007.

since the process—litigation or legislation—is not inherently participatory. Neither does individual employment law aim to alter the experience of work in the name of human dignity. Rather its focus is on the "bottom line", a mostly comparative numerical settling of accounts, again, at the end of the employment relationship, leaving the nature of the workplace in the duration of the working relationship in second place.

One might argue that this approach gives meaningful and concrete content to the idea of human dignity at work, guaranteeing an income that allows workers a reasonable standard of living and reasonable working conditions. However, this concept of human dignity is narrower than the one emerging from the collective labor law approach, with its emphasis on the process and experience of work life. The individualist approach, with its reliance on litigation, is more confrontational and crisis-centered, while the collectivist approach, with collective agreements as its tools, requires negotiation and cooperation.

Furthermore, it has been argued that rights-based groups, frequently working out of concern against discrimination, deepen individualist tendencies to the extent that they become almost separatist, as everyone "looks out for their own" (Lobel 2004). This effect was noted in the field of individual employment law, where "tailor-made" NGOs, while more dynamic than unions, deepened the segmentation of the workforce (Shafir and Peled 1998). So too, the employment law legislation focused on sub-groups of workers instead of establishing principles with a broad application that could be relevant to the full experience of work (Friedman 1991).

In that sense, individual employment law rights fall short of a broad conception of human dignity, since it is confined to a narrow results-based top-down approach that focuses on rights against mistreatment and unfair dismissal, as opposed to the broader process-based approach of collective labor law that directly endows workers with human dignity by empowering them to demand those same rights for themselves in the duration of the working relationship. This could explain the inability of individual employment law to rein in recent problematic phenomena undermining human dignity at work such as the "gig" economy and zero hour contract (Meryon et al. 2022). These phenomena have been justified as strengthening worker autonomy, a concept closely aligned with dignity. At the same time, these phenomena have been at the focus of much criticism for circumventing and undermining entrenched employment law rights (Aloisi and Cherry 2017; McKeown and Pichault 2019). While the flexibility and earning potential of both phenomena are at the root of their proliferation, they are also symptomatic of an atomistic individualism in line with the move away from collective labor law. In short, these sorts of phenomena could not occur in a predominantly collective labor law regime, whose concept of human dignity embodies not only dignity in terms of wage but also dignity in terms of self-governance and voice.

In other words, a system allowing workers to express their needs and coordinate their actions aiming at meeting those needs, while employed, would probably prevent the indignities of the above-described new forms of employment. There have been calls for labor law reform to strengthen worker voice in the workplace (Befort 2002), if not through increasing union membership then through other collectivist approaches that avoid the need to unionize yet allow for employee participation and effective self-governance (Lobel 2004). Grievance systems could advance that aim, as could employee representation in the board of directors (Abramowitz 1980). Another example of such a system is the Works Councils, which exist in some continental law jurisdictions such as France and Germany, or joint consultative committees, as they are known in common law jurisdictions. These are committees comprising of elected non-union worker representatives who meet with management over work rights, job training, and structural changes. While research has found their presence to correlate with workplace satisfaction (Barry et al. 2018), even whilst controlling for union presence, they exist in a minority of companies.

Given the above analysis, it can carefully be suggested that while the work law commitment to worker human dignity has changed, it has not faltered. However, the current multifaceted form, embracing both individualist and collectivist approaches to worker human dignity risks exposing vulnerable workers where individual employment law dominates (Bondy 2020). The emphasis on self-governance in the broad, collectivist approach to human dignity would most probably prevent the race to the bottom effect embodied by the "gig" economy and zero hour contracts, by emphasizing additional value to workplace human dignity beyond income, such as upholding participation and voice.

The idea of the centrality of self-governance to the concept of human dignity is applicable outside the context of work law as well, and it has been argued that denials of dignity occur throughout society, a fact that justifies a connected rather than atomized response (Yamada 2009). The collectivist approach to work law provides a voice to workers and a stage for their opinions, reaffirming their human dignity, even within the context of subordination inherent in the state of being an employee. For this reason, it is clear that work laws that protect the basic rights of workers to organize can help to reaffirm workers' dignity. While the litigation-based strategy of the individualist era of work law may achieve the same results from a narrow economic rights perspective, a broader perspective taking account of values and interests reveals that respect for human dignity in the workplace requires protections for self-governance, either in the form of organizing rights or other types of employee participation (Bondy 2020). The message of participation resonates in other forums of civic society and has the potential to advance human dignity on national thresholds as well as on a global scale.

8.6 Conclusion

This chapter looked at one of the central developments in the law of work, that of the move from collectivism to individualism, probing how this development affects the human dignity of workers. The discussion above revealed that while this transition helped workers by increasing the forms of protection available to them and improving standards at work, the protection individual employment law offers is limited as compared to that offered by collective labor law, because it fails to provide for worker voice, participation, or self-governance. In that sense, the shift from collectivism to individualism in the law of work has left workers at the threshold of a comprehensive idea of human dignity, since the concept of human dignity emerging from this analysis of individual employment law is limited to economic rights. Economic rights are important but insufficient, pertaining to a narrow concept of human dignity. In order to advance a broader form of human dignity for workers under the current individual employment law regime, this chapter suggests that policy and law makers address the need for workers to be "authors of their fate". Acknowledging the unique perspectives of collective labor law can contribute to a new broader paradigm of human dignity in the workplace. By finding new ways for the voices of workers to be heard in the era of individual employment law, the workers will be able to transition to a new concept of human dignity.

References

Abramowitz B (1980) Broadening the board: labor participation in corporate governance. Southwest Law J 34:963

Aloisi A, Cherry MA (2017) "Dependent contractors" in the gig economy: a comparative approach. Am Univ Law Rev 66:635–689

Barry, Bryson, Gomez, Kaufman, Lomas, Wilkinson (2018) The "good workplace": the role of joint consultative committees, unions and HR policies in employee ratings of workplaces in Britain. Discussion Paper Series, IZA Institute of Labor Economics

Beatty DM (1980) Labour is not a commodity. In: Reiter BJ, Swan J (eds) Studies in contract law. Butterworths, Toronto, p 313

Befort SF (2002) Labor and employment law at the millennium: a historical review and critical assessment. Boston Coll Law Rev 43:351

Bellace JR (2011) Achieving social justice: the nexus between the ILO's fundamental rights and decent work. Emp Rights Emp Policy J 15:5

Blackett A (2007) Situated reflections on international labour law, capabilities, and decent work. RQDI 223

Bondy A (2020) The creation and erosion of branch-specific collective negotiation: the development of hybrid work relations in the private sector. Work Soc Law 17:79. [Hebrew]

Collins H (1992) Justice in dismissal. Clarendon Press, Oxford

Collins H (2011) Theories of rights as justifications for labour law. In: Langille B, Davidov G (eds) The idea of labour law. Oxford University Press

Cox A (1958) The legal nature of collective bargaining agreements. Mich Law Rev 57:1

Davidov G (2004) Collective bargaining law: purpose and scope. Int J Comp Labour Law Ind Relat 20:81–106

Davidov G (2009) A purposive interpretation of the national minimum wage act. Mod Law Rev 72: 581

Davidov G (2010) Judicial development of collective labour rights – contextually. Can Labour Employ Law J 15:235–250

Davies ACL (2009) Perspectives on labour law. Cambridge University Press

Davies P, Freedland M (1993) Labour legislation and public policy. Clarendon Law Series

Deakin S, Morris GS (2012) Labour law, 6th edn. Hart Publishing

Dukes R (2008) Constitutionalizing employment relations: Sinzheimer, Kahn-Freund, and the role of labour law. J Law Soc 12:341

Ehrenreich R (1999) Dignity and discrimination: toward a pluralistic understanding of workplace harassment. Geo Law J 88:1
Estlund C (2005) Rebuilding the law of the workplace in an era of self-regulation. Colum Law Rev 105:319
Fredman S (2001) Equality: a new generation? Ind Law J 30:145
Freedland M, Kountouris N (2011) The legal construction of personal work relations. Oxford University Press, Oxford
Freeman R et al (eds) (2005) Emerging labour market institutions for the twenty-first century. University of Chicago Press
Friedman LM (1991) American legal culture: the last thirty-five years. St Louis Law J 35:529
Giddens A (1998) The third way: the renewal of social democracy. Polity Press
Hepple H (2005) Labour laws and global trade. Hart Publishing
Hirsch BT, Macpherson DA (2003) (updated annually at unionstats.com) Union membership and coverage database from the current population survey: note. Ind Labor Relat Rev 56:349–354
Israeli Central Bureau of Statistics. https://www.cbs.gov.il/en/Pages/default.aspx. Accessed 30 June 2023
Kahn-Freund O (1954) Legal framework. In: Flanders A, Clegg HA (eds) The system of industrial relations in Great Britain: its history, law and institutions. Blackwell
Kirton G, Healy G (2013) Commitment and collective identity of long-term participation: the case of women union leaders in the UK and USA. Work Emp Soc 27:195, 196
Klare KE (2014) Labor law as ideology: towards a new historiography of collective bargaining law. Berkley J Emp Lab Law 4:450
Lobel O (2004) Between individualism and solidarity: collective efforts for social reform in the heterogeneous workplace. Diversity in the Workplace, Res Sociol Work 14:131–164
Lurie L (2014) Do unions promote gender equality? Duke J Gender Law Policy 22:88
McKeown T, Pichault F (2019) Autonomy at work in the gig economy: analysing work status, work content and working conditions of independent professionals. New Technol Work Employ 34: 59–72
Meryon M, O'Reilly J, Rolf S (2022) Towards privatized social and employment protections in the platform economy? Evidence from the UK courier sector. Res Policy 51(5):104492
Mundlak G (2007) Fading corporatism: Israel's labor law and industrial relations in transition. ILR Press
Njoya W (2007) Property in work: the employment relationship in the Anglo-American Firm. Ashgate
Raday F (1996) Anatomy of trade unionism. Mishpatim 26:85. [Hebrew]
Radin MJ (1996) Contested commodities. Harvard University Press, Cambridge
Schultz V (2000) Life's work. Colum Law Rev 100:1881
Shafir G, Peled Y (1998) Being Israeli: the dynamics of multiple citizenship. In: Mautner M, Shamir R (eds) Multicultralism in a democratic and Jewish State: The Ariel Rosen-Zvi Memorial Volume. Tel-Aviv University Press [Hebrew]
Spector H (2006) Philosophical foundations of labor law. Fla State Univ Law Rev 33:1119
Teulings C, Hartog J (1998) Corporatism or competition? – Labour contracts, institutions and wage structures in international comparison. Cambridge University Press
Toth MA (2008) The right to dignity at work: reflections on Article 26 of the Revised European Social Charter. Comp Labor Law Policy J 29:275–316
Yamada DC (2007) Dignity, "rankism," and hierarchy in the workplace: creating a "dignitarian" agenda for American employment law. Berkeley J Emp Lab Law 28:315–324
Yamada DC (2009) Human dignity and American employment law. Univ Rich Law Rev 43:523
Yonai Y (1998) The law about sexual orientation: between history and sociology. Mishpat U-Mimshal 4:550–557. [Hebrew]
Ziv N (1998) Disability law in Israel and the United States – a comparative perspective. Isr Yearb Hum Rights 28:171–202

Chapter 9
Human Dignity and Labor Protection in South Africa

Marius van Staden

Abstract This chapter assesses the relationship between the notion of dignity and security in employment as well as dignity and the social protection offered following the loss of employment. It does so by exploring the specific instruments that have been utilized to protect employees against unfair dismissal and the social protection instruments that are available to support the dignity of workers following the loss of employment. The later enabling them to re-join the world of work and the dignity it affords them. Ultimately, this chapter argues that a person's dignity and entry into the employment relationship, the maintenance of the relationship through employment security measures and the appropriate social protection mechanisms established in the event of the termination of the employment relationship are interdependent factors.

9.1 Introduction

Human dignity is a key constitutional right and value in South Africa. Dignity is the first mentioned value in the founding provisions of the Constitution of the Republic of South Africa, 1996 (see section 1(a) of the Constitution); there are seven references to this key societal value (see sections 7(1), 10, 35(2)(e), 36(1), 37 and 39(1)(a)). Section 10 states: "[e]veryone has inherent dignity and the right to have their dignity respected and protected." The South African Constitutional Court in S v. Makwanyane (1995 3 SA 391 (CC), par 327) found that "without dignity, human life is substantially diminished." The Court described dignity as the public law value upon which the South African constitutional order is founded (para 58). The Court stated:

> [T]he importance of dignity as a founding value of the new Constitution cannot be overemphasised. Recognising a right to dignity is an acknowledgement of the intrinsic worth of human beings: human beings are entitled to be treated as worthy of respect and

M. van Staden (✉)
University of the Witwatersrand, Johannesburg, South Africa
e-mail: marthinus.vanstaden@wits.ac.za

S. N. Arel et al. (eds.), *Probing Human Dignity*,
https://doi.org/10.1007/978-3-031-42437-3_9

> concern. This right therefore is the foundation of many of the other rights that are specifically entrenched in [the Bill of Rights].

Dignity is one of only two rights in the Constitution (the other is the right to life) which is entirely non-derogable, albeit in the context of a state of emergency (section 37). The Constitution however has no provision which clarifies the meaning of "human dignity," and the responsibility for giving life to this central concept is left to the courts and their powers of interpretation. The exercise of this responsibility becomes even more pressing in the context of the Constitutional Court laying stress on the argument that the socio-economic rights in the South African Constitution are closely related to the foundational value of human dignity (Khosa v. Minister of Social Development; Mahlaule v Minister of Social Development 2004 6 SA 505 (CC), para 76).

South African labor law distinguishes between employees and other workers such as independent contractors. The primary purpose in this distinction is to exclude individuals from the ambit of South African labor legislation which extends protection only to those who are defined as "employees." In general, the view underlying labor laws is that employees are in a vulnerable position and in need of legislative protection. In contrast, these laws presume that those outside of the definition of employee, such as independent contractors, are in a commercial relationship and are less in need of protection. These workers have to rely on the law of contract and to resolve their disputes through the general court system.

As admittance to the category of employee in an important threshold for the advancement of the dignity of workers, this chapter focuses on the relationship between work and the loss or unavailability of work and the effect on a person's human dignity. First, the chapter considers the understanding by the South African Constitutional Court of the concept of human dignity. Second, the chapter explores the impact upon a person's dignity of being unable to enter into employment, as well as the legislative and judicial response adopted which encourages entrance to the employment relationship. Third, the chapter examines the manner in which the dignity of workers who already are party to the employment relationship can be protected through measures designed to promote security of employment. Fourth, the chapter considers how social protection mechanisms seek to protect the human dignity of persons in the event of the loss of employment. This chapter finds that dignity although inherent to the personhood of an individual nevertheless demonstrates a dependence upon entry into the employment relationship, the maintenance of such a relationship through employment security arrangements, and appropriate social protection mechanisms in the event of the termination of the employment relationship.

9.2 Understanding Dignity

According to Woolman, there are at least five primary "definitions" or "conceptions" of dignity in the jurisprudence of the Constitutional Court (see Woolman 2014, p. 2). These conceptions may be seen as formulations derived from dignity of what is required so as to achieve dignity. They are: the individual as an end in him or herself, equal concern and equal respect, self-actualization, self-governance, and collective responsibility for the material conditions for individual agency. The first conception of dignity (the individual as an end in him or herself) is based on Immanuel Kant's (1785) second formulation of the categorical imperative: act in such a way that you always treat humanity, whether in your own person or in the person of another, never simply as a means, but always at the same time as an end. Hill (1980) interprets Kant's theory as meaning that humanity is not a relative end but rather an objective end or an end in him or herself. Such an end means an end which serves the will as the "(subjective) ground of its self-determination." Humanity also is regarded as a self-existent and objective end (Hill 1980, p. 88); this end is "a supreme condition limiting the use of every means," "a condition limiting all merely relative and arbitrary ends", and "a limit on all arbitrary treatment." Importantly, this first conception of dignity in a South African context requires an interpretation which takes into account a history of racial exclusion in respect of the majority of South Africans prior to the advent of constitutional democracy. Ackerman (2004, p. 650) explains this idea as follows:

> [I]t is permissible and indeed necessary to look at the ills of the past which [the Constitution] seeks to rectify and in this way try to establish what equality and dignity mean? What lay at the heart of the apartheid pathology was the extensive and sustained attempt to deny to the majority of the South African population the right of self-identification and self-determination. Who you were, where you could live, what schools and universities you could attend, what you could do and aspire to, and with whom you could form intimate personal relationship was determined for you by the state. That state did its best to deny to blacks that which is definitional to being human, namely the ability to understand or at least define oneself through one's own powers and to act freely as a moral agent pursuant to such understanding of self-definition. Blacks were treated as means to an end and hardly ever as an end in themselves; an almost complete reversal of the Kantian imperative and concept of priceless inner worth and dignity.

In respect of the labor laws, black workers were dealt with primarily as a means to an end and hardly ever as an end in themselves. All labor legislation prior to 1971 had a distinguishing feature of excluding black workers from its ambit. Two mechanisms were used to achieve this aim; black workers either were excluded directly from the protections afforded by legislation, or workers were indirectly excluded from the provisions of an act due to their inability to comply with the statutory definition of the term "employee" (Wiehahn 1982, pp. xx–xxii). In practice, although some laws at face value were racially neutral, they applied only to non-white workers employed in a limited number of services (such as the agricultural and domestic sectors). The exclusion of many black workers was also achieved by means of pass and influx control laws that were designed to control the movements of black workers. Certain laws established quotas for black and white workers and reserved the better paying jobs for white workers (Le Roux 2008, p. 32).

South Africa's history of racial exclusion had the effect of treating black workers as a means. Twenty-six years after South Africa's first justiciable constitution was adopted black workers still are more likely either to be unemployed or in an atypical work relationship in which they are not viewed as employees.

The other four definitions of dignity are reformulations of Kant's "categorical imperative," and they are what is required if workers are to be treated as an end in themselves. The second definition of dignity (equal concern and equal respect) is based on Kantian moral law. Kant (1797, p. 230) stated that "[a]ny action is right if it can coexist with everyone's freedom in accordance with a universal law, or if on its maxim the freedom of choice of each can coexist with everyone's freedom in accordance with a universal law." This negative obligation not to interfere with the freedoms of others means that others should not be treated merely as a means to an end but as autonomous moral agents. An acceptance of acts as being the product of an autonomous moral agent entails the recognition that individuals are entitled to equal concern and to equal respect (Woolman 2014, p. 10). Human dignity requires a society to respect the equal worth of marginalized workers by marshalling its resources to redress the conditions that perpetuate their marginalization (see Liebenberg 2005). Ackerman (2003, p. 105) affirms that the purpose of the South African constitutional order is "the establishment of a society in which all human beings will be accorded equal dignity and respect." The Constitutional Court confirmed that "under our Constitution all human beings, regardless of their position in society, must be accorded equal dignity" (Hoffmann v. South African Airways (2001 1 SA 1 (CC), para 27; see also President of the Republic of South Africa v. Hugo 1997 4 SA 1 (CC), para 41).

Dignity as demonstrating the principle of equal concern and equal respect is highlighted by the decision of the Labor Appeal Court in ARB Electrical Wholesalers v. Hibbert (2015 36 ILJ 2989 (LAC), para 23) where it was held that compensatory relief in terms of the Labor Relations Act (LRA) (55 of 1996) is payment for the impairment of an employee's dignity and that such payment constitutes solace in that it provides satisfaction to an employee whose constitutionally-protected right to fair labor practice has been violated. In South Africa, not being afforded the label "employee" marginalizes workers in respect of the protection provided by legislation; workers who are not defined as "employees" will be denied equal concern and equal respect. In South African Informal Traders Forum v. City of Johannesburg (2014 4 SA 371 (CC), para 31), the Constitutional Court highlighted the importance of the ability to earn money and to support oneself, describing this possibility as an important component of the right to human dignity without which persons face "humiliation and degradation." "The ability to earn money and to support oneself" often is a feature protected in legislation that is limited to workers who are "employees."

According to the third definition of dignity, there is a requirement that the concept secures a space for self-actualization. The Constitutional Court in Ferreira v. Levin NO; Vryenhoek v. Powell (1996 1 SA 984 (CC), para 49) held that "[h]uman dignity cannot be fully valued or respected unless individuals are able to develop their humanity, their 'humanness' to the full extent of its potential." In South African Police Service v. Solidarity o.b.o. Barnard (2014 6 SA 123 (CC), para 173), the Court stated:

> [T]he value of the individual is safeguarded in our jurisprudence. Every person should be treated as an end in herself and not as a means to an end only. This is what blunt utilitarianism would allow. The concept of dignity also concerns an individual's sense of self-esteem, and encompasses the idea that one is permitted to develop one's talents optimally.

The South African Constitution secures a space for self-actualization that demands the extension of labor protection to as broad a range of workers as possible. A policy responsive to this demand will ensure the attainment of human dignity as it creates an environment in which every person can achieve his or her own maximum potential and possibilities (Woolman 2014, p. 11). In Minister of Home Affairs v. Watchenuka (2004 1 All SA 21 (SCA), para 26), the Supreme Court of Appeal found:

> The freedom to engage in productive work – even where that is not required in order to survive – is indeed an important component of human dignity ... for mankind is pre-eminently a social species with an instinct for meaningful association. Self-esteem and the sense of self-worth – the fulfilment of what it is to be human – is most often bound up with being accepted as socially useful.

The finding in this case highlights the claim that, for most, access to an enabling environment where individuals are able to develop their humanity is dependent on gaining access to the protection an employment relationship provides.

The fourth conception of dignity involves the recognition of the ability of all persons to set ends for themselves through their capacity to reason (Woolman 2014, pp. 12–13). Due to the nature of the employment relationship, it is the shareholders and employers who set ends chiefly in terms of the pursuit of profit, and generally, employees do not set their own ends. This conception of dignity can be employed in the advocacy of establishing a workplace democracy, collective bargaining, and social dialogue, which to a greater or lesser extent, allows employees collectively to set ends (or goals). This capacity also is dependent on participation as a party to the employment relationship. The Constitutional Court has highlighted the importance of collective bargaining in advancing the human dignity of workers, "who in [the South African] constitutional order may not be treated as coerced employees" (National Union of Metal Workers of South Africa and Others v. Bader Bop (Pty) Ltd and Another 2003 (2) BCLR 182, para 13).

The final conception of dignity acknowledges a focus on broader societal ends. In this view "[d]ignity is that which binds us together as a community, and it occurs only under conditions of mutual recognition" (Woolman 2014, pp. 12–13). The Constitutional Court held in Port Elizabeth Municipality v. Various Occupiers (2005 1 SA 217 (CC), para 18) that it is not only the dignity of the marginalized that is assailed when marginalized people are inadequately treated but also society as a whole is demeaned when state action intensifies their marginalization (see also MEC for Education: KwaZulu Natal v. Pillay 2008 1 SA 474 (CC), para 150). Although this case dealt specifically with the treatment of homeless persons, the logic the court applied in its finding can be extended to those who find they are unable to transit to the situation of an "employee," the inability to do so inevitably has broad-ranging societal consequences. So too in Khumalo v. Holomisa (2002 5 SA 401 (CC), para 27), the Constitutional Court found dignity is concerned not only with an individual's sense of self-worth but also with the worth of all in society. In South African Police Service v. Solidarity o.b.o. Barnard (2014 6 SA 123 (CC), para 174), the Constitutional Court again emphasized that

> "we are not islands unto ourselves," that the individual as the bearer of the right to dignity "should not be understood as an isolated and unencumbered being" and that dignity "contains individualistic as well as collective impulses."

On this final conception of dignity, the link is drawn between the concept of dignity and the African value of Ubuntu. Ubuntu requires that those outside an employment relationship should have their dignity recognized. For instance, the Labor Court in Department of Health: Gauteng Provincial Government v. National Education Health and Allied Workers Union (case no J2864/16 (LC) (unreported) par 1) highlighted the interrelationship between the right to fair labor practices and the constitutional right to dignity in holding that the right to dignity extends to situation of deceased persons. The case involved a proposed strike action by forensic pathologists that would delay the funerals of several deceased persons. The Court declared the proposed strike action unprotected and held that the right to human dignity arises out of our very existence as human beings and is based on values held in the concept of Ubuntu, which Archbishop Desmond Tutu defined as "the essence of being human. It speaks of the fact that my humanity is caught up and is inextricably bound up in yours. I am human because I belong. It speaks about wholeness, it speaks about compassion" (par 9). Ubuntu embraces "humaneness, group solidarity, compassion, respect, human dignity, conformity to basic norms and collective unity, humanity, morality and conciliation" (Du Plooy v. Minister of Correctional Services & Others 2004 3 All SA 613 (T), par 18). It embraces the "communality" and "interdependence of the members of a community" (S v. Makwanyane 1995 3 SA 391 (CC), para 224). The Department of Health case illustrates how the values that are an attribute of Ubuntu are a link forged between the constitutional value system and social values.

Although not explicitly mentioned in the Constitution, 1996, Ubuntu is explicitly mentioned in the post-amble of the interim Constitution (Act 200 of 1993). The Constitutional Court has held that Ubuntu is a key constitutional value and is a fundamental commitment of the Constitution (Hoffman v. South African Airways 2001 1 SA 1 (CC), para 38). This final conception and the tie to the notion of Ubuntu implies that workers or employees are not the only persons who have a vested interest in the protection afforded as a consequence of labor legislation; the dignity of workers, their family, community and society at large are also affected by the risks associated with the life-work cycle.

In order to advance the values expressed as dignity, South African labor law must be responsive to all five conceptions of dignity. First, labor law mechanisms must be responsive to the history of racial exclusion affecting the majority of South Africans prior to the advent of constitutional democracy. Second, all workers should be afforded equal concern and equal respect. Third, people need access to an enabling environment in the workplace where individuals are able to develop their humanity. Fourth, forms of workplace democracy would make it possible for employees to set ends for themselves. Fifth, society also has a vested interest in protecting the dignity of workers.

9.3 Dignity and the Employment Relationship

The value of dignity and its association with the values attributed to the notion of Ubuntu are important considerations regarding who is a party in the employment relationship because a person's work is a part of identity and also is constitutive of one's dignity. The designation of "employee" is a badge of dignity and of personhood. For all practical purposes, those who fall outside the employment relationship, such as independent contractors, are not afforded the legislative protection granted those deemed to be "employees," even though formally their dignity is recognized.

The protection supplied in labor legislation extends only to those defined as "employees." Labor law generally views employees as in a vulnerable position and in need of legislative protection. In contrast, however, these laws presume that workers not covered in the definition of employee, such as independent contractors, are in a commercial relationship and less in need of protection. These workers rely upon the law of contract and must resolve disputes through the general court system. As Deakin and Wilkinson (2005, p. 4) show "[i]t is no exaggeration to think of the classification of work relationships as the central, defining operation of any labor law system. Without classification, the law cannot be mobilized." Thus, it is imperative that as many workers as possible should be drawn into the protective ambit of the employment relationship. In Affordable Medicines Trust v. Minister of Health (2006 3 SA 247 (CC), para 59) the Constitutional Court commented on the importance of the relationship between work and human dignity. In the view of the Court, work is part and parcel of a person's dignity. The Court stated "there is a relationship between work and the human personality as a whole." As a consequence, the inability to find employment, the loss of employment, insufficient social protection in circumstances of unemployment, and the inability to be admitted to the employment relationship in the first place violates the dignity of a person, their family, and society. All five "conceptions" of dignity in the jurisprudence of the Constitutional Court therefore are dependent on classification as an "employee" in order to access the protections afforded by labor legislation.

A significant percentage of the South African working-age population is unable to transit the threshold into employment and the dignity it affords, either because they are unable to find employment, or they work in the informal economy where they are not regarded as "employees." In South Africa, as of the first quarter of 2020, only 16,383,000 out of a population between the ages of 15 and 65 of 38,874,000 had jobs. Of these, only 11,282,000 are employed in the non-agricultural formal sector. In addition, although the unemployment rate formally stands at 30.1%, the labor force participation rate is 60.3% (Statistics South Africa 2020, p. 1). These statistics point to the fact that many South Africans are unable to transit to an employment relationship. Even more alarmingly, these statistics encapsulate unemployment in South Africa prior to the COVID-19 pandemic which eliminated an estimated further 3,000,000 jobs in the formal economy between February and April of 2020. Another 1,500,000 employees were furloughed (Spaull 2020). These statistics point to the dire state of the South African economy and the inability to create jobs that will advance the dignity of workers, their families, and society. The law in general and labor law in particular are not vehicles for the creation of (formal) employment in an economy, but have the task of shaping the legal foundation of the employment relationship in accordance with the dignity of persons. Labor law and especially the judiciary and the legislature can do much more to make the protected field of employment more inclusive.

The chief judicial mechanism used to include workers into the definition of employment has been to interpret the concept "employee" broadly. In addition, the courts have done away with requiring that there be a valid contract of employment as a prerequisite for the existence of an employment relationship (see for example Discovery Health Limited v. CCMA 2008 29 ILJ 1480 (LC) and "Kylie" v. CCMA 2010 31 ILJ 1600 (LAC)). Similarly, the courts have interpreted liberally legislative provisions designed to extend adequate protection to vulnerable categories of workers. However, there are cases where the labor courts have been unwilling to deem workers employees, such as in the case of Uber drivers (Uber South Africa Technology Services (Pty) Ltd v. National Union of Public Service and Allied Workers 2018 39 ILJ 903 (LC)) and in a case where employees and employers occupy relatively equal bargaining positions (see Vermooten v. Department of Public Enterprises 2017 38 ILJ 607 (LAC)). Notwithstanding the capacity of the courts to contribute to the advancement of dignity and the transformation of society through their powers of interpretation, the courts have not always succeeded in doing so.

The legislative mechanisms that primarily have been employed in regard to the extension of protection are fourfold. First, the legislature seeks to provide greater guidance as to who should be regarded as employees; the legislature adopted a definition of employment (section 213 of the LRA) introducing a presumption of employment (section 200A of the LRA) and a code of good practice as to who is an employee. Additionally, section 23(1) of the Constitution provides protection to non-standard employees who do not fit the definition of employee as provided for in labor legislation because section 23(1) grants the right to "everyone." The Constitutional Court has found that the term "everyone" engages "broadly speaking, the relationship between the worker and employer" (NEHAWU v. UCT 2003 3 SA 1 (CC): para 40) with the result the term encompasses persons on the margins of the employment relationship including those in employee-like relationships. For example, the Constitutional Court has found that section 23 encompassed members of the South African National Defense Force even though they specifically are excluded from the definition of "employee" in labor legislation. The Court concluded that the relationship between the soldiers and the military was "akin," although not identical, to a normal employment relationship that would entitle the members to the protections of section 23 (South African National Defense Union v. Minister of Defense 1999 4 469 (CC): para 35–36).

Second, the legislature prohibited or imposed strict conditions on certain employment relationships. The employment of vulnerable, lower-paid workers by a temporary employment service is restricted to situations of genuine and relevant temporary work and various measures protect workers employed in this way (sections 189 and 189A of the LRA). For example, an employer is permitted to employ an employee on a fixed-term contract or successive fixed term contracts for up to six months (section 189B of the LRA). An employee may be employed on a fixed term contract for longer if the nature of the work is of limited or definite duration or the employer can demonstrate any other justifiable reason for fixing the term of the contract (section 189(3)(a)-(b) of the LRA). If this is not done, employment will be deemed to be of indefinite duration. As a further example, an employer must treat a part-time employee (section 189 C(1)(a) of the LRA defines a part-time employee as "an employee who is remunerated wholly or partly by reference to the time that the employee works and who works less hours than a comparable full-time employee") on the whole not less favorably than a comparable full-time employee doing the same or similar work.

Third, in terms of section 83 of the Basic Conditions of Employment Act 75 of 1997 (BCEA) on advice of the Employment Conditions Commission and by notice in the Government Gazette the minister may deem any category of persons specified in the notice to be employees for the purposes of the whole or any part of the BCEA or any other employment law or sectoral determination. Fourie (2008, p. 125) however questions "why the act does not regulate the position of non-standard workers directly, and whether or not it is wise to leave a matter of such importance up to the discretion of the Minister to adopt measures when he/she deems it appropriate." Determinations where the minister has deemed categories of persons as employees have been politically unpopular and therefore generally have not been utilized.

Fourth, to draw especially black workers (but also women and disabled persons) into the domain of protection reserved for employees, the legislature mandates employers to implement affirmative action measures (section 13 of the Employment Equity Act 55 of 1998 (EEA)) and provides that affirmative action is a defense to a claim of unfair discrimination (section 6(2) of the EEA). Affirmative action measures are meant to advance substantive equality in society in general and in the workplace in particular. Affirmative action measures take cognizance of South Africa's history of racial exclusion under which black workers were treated as a means to an end and therefore seek to advance the dignity of black workers as per the first conception of dignity adopted by the Constitutional Court. The Court has held that the dignity of those negatively affected by affirmative action measures should not be unduly impinged (South African Police Service v. Solidarity obo Barnard 2014 6 SA 123 (CC) para 28 and 30). Notwithstanding affirmative action measures, the South African Human Rights Commission notes that especially the private sector remains substantially untransformed and that rigid and absolute quotas in the context of affirmative action are misaligned to the constitutional object of achieving equality. In addition, the EEA uses a rigid system of classification which excludes indigenous peoples, those born from mixed race marriages and linguistic or tribal minorities within designated groups. The failure of government to calculate the impact of affirmative action measures has been the subject of criticism (South African Human Rights Commission 2018, p. 38).

Notwithstanding the great strides to make employment more inclusive that are the consequence of the efforts of the judiciary and the legislature, Le Roux (2014, p. 33) argues inevitably there is pushback against these interventions "pushing more and more workers beyond the reach of protective labor legislation." The potential to have an impact, especially of the judiciary, should not be underestimated; emboldened by their powers of interpretation and by applying a broad approach to the interpretation of labor laws, South African courts are able to do more to protect vulnerable workers and bring workers under the protection of labor legislation. So too, the legislature can do more to deal with specific categories of vulnerable workers directly. The minister of labor has powers in terms of section 83 to include more categories of workers under the definition of "employees." These existing strategies will do much to advance the dignity of vulnerable workers.

9.4 Dignity and Security of Employment

If a worker has transitioned to the status of an employee, the dignity that relationship bestows depends on the continuation of employment. Security of employment therefore is an important element in the advancement of the five conceptions of dignity identified by the Constitutional Court (refer to Sect. 9.2 above). The International Labor Organization (ILO) defines employment security as "the protection of workers against fluctuations in earned income as a result of job loss. Job loss may occur during economic downturns, as part of restructuring, or be related to other various reasons for dismissals" (ILO 2019). Security of employment is achieved primarily through protection against dismissal and is supplemented by social protection in the event of loss of employment. According to Cheadle (2006, p. 668), the broader term "security" includes labor market security such as opportunities for employment; employment security, such as protection against the arbitrary loss of employment; job security, such as the protection against arbitrary loss of or alteration to the job; work security, which includes health and safety in the workplace, and representation security, which deals with representation in the workplace. This section of the chapter considers security of employment in terms of protection against job loss. The following section will address aspects of social protection that may impact the dignity of workers in the event of a loss of employment (refer to Sect. 9.5 below).

The Constitutional Court found security of employment to be a core value of the LRA (NEHAWU v. UCT 2003 3 SA 1 (CC), par 42). An important objective in the LRA is to enhance security of employment primarily through protection against dismissal (Grogan 2014, p. 164). The right not to be unfairly dismissed, said the Court, is "essential to the constitutional right to fair labor practices." The judiciary frequently has viewed the unfair dismissal of employees as a fundamental affront to the dignity of employees (Parry v. Astral Operations Ltd 2005 10 BLLR 989 (LC), para 137). The dignity of workers is protected primarily by means of the following measures which are designed to protect employees from unfair dismissal: strictly defining the conditions under which employees may be dismissed (section 186(1) of the LRA), prescribing the circumstances in which a dismissal is adjudged to be fair or unfair (section 187(1) of the LRA), creating specialized forums who are tasked with determining if a dismissal has occurred and whether the dismissal is unfair (the LRA establishes the Commission for Conciliation, Mediation and Arbitration (section 112) and the Labor Court (section 151)) and extending remedies against unfair dismissal (section 193(1) of the LRA). Employees may be dismissed only for reasons related to misconduct, capacity, and the operational requirements of the employer. Also, dismissals may be effected only in accordance with a fair procedure.

Three remedies can be utilized by employees when a dismissal is found to be unfair. They are reinstatement, re-employment, and compensation. Reinstatement is the primary remedy in the event of an unfair dismissal and is to be preferred over and above compensation. This position reflects the premium placed by the constitutional right to fair labor practices on security of employment. The primacy of this remedy also reflects the economic reality in South Africa where the number of jobs is finite. The primacy accorded this remedy underscores the fact that loss of employment has a profound influence on the dignity of employees and their families and on the dignity of society. Compensation is an appropriate remedy only if the employee does not wish to be reinstated or re-employed. If the circumstances surrounding the dismissal are of a nature that continuing the employment relationship would be intolerable, it is not practicable for the employer to reinstate or re-employ the employee. Similarly, compensation is the correct remedy if the dismissal is unfair only because the employer did not follow a fair procedure (section 193(2) of the LRA). When a court or tribunal decides that compensation should be awarded an infringement of a person's dignity should be a consideration in determining fair compensation in a given set of circumstances (Vettori 2012, p. 104).

In relation to dismissals for operational requirements or retrenchments, the judiciary has interpreted the relevant provisions largely to the detriment of the interests of employees resulting in a limitation on the protection available and negatively affecting the dignity of workers. From a substantive viewpoint, the courts, for example, have held that retrenchments may be affected not only to avoid financial ruin but also to increase profits (Fry's Metals (Pty) Ltd v. National Union of Metalworkers of SA 2003 24 ILJ 133 (LAC)); in doing so, the courts place commercial interests above the protection of the dignity of employees. From a procedural angle, too, the courts have lowered the protection afforded employees. Recently, the Constitutional Court held that there was no obligation on employers to consult with individual employees or minority unions during a retrenchment consultation processes (Association of Mineworkers and Construction v. Royal Bafokeng Platinum Limited 2020 3 SA 1 (CC)). This decision is profoundly negative in its general effect on the notion of dignity, particularly upon an aspect of dignity relating to a person's ability to set ends for him or herself.

Dismissal protection mostly has application to the situation of workers protected by an employment relationship. In order for protection against dismissal to be actively pursued, a claimant first has to demonstrate fulfilment of the conditions of being an employee as only employees may be dismissed (Grogan 2014, p. 164). Workers who are not included in the definition of "employee" are not afforded protection against unfair dismissal. Consequently, it is an essential requirement to qualify if a worker is to enjoy security of employment under current legislation; the dignity of employees is deemed more worthy of protection than that of workers outside the employment relationship.

9.5 Dignity and Social Protection

Security of employment is insufficient to offer real protection against the consequences of dismissal. Many other factors impact the security of employment of workers (Cheadle 2006, p. 668). For example, an enabling market economy which allows workers to find alternative employment quickly following the loss of employment and appropriate social protection mechanisms for the unemployed, also impact on security of employment. Social protection is an essential feature in the ILO's decent work agenda (Saith 2004, p. 1). The ILO (2017, p. 2) defines social protection as:

> the set of measures provided by society to protect its members from: (1) poverty and social exclusion, (2) the financial consequences of "life cycle risks" (ill health, sickness, disability, maternity, employment injury, unemployment, old age, or death of a family member) and (3) insufficient family support particularly for children and adult dependents.

Several constitutional provisions offer guarantees arising out of social protection. Section 27(1)(c) of the Constitution states: "[e]veryone has the right to have access to social security, including, if they are unable to support themselves and their dependents, appropriate social assistance." Section 27(2) requires that "[t]he state must take reasonable legislative and other measures, within its available resources, to achieve the progressive realization of each of these rights." Nyenti (2016, p. 202) described the purpose of this right to be a means enabling people to avoid destitution and affording them a way to meet basic needs upon stoppage or disruption of their income or their earning potential never developing. The Constitution further provides for rights to adequate housing (section 26) and health care, food and water (section 27).

Social protection mechanisms are a means of avoiding destitution and protect human beings against poverty and material insecurity. Put differently, these measures seek to advance the dignity of those who live under conditions of profound indignity; social protection measures support the rights of the vulnerable to live in dignity (Fourie and Van Staden 2022). In Khosa v. Minister of Social Development; Mahlaule v Minister of Social Development (2004 6 SA 505 (CC): para 76) the Constitutional Court held that the exclusion of permanent residents from the class of persons entitled to a variety of social security grants was unconstitutional:

> The exclusion of permanent residents in need of social-security programs forces them into relationships of dependency upon families, friends and the community in which they live, none of whom may have agreed to sponsor the immigration of such persons to South Africa. Apart from the undue burden that this places on those who take on this responsibility, it is likely to have a serious impact on the dignity of the permanent residents concerned who are cast in the role of supplicants.

Article 22 of the Universal Declaration of Human Rights establishes a connection between social protection and human dignity:

> Everyone, as a member of society, has the right to social security and is entitled to realization through national effort and international cooperation and in accordance with the organisation and resources of each State, of the economic, social and cultural rights indispensable for his dignity and the free development of his personality.

Art 23.3 of the Declaration states:

> Everyone who works has the right to just and favorable remuneration ensuring for himself and his family an existence worthy of human dignity, and supplemented, if necessary, by other means of social protection.

In respect of advancing these rights, the South African social security system protects workers from the following contingencies: employment injuries and diseases (the Occupational Diseases in Mines and Works Act 78 of 1973, the Occupational Health and Safety Act 85 of 1993, the Mine Health and Safety Act 29 of 1996 and the Compensation for Occupational Injuries and Diseases Act 130 of 1993), unemployment (the Unemployment Insurance Act 63 of 2001 and the Unemployment Insurance Contributions Act 4 of 2002), old age and retirement, and health. There is not a public insurance scheme in South Africa; however, section 10 of the Social Assistance Act 13 of 2004 provides for a means-tested old-age grant at the age of 60 years. Employees have an option to join a private retirement scheme, but there is not a statutory obligation on employers to grant it as a benefit. Most people employed in the informal economy or in an atypical employment relationship rely on the old-age grant rather than a private retirement scheme. The social protection measures primarily are employment-based with the effect they support the dignity only of those regarded as employees (Fourie and Van Staden 2022). Indirectly, the measures that exist have positive consequences for their families and communities and for society.

Additionally, there is legislation in South Africa to advance skills development and (re)training (such as the Skills Development Act 97 of 1998, the Skills Development Levies Act 9 of 1999, the Employment Services Act 4 of 2014 and the

Employment Tax Incentive Act 26 of 2013). The purpose of the Skills Development Act is to develop skills in the South African workforce in order to improve the quality of life of workers. The aim to develop skills also is a means elevate the unemployed and protect their dignity. A key goal in the social security mechanisms is the encouragement to seek employment among those who receive or apply for social security benefits. South Africa is regarded as having a skills shortage; thus, skills development measures are an effort to deliver the necessary skill set to enable workers to transition to a level of employment and gain the protection of the benefits that situation offers. The current approach in skills development successfully addresses poverty, inequality, and unemployment, and, therefore, contributes to enhance the dignity of persons; however, there is a need for explicit reference to specific target groups, particularly the youth who are unemployed, uneducated, and untrained, as well as other key marginalized groups such as the rural poor (Human Sciences Research Council 2017, p. 56).

9.6 Conclusion

There is a fundamental relationship between work and the aspiration to human dignity. The loss of employment, insufficient social protection in circumstances of unemployment and an inability to enter an employment relationship have severe consequences for a worker's sense of dignity and of respect by their families and society. Legislative and judicial responses to this circumstance have been adopted to assist in the transition to employment and the protections that situation provides as a means to further the five conceptions of human dignity expressed by the Constitutional Court and serve to highlight the interrelationship between work and human dignity. The five key conceptions of dignity adopted by the South African Constitutional Court (the individual as an end in him or herself, equal concern and equal respect, self-actualization, self-governance and collective responsibility for the material conditions for individual agency) require the extension of the basic protection afforded by law to all workers. Although, at present, the protections that safeguard the dignity of workers is afforded only those viewed as "employees."

The dignity of persons will be safeguarded only when judicial and legislative "policy" actively enlarge the category of workers protected as employees. Although the liberal interpretation by the judiciary of the term "employee" has broadened the scope of the protection that is available, there are cases where the courts have acted hesitantly. The judiciary has the power and a responsibility to accelerate the transformation of society through the advancement of dignity. The legislature has clarified the definition of "employee" and has prohibit or imposed strict conditions on certain types of employment relationship, but the measures introduced that permit government to designate categories of workers as "employees" are unpopular. The legislature has failed to deal directly by means of legislation with categories of vulnerable workers. The affirmative action measures designed to advance black participation in the economy have been ineffective in transforming the private sector.

The dignity of workers will be guaranteed only if there are measures which protect their status and are supported by social protection mechanisms to cover the loss of employment. Instances where the courts interpret key provisions relating to the protection of employment restrictively, negatively affect the notion of dignity. Limiting the application of protection has an undermining effect because it excludes some workers from benefitting from the protection reserved for those defined as employees and the problem is exacerbated as a result of inadequate access to social protection measures. The labor courts must take cognizance of the situation in which unfair dismissal is an affront to dignity. The value of dignity will gain support only if there are forms of protection following the loss of employment and workers are assisted to transition to the category in which they enjoy the privileges of the employed. The skills-development programs are aimed at addressing poverty, inequality and unemployment and thus assisting in the attainment of dignity but require a greater focus on the most vulnerable if they are to redress the plight of those who live under the most undignified of circumstances.

References

Ackerman L (2003) Equality under the 1996 South African Constitution. In: Wolfrum R (ed) Gleichheit und Nichtdiskriminierung im nationalen und internationalen Menschenrechtsschutz (Beiträge zum ausländischen öffentlichen Recht und Völkerrecht). Springer, Berlin, pp 105–117

Ackerman L (2004) The legal nature of the South African constitutional revolution. N Z Law Rev:33–64

Cheadle H (2006) Regulated flexibility: revisiting the LRA and the BCEA. Ind Labour J:663–703

Deakin S, Wilkinson F (2005) The law of the labour market: industrialization, employment and legal evolution. Oxford University Press, Oxford

Fourie E (2008) Non-standard workers: the South African context, international law and regulation by the European Union. Potchefstroom Elektroniese Regsblad:110–184

Fourie E, Van Staden M (2022) Labour market segmentation in Southern Africa and its impact on vulnerable workers. Int Labour Rev:555–571

Fry's Metals (Pty) Ltd v. National Union of Metalworkers of SA 2003 24 ILJ 133 (LAC)

Grogan J (2014) Workplace law. Juta, Cape Town

Hill TE (1980) Humanity as an end in itself. Ethics:84–99

Human Sciences Research Council (2017) Skills development legislation as a lever of change to reduce poverty, inequality and unemployment. Accessed 30 June 2023

ILO (2017) The ILO DW for SDGs notes series: social protection. International Institute for Labour Studies, Geneva

International Labour Organisation (2019) Employment security. https://www.ilo.org/global/topics/employment-security/lang%2D%2Den/index.htm. Accessed 30 June 2023

Kant I (1785) Groundwork of the metaphysics of morals (trans: Wood AW). Cambridge University Press, Cambridge

Kant I (1797) Metaphysics of morals (trans: Gregor M). Cambridge University Press, Cambridge

Le Roux R (2008) The regulation of work: whither the contract of employment? An analysis of the suitability of the contract of employment to regulate the different forms of labour market participation by individual workers. 2008 thesis University of Cape Town

Le Roux R (2014) Employment: a Dodo, or simply living dangerously? Ind Law J:30–46

Liebenberg S (2005) The value of human dignity in interpreting socio-economic rights. S Afr J Hum Rights:1–31
Nyenti MAT (2016) Role of constitutional principles and values in the development of social protection in South Africa. Glob Soc Policy:201–217
Saith A (2004) Social protection, decent work and development. International Institute for Labour Studies, Geneva
South African Human Rights Commission Annual Equality Report for the period 2017/2018. https://www.sahrc.org.za/home/21/files/SAHRC%20Equality%20Report%202017_18.pdf. Accessed 30 June 2023
Spaull N (2020) The jobs reckoning is here: 3-million jobs lost. https://www.businesslive.co.za/fm/features/cover-story/2020-07-15-the-jobs-reckoning-is-here/. Accessed 30 June 2023
Statistics South Africa (2020) Quarterly Labour Force Survey Quarter 1: 2020. http://www.statssa.gov.za/publications/P0211/P02111stQuarter2020.pdf. Accessed 30 June 2023
Vettori S (2012) The role of human dignity in the assessment of fair compensation for unfair dismissals. PER: Potchefstroomse Elektroniese Regsblad:101–124
Wiehahn Commission (1982) The Complete Wiehahn Report with Notes by Prof NE Wiehahn. Lex Patria, Pretoria
Woolman S (2014) Interpretation of the Bill of Rights. In: Woolman S, Roux T, Bishop M (eds) Constitutional law of South Africa. Juta, Cape Town, pp 1–75

Chapter 10
Same-Sex Marriage: The Structural Articulation of "Equal Dignity"

Connor M. Ewing

Abstract The United States Supreme Court's 2015 decision in *Obergefell v. Hodges*, establishing a constitutional right for same-sex couples to marry, was grounded in the "equal dignity" of gay and straight couples. This decision, in turn, built on and extended a jurisprudence developed principally in the earlier cases of *Lawrence v. Texas* (2003) and *United States v. Windsor* (2013). While human dignity is a central value in all three of these cases, in each of them the Court advanced a distinct conception of dignity: dignity as autonomy (*Lawrence*), variable dignity (*Windsor*), and democratic dignity (*Obergefell*). This chapter demonstrates how the pivotal move in this jurisprudential trajectory—the development of *Windsor*'s conception of variable dignity—was decisively shaped by the structure of the American regime. The federal structure, and the specific position of the Supreme Court therein, occasioned the development of an understanding of dignity rooted in the power of subnational governments to augment the dignity of their citizens. Even as variable dignity facilitated the expansion and ultimate constitutionalization of same-sex marriage rights, this variable conception was starkly different from how human dignity had traditionally been defined in American rights jurisprudence. Engaging human dignity at a threshold of American constitutional law, this chapter reveals the role of political structure in the evolution of dignity's meaning and significance.

10.1 Introduction

On April 28, 2015, the United States Supreme Court heard oral arguments in *Obergefell v. Hodges* and three consolidated cases. Though distinguished by everything ranging from geography to personal detail, the cases nonetheless presented the same legal questions. Did the U.S. Constitution afford same-sex couples the right to marry? If so, were states required to recognize those marriages? The petitioners urged the Court to answer "yes" to both questions; the respondents, "no." Two

C. M. Ewing (✉)
University of Toronto, Toronto, ON, Canada
e-mail: connor.m.ewing@gmail.com

S. N. Arel et al. (eds.), *Probing Human Dignity*,
https://doi.org/10.1007/978-3-031-42437-3_10

months later the Court would announce its decision, holding that same-sex couples had a constitutional right to marry and that states could not withhold legal recognition. As Justice Anthony Kennedy wrote in the closing lines of his majority opinion, the petitioners "ask for equal dignity in the eyes of the law. The Constitution grants them that right" (576 U.S. 681).

But on that April morning, the ultimate resolution of the case was still unknown, and attention turned to the advocates charged with presenting each side's arguments. Representing the petitioners were Mary Bonauto, a longtime civil rights lawyer, and Donald Verrilli, the Solicitor General of the United States. In her opening statement, Bonauto cast the case in terms that anticipated the Court's ultimate judgement. Drawing a connection between same-sex and heterosexual couples, she argued, "If a legal commitment, responsibility and protection that is marriage is off limits to gay people as a class, the stain of unworthiness that follows on individuals and families contravenes the basic constitutional commitment to equal dignity" (*Obergefell* Oral Argument Transcript 2015, p. 4). Verrilli was even more direct, beginning his statement as follows: "The opportunity to marry is integral to human dignity. Excluding gay and lesbian couples from marriage demeans the dignity of these couples" (*id.*, p. 28). At least as far as the petitioners were concerned, the question of the status of same-sex marriage under the Constitution was a question about human dignity.

If one looks backwards from *Obergefell* across earlier episodes of constitutional litigation, it becomes clear that dignity played an important role in the Supreme Court's decisions in the area of gay rights. Indeed, over the course of these cases, dignity emerged as a fundamental component—if not the essential ground—of the Court's gay rights jurisprudence. This jurisprudence was developed principally in the "gay-rights triptych" of *Lawrence v. Texas* (2003), *United States v. Windsor* (2013), and *Obergefell* (2015) (Tribe 2015, p. 22). In each of these cases, dignity was at the heart of the Court's decision. Crucially, though, these cases developed not one but three different conceptions of dignity: dignity as autonomy (*Lawrence*), variable dignity (*Windsor*), and democratic dignity (*Obergefell*). Despite the considerable attention devoted to these cases and the developments to which they contributed, this discontinuity has yet to be addressed, much less explained.

Dignity's role in gay rights jurisprudence is made all the more remarkable given the odd place of human dignity in American constitutional law. Even as dignity is routinely identified as a foundational commitment of constitutional government (*e.g.*, Murphy 2007, pp. 6–12), the term does not appear in the text of the U.-S. Constitution, distinguishing the American governing charter from the vast majority of national and international legal systems which explicitly invoke the concept of dignity. More to the point of the present inquiry, the historical and doctrinal lodestars of American rights jurisprudence are liberty and equality, not human dignity. And yet, dignity has been the touchstone of the Court's gay rights opinions. The decision in *Obergefell* thus represents the culmination of a process characterized by both continuity and discontinuity. Furthermore, the history of the relevant cases traces the emergence into American constitutional law of a value that is simultaneously foundational to legal protections for individual rights and equal standing yet skeptically greeted by even those who welcome the results. Accordingly, the three conceptions of dignity advanced by the Supreme Court illustrate the contingency of one of the most significant developments in American constitutional law, a contingency that has yet to be satisfactorily evaluated.

In what follows, I sketch the contours of these three conceptions of human dignity and demonstrate how the judicial articulation of "equal dignity" was decisively shaped by the structure of the American constitutional order. I term this process the "structural articulation" of the Court's equal dignity jurisprudence. The American Supreme Court's role in the federal system, specifically its review of state actions in the areas of substantive due process and equal protection, occasioned the elaboration of a conception of dignity predicated on subnational governments' ability to augment the dignity of their citizens. While this understanding broke sharply from dignity's traditional meaning in American constitutionalism, as expressed in *Lawrence v. Texas,* it nonetheless served as the basis for the constitutionalization of same-sex marriage rights in *Obergefell.*

The following analysis proceeds in two principal steps. The first section begins by presenting a brief account of the construction and development of the jurisprudence of "equal dignity." Whereas previous scholarship has documented the continuities evident in this jurisprudence (Tribe 2015; Ewing 2018; *Harvard Law Review* 2019), I highlight in this section the underlying discontinuities by providing a theoretical categorization of the different conceptions of human dignity advanced by the Court. Beginning with *Lawrence* and proceeding through *Windsor* to *Obergefell*, I document the emergence of "equal dignity" and identify three discrete conceptions of dignity at play in these cases: dignity as autonomy (*Lawrence*), variable dignity (*Windsor*), and democratic dignity (*Obergefell*). With these three conceptions as context, I turn in the next section to a closer examination of variable dignity, the conception at the center of the Court's holding in *Windsor*. The understanding of dignity advanced in *Windsor*, along with the decision it supports, serves as a link between *Lawrence* and *Obergefell*. For this reason it is a crucial step in the development of the jurisprudence of "equal dignity." In order to clarify the meaning and significance of dignity as it figures in Windsor, I engage critically with a prominent interpretation of the Court's opinion, namely that dignity, as it is used in that case, is best understood as a right of recognition. I argue instead that because of the underlying legal and political dynamics the Court engaged not in first-order but second-order recognition, a distinction that renders the characterization of Windsor's dignity as a right of recognition inaccurate. Moreover, the distinction between first- and second-order recognition highlights the ways in which political structure, specifically the structure of the American federal system, shaped the articulation of dignity in *Windsor* and, as a result, the broader jurisprudence of "equal dignity."

In the fields of law and political science, it is common, as a matter of both analysis and pedagogy, to distinguish between two fundamental aspects of the U.-S. Constitution: structure and rights. Courses in constitutional law proceed along these lines, while academic treatments of one rarely stray into the other. Only infrequently is the connection between political structure and rights jurisprudence the focus of scholarly inquiry (but see, *e.g.*, Katz and Tarr 1996). The relatively few accounts that do acknowledge a relationship between federalism and rights stop short of examining if and how political structure influences the substantive content or development of rights jurisprudence. Many instead consider the ways in which federalism either enhances or imperils individual rights (Riker 1964, 1975; Elazar 1987; Watts 1999; Epstein 1992; Buchanan 1995). Others have examined the relationship between federalism and civil rights, documenting how the federal system imposed obstacles to the realization of equal protection before the law (Klarman 2004, pp. 23 and 98–170). In a similar vein, scholars have observed that the expansion of formal racial equality entailed the "pruning back [of] federalism" (Michelman 1993, p. 303).

At their most optimistic and probing, these studies ascribe an iterative relationship to constitutional rights and constitutional structure, concluding that "rights and structure are like two interlocking gears, moving the grand project of constitutional integration forward" (Gerken 2015, p. 588). [1] Similarly, other observers have noted the strategic opportunities presented by federalism: by offering multiple fora, federal structures furnish a range of opportunities—legislative, legal, and political—for advancing rights claims (Knauer 2018). But the connection is much more fundamental and, indeed, consequential than this. The structure of the American regime not only occasions jurisprudential development through the generation of legal conflict and the provision of multiple fora where those conflicts can play out. It also directly shapes the content of that jurisprudence. In this way, the Court's jurisprudence is articulated not just conceptually but also structurally, with the institutional arrangement of the constitutional order conditioning the substantive elaboration of legal doctrine. At its most basic, that is the central argument of this chapter.

10.2 "Equal Dignity"

Continuity is an exalted virtue—though perhaps at times also a conceit—of constitutional jurisprudence. As such, Court opinions on constitutional questions frequently evince an effort to tightly stitch a decision's arguments into the tapestry of precedent so the conclusions offered appear to follow seamlessly from what has come before. The holding of the case at hand thus seems to follow as a natural, if not necessary, implication of previous caselaw. It should not be surprising, then, that one

[1] Despite the shortcomings noted here, the approach to federalism ushered in by Gerken—"-federalism as the new nationalism" (2014)—contains within it the seeds of precisely the kind of focus I am urging. Though they have to this point largely treated subnational governments principally as fora for political contestation and representation, works in this vein underscore the ways in which federal systems not only facilitate but can also structure jurisprudential developments (e.g., Bulman-Pozen and Gerken 2009; Gerken 2010). In short, the "New Nationalist" project does not preclude what I fault them for here; in this respect, it has not yet made good on its full potential.

account of the jurisprudence of "equal dignity" stresses its continuity with prior decisions. Indeed, this is the account that the Court itself attempts to establish in *Obergefell*. Writing for the majority, Justice Kennedy grounds the dignity interest of the plaintiffs in the foundation recognized in and established by, among other cases, *Lawrence v. Texas* and *United States v. Windsor*. Even observers attentive to the use of dignity in constitutional jurisprudence have largely bought into this narrative of continuity, opting either to criticize *any* use of dignity in constitutional jurisprudence or to assimilate the new wine of dignity jurisprudence to the old wineskins of substantive due process and equal protection doctrine (Yoshino 2011, 2015).

Upon closer examination, though, it becomes clear that across these cases the value at the heart of the jurisprudence of "equal dignity" underwent significant development. Indeed, "equal dignity" as it emerges from *Obergefell* rests on an assemblage of cases that present discrete and divergent conceptions of human dignity and its place in the American constitutional tradition. Though later usage draws on and even bears a residue of earlier usage, each case presents an independent understanding, one that not only stands on its own but also stands in varying degrees of contrast with the other conceptions employed.

To be clear, I am not arguing that dignity jurisprudence was an innovation of the gay rights cases that culminated in *Obergefell*. There is a long and well documented tradition of dignitary reasoning by the Supreme Court. As numerous scholars have observed, the absence of "dignity" from the American constitutional text has done little to prevent its appearance in constitutional jurisprudence (Henry 2011; Goodman 2006; Resnik and Suk 2003; Barak 2015, pp. 185–208). Moreover, considerable attention has already been paid to the use of dignity in the cases on which I focus (Tribe 2003, 2015; Yoshino 2015; Finck 2016, pp. 32–37).[2] But viewing this tradition as the coherent elaboration or univocal development of the underlying value of human dignity, as has too often been the case, conceals significant and consequential discontinuities. Discernible in the jurisprudence of "equal dignity" are three conceptions of dignity, each corresponding to a different case: dignity as autonomy (*Lawrence*), variable dignity (*Windsor*), and democratic dignity (*Obergefell*). Accordingly, the jurisprudence of "equal dignity" is marked by both consistency and departure, continuity and discontinuity.

---

[2]Like invocations of dignity in other areas of constitutional and human rights law, the Supreme Court's dignity jurisprudence has come under intense criticism. While much of the resulting literature draws from a familiar set of critiques (see, *e.g.*, Weinrib 2018), two recent works offer particularly illuminating critical assessments of the Supreme Court's use of dignity in and beyond the domain of gay rights. The first is Engel and Lyle's *Disputing Dignity*, in which they argue that dignity, as deployed by the Supreme Court in *Obergefell*, functions not only as an instrument of power but one that furthers both neoliberal and heteronormative aims (2021; see also Engel 2018). The second is a recent article by Moore and Rodman (2022) that construes the Court's use of dignity as defining a right to recognition. This recognition, they argue, "centers state recognition as the solution to discrimination, inequality, and unfreedom" and, in so doing, "elides harms that originate with the state, positions state power as innocent, and may exacerbate injustices of marginalization" (*id.*, 699). Despite their differences, both of these works take seriously the broader political projects to which the jurisprudence of dignity has—intentionally or not—contributed.

For our purposes, we can begin with *Lawrence v. Texas*, a case in which the Court held that a state law prohibiting sodomy unconstitutionally infringed the Fourteenth Amendment's due process guarantee. This decision not only directly conflicted with but explicitly and in no uncertain terms rejected the Court's decision just seventeen years earlier in *Bowers v. Hardwick* (1986). In the course of clarifying the liberty interest at stake in the case, Justice Kennedy reached back to *Bowers*, quoting from Justice Stevens's dissenting opinion. There, Stevens had grounded the relevant due process liberty interests in what the Court recognized as privacy but what he thought was better expressed by human dignity, a value intimately connected to individual choice. Quoting from an opinion he had written in 1975 while on the Seventh Circuit, Stevens wrote:

> Guided by history, our tradition of respect for the dignity of individual choice in matters of conscience and the restraints implicit in the federal system, federal judges have accepted the responsibility for the recognition and protection of these rights in appropriate cases (523 F.2d at 720; emphasis added).

Kennedy's *Lawrence* opinion elevated this connection between dignity and autonomy to the majority opinion. The resulting conception of dignity emphasized the individual's decisional freedom and capacity for self-determination in specific spheres, both of which were given greater jurisprudential significance by Kennedy's opinion in a case decided between *Bowers* and *Lawrence*. In *Planned Parenthood v. Casey* (1992), Kennedy had elaborated the relationship between dignity and autonomy, stating that "choices central to personal dignity and autonomy, are central to the liberty protected by the Fourteenth Amendment" (505 U.S. at 851). These choices, which he called "the most intimate and personal choices a person may make in a lifetime," included those "relating to marriage, procreation, contraception, family relationships, child rearing, and education" (*ibid.*). Thus, in *Lawrence* Texas's sodomy prohibition infringed constitutionally protected liberties because it encroached on the inviolable sphere of individual decisions, a sphere simultaneously necessitated and constituted by the dignity that inhered in each individual.

Ten years after *Lawrence* was handed down the next significant gay rights case came before the Supreme Court. *United States v. Windsor* presented a challenge to Section 3 of the Defense of Marriage Act (DOMA), which defined "marriage" and "spouse" in exclusively heterosexual terms for the purposes of federal law. The opinion of a closely divided (5-4) Court was again delivered by Justice Kennedy. At a surface level, this opinion is striking for the sheer emphasis on dignity. While "equality" or "inequality" appears seven times in the opinion and "liberty" just five, some form of "dignity" appears ten times—a remarkable fact when one considers that the case was decided on due process grounds, while also addressing the equal protection dimensions of the questions presented.

But something even more striking and consequential lies beneath this linguistic surface phenomenon, in the substance of the reasoning about human dignity. The majority opinion in *Windsor* departed almost entirely from the conception of dignity as autonomy laid out in *Lawrence*. This break was signaled very early in the opinion, when Kennedy wrote that it was only just beginning to dawn on many people "that two persons of the same sex might aspire to occupy the same status and dignity as that of a man and woman in lawful marriage" (570 U.S. at 763). The language of aspiring to occupy a place, condition, or status of dignity is quite different from the picture of dignity presented in *Lawrence*, which was inherent in and thus (in some sense) possessed by the individual. Had the Court adhered to the logic of the conception of dignity advanced in *Lawrence*, it might have observed that it was only a recent revelation that two persons of the same sex *have* or *possess* the same dignity as two persons of the opposite sex who are joined in marriage. This movement away from inherence in *Windsor* presents a set of complicated questions. If dignity is not inherent in individuals, whence does it come? Who or what can fulfill one's aspiration "to occupy the same. . .dignity" as one's peers? And finally, is dignity indivisible, or does it permit of variation?

Kennedy answers each of these questions over the course of his opinion and in the process lays out a conception of dignity that, because of its susceptibility to bestowal and augmentation, I term *variable dignity*. At the heart of this understanding is the role of the state, which he identifies as the entity empowered to grant or confer dignity. The dignity interest at stake in the case was constituted by New York's decisions to recognize same-sex marriages performed out-of-state and, ultimately, to authorize same-sex marriages within the state. As regards the affected individuals and couples, these decisions "*conferred* upon them a dignity and status of immense import" and, as a result, "*enhanced* the recognition, dignity, and protection of the class in their own community" (*id.* at 746 and 768; emphasis added). We see in this description two ways in which dignity is variable. First, it can be given by the state to individuals who, presumably, suffer from a deficit or shortage relative to others. Hence, dignity can vary across individuals within a jurisdiction, with some enjoying its benefits or advantages while others do not. Second, according to the logic of the majority opinion, dignity can be incrementally adjusted, such that individuals can have their dignity "enhanced" or similarly modified. Importantly, as is illustrated by *Windsor*, the state governments possess this power of enhancement and modification. This second feature of *Windsor*'s presentation of dignity highlights why one must say that *Lawrence*'s notion of dignity as autonomy is almost entirely absent from *Windsor*. Nowhere in the *Windsor* majority opinion does Kennedy suggest that any individuals are wholly without dignity. In fact, though it is not entirely clear, he can be read to argue that state action modifying individuals' dignity occurs alongside and in addition to their preexisting—though perhaps not fully recognized—inherent dignity.[3]

But there is considerable ambiguity on this point, and for good reason. The *Windsor* Court did not forthrightly acknowledge a latent and unrecognized dignity

[3]I say that it is not entirely clear because Kennedy's formulations of the dignity interest implicated by the case can be read in multiple ways. To take one characteristic example, he says the following of same-sex relationships: ". . .New York sought to give further protection and dignity to that bond." While this could be read to say that New York gave "further. . .dignity to that bond" is could also be read to say that the state "sought to give. . .dignity to that bond." Whereas the former acknowledges some underlying or extant dignity interest, the second does not (though it also does not preclude it).

interest in same-sex couples or gay individuals. Nor even did the Court indicate that New York had acknowledged such an interest. Rather, in giving effect to New York's actions, the *Windsor* majority constructed a new conception of dignity, one that involves the state granting and enhancing the dignity interests possessed by individuals and borne by the relationships they enter. Recognizing a latent interest would have been nearly untenable, as it would have presented an unavoidable question: If gay individuals and same-sex couples in New York possessed a dignity interest independent of state action, why not elsewhere? If the dignity in question was inherent, it would extend far beyond state boundaries. And if that was the case, what basis would there be for limiting its possession or enjoyment to the individuals of one jurisdiction?

A case from the same term that the Court declined to decide on the merits further illustrates the questions left unresolved by *Windsor*. *Hollingsworth v. Perry* presented a challenge to California's Proposition 8, a state ballot initiative that banned same-sex marriage in reaction to a state court decision that struck down a statute forbidding the recognition of such unions. The case came to the Supreme Court after a district court held and circuit court affirmed that Proposition 8 violated the equal protection and due process clauses of the Fourteenth Amendment. A bare majority of the Supreme Court rejected the challenge on the grounds that the petitioners, the initiative's official advocates who had intervened when the state demurred from continuing to defend Proposition 8, lacked standing to sue.

The author of the dissenting opinion was none other than Justice Kennedy, who wrote that "[t]he essence of democracy is that the right to make law rests in the people and flows to the government, not the other way around" (570 U.S. at 727). The initiative's supporters were thus entitled to their day in court. But had Kennedy's side prevailed, he would have faced the question of how to reconcile democratic processes that in one state legalized, and in another state forbade, same-sex marriage. Could state-level democracy enhance the dignity of same-sex couples in New York but refuse to do so—even actively rescind the dignity of official recognition and legal benefits—in California? Could the people of California retract through ballot initiative the dignity that had been conferred through decisions of that state's courts, or was dignity a one-way ratchet? Perhaps the chief expositor of the jurisprudence of "equal dignity" had in mind answers to these questions that would further clarify the conception of variable dignity advanced in *Windsor*. But Kennedy's opportunity to engage such questions would have to wait until a later date. In this respect, then, it is an open question whether the majority opinion in *Windsor* is most fundamentally an argument about the nature of constitutional politics or about the meaning of human dignity in American constitutional law.

We will have occasion to return to these questions shortly. For now, the important point is the distinction between *Lawrence*'s dignity as autonomy and *Windsor*'s variable dignity. Whereas in *Lawrence* the Court recognized a constitutionally cognizable dignity interest possessed by and thus guaranteed to all individuals, in *Windsor* it recognized the consequences of a state's efforts to equalize the dignity enjoyed by those within its jurisdiction. This contrast highlights the salience of equality in *Windsor*, as well as the connection between equality and dignity.

New York's actions were oriented towards, in effect, elevating those who enjoyed less dignity to the level of those who enjoyed more. This involved granting and enhancing the dignity of the former group. "This status," Kennedy wrote of the consequence of New York's protections for same-sex relationships, "is a far-reaching legal acknowledgement of the intimate relationship between two people, a relationship deemed by the State worthy of dignity in the community equal with all other marriages" (570 U.S. at 769). In *Windsor*, the equality-regarding dimensions of dignity were elaborated and moved to the constitutional foreground. In stark contrast with *Lawrence*, dignity in *Windsor* was understood to be susceptible to augmentation by the state in order that discrepancies between individuals and relationships could be redressed. However, the application of this conception of dignity was limited by the jurisdictional boundaries implicit in the logic of variable dignity and the democratic politics on which it was predicated. For this reason, the conceptual development of dignity from *Lawrence* to *Windsor* is central to the jurisprudence of "equal dignity."

Windsor, of course, was not the last word. In fact, soon after the decision's announcement, the case came to be seen as an intermediate step on the way to another, likely more expansive, decision (Marcus 2014). The next fall the Court denied cert in a host of cases challenging rulings by lower courts permitting (or requiring) the recognition of same-sex marriage, thus allowing those decisions to stand. This created the conditions for *Obergefell v. Hodges*, the consolidated action that directly presented the question of the constitutionality of prohibitions on same-sex marriage. Again, Justice Kennedy wrote for the majority. And again, dignity was a—arguably the—central value. By a 5-4 majority the Court held that prohibiting same-sex marriage violated the Fourteenth Amendment and, as a result, that all states were bound to recognize such marriages.[4]

The principal argument of the decision is aptly summarized in the concluding passage of the majority opinion, a passage that reveals how much the Court's jurisprudence had changed since *Lawrence*. Of the petitioners and those whom they represented, Kennedy wrote, "They ask for equal dignity in the eyes of the law. The Constitution grants them that right" (576 U.S. at 681). For the Court, "equal dignity" compelled the identification of a constitutionally protected right to same-sex marriage. But this "equal dignity" is not identical with what carried the same label in *Windsor*; nor is it wholly consistent with the Court's understanding of dignity in *Lawrence*. Rather, it is an attempted fusion of the conceptions laid out in *Lawrence* and *Windsor*, one that because of its emphasis on dignity's liberty- and equality-regarding dimensions can be termed *democratic dignity*.

[4]While the discussion that follows focuses on Kennedy's opinion for the majority in *Obergefell*, it is important to acknowledge that Clarence Thomas' dissent marked the first time in the Court's history that justices openly disagreed about the definition of dignity. The different conceptions advanced by Kennedy and Thomas, and the broader constitutional theories that those conceptions support, underscore "how dignity has served as an extra-textual value that informs the interpretation of the Constitution's text and history" (Ewing forthcoming).

Democratic dignity, as set out in *Obergefell*, combines the constitutional centrality of decisional autonomy and self-determination, on the one hand, with the legal and political commitments to equality, on the other. This understanding parallels those offered by constitutional scholars like Walter Murphy:

> Democratic theory is based on a notion of human dignity: as beings worthy of respect because of their very nature, adults must enjoy a large degree of autonomy, a status principally attainable in the modern world by being able to share in the governance of their community (1993, p. 3).

While Murphy's definition is oriented towards political participation, the majority's argument in *Obergefell* stressed the broader social dimensions of equal political standing. Autonomous decisions implicate one's standing as a citizen of a socio-political world structured, in part, by government regulation and recognition (Engel 2016, pp. 683–684). The ability "to share in the governance of [one's] community" requires the ability to confront members of that community as an equal in the capacities collectively deemed important and worthy of recognition. The dignity of individuals and their relationships was not subject to the whims of political majorities, the *Obergefell* opinion argued; that dignity was borne by those individuals and, in the context of marriage, the unions they entered. Nonetheless, this dignity interest was realized in a socio-political and socio-legal context, relative to other individuals and the entitlements they could claim. One's dignity was thus assessed and made meaningful by comparison with similarly situated persons and relationships.

The majority opinion in *Obergefell* can be understood as an attempt to show that—without explicitly acknowledging their differences—the conceptions of dignity set forth in *Lawrence* and *Windsor* are, in fact, two sides of the same coin. While such an interpretation entails reintroducing the inherence that characterized *Lawrence*'s treatment of dignity, it also requires a significant departure from the variability that was at the heart of *Windsor*'s treatment. For the very reasons (discussed above) why *Windsor* did not forthrightly recognize a latent dignity interest of gay individuals and couples, *Obergefell* could not ground that interest in the actions of states. Instead, the majority opinion located the dignity interest at stake in a foundation beyond the reach of individual states, vesting it in individuals themselves and their relationships. What enabled this shift (at least in part) is that in the intervening period between *Windsor* and *Obergefell* the community of reference had expanded. Through political action and lower court decisions, the jurisdictional sphere in which gay couples enjoyed the dignity of legal marriage had increased dramatically, to the point that by the time oral arguments in *Obergefell* were heard same-sex marriage was an on-the-ground legal reality in twenty-four states and multiple federal districts (Haddad 2016, pp. 1502–1507).

The conception of dignity presented in *Obergefell* reflected these changes. The dignity interest that was in *Windsor* conferred upon same-sex relationships now inhered in those relationships and, more fundamentally, in the individuals that composed them. Following *Windsor*'s logic, because the discrepancies in dignity were not limited to an individual state but instead cut across their boundaries, the questions presented in *Obergefell* were national in scope, implicating all individuals.

As a result, there is no mention whatsoever of the state's role in enhancing, much less conferring, dignity. After all, recognizing the power of states to control the dignity interests of their citizens would risk undermining the very interest for which the majority sought a firm constitutional foundation. Thus, just as *Windsor* departed from the conception of inherent dignity advanced in *Lawrence* in favor of a conception more conformable to the dynamics of the case, *Obergefell* departed from the variable conception of dignity advanced in *Windsor* for the sake of a conception that was more responsive to the logic of the legal questions presented.[5]

This final step in the conceptual development of dignity reveals why *Windsor* is the lynchpin of the jurisprudence of "equal dignity," providing the bridge between the inherent dignity of decisional autonomy, on the one hand, and the dignity of all marital relationships and the individuals included in them, on the other. By bringing together *Lawrence*'s dignity as autonomy and the consequences of *Windsor*'s variable dignity, the *Obergefell* Court set "equal dignity" on the constitutional foundation of liberties protected by the guarantee of due process. This, taken in conjunction with the formulation of the term itself, demonstrates that "equal dignity" is not merely a composite of equality and dignity but rather the doctrinal representation of a dynamic relationship among liberty, equality, and dignity (Ewing 2018). This relationship was constructed across the central gay rights cases and, more importantly, through the three conceptions of dignity identified along the way. The crucial steps in this development were first a movement away from and then a return to the inherence of dignity occasioned by the recognition of the dignity-regarding consequences of state action. The turning point, in other words, was *Windsor*'s identification of variable dignity.

10.3 Structural Articulation

That there are multiple conceptions of dignity underlying the jurisprudence of "equal dignity" is just one part of the story. The diversity of usage across the central cases raises a further question: Why did these modulations occur? What, in other words, accounts for the significant changes in the meaning of the key term in these cases? After all, much of the criticism of dignity jurisprudence follows from the observation that dignity has been used so many different ways. How, this criticism runs, can one

[5]This aspect of the *Obergefell* decision is all the more remarkable given Justice Kennedy's emphasis on (what I call) variable dignity at oral argument. In his questioning of the respondent's counsel, John Bursch, Kennedy pointedly objected to the argument that marriage was not "dignitary [*sic*] bestowing" (*Obergefell* Oral Argument Transcript, 71). To this Kennedy interjected, "I don't understand [how] this is not dignity bestowing. I thought that was the whole purpose of marriage. It bestows dignity on both man and woman in a traditional marriage" (*id.*, 72). As we see in this passage, though, the role of the state in conferring this dignity has receded in favor of an emphasis on the institution of marriage itself. As I argue here, this was at once a principal consequence of *Windsor* and an imperative for the *Obergefell* majority.

speak of dignity in a legally cognizable and enforceable way when it can mean seemingly anything? If dignity can mean anything, it means nothing at all. Surely the variety in usage from *Lawrence* to *Obergefell* does little to counter this line of attack. One plausible explanation is aimed at rebutting this criticism directly. The various conceptions of dignity at play in the gay rights cases and, indeed, in dignitary jurisprudence well beyond the United States, represent efforts to instantiate a "mother right" or framework right, one that entails a range of legal protections and guarantees (Barak 2015, pp. 156–169). What may appear to be ambiguity or abstraction, this defense would insist, is really an indication of dignity's robustness and fundamental legal importance.

While there is much to recommend this explanation, it is ultimately incomplete, especially in the context of the jurisprudence of "equal dignity." Left unaccounted for by this argument is, most pressingly, why the conceptions of dignity identified in the previous section appeared when they did. Put differently, conceptual breadth or complexity explains only that multiple usages may arise. It does not explain why they arise when they do. Those matters can be clarified, at least in part, by taking account of the political and institutional context of the Court's decisions. More specifically, the structure of the federal system conditioned the conceptual development of dignity and, as a result, the broader development of the jurisprudence of "equal dignity."[6] To begin understanding the structural dimensions of the jurisprudence of "equal dignity," we can look to one of the most sophisticated, yet ultimately flawed, efforts to understand the role of dignity in American constitutional jurisprudence. I refer here to the argument that the Court's dignity jurisprudence established a "right of recognition," which was presented most forcefully by then-law professor and current federal judge Neomi Rao in her critical response to the decision in *Windsor*. Rao's account is a particularly useful contrast to the argument I will advance here because, while we come to different conclusions about the nature of the dignity interests identified by the Court, her analysis helps isolate a number of important dynamics underlying the jurisprudence of "equal dignity."[7]

---

[6]Though it is not addressed in the analysis that follows, it is nonetheless necessary to note the robust body of state dignitary jurisprudence that preceded and fed into changes at the national level. See, for example, *Goodridge v. Department of Public Health* (798 N.E.2d 941, Mass. 2003), *In re Marriage Cases* (43 Cal. 4th 757, 2008), and *Kerrigan v. Commissioner of Public Health* (957 A.2d 407, Conn. 2008). These cases are omitted in order to focus on the discursive development of "equal dignity" within federal constitutional law, which though related to developments in state law nonetheless depended on a different set of institutional and legal dynamics. More importantly, the evolution of dignity's meaning was instrumental to the emergence of a national constitutional right to same-sex marriage. The developments underlying this emergence occurred not in state courts but in the briefs, arguments, and opinions of the Supreme Court.

[7]Although the following analysis focuses on the conception of dignity presented in *Windsor*, my larger argument about the relationship between political institutions and political discourse should lead us to inquire into the structural dimensions of *each* conception of dignity present in the jurisprudence of "equal dignity." However, the justification for the focus on variable dignity rests on (1) the significance of that conception in the jurisprudential developments to which it contributed and (2) the distinctiveness of that conception relative to the American constitutional tradition.

Writing shortly after *Windsor* was decided, Rao argued that Kennedy's use of dignity there was "dignity as recognition" (2013), one of the three concepts of dignity she identified in an earlier piece as operative in constitutional law (Rao 2011; see also Rao 2008). Briefly identifying inherent dignity and substantive dignity clarifies what Rao means by dignity as recognition. Inherent dignity "focuses on the inherent worth of each individual…such dignity inheres in all individuals without appraisal by any other standard" (Rao 2011, p. 187). In American constitutional law, as illustrated by the discussion of *Lawrence* in the previous section, "intrinsic dignity is reflected in decisions about freedom from interference by the state in areas such as freedom of speech, privacy, and sexual relationships. This dignity encompasses the liberal notion of negative freedom—of creating a space for individual choice" (*ibid.*). Substantive dignity, on the other hand, "embodies a particular view of what constitutes the good life for man, what makes human life flourish for the individual as well as the community" (*ibid.*). This notion of dignity requires particular ways or standards of living. Whereas inherent dignity corresponds to negative freedoms, substantive dignity corresponds to positive freedoms, including (but not limited to) government provided social services like education and housing. Unlike inherent dignity, substantive dignity has not found much traction in American law, though it is arguably the dominant conception in the global constitutional context (Rosen 2008, p. 28; Kretzmer and Klein 2002).

Finally, in contrast to both of these notions, for Rao, dignity as recognition "requires esteem and respect for the particularity of each individual…It creates a political demand for the state and other individuals to accept and approve of one's lifestyle and personal choices" (Rao 2011, p. 243). Here Rao relies on Charles Taylor's explication of the "politics of difference," arguing that according to dignity as recognition, human dignity must be realized only through the acts of the state which in their acknowledgement and validation of differences aid the social construction of group identity (*id.* at 243–244; Taylor 1994). Though Rao's initial taxonomy predated the decision in *Windsor*, the striking down of DOMA's Section 3 occasioned a return to her three concepts of dignity. The title of that piece, "The Trouble with Dignity and Rights of Recognition," captures much of the flavor of her argument. *Windsor*, she argued, introduced into American law a new form of dignity predicated on a right to government recognition. Of the decision she wrote, "Dignitary themes of inclusion and recognition are at the heart of Justice Anthony Kennedy's opinion for the Court. Commentators, however, have failed to appreciate the extent to which the Court's use of dignity identifies a novel constitutional right to recognition unconnected to any substantive right" (2013, p. 30). As this quotation hints, the "trouble" with the right of recognition announced in *Windsor* is that it is not grounded in any substantive individual right, unlike other dignity claims in American constitutional law. Had the Court held that there was a right to same-sex marriage, she maintained, then there would be a clear right from which a dignity claim could derive. But *Windsor* did not go that far. Despite its ruling striking down the exclusion of same-sex couples from federal marriage benefits, the Court stopped short of identifying a right to marriage for those same-sex couples. Thus, on Rao's argument, no basis existed for a judicially cognizable dignity claim.

There is much truth in this conceptualization of dignity and its various manifestations in constitutional law. At least on the surface, conceiving of dignity in *Windsor* as a right of recognition seems to make sense of what the Court did. It quite literally recognized the claim of a same-sex couple's surviving member, acknowledging the value of and respect due that intimate relationship as regards federal law. Rao's argument also captures the liberty interest at play in *Lawrence* through its identification of dignity's connection to autonomy and choice free from government coercion. In the end, though, understanding the evolution of dignity from *Lawrence* to *Windsor* (and beyond) as the arrival of a new right of recognition obscures more than it illuminates. Rao's tripartite typology ignores subtle though consequential differences between *Windsor*'s dignity and traditional rights of recognition. Those differences, in turn, identify the decisive role played by the structure of the federal system in the articulation of the jurisprudence of "equal dignity."

To begin, Rao's notion of dignity as recognition drastically simplifies what was going on in *Windsor*. Only at a very abstract level can one say that Edith Windsor was seeking the Court's recognition of her or her relationship's dignity. To do so would require ignoring the social and legal context out of which her claim emerged, the very context which endowed her relationship with the dignity that Kennedy acknowledged in the majority opinion. And even if we grant that Windsor sought the Court's recognition, strictly speaking that is not what the Court in fact did. To respond to both of these points we need only understand that what the Court recognized was the dignity interest that *New York* had "extended" to Edith Windsor, her spouse Thea Spyer, and all other same-sex couples under its jurisdiction through its official actions—the first being an executive order mandating the recognition of same-sex marriages from other jurisdictions, and the second the legalization of same-sex marriage. Thus, what *Windsor* presents is not a right to recognition but *the recognition of a right to recognition*, a difference rooted in the structure of the federal system and the place of the Supreme Court therein.

In his opinion, Kennedy put great stock in the ways New York's actions had changed the status of same-sex couples and, buttressed by an analysis of the states' traditional role in defining and regulating the marital relationship, he presented an argument for why the effects of those actions—extending and enhancing dignity—must be preserved. Indeed, the vast majority of references made to dignity in the opinion come in the context of the state's actions (570 U.S. at 746, 768–769, and 775). The most compelling such use draws a clear causal connection between the actions of the State of New York and the dignity at stake in *Windsor*: "The history of DOMA's enactment and its own text demonstrate that interference with the equal dignity of same-sex marriages, a dignity conferred by the States in the exercise of their sovereign power, was more than an incidental effect of the federal statute. It was its essence" (*id.* at 770). In so far as recognition played a role in the Court's reasoning, it was the federal recognition of a dignity interest that was, in the first instance, recognized, extended, and enhanced by a state.

Thus, it is more accurate to think of the Court as engaging in second-order reasoning about dignity than establishing a right to recognition.[8] Rather than engaging a claim for recognition head-on, as it would have in the case of a traditional right of recognition, the majority opinion addressed separate questions concerning the origins and significance of dignity claims in the American federal system. An answer could be given to the case's primary question regarding DOMA's exclusion of same-sex couples only after those separate questions were resolved. Indeed, if *Windsor* truly presented a right of recognition, one wonders why a federalism analysis was necessary at all. Surely such an analysis would not have persuaded any other members of the Court to join the majority opinion, as those to whom the arguments would presumably appeal not only ended up on the other side but even criticized the notion that the decision was about federalism principles. As Justice Scalia wrote in dissent, the majority opinion's "seven full pages about the traditional power of States to define domestic relations" likely had the effect of "fooling many readers, I am sure, into thinking that this is a federalism opinion" (*id.* at 791). It is clear from the dynamics underlying the decision and the political structures in which those dynamics were rooted that *Windsor* did not protect dignity by establishing a right of recognition but rather by recognizing the actions taken by a state to vest its citizens with a dignitary interest.[9] Those actions, moreover, were incorporated into the Court's articulation of the dignity interests of same-sex couples, producing a conception of dignity that hinged on the state's capacity and decision to confer dignity on its citizens. In this way, the position of the Supreme Court as both adjudicator and observer of subnational actions constituted variable dignity.

What was absent in *Windsor*, however, was present in *Obergefell*, and Kennedy's opinions in the two cases make that clear. As the previous section demonstrated, in *Obergefell* the majority's emphasis shifted from the dignity conferred by the states to the dignity of individuals and relationships. But the reasoning in *Obergefell* depended on dignity as it was employed in *Windsor* to the extent that the dignity of marriage was made manifest by and in the unions recognized by that decision and the subsequent political developments it occasioned. The dignity of marriage, Kennedy seems to suggest in *Obergefell*, inhered in its actualization—the dignity interest crystallized when marriages were actually entered into—and that necessitated state sanction, which *Windsor* acknowledged. By the time *Obergefell* came around, the Court could point directly to the dignity of marriage—gay and straight—

[8]On this point I follow David O. Brink's distinction between first-order and second-order principles. Whereas the former are "legal rules" that are "typically. . .the result of authoritative enactments," the latter "play an essential role in the interpretation of first order legal standards" (1988, pp. 109 and 125).

[9]Another way of stating the critique presented in this section is as follows: To hold that *Windsor's* dignity is a right to recognition, one must also hold that the decision would have been the same for a fictional Edith Windsor who lived not in New York but Wisconsin or Texas, states that had not taken affirmative steps to recognize same-sex marriages. For it is in a situation such as that, where there are no state actions through which dignity claims are refracted and articulated, that the conditions for a traditional right of recognition would be present.

instead of citing the state's authoritative role in conferring dignity. And as the Court faced a question about the states' ability to refuse recognition of same-sex marriages performed in other jurisdictions, it is understandable that the role of state governments in altering dignity was downplayed almost entirely. At the time, and certainly in retrospect, *Windsor* was viewed as an incremental step, a decision that would lead to yet another holding about the constitutional right of same-sex couples to marry. The crucial jurisprudential move in the development of "equal dignity," then, was *Windsor*'s recognition of the dignity interest conferred and enhanced by New York's actions. That conception of dignity broke starkly from the Court's earlier articulation in *Lawrence* and was, at least in part, structured by the institutional position and role of the Court in the federal system.

10.4 Conclusion

The jurisprudence of "equal dignity" is far from settled. Such is the nature of constitutional jurisprudence. Like the constitutional law of liberty and equality in which the Court's gay rights decisions intervened, the jurisprudence of "equal dignity" was iteratively constructed, taking shape as it was put to use. But as it developed, subsequent usage was—at least to some extent—constrained by what came before. While the venerated principle of *stare decisis* may be honored more often in the breach (Segal and Spaeth 1996), the imperatives of doctrinal coherence and jurisprudential continuity at work in the majority opinion in *Obergefell* entailed turning away from *Windsor*'s variable dignity and back to the more traditional foundation in autonomy, along the lines set out in *Lawrence*. The result was democratic dignity, an understanding that emphasized both the liberty- and equality-regarding dimensions of human dignity.

In this respect, dignity's emergence in this area of American constitutional law reflects the more general phenomenon observed by Novkov: claims for equal treatment have often been "most successful when the substantive equality being sought is access to a fundamentally conservative right or institution" (2015, p. 473). As the legal developments recounted in this chapter show, the ultimate identification of the right for same-sex couples to marry entailed leveraging the language of dignity even as its meaning and requirements shifted. Those shifts, and most significantly the Court's temporary embrace of a variable understanding of dignity, were occasioned, in part, by the structure of the political order through which legal disputes were channeled.

Even if future rights jurisprudence rejects or departs from the conceptions of dignity employed in the central gay rights cases, a residue will remain, furnishing legal and conceptual resources from which judges, advocates, and citizens can draw.[10] There is little reason to believe that what I have called structural articulation is unique to the cases discussed here. Future inquiry should, therefore, seek to determine when and how institutional characteristics or interactions affect the content and development of judicial discourse. As I have argued in this chapter, the substance of the Supreme Court's dignity jurisprudence has been fundamentally influenced by the structure of the American regime. Because of the structural and process-based dynamics it entails, the federal system occasioned the development of a conception of dignity that departed from earlier understandings. That new understanding—variable dignity—facilitated the Court's eventual decision in *Obergefell* granting "equal dignity in the eyes of the law" to same-sex couples seeking to marry. Constitutional jurisprudence is, as these cases demonstrate, articulated both conceptually and structurally. As such, the future of "equal dignity" and its consequences for American rights jurisprudence will be shaped not only by the facts of the legal questions that arise but also by the political and institutional contexts in which those questions are addressed.

References

Barak A (2015) Human dignity: the constitutional value and the constitutional right. Cambridge University Press, New York

Brink DO (1988) Legal theory, legal interpretation, and judicial review. Philos Public Aff 17(2): 105–148

Buchanan JM (1995) Federalism as an ideal political order and an objective for constitutional reform. Publius 95(2):19–27

Bulman-Pozen J, Gerken HK (2009) Uncooperative federalism. Yale Law J 118:1256

Elazar DJ (1987) Exploring federalism. University of Alabama Press, Tuscaloosa

Engel SM (2016) Seeing sexuality: state development and the fragmented status of LGBTQ citizenship. In: Valelly R, Mettler S, Lieberman R (eds) The Oxford handbook of American political development. Oxford University Press, New York, pp 682–698

Engel SM (2018) Dynamics of constitutional development and the conservative potential of U.S. Supreme Court gay rights jurisprudence, or why Neil Gorsuch may stop worrying and learn to love same-sex marriage. Const Stud 3(1):1–40

Engel SM, Lyle TS (2021) Disrupting dignity: rethinking power and progress in LGBTQ lives. NYU Press, New York

Epstein RA (1992) Exit rights under federalism. Law Contemp Probl 55(1):147–165

Ewing CM (2018) With dignity and justice for all: the jurisprudence of equal dignity and the partial convergence of liberty and equality in American constitutional law. Int J Const Law 16(3): 753–775

[10] An important development in this respect is the Court's recent decision in *Dobbs v. Jackson Women's Health Organization* (2022). On the way to finding that the Constitution did not guarantee a right to abortion, the majority directly criticized how previous decisions, particularly *Planned Parenthood v. Casey*, had grounded that right in "the freedom to make 'intimate and personal choices' that are 'central to personal dignity and autonomy.'" Accordingly, *Dobbs*' overruling of *Casey* has cast doubt on cases, like *Lawrence* and *Obergefell*, that rely on *Casey*'s account of due process rights.

Ewing CM (forthcoming) Dignity disputed. J Law Courts
Finck M (2016) The role of human dignity in gay rights adjudication and legislation: a comparative perspective. Int J Const Law 14(1):26–53
Gerken HK (2010) Foreword: federalism all the way down. Harv Law Rev 124:4
Gerken HK (2014) Federalism as the new nationalism: an overview. Yale Law J 123:1889
Gerken HK (2015) Windsor's mad genius: the interlocking gears of rights and structure. Boston Law Rev 95:587
Goodman M (2006) Human dignity in Supreme Court constitutional jurisprudence. Nebraska Law Rev 84:740
Haddad JJ (2016) The evolution of marriage: the role of dignity jurisprudence and marriage equality. Boston Univ Law Rev 96:1489
Henry LM (2011) The jurisprudence of dignity. Univ Pa Law Rev 160:169
Katz E, Tarr GA (eds) (1996) Federalism and rights. Rowman & Littlefield, Lanham
Klarman MJ (2004) From Jim Crow to civil rights: the Supreme Court and the struggle for racial equality. Oxford University Press, New York
Knauer NJ (2018) Federalism, marriage equality, and LGBT rights. In: Banks CP (ed) Controversies in American federalism and public policy. Routledge, New York, pp 93–113
Kretzmer D, Klein E (eds) (2002) The concept of human dignity in human rights discourse. Kluwer Academic Publishers, New York
Marcus NC (2014) Deeply rooted principles of equal liberty, not 'Argle Bargle': the inevitability of marriage equality after Windsor. Tulsa J Law Sex 23:17
Michelman FI (1993) Property, federalism, and jurisprudence: a comment on Lucas and judicial conservatism. William Mary Law Rev 35:301
Moore C, Rodman E (2022) 'It would "mean little" absent governmental recognition': theorizing state power and the new jurisprudence of dignity. Law Cult Humanit 18(3):698–715
Murphy WF (1993) Constitutions, constitutionalism, and democracy. In: Greenberg D, Katz SN, Oliviero MB, Wheatley SC (eds) Constitutionalism and democracy: transitions in the contemporary world. Oxford University Press, New York, pp 3–25
Murphy WF (2007) Constitutional democracy: creating and maintaining a just political order. Johns Hopkins University Press, Baltimore
Note (2019) Equal dignity—heeding its call. Harv Law Rev 132:1323
Novkov J (2015) Equality. In: Tushnet M, Graber MA, Levinson S (eds) The Oxford handbook of the U.S. constitution. Oxford University Press, New York, pp 455–478
Rao N (2008) On the use and abuse of dignity in constitutional law. Colum J Eur Law 14(2): 201–256
Rao N (2011) Three concepts of dignity in constitutional law. Notre Dame Law Rev 86:183
Rao N (2013) The trouble with dignity and rights of recognition. Va Law Rev Online 99:29
Resnik J, Suk J C-h (2003) Adding insult to injury: questioning the role of dignity in conceptions of sovereignty. Stanford Law Rev 55:1921
Riker WH (1964) Federalism: origin, operation, significance. Little, Brown, Boston
Riker WH (1975) Federalism. In: Greenstein F, Polsby N (eds) Handbook of political science, vol 5. Addison-Wesley, Reading, pp 93–172
Rosen M (2008) Human dignity: its history and meaning. Harvard University Press, Cambridge
Segal JA, Spaeth HJ (1996) The influence of stare decisis on the votes of United States Supreme Court Justices. Am J Polit Sci 40(4):971–1003
Taylor C (1994) The politics of recognition. In: Gutmann A (ed) Multiculturalism: examining the politics of recognition. Princeton University Press, Princeton, pp 25–73
Tribe LH (2003) Lawrence v. Texas: the 'fundamental right' that dare not speak its name. Harv Law Rev 117:1893
Tribe LH (2015) Equal dignity: speaking its name. Harv Law Rev Forum 129:16
Watts RL (1999) Comparing federal systems. McGill-Queens University Press, Montreal

Weinrib J (2018) Human dignity and its critics. In: Jacobsohn GJ, Schor M (eds) Comparative constitutional theory. Edward Elgar Publishing, Cheltenham, pp 167–186
Yoshino K (2011) The new equal protection. Harv Law Rev 124:747
Yoshino K (2015) Comment: a new birth of freedom? Obergefell v. Hodges. Harv Law Rev 129: 147

Part IV
Human Dignity and Trauma

Chapter 11
The Role of Art in Restoring Human Dignity at the Threshold of Forgetting Traumatic Pasts

Caterina Preda

Abstract This chapter analyzes the role artistic renderings of a traumatic past play in restoring human dignity after dictatorships with specific examples from the Chilean and Romanian experiences and at the threshold of forgetting the past. Although after the Second World War human dignity was established as a foundational concept for human rights, several dictatorial regimes did not respect this assertion. Moreover, while human dignity is often considered inalienable, several artworks analyzed in this chapter have the goal to restore human dignity to the victims of dictatorial regimes, thereby illustrating that human dignity can be violated. Anchored in cultural memory studies, this chapter analyzes the role art plays in restoring human dignity of the victims of dictatorships. I argue that artistic strategies aspire to restore dignity to the victims of dictatorships through a personalization of victimhood, and by giving victims "visual dignity," or as a form of symbolic reparation.

11.1 Introduction

This chapter engages two very different examples of artistic memorialization, which invoke the restoration of the human dignity of the victims of dictatorships. The first case I consider is in Eastern Europe, in the Romanian context, and refers to the memory of the victims of the communist regime. The second case is in the South American, specifically Chilean, context and considers the memory of the victims of the Pinochet dictatorship. Both cases illustrate how artists respond to dictatorships 30 years after their end, to remember the victims, to restore their dignity. This happens at what I call the "threshold of forgetting," when sufficient time has passed since the end of the regimes, and in the absence of proper public policies to deal with the traumatic past.

C. Preda (✉)
University of Bucharest, Bucharest, Romania
e-mail: caterina.preda@unibuc.ro

S. N. Arel et al. (eds.), *Probing Human Dignity*,
https://doi.org/10.1007/978-3-031-42437-3_11

The regimes in Romania and Chile serve as oppositional case studies for a broader phenomenon in the two regions: non-democratic regimes which appeared in the second half of the twentieth century, after World War II. They represent contrasting examples of how countries in Eastern Europe and South America, respectively, deal with the past, illustrating what has been called "the third wave of democratization" (Huntington 1991), countries that witnessed transitions to democracy in the 1970s and 1980s. According to the theorization on Transitional Justice (TJ), the process of dealing with the past should encompass in the case of the countries of the third wave of democratization three stages: truth, justice, and reconciliation (De Brito et al. 2001). Following this approach, the new democratic regimes should identify what happened in their recent pasts, send to trial those identified as guilty, and then proceed with societal reconciliation.

These two cases can also work as theoretical landmarks that could be further tested in the same regions, or across other regions. On the one hand, Romania witnessed a bloody revolution in 1989, which ended the harsh personal dictatorship of Nicolae Ceaușescu (1965–1989) leading to a democratic regime that has not been able to confront its recent past. On the other hand, the Chilean regime represents a good example of dealing successfully with the past and consolidating a democratic regime after a traumatic dictatorship (1973–1990). In this chapter, I argue that the analysis of artistic discourses which confront the recent dictatorial pasts in these countries shows the limits of the processes of TJ and brings forward a more in-depth understanding of how societies deal with their traumatic experiences. In art emerging from Romania and Chile in the 1990s and 2000s, artists contradict the forgetting the past (Romania), or the official memory that emphasized reconciliation with the past (Chile), showing there are unresolved issues connected to the wrongdoings of the dictatorships.

The chapter explores, how artworks can help restore human dignity through their mediated experiences and examines which aesthetic strategies artists use to achieve this restoration.

Human dignity has been defined both as "the source from which all the basic rights derive their substance" (Habermas 2018, p. 54) and in a "post-Kantian tradition as an unconditional feature of the human condition, inherent in and owed to every human being irrespective of race, gender, age, status, profession or nationality, and as such dependent on mutual recognition and thus other-regarding demeanour" (Pless et al. 2017, p. 223). Some authors stress how human dignity is both the "premise and the practice of human rights" (Garnsey 2016, p. 86).

After the Second World War, the Universal Declaration of Human Rights (1948) established human dignity as a foundational concept: "a statement against the Shoah, against totalitarianism, and against the atrocities of the war" (Düwell et al. 2014, p. xix); however, several non-democratic regimes, organized in the second half of the twentieth century, failed to adopt this notion of human dignity. Authoritarian or totalitarian regimes inspired by both right wing and left-wing ideological projects emerged in Europe and the Americas committing several forms of human rights violations. Human dignity was denied to the citizens during the dictatorships in Eastern Europe and the Southern Cone of South America in several ways: citizens were incarcerated in terrible conditions, arrested without any warrant, tortured, and, in the case of the dictatorships of South America, many remain *disappeared* (that is their families do not have any information of their whereabouts).

Although many conceptualizations of human dignity consider the value intrinsic to human beings (Gewirth 1992) and impossible to be taken away, I argue artists see human dignity eradicated in victims of dictatorial regimes who were abused and killed by the dictatorships. In response to this removal, artists in each context attempt to restore human dignity through the use of different visual strategies.

My approach in this chapter lies at the intersection of cultural memory studies and research that explores the role of art in TJ, a topic of increasing interest in the last decade (Rush and Simić 2016; Atencio and Gates-Madsen 2013; Bahun 2015; in addition see Barat 2020, pp. 242–250; Shefik 2018, pp. 314–333; Garnsey 2019).

Cultural memory is an interdisciplinary study that associates history with political science, philosophy, psychology, media or literary studies; it is a term that encompasses social memory, material memory and mental or cognitive memory (Erll 2010). According to Alexander Etkind, cultural memory includes two types of memory, which mirror the memory system of a computer: soft and hard memory (2013, p. 177). "Soft memory" is formed by texts (literary, historical and other narratives), while "hard memory" is primarily shaped by monuments (177); if sites of memory structure cultural hardware, then events, or what Etkind calls "memory events," constitute its software (178). Moreover, the new memory studies, starting with the 1980s, have increasingly dwelt into cultural memory practices, which are understood here as the residues of dictatorships (in addition see Cento Bull and Hansen 2020; Gutman and Wüstenberg 2023).

The studies that analyze the role of art in TJ have considered it from the point of view of its therapeutic, or healing role for the victims of atrocities. In this analysis I want to rather focus on the role of contemporary artists in showing the limits of the TJ processes (truth commissions, reconciliation practices, memory policies). In certain cases, such as the Chilean one, which is considered to have had an exemplary transition to democracy and has organized truth commissions to work toward reconciliation, there are limits to the process of dealing with the past. Contemporary Chilean artists indicate these limits by acknowledging the difficult memory of the dictatorship and by evoking those that are still missing, the *disappeared*.

Furthermore, while there are studies in cultural memory and TJ that analyze how artistic expressions deal with traumatic experiences, the link to how human dignity connects to this focus remains largely unexplored. Only limited research that studies the role arts have in restoring human dignity after traumatic experiences has been produced, although the link between the development of human dignity and the arts has been illustrated. As Pless et al. (2017, p. 223) acknowledge, visual and performing arts can play a crucial role in the actualization of dignity. Theatre and music served as a means for Holocaust victims to endure suffering and helped them to experience dignity and pride under dehumanized conditions (Audhuy 2015). More contemporary examples of the role of the arts in promoting dignity include the visual arts produced in indigenous communities [for example in] Australia.

In this sense, a scholar of the role of art in TJ studies, Garnsey (2016) analyzed the role artworks play in relation to human dignity in the context of the "visual jurisprudence" of the art collection of the Constitutional Court in South Africa. For her, the artworks "serve as reminders of past violations of human dignity, underscored by a norm of nonrepetition" and function "as a kind of symbolic reparation – memorializing... and returning a sense of visual dignity which ... death denied" (2016, pp. 84, 95). Thus, "the value of individual human dignity is preserved through these acts of resistance and in the commemoration of these acts. ...While the value of human dignity is preserved in the artwork" (95). Garnsey underlines how "each artwork offers a perspective on human dignity and probes the notion of what human dignity as the promise of human rights means and entails" (2016, p. 97).

Drawing on Garnsey (2016, p. 84), in this chapter, I examine how artworks realized after dictatorships in Romania and Chile help us conceptualize how artists evoke human dignity, contributing to its development after traumatic experiences. The artworks analyzed in what follows grant a form of poetic or symbolic reparation to the victims, which were denied human dignity, giving them visual dignity and therefore serving as a form of symbolic, poetic reparation.

Because the dictatorships denied human dignity to their victims, I contend artists seek to return dignity to the victims through a personalization of victimhood; they recreate "the biographies of the victims and thus break the decades of silence and grant them, even if only symbolically, their human dignity" (Brodsky 2015, p. 11). They address personal histories that help avoid the abstract depiction of the victims by other TJ mechanisms such as the Truth commissions' reports. Artists through their "pensive images" (Rancière 2008) can produce a form of *dissensus* of the memorial consensus.

The first section of the chapter briefly explores the Romanian situation concerning the process of dealing with the communist past, and the second section looks at the role contemporary artworks have played in providing a more complete outlook onto the communist regime in Romania. To show that artists contribute to the missing memory of the victims of the communist regime, I will analyze two artworks that employ documentary forms to discuss restoring human dignity through the personalization of suffering; this includes the artistic documentation of the extensive 12 interviews with victims of the communist regime in *The Archive of Pain* (Ştefan Costantinescu, 2000) and the dignified portrait of the imprisoned artist Lena Constante realized by Thomas Ciulei in *The craziness of the heads* (1997). In the third section of the chapter, I turn to Chile focusing on the process of dealing with the Pinochet dictatorship. The fourth section analyzes the role of two artworks from Chile, *Geometry of Conscience* (2010) by Alfredo Jaar and the video-triptych by Enrique Ramirez formed of *Breezes, Pacific and The Sleepers*, in contradicting official memory. I argue the artistic gaze forces the acknowledgement of what the dictatorship wanted to be erased: the memory of those killed in illegal, unknown conditions and who up to today remain *disappeared*. Through their work, Ramirez and Jaar grant the victims a form of visual dignity.

11.2 "Communism Never Happened": Official Memory in Romania

Eastern Europe was dominated for over four decades by communist regimes, imposed by force and using different types of repression to remain in power until 1989. Ruled by a communist regime from 1948 to 1989, Romania had become one of the most closed-in countries in Eastern Europe. It was dominated by a personal dictatorship established by the Nicolae Ceauşescu regime (1965–1989) that developed an exaggerated cult of personality; the government allowed no freedom of expression; food and energy shortages abounded, and travelling abroad was a practical impossibility for most Romanian citizens.

Evidencing of the most dramatic ends of the communist regimes in December 1989, Romania had a revolution, which started in Timişoara on December 16th, 1989 and then extended to the entire country including Bucharest. As a result, the Ceauşescu regime ended, and Nicolae Ceauşescu, and his wife Elena Ceauşescu were put on trial and condemned to death. Both were shot on December 25, 1989. During the events of that fateful December, 1104 people were killed, and 3352 persons were wounded.

Subsequently, the approach of the Ion Iliescu regime (1990–1996, 2000–2004) which was formed of the second echelon of the Romanian Communist Party nomenklatura, and that established its legitimacy on the revolutionary moment, emphasized the need to move forward, to not interrogate the recent past and focus on the future. It was only in the mid-2000s, that a different approach of the communist past was put forward by an alliance of the right-wing parties formed by the National Liberal Party and the Democratic Party. Thus, in December 2006 the Romanian president Traian Băsescu (2004–2014) condemned the "communist dictatorship as a criminal regime" on the basis of the report prepared by the Presidential Commission for the Study of the Communist Dictatorship in Romania (2006) also known as the Tismăneanu Commission. This report was criticized for its lack of rigor, and legal consequences, and Băsescu's assembling such a report was questioned because he has been accused of having collaborated with the former secret police, the *Securitate*.

One of the criticisms of the Tismăneanu Report refers to the number of victims of the communist dictatorship it put forward. Because there was a lack of access to the archives from the former secret police as well as from other state institutions, such as the militia or the Ministry of Internal Affairs, that dealt with the repression of those opposing the regime, the Tismăneanu Commission estimated the number of victims of the communist regime totaled between 500,000 to 2 million. As Lavinia Stan (2012) observes, other civic organizations investigated the number of the victims and evoked smaller numbers. For example, the Civic Academy mentions the 93,000 penal transcripts of detainees from a larger number of documents, which were lost (Memorial to the Victims). Stan (2012, p. 142) also recalls the numbers given in the *Dictionary of Victims of Communist Terror* by the former prisoner Cicerone

Ioniţoiu, which identifies 100,000 victims "who were arrested, tortured, jailed and killed during the 1945–1989 period."

As a result of both this imposed forgetting of the past and the lack of information on the communist regime's crimes, opinion polls have registered appreciation from nearly half of all Romanian citizens for the regime. The percentages of those who consider communism good for the country, vary between 53% of the population in 2006, to 61% in 2010, 44% in 2014, and 40% in 2018 (Besliu 2014).

Both public memory projects supported by the Romanian state, and the memory of the victims are expressed through monuments or memorials, or what Alexander Etkind (2013) calls "hard memory." While there still is no Museum of Communism as in other countries of the region (Hungary, the Czech Republic), there are several museums that offer a space for the memorialization of different aspects of communism in Romania, from the commemoration of its victims to the nostalgic approach to the communist period. The Memorial to the Victims of Communism and to the Resistance in Sighet (1993), inaugurated by the Foundation the Civic Academy on the site of a former prison, commemorates its victims. Another site of memory is the Ceauşescu House (2016) in Bucharest, which was the former residence of the Ceauşescu family (1970–1989), and which safeguards part of their personal effects and showcases their lifestyle. Several private initiatives also display symbols of communism, such as the Museum of the Communist Consumer in Timişoara, the Museum of the Dacia Car in Satu-Mare, or Ferestroika, the communist apartment in Bucharest.

In fact, nostalgic practices have multiplied in Romania. Music bands use communist reenactments such as *Romarta* to invoke a positive attitude toward the communist past; ads that use symbols of the past (the chocolate Rom) to sell their products, while bars and parties employ the specific attire of the pioneers calling their guests to dress as during communism and promote an ironic perspective on the past. Recent films have also discussed nostalgic practices. The collective work *Tales from the Golden Age* (Cristian Mungiu, Hanno Höfer, Constantin Popescu, Ioana Uricaru, Răzvan Mărculescu, 2009) presents a collection of urban myths popular during the last period of communism to encourage spectators to use laughter as a strategy of remembrance. Several contemporary artists such as Ciprian Mureşan (*Communism never happened* 2006), Mona Vătămanu, and Florin Tudor (*Long live and thrive capitalism!* 2009) have also engaged with nostalgia for the communist regime. In his work *Communism never happened* (2006), Ciprian Mureşan cut the words of this title from propaganda music discs of the Ceauşescu regime; this artwork ironically questions the approach of the postcommunist regime in Romania in relation to the communist past.

Thus, in the Romanian cases, there is no comprehensive public policy of memorialization of the communist regime. This lack of policy has provoked nostalgic reactions that have been reinterpreted by several artistic means. The artists whose artworks that use documentary forms, I analyze further, react to this absence of a memorial consensus in what regards the communist past.

11.3 Restoring Visual Dignity Through the Artistic Memorialization of the Victims of the Communist Regime in Romania

Romanian contemporary art discourses have tackled the communist past in several ways. Along with a critical perspective on the nostalgic approach, which challenges the positive outlook on the recent past, artists have focused on portraying Nicolae Ceaușescu and have presented the complexity of this historical figure. Moreover, they have engaged extensively with the end of the communist regime, the December 1989 revolution. A smaller number of artists have confronted issues related to human rights violations, or the mistreatments suffered during the communist regime such as those related to forced labor, the loss of (property) rights, censorship, or the lack of the freedom of movement, etc.

The memory of the victims of communism has not been an official topic of memorialization except for the NGOs of the victims. One of the best known is the documentary series *Memorialul durerii/The memorial of pain* (Lucia Hossu Longin, 1991). In 36 episodes it documents the repression of opponents of the Communist regime in Romania, showing prisons, enforced labor camps, and the persecution by the secret police, the *Securitate*. The series emphasizes the recuperation of a part of history, which was largely unknown during the communist regime, that of the fate of its victims. At the same time, the documentary has been criticized because it showcases among the heroes of the anti-communist resistance members of the fascist organization the Legion of Archangel Michael (Iron Guard), which was influential during the inter-war period. Thus, the different traumatic history strata come together in the post-communist period and render the memory of suffering more complex than how it is remembered at the official level.

The artwork *The Archive of pain* (2000, see Fig. 11.1) is a collective work to which Ștefan Constantinescu participated together with the director Cristi Puiu and the graphic designer Arina Stoenescu. It documents through archive images, propaganda material, and interviews with former political prisoners the period 1945–1965.[1] The video installation formed of four screen projections includes interviews with twelve former prisoners, who are shown sitting and talking about their experience. The former prisoners are both women (3) and men (9) recounting their experience of pain both during the imprisonment and afterwards. The artwork constitutes a supplementary source of information about the communist regime in Romania as it was realized at a time when interest in the past, and especially in the regime of the first communist leader of Gheorghe Gheorghiu Dej (1948–1965), was rather absent. The approach of the artistic project, which has as a subtitle, "Testimonies of the Red Terror," is openly anti-communist and focuses on the criminal character of the regime.

[1] http://www.stefan-constantinescu.com/index.php/work/archive-of-pain/.

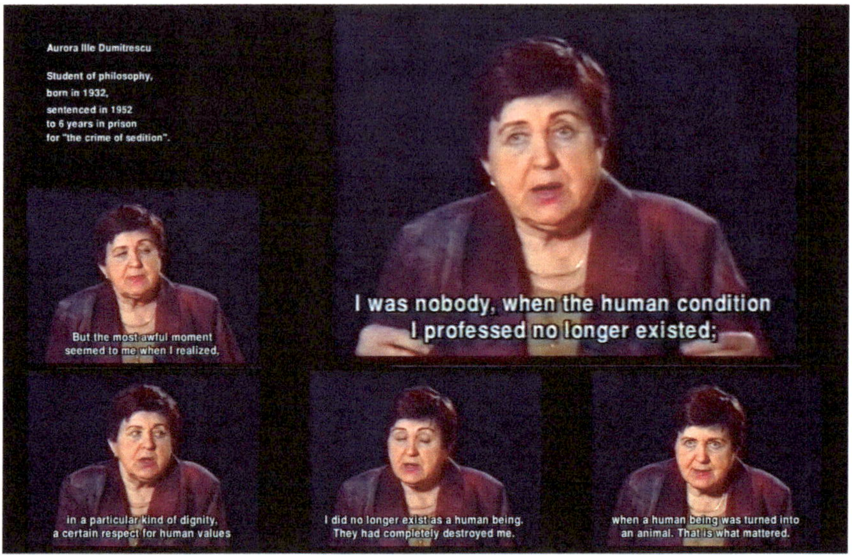

Fig. 11.1 Ştefan Constantinescu, The Archive of Pain (2000)

One of the students portrayed is Aurora Ilie Dumitrescu, who was a philosophy student, born in 1932 and sentenced in 1952 to 6 years in prison for "the crime of sedition." As she recounts:

> the most awful moment seemed to me when I realized, I became aware and it was a strong feeling that in fact I was nobody, when the human condition I professed no longer existed, that I was like a hunted animal in their clutches (. . .) I did no longer exist as a human being. They had completely destroyed us. (. . .) We were. . .as I said our generation was raised in a particular kind of dignity, a certain respect for human values, and man himself, and when I got there I saw the status they enforced upon me: you did not mean anything to them. (. . .) when a human being was turned into an animal. . .they would treat you as a kind of beast.[2]

Aurora Ilie Dumitrescu's prison experience was terrible because, as she articulates, she was treated as sub-human. She recounts her trial as a farce because prior to it a decision was already made by the Secret police (the *Securitate*) to keep her under house arrest for two years.

The testimonies of the former prisoners that we witness in the video-work of Constantinescu are all frontal portraits of now older persons, but all recount their arrest at a young age, their sentencing to hard labor and imprisonment, and their difficulties after being released, including the efforts to reorganize their lives. The artist does not intervene in the interviews, which last more than 15 h (with every interview between 40 min and one hour). The absence of any guidance by the artist alongside the length of the testimonies accomplishes a sort of reenactment of the

[2] Aurora Ilie Dumitrescu as part of "The Archive of pain", video installation and book (2000), edited by Arina Stoenescu with texts by Lucian Boia, Adrian Cioroianu and Tom Sandqvist.

whole experience for the spectator. In this process, Constantinescu grants human dignity to his interviewees who are given ample time to recount their story in full, without being disturbed or interrupted.

The second artistic example I want to focus on is the documentary film *The Craziness of the Heads* (1997) by the film director Thomas Ciulei in which he focuses on the portrait of the Romanian artist Lena Constante (1909–2005). A visual artist, Lena Constante interprets herself in the film, inspired by her personal prison experience. She was arrested as part of the "Pătrăşcanu batch" (1948), condemned by the communist regime in 1950 and released in 1961. She was jailed for 12 years, eight of which were spent in solitary confinement. Although she was rehabilitated in 1968, she could no longer exhibit her artworks. The regime marginalized her. Still, she discovered a way to recount her prison experience in a memoir, *The Silent Escape* published first in French, and then in Romanian after 1990,[3] and she explained her choice to write about her experience by saying she wanted to talk about detention as such, perfectly knowing the facts.

> Daily life in a cell. I think I lived a unique experience. A woman, alone, for many years. Years made of hours, of minutes, of seconds. These seconds I would like to recount, these 3600 seconds in an hour, these 86400 seconds in a day, that slowly drags, along the body, slobbery snakes that climb in spirals from your feet to your neck, without a break, without mercy, from morning to evening and in the nights of insomnia, too often, continuing to enchain you without rest, and without stop, endlessly. Because I want to talk also of human dignity. And of those women, later my prison comrades, that against everything and everybody, remained profoundly human beings. And to affirm a hope. The hope that some far away day, man will conquer nature. Not by changing the course of waters, or the desert, or by conquering the cosmos, but by changing himself. Changing his heart and mind.[4]

The Craziness of the Heads portrays Lena Constante in very tight shots showing only her face, where the artist reads from her memoir and evokes the "craziness of the heads, the visual hallucinations she had following her physical and psychological depletion."[5] Constante is filmed in her room, which, according to Ciulei is the projection of her cell outside prison, as she can never escape. Through this manner of filming her, Ciulei wanted to force the spectator to imagine a space as Lena Constante had done when she was imprisoned. Ciulei alternates the tight portraiture of Lena Constante with images of the prison corridors, of piles of uniforms and boots and poetic images close to the Doftana prison. [6] In the film she recounts how she remained sane by composing shows and reciting poems to keep her mind alive and

---

[3] Lena Constante, *L'évasion silencieuse: trois mille jours, seule, dans les prisons roumaines* (Paris, La Découverte, 1990).

[4] Lena Constante, The silent escape quoted http://ler.is.edu.ro/~cr/index.php?page=person&id=168.

[5] Andreea Vlad, "Thomas Ciulei relansează Nebunia capetelor, documentarul Lenei Constante", 29 November 2013. http://www.bewhere.ro/features/thomas-ciulei-relanseaza-nebunia-capetelor-documentarul-lenei-constante-5058/ (accessed May 30th 2019).

[6] Ibidem.

escaping into her imagination as a form of surviving. [7] So, Constante confirms the conclusion of Audhuy (2015) quoted by Pless et al. (2017, p. 223) and that we recalled in the introduction, who affirmed, art can and has been a form to "experience dignity and pride under dehumanized conditions."

Moreover, the artistic evocation by Ciulei of Constante restores her human dignity because we are confronted with the powerful story of an artist who used her imagination and her inner strength to resist extreme forms of torture, among which included the threat of being thrown into a hole with rats. She recounts the tens of thousands of seconds of loneliness that passed through poetic recitation and artistic creation. Visual dignity is conveyed to Lena Constante's dramatic experience through the gracious portrayal Ciulei creates of her, by recapturing how together with her fellow women prisoners, they refused to concede to their torturers.

The two artistic projects discussed, *The Archive of pain* (Stefan Constantinescu, 2000) and *The Craziness of the Heads* (Ciulei 1997) portray victims of the Romanian communist regime who were imprisoned in the 1950s and whose experience has been largely erased from the public space after the democratic transition of 1990, as if communism never happened. Through their documentary gestures, both Constantinescu and Ciulei restore dignity to the victims. Constantinescu offers visual dignity to the prisoners as a sort of symbolic reparation for their experiences by not intervening at all in the interviews, whereas Ciulei's portrayal of Constante poetically accentuates her unique worldview. So, in the Romanian case, despite the official willingness to forget the communist past as if it never happened, artists such as Constantinescu and Ciulei, through their artworks, document the suffering of the victims of communism, insert a missing history into the public realm, and grant victims visual dignity.

11.4 The Official Memory Policy in Chile: (Partial) Truth and (Imposed) Reconciliation After the Dictatorship

In the 1960s–1980s South America was marked by a wave of authoritarian coups by an alliance between the military and civilian sectors, which took power and governed by force. Chile witnessed the most violent intervention by the Armed forces on September 11th, 1973, which led to the gradual domination by the General Augusto Pinochet U. between 1973 and 1990 with the help of the secret police DINA (National Intelligence Directorate). At the same time, the country was transformed not only with repression against opponents, but also, beginning in 1975, through a neoliberal revolution, with a state giving up its role in most of the areas from education to pensions.

Several Truth Commissions organized after the return to democracy documented human rights violations in the region during Pinochet's rule, detailing how human

[7] Ibidem.

dignity was denied to those arrested and detained.[8] The reports of the two Truth Commissions concluded that there were around 40,000 victims of the dictatorship: 1100 disappeared, 2116 persons executed for political reasons, and 38,256 victims of prison and torture in 1132 detention and torture centers (Cardenas Hernandez 2017, p. 8). The reports include descriptions of the types of human rights violations suffered by the victims (children, women, men) described during the hearings of the commissions. The 1100 disappeared remain unaccounted for until today despite the efforts of the families and of the victim led NGOs to receive answers from the authorities. Human dignity was denied to those that became victims of the dictatorship in Chile, as the military took people from their homes and from the streets, detaining them illegally; many disappeared without a trace.

After the end of the dictatorship, memorial practices include a "hard memory" in the sense of Etkind (2013) that incorporates the Museum of Memory and Human Rights inaugurated in Santiago in 2010. Of the 1132 detention centers recognized by the truth commissions, only twenty have been acknowledged as historical monuments, and not as sites of memory (Lawner 2017, p. 19). Such an example is the house of the street Londres, 38 in the center of Santiago, which was the first center of torture used by the secret police, DINA, and which was recuperated as a memory site in 2010; it is now administered by an NGO, "Londres 38, Espacio de Memorias" (London 38 Space of Memories) that organizes several activities of memorialization (Cabeza Monteira et al. 2017, p. 99). One of the most emblematic sites of memory is Villa Grimaldi or The Park of Peace Villa Grimaldi. Called Cuartel Terranova during the Pinochet regime. Between 1973 and 1978 it served as a detention center holding more than 4500 people, 226 of whom disappeared, and 18 were executed (Cabeza Monteira et al. 2017, p. 81). Villa Grimaldi was a former restaurant for the elite in the 1950s, taken over in 1973 by the Chilean Secret Police, the DINA. In 1987, the Secret Police (called at the time CNI) sold it to a firm that demolished the villa in preparation for building new residences. In 1990, the association "Corporación Parque por la Paz Villa Grimaldi" requested to retake the site, and in 1997, it was inaugurated as a park of memory. In 2004, it became a historical monument.

Despite the official efforts of dealing with the past, the memory of the Pinochet dictatorship is not settled and is contested by those still supporting the former dictator. As such, in Santiago de Chile, there is also a site of memory, hosted by the Foundation President Pinochet (1995), that celebrates the positive memory of the dictatorship. It includes a small museum that portrays the military dictator as a hero who saved Chile from communism.

Thus, the artworks, films, and theater works that deal with the memory of the victims of the dictatorships in Chile are important because they insert into public

[8]The National Commission for Truth and Reconciliation (Rettig Commission, 1990), the National Corporation of Reparation and Reconciliation (1992), the Table of Dialogue for Human Rights (1999), the National Commission about Political Prison and Torture (Valech Commission, 2003), which included a second stage, the Consultative Commission to the Presidency for the Qualification of Disappeared Detainees, Political executed and victims of political prison and torture (Valech Commission II, 2010).

discourse the topic of the memory of the wrongdoings of the dictatorship that is otherwise being marginalized by the new democratic regime. These artistic recollections use different types of media (from archives, performance, photography, film, or sounds), and the artworks that participate to this effort of memorialization discuss several topics. One of the recurrent themes of these artistic renderings is that of the *detenidos desaparecidos* (detainees that were illegally arrested and became disappeared). Chilean artists underline their humanity and try to individualize their pain showing us their portraits, their stories. In fact, even during the dictatorship, artists who were personally concerned by the phenomenon of "disappearances" or simply reacted to their specific social context created artworks related to this issue. For example, the artist Luz Donoso in *Support Action in a Commercial System* (1979) inserted images of those disappeared on the television screens of a commercial street in downtown Santiago, and in another work, *Endless Band* (1978) she put together photographs and repeated the phrase "Where are they?" together with pamphlets, flyers from the protests against the dictatorship (Giunta 2017, p. 255). After the return to democracy, Chilean artists like Donoso continued to insist on displaying the portraits of those disappeared. Works by Guillermo Cifuentes (*Rumor* 2000, *Rumors* 2012), Claudio Pérez (*Saying Goodbye Love Before Forgetting* 2007), or Carlos Altamirano in his series of *Portraits* (1989–2007) reflect the insistence of exposing images of the disappeared.

Connected to this artistic focus on the disappeared, I will now analyze in more detail, the artworks Geometry of Conscience (2010) by Alfredo Jaar which deals with the memory of the victims as part of the general experience of Chilean society, and the artworks of Enrique Ramirez's, *The Sleepers, Pacific, and Breezes* (2008) which offers a poetic understanding of the weight of the memory of those that are still disappeared.

11.5 The Permanent Presence of Their Absence: The Memory of the Disappeared in Chilean Visual Art Discourses as Poetic Reparation

The artwork *Geometry of conscience* (2010, see Fig. 11.2) by Alfredo Jaar is part of the corpus of artworks that are concerned with the victims of the dictatorship. His installation creates an infinite illuminated afterimage of the victims that brings together both the silhouettes of those that were killed, and those that are still alive. Housed in the underground gallery of the Museum of Memory and Human Rights in Santiago, Chile, inaugurated in December 2010 by president Michelle Bachelet (2006–2010, 2014–2018) in a powerful gesture by a former detainee and a victim of torture during the Chilean military dictatorship, Jaar's piece has to be descended into from the plaza that surrounds the museum down a stairway.

After going underground, the visitor enters a room. The door closes eliminating the possibility of exit and, the visitor experiences complete darkness for three

Fig. 11.2 Alfredo Jaar, Geometry of conscience (2010)

minutes. 462 white silhouettes, multiplied infinitely by the mirrors situated on the walls on the right and on the left side of the room, break the darkness. The silhouettes belong both to victims of the dictatorship, as well as to persons living at the time of the creation of the artwork in 2010. The visitors' mirrored image accompanies this infinite row of white silhouettes emerging from complete darkness. After a minute, the darkness returns, the doors open, and the visitor can walk back up the stairs to the plaza. Jaar's artwork intentionally

> [makes] visible the human rights violations committed by the state during the period 1973-1990, to give back dignity to the victims and to their families and stimulate reflection and debates on the importance of respect and tolerance so that this kind of events don't repeat themselves. It participates to the ethical imperative of the obligation to remember (Mora 2016, p. 33).

Usually, the *disappeared* are represented as absent, and artists use their black and white photographs to evoke their loss. In this case, the artist refers to the absence by showing the shapes of both the detained and persons alive in 2010 and supports the idea that the dictatorship affected everybody because, as Jaar said, "we have all lost something with the dictatorship" (Mora 2016, p. 34). Surpassing the traditional form of memorials, which are consecrated exclusively to the victims, Jaar proposes a memorial that includes the entire Chilean society, not only the victims and their families (Mora 2016, p. 34). By choosing to eliminate portraits and including only their silhouettes, the identification of the spectator with the artwork is achieved (Mora 2016, p. 35) through the use of the mirror. As Alfredo Jaar himself recognized: "I wanted to create a sort of geometry, of symmetry between the ones alive and the dead, to suggest with that that we can understand ourselves, the past, and the future only if we are illuminated by both: those alive and those dead" (Mora 2016, p. 35). Rancière considers Jaar's images "pensive" as they lie "outside of the system of information," becoming "post-images of human rights that have left their memory...in a sort of aesthetic unconscious where the duty of the human being is to see a reality that nobody wants to see" (Gomez-Moya 2012, p. 50).

In the total darkness concerning the dictatorial past, Jaar intervenes using aesthetic strategies such as the use of light to emphasize the silhouettes of those that constitute the Chilean society, that is both those that were killed and remain disappeared and those that are still alive and must remember those that are no longer here. Visual dignity in this case translates into the use of light as a metaphor to disrupt the darkness of the past.

The second Chilean example is that of Enrique Ramirez' works that deal with forgetting and insists on how "memory does not forget anything" (*Breezes*). In Chile, 1100 persons are still considered disappeared by the reports of the Truth commissions. According to the information received by the Chilean government in 1999, 200 bodies of those illegally detained were thrown by the military into the Pacific Ocean. The artist has reflected in his artworks this horrendous fact, and in three video-works titled *Breezes*, *Pacific*, and *The Sleepers*[9] (2014), he links his work to that of the TJ mechanisms in Chile, as the artist says in his statement presenting the latter work:

> The second objective [of the Table of Dialogue of 1999], was to obtain information about the fate of the arrested missing people (officially around one thousand cases). These disappearances have clouded the national collective imagination. The army took over the brutality of the past: first there was a real admission of guilt, but the most striking in this confession is that the Army insisted on the inevitable disappearance of the bodies. The sentence « thrown into the sea » is written along most of the names that were in the list (list that was incomplete). This is the most recent image that the Army offers to the nation to settle a common vision of the history: the Chilean sea the only place that is not one: the Pacific Ocean.[10]

The Sleepers evokes "a particularly abominable episode of the Chilean dictatorship: victims—some still alive—were thrown into the sea from helicopters, tied to railway ties."[11] We see three stages of their story on a triptych. The video at the center shows an older man that carries a fish, while the video on the left displays images of the ocean, and the video on the right side accompanies them with images of the crosses in the ocean. A voice that accompanies the images tells us:

> Look at how things fall apart (...) a train, the oblivion, the silence, The salty mouth, Eyes open under the water, The life we have never seen, Leave a trace in the sea, Search for something that is not seen, there where the history is silent, there where the history would seek silence.

[9]This translates in Spanish as both sleepers and railway ties.

[10]https://enriqueramirez.net/portfolio/pacifico/.

[11]https://enriqueramirez.net/portfolio/los-durmientes/.

Fig. 11.3 Enrique Ramirez, *Breezes* (2008)

A younger man who continues to walk along the ocean replaces the old man, and the voice continues to tell us: "Fabricate the silence, fabricate forgetting, fabricate fear, fabricate the return, fabricate the search, fabricate the time." The two men meet and embrace each other. On the screen to the left a helicopter appears, and we hear the sound as the two men reach water, while the screen on the right shows the crosses in water decorated with the flag of Chile. The video *Pacific* also part of this triptych shows us the waves of the ocean, the final point for the victims of the military dictatorship in Chile.

In these video pieces, Ramirez recalls how the military used train rails to make the bodies they threw into the ocean stay on the bottom of the ocean. Through the speaking narrator, the artist emphasizes how the military enforced silence, and how families continued to search for their missing relatives. Ramirez' video works poetically to reinsert into the public realm terrible acts of the dictatorship that have been erased from the public memory, and this video piece grants victims a form of symbolic or poetic reparation: the dignity of being remembered.

Finally, in the video artwork *Breezes (see Fig. 11.3)*, which lasts eleven minutes, the viewer accompanies a man dressed in a costume with water dripping on his clothes as he walks in downtown Santiago towards the presidential palace of *La Moneda*. He enters the building crossing the interior yard, to exit on the other side. The voice over that accompanies the man's walk reflects on the memory of the past mixing personal memories with more general ideas. "Healing takes time, Curing takes time (...) The history is ours; History is mine (...) Is it possible to look back at the past? How can we understand what we were? (...) The memory does not forget anything." The artist as narrator asks these questions, and others, reflecting on how the memory of the past makes people grey, in a grey city, and how this overflow of memory in this place influences their lives still today.

Thus, the first artwork, the installation by Jaar, illuminates the geometry of the conscience of those that are alive by including in the societal narrative of those that are missing. This type of aesthetic strategy of memorialization of the Chilean dictatorship disrupts official policy, highlighting the necessary reconciliation with the dictatorial past, and implicit forgetting, as a way to move forward, of avoiding conflicts of interpretation of the past. Jaar acknowledges those missing and places them next to those that remain alive as a form of poetic reparation, emphasizing their permanent absence as a lasting scar in the collective narrative.

In his artwork *The Sleepers*, Ramirez choses to represent the killing by the military of those who were detained illegally, tortured, and thereafter thrown from helicopters into the Pacific Ocean. The artist recreates in a very cinematic approach the violence used by the military dictatorship, and by transforming its protagonist from an old man to a young man, he personifies the memory of those killed in terrible conditions. Finally, in *Breezes,* Ramirez reflects on the relationship the Chilean society, shown in the video through the emblematic image of the presidential palace (where the former president Salvador Allende was killed on the day of the military coup of September the 11th, 1973), has with the memory of the suffering of victims during the dictatorship. Ramirez reflects on the status of the memory of the suffering in a poetic, cinematic approach.

11.6 Conclusion

30 years ago, two regions of Eastern Europe and South America avoided confrontation with the dramatic past through officially imposed policies of forgetting and reconciliation. Yet, unresolved issues, related to restoring Human Dignity to the victims, remain.

This chapter highlights the role artistic renderings of the dictatorial past can play in restoring human dignity to the victims. I argued, visual artists in Romania and Chile question the official memory, which emphasizes forgetting (in Romania), or reconciliation (in Chile), and use different aesthetic strategies to grant human dignity back to the victims of the dictatorships. This symbolic reparation is possible through offering victims a form of visual dignity, with each artwork providing a perspective on the human dignity of the victims (Garnsey 2016, p. 97).

Artists use the personalization of suffering by showing us specific portraits of the victims; artists constitute a collective narrative which includes not only the victims but also the survivors to offer a form of poetic reparation to those forgotten, whose dreadful deaths have been erased from collective memory.

In Romania, remembering the victims of communism is not and has not been a priority for the postcommunist regime. Through the documentation of the individual stories of the victims of repression during communism, Constantinescu in *The Archive of Pain* (2000) and Thomas Ciulei in *The craziness of the heads* (1997) restore visual dignity to the victims. Their suffering is now part of the memorialization of communism through an artistic documentation.

In Chile, Alfredo Jaar's underground installation, *Geometry of Conscience* (2010) proposes an infinitely illuminated series of white contoured silhouettes of both the victims of the Chilean dictatorship and the survivors. Jaar's aesthetic strategy of using the endless white silhouettes dignifies the victims by inserting their story in the collective history and supports the idea that everybody was affected by the dictatorship, and thus, there is a responsibility in remembering.

By recreating in a poetic light, the Chilean state's approach to the memory of the victims in his video triptych (*The Sleepers, Pacific, Breezes*), Enrique Ramirez grants back human dignity to the victims, to those otherwise forgotten, ignored by the democratic regime by reinserting their story into public discourse. Ramirez's video works provide additional information on what happened to the victims, specifically to those that were killed by the military by being thrown into the Pacific Ocean. Ramirez reflects on the erasure of memory and on the imposed silence, as well as questions if we can look back at the past.

To conclude, in this chapter I have argued that these two cases, although opposed extreme cases, represent models of how contemporary visual discourses engage with a traumatic past, which is otherwise marginalized or erased by official policies. I argue artistic evocations such as those analyzed help us remember the details of a past that the official memory would like us to forget. Artists in different post-dictatorial contexts employ poetic instruments such as metaphors, or on the contrary use brutal images of a recent past to conjure remembrance of those victims whose dignity was taken by the predatory states. At the threshold between forgetting and remembrance, artists in Romania and Chile insist on the memory of those that were victims of their respective dictatorships and stress the need to recall their experiences as an obligation.

References

Atencio R, Gates-Madsen N (2013) Art and transitional justice. In: Stan L, Nedelsky N (eds) Encyclopedia of transitional justice. Cambridge University Press, Cambridge, pp 117–123

Audhuy C (2015) Freud und Leid: theater im Konzentrationslager. TV Documentation ARTE, April 20, 2015. http://info.arte.tv/de/theater-im-kz

Bahun S (2015) Transitional justice and the arts: reflections on the field. In: Eisikovits N, Corradetti C, Volpe J (eds) Theorizing transitional justice. Ashgate, UK, pp 153–166

Barat CR (2020) The path to social reconstruction: between culture and transitional justice. Int J Transit Justice 14(1):242–250

Besliu R (2014) "Communist nostalgia in Romania", Open Democracy, 13 April. https://www.opendemocracy.net/en/can-europe-make-it/communist-nostalgia-in-romania/. Accessed 30 June 2023

Brodsky R (2015) Presentación. In: Operación Condor. Historias personales, memorias compartidas. Museo de la Memoria y los Derechos Humanos, Santiago, p 11

Cabeza Monteira Á et al (eds) (2017) Patrimonio de la memoria de los derechos humanos en Chile Sitios de memoria protegidos como Monumentos nacionales 1996/2016. Dibam, Santiago

Cardenas Hernandez AP (2017) La puesta en valor de la memoria de las violaciones a los derechos humanos. In: Cabeza Monteira Á et al (eds) Patrimonio de la memoria de los derechos humanos en Chile Sitios de memoria protegidos como Monumentos nacionales 1996/2016. Dibam, Santiago, p 8

Cento Bull A, Hansen HL (2020) Agonistic memory and the UNREST project. Mod Lang Open 1. https://doi.org/10.3828/mlo.v0i0.319

De Brito AB, Enriquez CG, Paloma A (eds) (2001) The politics of memory and democratization : transitional justice in democratizing societies. Oxford University Press, Oxford

Düwell M, Braarvig J, Brownsword R, Mieth D (2014) Why a handbook on human dignity. In: Düwell M et al (eds) The Cambridge handbook of human dignity. Cambridge University Press, Cambridge, pp xvii–xxii

Erll A (2010) Literature, film and the mediality of cultural memory. In: Erll A, Nunning A (eds) A companion to cultural memory studies. De Gruyter, Berlin, pp 389–398

Etkind A (2013) Warped mourning stories of the undead in the land of the unburied. Stanford University Press, Stanford

Garnsey E (2016) Framing human dignity: visual jurisprudence at South Africa's Constitutional Court. Aust J Hum Rights 22(2):81–101. https://doi.org/10.1080/1323238X.2016.11910943

Garnsey E (2019) The justice of visual art creative state-building in times of political transition. Cambridge University Press, Cambridge

Gewirth A (1992) Human dignity as the basis of rights. In: Meyer MA, Parent WA (eds) The constitution of rights: human dignity and American values. Cornell University Press, Ithaca, pp 10–28

Giunta A (2017) Poetics of resistance. In: Fajardo-Hill C, Giunta A (eds) Radical women: Latin American Art, 1960-1985. Prestel Publishing, Hammer Museum, pp 251–259

Gomez-Moya C (2012) Derechos de Mirada. Arte y visualidad en los archivos desclasificados. Palinodia, Santiago

Gutman Y, Wüstenberg J (eds) (2023) The Routledge handbook of memory activism. Routledge, London

Habermas J (2018) Human dignity perspectives from a critical theory of human rights. In: Nascimento A, Bachmann ML (eds) Human dignity perspectives from a critical theory of human rights. Routledge, London, pp 52–70

Huntington SP (1991) The third wave: democratization in the late twentieth century. University of Oklahoma Press, Oklahoma

Lawner M (2017) Arquitectura y memoria histórica. In: Cabeza Monteira Á et al (eds) Patrimonio de la memoria de los derechos humanos en Chile Sitios de memoria protegidos como Monumentos nacionales 1996/2016. Dibam, Santiago, pp 19–24

Mora M (2016) Éthique et esthétique. Une approche possible de la lisibilité de l'histoire. In: Medina J, Mora M, Soulages F (eds) Frontières et dictatures Images, regards – Chili, Argentine. L'Harmattan, Paris

Pless NM, Maak T, Harris H (2017) Art, ethics and the promotion of human dignity. J Bus Ethics 144(2):223–232

Rancière J (2008) Le spectateur emancipé. La Fabrique, Paris

Rush PD, Simić O (2016) The arts of transitional justice culture, activism and memory after atrocity. Springer, New York

Shefik S (2018) Reimagining transitional justice through participatory art. Int J Transit Justice 12(2):314–333

Stan L (2012) Reckoning with the communist past in Romania: a scorecard. Europe-Asia Stud 65(1):127–146. https://doi.org/10.1080/09668136.2012.6980

The Memorial to the Victims of Communism and to the Resistance. http://www.memorialsighet.ro/recensamantul-populatiei-concentrationare/#fise_matricole_penale. Accessed 30 June 2023

Chapter 12
Shame, Trauma, and Guilt: Restoring Dignity Through Empathy

Stephanie N. Arel

Abstract This chapter explores human dignity from two disciplinary perspectives: theology and psychology. In the western Judeo-Christian framework dignity emerges as the human created in God's image or as the *Imago Dei*. From a psychological standpoint, self-worth, both conceived and perceived, constitutes human dignity. The two disciplinary perspectives illuminate a dual conception of dignity, as (1) inherent or internally developed and (2) acquired or externally confirmed. Inherent dignity assumes an unassailability, while acquired or perceived dignity remains assailable: one person or persons can diminish or externally destroy another's perceived dignity. Trauma enacted by human design undermines the perception of self-worth and dignity, despite the assurance of human dignity inherent in notion of humanity's creation in the image of God. Exploring trauma perpetuated by human design underscores a tension in dignity, between the internal and external worlds. Trauma affects dignity internally related to human affect and externally related to approbation and empathy. Internally, shame affectively impairs dignity as an outcome of trauma. Restoring dignity, and lessening the shame experience, requires the internal belief of self-worth. Human relationships facilitate the development of such worth. The internal belief instills itself through the external approbation of another, here outlined as empathic connection. A cycle emerges; structural parallels between shame and empathy intertwine at a threshold where a dearth of empathy feeds into more shame and less dignity. When shame goes unaddressed, the affect inhibits empathy and undermines human dignity both intrinsically, as self-worth, and extrinsically, as part of the social fabric of human life. The chapter thus argues that a connection with others, considered as shared empathy, combats the violation of human dignity enacted by shame and trauma.

S. N. Arel (✉)
Fordham University, New York City, NY, USA
e-mail: sarel@fordham.edu

S. N. Arel et al. (eds.), *Probing Human Dignity*,
https://doi.org/10.1007/978-3-031-42437-3_12

12.1 Introduction

Throughout this volume, authors negotiate varying interpretations of human dignity, from the perspective of law, political theory, art, anthropology, etc. This chapter begins with definitions of human dignity from two different perspectives: theology and psychology. In theology, dignity transpires from the Judeo-Christian framework that God creates humans in God's own image as the *Imago Dei*. Inherent dignity cannot be lost as dignity encapsulates the notion of the human in the likeness of God.[1] Human dignity develops in modern Catholic thought as both substantive—constituting the image of God in the human person—and relational—comprising the image of God in others. The relationality reflects as the triune nature of God in three persons, the Father, the son and the Holy Spirit, each related to the other in mutual love (Hollenbach 2014, p. 253). In psychology, the conception and perception of a person's self-worth constitutes human dignity. Both disciplines envision dignity as an interior phenomenon—conceiving oneself as made in God's image and worthy—and exteriorly associated with a relationship—being seen as *Imago Dei* or as having worth that demands respect.

These two definitions illuminate a dual concept of dignity, as inherent or internally developed and as developed in response to external experiences or another. One enters the world with internal "worth" or dignity simply by nature of being human. But external experiences possess potential to diminish or destroy dignity, at least insofar as that dignity rests in the realm of perception. This chapter argues that incidences of trauma undermine the perception of self-worth, and yet the inherent nature of presumed self-worth perpetuated in the Judeo-Christian tradition by the notion of the *Imago Dei* establishes a platform denying the possibility of human dignity's complete eradication, from psychological and theological point of views.

Exploring trauma perpetuated by human design underscores this tension in dignity, between the internal and external worlds. Examining trauma reveals how its effects relate internally to human affect and externally to approbation and empathy. Shame rests at the heart of this interconnection. Clarifying the correlations between shame and trauma requires presenting shame as a biological and social phenomenon to distinguish it from guilt; confusion between shame and guilt obscure the impact of the former and its amelioration. Distinguishing between guilt and shame underscores the debilitating nature of shame and the experienced loss of dignity. To restore dignity requires reducing the shame experience and promoting the internal belief of self-worth. This belief instills itself through the external approbation of another, here outlined as empathic connection.

This new threshold of understanding dignity comes to the fore in the argument that trauma perpetuates shame and humiliation, the most intense form of the shame affect. Unaddressed shame inhibits empathy attenuating human dignity both

[1] Gaudium et Spes (Pastoral Constitution on the Church in the Modern World), no. 29. https://www.vatican.va/archive/hist_councils/ii_vatican_council/documents/vat-ii_const_19651207_gaudium-et-spes_en.html.

intrinsically, as self-worth, and extrinsically, as part of the social fabric of human life. Shared empathy, or human connection, ameliorates the violation of human dignity endured through shame and trauma. To resurrect dignity in both internal and external domains requires understanding the contiguity of shame and empathy.

12.2 Human Dignity: Intrinsic and Extrinsic

The *Imago Dei* has its roots in Genesis 1:27: "God created humankind in His image, in the image of God He created them; male and female He created them." The passage clarifies God's participation with humanity in creation: God makes God's self seen through humankind, and humankind shapes the world alongside God. Humankind, therefore, must behave like God—loving others for instance. Theological anthropology on this topic highlights the concept of the *Imago Dei* in the patterning of human dignity as within the self but also reliant on relationality. The *Imago Dei* reflects the dual ideas that the "invisible" image of God which "someone is, represents, or embodies" illustrates an internalization of that God, and that the "the image someone else perceives, which poses the challenge of seeing more than one can see optically" illustrates the external perception of that God (Welz 2016, p. 2).

The Judeo-Christian notion of the Imago-Dei emerges in various cultural interpretations of dignity. For instance, the Anglican Archbishop Desmond Tutu integrates the western notion of *Imago Dei* into the traditional Nguni Bantu concept of Ubuntu. Tutu writes,

> Each one of us has been created in the image of God. This is something intrinsic. It means that each one of us is a God-carrier, God's viceroy, God's representative (Tutu 2004, 93).

This definition of the *Imago Dei* implicates *how* persons should treat one another. This reliability on and relationship with others intertwine with Ubuntu, "which speaks to the very essence of being human" (Tutu 2004, p. 31). The depth of the term exceeds one English summation, and so Tutu offers several expressions to explain it: "My humanity is caught up, is inextricably bound up, in yours", "A person is a person through other persons," and "I am human because I belong. I participate. I share" (Tutu 2004, p. 31). Viewed through this lens, a person experiences dignity internally as a carrier of God and externally as having one's humanity entangled with the humanity of another.

From a psychological point of view, human dignity continues to carry this duality: dignity represents both a foundational concept related to the perception of self-value built on the concept of intrinsic self-worth and the self's being in constant relationship with other persons (Kirchhoffer 2017). This interpretation of dignity intertwines with theological anthropological interpretations of the term. Dignity corresponds with self-value or self-worth, theologically the *Imago Dei,* but relies on the perception of value that arises related to human connection.

Psychiatrist Eli Markovitz underscores this binary nature of dignity in its conception as both an intra-psychic (intrinsic) and a social phenomenon (extrinsic). Feeling dignified or worthy, and recognizing oneself as having innate worth, couples with a state of being recognized as worthy or dignified (Markovitz 2016, pp. 62–71). Recognizing the connection between self-worth and treatment by others facilitates an understanding of dignity's evolution, stabilization, and restoration in situations that undermine dignity.

Markovitz also considers dignity a developmental phenomenon—emerging internally at age two with mastery of the body: walking, running, and bodily functions, then in the attainment of skills and adaptation—to the world and in adjusting the world to fit oneself. This mastery leads to self-respect, and a sense of power and agency. In the face of external life challenges, dignity requires implementation of this power manifesting in self-assertion. Markovitz locates within dignity a mix of pride and humility—a high self-regard combined with a knowledge of one's limitations. The internal manifestations of dignity and its experience as an internal reality culminate in the experience of affinity which relies on others. Thus, dignity in this psychological framework arises when "one feels as part of something, generating a perception of worth in living for something" (p. 71).

In Markovitz's observations dignity depends on "Being, Knowing, Doing, Creating, and Impressing" (p. 69). Most of these relate to action, but the concept of "being" carries with it a meaning that worthiness in the form of dignity relies simply on the state of being alive, just as does the *Imago Dei.* De Rosis (1973) underscores this concept when she equates dignity with psychic wholeness or a "sense of being" distinguished from self-esteem (p. 22). In this construction, wholeness and dignity emerge in the individual capacity to maintain a sense of self and tolerate the influence of others. The opposite emerges in the case of humiliation "the destroyer of dignity" (Markovitz 2016, p. 66). "To humiliate," Marcovitz writes, "is to dishonor, to degrade, to expose weakness" (p. 66). Humiliation comes from the outside, but shame, connected directly with humiliation, is "carried around inside" and is a "constant drain on dignity" (p. 66). From a more ethical view, Avishai Margalit articulates the same interplay where humiliation violates a person's or victim's dignity, felt internally as shame (Margalit 2004, p. 86).

In both theological anthropology, which aims to diagnose the religious person, and psychology, which aims to understand the human psyche, human dignity evolves as both an intrinsic concept and an extrinsic one. Theoretically, the intrinsic sense of dignity refutes erasure; inherency prohibits erasure. However, the intrinsic interpretation of dignity relies on others. This reliance reinforces vulnerability with the potential to eradicate dignity. Furthermore, extrinsic violations possess the power to alter the *perception* of innate dignity.

12.3 Trauma: An Extrinsic Violation

Definitions of trauma in psychological literature vary. This chapter focuses on trauma related to its impact on the body, building on the most recent research in neuroscience, neurobiology, and developmental psychopathology. From this vantage point, trauma constitutes an extrinsic event that produces intrinsic physiological changes, altering how the body signals external threat to the brain, increasing stress hormones, and interfering with the brain's ability to filter information to distinguish what is relevant from what is irrelevant (Van der Kolk 2015; Perry 2021). Bruce Perry's concise definition applies: trauma is an experience that influences the way that stress systems work and therefore has a long-term impact (Perry 2021).

Thus, trauma engenders an interior experience of an exterior event. The external circumstances alter a person's biological and neurological stasis based on a variety of factors including but not limited to personal history, individual genetic makeup, prior trauma, and ability to manage cognitive processes. Therefore, one person's trauma distinguishes itself from another's; people have different abilities to manage extrinsic events, based on inherited traits and past experiences, and therefore they will emerge from a traumatic event with different effects. These effects depend on the age at which the trauma occurred, the length of time that the traumatic event lasted, and the degree of social or familial support an individual receives during and after a trauma (van der Kolk 2015, pp. 2–3). When the traumatic experience remains central to a person's identity or when a person continues to experience life as if the traumatic environment persists, the trauma stays interior to the self. The self perceives every exterior event informed by that trauma. The war veteran provides a classic example: when a car backfires the sound triggers, and fails to be discriminated from, the sounds of combat. The veteran responds as if the war happens in real time. Traumatic triggers emerge in flashbacks, nightmares, and similar sensory intrusions. Generally, the long-term impact of traumatic triggers relates to the inability to integrate a traumatic event, or to make sense of it.

Trauma influences the brain. Symptomatology of PTSD includes long-term dysregulation of norepinephrine and cortisol systems as per the Diagnostic and Statistical Manual of Mental Disorders (DSM-5 1994; Sherin and Nemeroff 2011). Populations who experience PTSD vary, including war veterans and persons who have endured abuse, accidents, disasters, or assaults. Children are particularly vulnerable to trauma and have increased neuropsychiatric reactions such as PTSD; the fragility of the brain in childhood contributes to such sensitivity, as the organ most rapidly develops and organizes in childhood (Ludy-Dobson and Perry 2010, 28). Trauma, therefore, effects brain development (Perry 2021).

In most cases of PTSD, a person experiences a sense of being persistently on high alert, emotionally reactive, and intense. Vulnerable areas of the brain—the hippocampus, amygdala, and medial prefrontal cortex—manifest an inhibition of learning, changes in memory, alterations in the fear response, and erratic responses to others (Sherin and Nemeroff 2011). On one end of the spectrum, a persistent negative emotional state ensues such as fear, horror, and anger. Memories of the event intrude in the form of flashbacks (Van der Kolk et al. 1989; Herman 1982). On the opposite end of this spectrum, a person constricts having diminished interest or participation in significant activities. Feelings of detachment or estrangement from others emerges alongside a persistent inability to experience positive emotions (e.g., inability to experience happiness, satisfaction, or loving feelings; Center for Substance Abuse Treatment 2014).

Exaggerated negative beliefs or expectations about oneself, others, or the world such as, "I am bad," "No one can be trusted," "The world is completely dangerous" accompany negative emotional states (DSM-5 1994). Persistent, distorted cognitions about the cause or consequences of the traumatic event(s) evolve leading the individual to blame himself/herself; persistent negative emotional states of guilt or shame also erupt. Self-blame represents an inwardly directed impetus that mars a sense of one's dignity, while the belief of an inherently dangerous world provokes behaviors—defensiveness, withdraw, violence—that affect the external conceptions or perceptions of dignity.

Shame arises. Its presence in the response to traumatic events highlights its importance to this examination, because of the affective link between shame and humiliation, where humiliation plays a central role in the depreciation of human dignity and connects to the central effect of trauma. The argument for shame as central in the response to a traumatic event emerges in Judith Herman's 2011 essay: "Posttraumatic Stress Disorder as a Shame Disorder." Here, Herman argues that the usual assumption of anxiety and fear as central to PTSD applies in trauma as a one-time event, such as an auto accident, but the explication fails to be sufficient when considering other types of traumas: sexual abuse, domestic violence, war, the state of being a refugee, or enduring racism or any other kind of constant discrimination or abuse for instance. These traumas by human design persevere over a long-term as insidious, sometimes cumulative, shame experiences.

12.4 Shame

Considering PTSD as a shame disorder shifts the focus from addressing indicators of fear and anxiety towards behaviors that indicate shame such as withdrawal or enacting violence on the self or others. Shame and humiliation influence dignity (Markovitz 2016; Tomkins 2008; Margalit 2004), manifesting internally—where humiliation represents the most extreme felt response of shame and externally to humiliate a person by violating body or soul induces shame. Interiorly felt humiliation/shame provoked by exteriorly imposed humiliation/shame approaches dignity's threshold. Felt, destroyed, and maintained dignity meets shame at the center of discourse around trauma and its recovery.

Shame is a biologically intrinsic and socially extrinsic phenomenon. Shame shares with fear and horror the ability to effectively impact all mammals and, as an affect, to cross cultural divides. This does not mean that the same social cues that inspire shame in one cultural context inspire it in another, but that shame instigates a similar visceral experience, an immediate and overwhelming physiological response. The outward physical manifestations include a bowed head, blushing, a turning under of the lips or sucking them in, averting the eyes downward, slumping the shoulders, covering of the face, and turning away (Tomkins 2008, p. 159). Children experiencing shame suddenly go limp, losing all tonicity in their muscles (Schore 2016).

Shame emerges in human development prior to the ability to use verbal language. Humans and non-humans share the shame experience as evidenced by the appeasement display when an animal in a fight surrenders by lying on its back and exposing its belly in a gesture of vulnerability and submission (Maibom n.d., pp. 12–14). Thus, shame lies at the center of behavior and in relation to others. Shame functions to preserve social bonds and thus represents a normal physiological response; it manifests to signal threat but also to indicate interest in another and therefore evidences an investment in that person's perception (Williams 2008; Dickerson et al. 2004). The shame affect arises in the experience of being seen, provoking a sense of withdrawal, embarrassment, vulnerability; but tension arises due to an investment in the relationship with the other and a desire to stay. Trauma distorts these normal exchanges and therefore disrupts the social functions of shame.

When shame swings to the more intense end of the affective spectrum and moves into the field of humiliation, often a result of trauma, its subjective experience manifests as shock. Painful emotions overwhelm the nervous system, and a loss of language ensues, returning the self to the preverbal state of the initiation of shame. This response parallels the freeze response initiated by the amygdala which works to have an organism fight, flee, or freeze in the face of danger.

Feeling afraid, small, powerless, and having the impulse to hide evinces the inability to maintain eye contact, the inability to speak, and in extreme cases, the inability to escape harm. This posture facilitates an internal sense of feeling unworthy, or as lacking dignity, but also influences the perceptions of others in viewing someone as dignified. Sometimes, a person in such shame will, instead of withdrawing, fleeing, or freezing, assume the posture of fighting, enacting violence on another. Violent behavior intimates shame (Scheff 1987). In traumatic circumstances, shame may also provoke a bifurcation of the self, or experiencing and observing the self simultaneously, as in the event of dissociation.

Embarrassment registers shame at its minimum; in a moderately healthy person the feeling—the blushing—fades quickly, and life continues as normal. However, traumatic external environment or exterior relationships increase shame's potency and longevity. On the affective spectrum, humiliation signifies the maximum expression of shame. Trauma by human design humiliates. For Markovitz, humiliation destroys dignity (Markovitz 2016). In a manual for treatment of childhood sexual abuse, Cloitre et al. (2006) explain that stories that trigger shame lead to humiliation in their recounting. Thus, simply sharing a traumatic memory (in the absence of safety protocols, capable therapists, secure attachments, etc.) has the potential to recreate the experience of shame and humiliation, undercutting human dignity. Avoiding this dynamic requires creating a situation where human connection alleviates shame and encourages dignity or the sense being dignified. Therapeutic encounters work to facilitate the felt effects of dignity, but an empathic, secure human connection can provide the same.

A critical move includes establishing the grounds for safety which fosters a sense of control of the body and the environment. Establishing control enables the telling of the trauma story while granting a sense of autonomy to the teller.

> In the same way that narratives of fear must be titrated so that the client experiences mastery over fear rather than a reinstatement of it, so too, narratives of shame should be titrated so that the client experiences dignity rather than humiliation in the telling, (De Young 2015, p. 122).

The titration occurs when exposure to the shame affect occurs in the smallest possible dosages, so that, in the therapeutic environment, a person can confront the shame, within an ongoing connection. As will be shown later, the restitution of dignity demands this connection, critical to a trauma survivor. Thus, in the affective spectrum of shame-embarrassment-humiliation, shame degrades with human dignity. Mediated shame produces dignity rather than humiliation. But shame confused and conflated with guilt inhibits access to the process. Distinguishing shame from guilt elucidates how shame intertwines with dignity in a way that guilt does not.

12.5 Guilt

Moral philosopher Bernard Williams roots guilt in the sensation of hearing, in the sound of the voice of judgment (2008, p. 89). Guilt operates, within this framework, on the level of the audible. Categorized as moral emotion, guilt appears at the age of three in children, with the cognitive ability to acknowledge and modify behavior (Erickson 1950, pp. 255–258; 1959, pp. 71–80. See also Schore 2003, p. 153). The child understands his/her capacity to take initiative and to "do" something, while realizing that attached to the thing done is some qualifier; an authority determines behavior as either good or bad, and the child can articulate this. In Williams' framework, the voice of God supports the discernment (Williams 2008, pp. 89–95). Guilt includes realizing, accurately or not, a misstep in a wrongdoing, a violation of a moral or ethical standard, or a transgression of a relational boundary. Thus, guilt points outward toward an act—the misstep—and therefore focuses on action. This act may elicit anger in another party or in the self. No matter what the guilty party does, the guiltiness of the act remains, unless an apology or atonement occurs. Guilt's logic echoes: "Even if I disappear, what I have done wrong goes with me." The consequences of guilt leave people feeling either regret for wrongdoing or denying any wrongdoing which subsequently evokes a level of hostility. Treating guilt requires forgiveness and absolution. Unaddressed guilt, that for which no repentance is sought, turns into shame.

Table 12.1 Ways to distinguish guilt from shame according to the work of English moral philosopher Bernard Williams in *Shame and Necessity* (2008)

	Shame	Guilt
Sense Orientation	Visible	Audible
Conceptualization	Covering, hiding	Realizing
Location	Points inward	Points outward
Aroused by	Defect, failure	Act that elicits anger
Logic	Disappearing	Disappearing fails
Consequences	Diminishment	Regret (positive) or Denial (negative)
Treatment of	Therapy	Absolution/Forgiveness
Dangers	Turns into violence to self or others	Turns into shame

12.6 Shame, Guilt, and Dignity

In terms of sense orientation, shame connects to sight and being seen. In a previous work, this author detailed how the Christian formation of the self, embodied by the lonely sinner seeking God's mercy, forms from the personification of Adam and Eve in the garden as sinners in shame—not in guilt (Arel 2016). Thus, the notion that shame implies an experience of the inferior self in the eyes of another locates shame's transpiration in a logic of exposure. In shame, a person finds ways of avoiding exposure—seeking concealment (Gilligan 1996, p. 64). Being seen when we perceive ourselves as inferior—or in shame—magnifies the shame experience, leading to humiliation and opposing dignity. A logical response to this sense of shame when in the gaze of the other is to cover-up, withdraw, or hide. As such, in shame, focus points inward to a perceived diminished or passive self, lacking dignity. The logic behind shame proceeds: "If I disappear, then no one will see me, and my shame will go away." The consequences of shame include feeling diminished or lessened. In a theological framework, shame in this construction undermines the *Imago Dei*. Psychologically, treating shame requires invention, therapeutic or otherwise. Guilt requires a simple apology for its amelioration. And while guilt unaddressed can morph into a shame response, unaddressed shame dangerously turns into violence directed towards the self or others (Table 12.1).

The table distinguishes the two affects in their structure and in their lived experience. Ultimately, shame and guilt can be understood through the articulation of two simple ideas which connect to human dignity. In guilt, a person identifies as having done something wrong. This act lies external to the self, as does perceived dignity, and while guilt implicates the self, it does not define the internal state of self-worth or dignity. Conversely, in shame, the self perceives itself as bad, disgusting, and shameful. The alarming, painful, or disgusting turns inward to define the self; self-worth diminishes, as does the perception of dignity. The actual physiological expression of shame underscores this perceived loss of dignity: persons who experience an internal sense of dignity or persons treated as dignified rarely cower, bow their heads, look downtrodden, slump their shoulders or avert their gaze. In the Christian tradition, at this juncture between shame and guilt lies the understanding of sin. Interpreting sin as an inner defect aligns it closely to shame. This author discussed elsewhere how this presents a psychological obstacle (Arel 2016) and interferes to the upholding of dignity as the *Imago Dei* or as inherent.

The internalization of some inner defect—psychologically buttressed by shame, theologically buttressed by notions of sin—manifests externally as an exterior symbolization. This symbolization leads to more shame and withdrawal or manifests as violence. Shame's power derives from an ability to diminish pride, not pride understood as hubris, but pride derivative of self-confidence and self-worth. James Gilligan studies this phenomenon at length in his research of the American penal system (Gilligan 2003). In his work with violent criminals, he interprets violence as the result of a deep desire to eradicate shame from the body and to reinstate pride. Gilligan writes that

> the basic psychological motive, or cause, of violent behavior is the wish to ward off or eliminate the feeling of shame and humiliation—a feeling that is painful and can even be intolerable and overwhelming—and to replace it with its opposite, the feeling of pride (2003, p. 1153).

Further, feeling shamed equates to feeling "dissed" in Gilligan's terms, and he argues that the prison system perpetuates such shame (2003, p. 1149). Being dissed, shamed, or humiliated relies on two important aspects of the shame experience: the internal experience of feeling unworthy—without dignity—and the exterior, social experience of being told that one is not worthy (as in the prison system)—treated without dignity.

Highly implicated in social relationships, even within the confines of a prison, shame emerges and fluctuates in social situations. In fact, shame hinges on the presence of the other, even though the affect can be experienced in isolation. Simply imagining a situation of feeling shame before the other elicits shame. The situation signifies shame in the presence of a real or imagined other, where shame occurs as a consciousness of a loss or failure of the self to live up to the expectations of the idealized other (Williams 2008, pp. 219–220).

The real or imagined disapproval of the other provokes the shame affect marking shame's "transition from a preexisting positive state to a negative state" (Herman 2011, p. 6). In its positive state, mediated by the parasympathetic nervous system, shame functions like a "brake" to excited arousal states. In some situations, this maintains personal safety of the self. The state regulates social investments and dissipates. However, when shame floods the body and transforms excited joy into something sober, or completely shuts down the body's capacity to act, the affect progresses to indicate a more deleterious aspect. This generally emerges in the face of a serious threat. For survivors of trauma, numerous and detrimental triggers result. Just as fear and its physiological correlates represent integral components of the response when the physical self-endures threat, shame and its accompanying physiology constitute components of a coordinated psychobiological response triggered with the threat of the social self (Dickerson et al. 2004, p. 1194).

Shame's power stems from its capacity to control behavior biologically according to social cues. The mores of society, for instance those that qualify someone or something as good or bad, or tasteful or disgusting, can shape a person in shame. In more extreme forms, being treated in a degrading manner ignites shame. The extreme family of shame emotions includes humiliation and feelings of defilement, disgrace, or dishonor. In hierarchical societies, disgust and contempt signify "emotions of status demarcation" that consign to lower status those against whom they are directed (Miller 1997). Relationships of dominance and subordination are inherently shaming. The social signals of subordinate status (bowed head and body, lowered eyes) signal elaborate and ritualized expressions of the biological signals of shame. In slavery, the most extreme form of social subordination, the enslaved person exists in a permanently dishonored status that Patterson (1982) describes as "social death" (Herman 2011, p. 265).

Herman (2011) asserts shames identifiability across cultural divides as coercive control and methods of domination generate shame. She illuminates this through a consideration of the *Amnesty International Report on Torture* (1973). In a discussion of this paper, Herman outlines torture treatments according to their consequences. For instance, the capricious endorsement of petty rules and intermittent rewards shape behavior and establish patterns; violence enacted on prisoners and the threat of violence instill fear; and control of bodily functions, social isolation, degradation, and enforced participation in atrocities stimulate the shame response (2011).

Shame can thus be distinguished from guilt and identified as a part of humiliation and trauma. Guilt for wrongdoing has little place in the enactment of trauma. Nor can guilt, as shame can, be culturally produced through disgust or things labeled as disgusting. Research distinguishes shame and guilt cultures, building from Ruth Benedict's 1946 work *The Chrysanthemum and the Sword.* She establishes the United States as a guilt culture, while addressing Japan as a shame culture. The categories, while outdated, emphasize a difference between shame and guilt. Salmon Rushdie departs from Benedict's distinctions asserting "Shame, dear reader, is not the exclusive property of the East" (Rushdie 1983, p. 22). He underscores the cultural production of shame across the globe, asserting its power to shape behavior in ways not obtainable by guilt. Rushdie also alludes to the fact that shameful behavior may differ in divergent cultures, but the shame dynamic operates in every culture: social mores establish the disgusting and that which produces shame.

Guilt, unless it goes unaddressed, does not respond to cultural mores around the disgusting and "shameful;" therefore, guilt fails to reach the heart of the self—fails to threaten dignity, its perception, self-worth, or the *Imago Dei*—in the way that shame does. Shame attacks the heart of the self, inhibiting self-worth and dignity; Silvan Tomkins delineates the experience of the affect:

> Shame is felt as an inner torment, a sickness of the soul. It does not matter whether the humiliated one has been shamed by derisive laughter or whether he mocks himself. In either event he feels himself naked, defeated, alienated, lacking in dignity or worth (2008, p. 351).

Erving Goffman's 1963 text *Stigma* also highlights the deep emotional effect of shame on the inherent notion of dignity. He quotes an unemployed German man during the Depression:

> When I go out, I cast down my eyes because I feel myself wholly inferior. When I go along the street, it seems to me that I can't be compared with an average citizen, that everybody is pointing at me with his finger. Instinctively I avoid meeting anyone (p. 17).

Feeling inferior, undignified, exposes a person in shame. Unfortunately, the manifested behavior—downcast eyes and avoidance—perpetuates shame. Further, since relationships with the other externally support dignity, by recognizing a person as dignified, the social isolation and withdrawal evident of shame impede the establishment or self-perception of dignity, either internally felt or externally experienced.

The shame that undermines self-worth leads to the internalized belief that the self is not whole. This toxic shame inhibits the individual's ability to recognize a need for contact that expresses remorse or gratitude; to a self absorbed by the pain of understanding him/herself as deficient, these words become nearly unspeakable. The self ceases to imagine another's pain or to be present for another. Along with impediments to remorse or gratitude, the self in shame can turn to anger or rage to break free from said shame. The exchange of shrinking and disappearing for externalized rage and violence takes place to fight the overwhelming destruction of self-esteem. This struggle emerges in Gilligan's study where the imprisoned men who felt "dissed" or shamed attempted to eradicate the affect through violence (2003).

In this struggle, social bonds disrupt. The internal sense of dignity—in the form of self-worth both felt internally and communicated externally—erupts. Shame and more shame results. Perhaps the most egregious obstacle when the self-experiences toxic levels of shame is the inability to restore dignity through external relationships; the self in shame does not, even physiologically cannot, reach out and connect with others in order to be treated as dignified so that the perception of self-worth increases. The self with downcast eyes, as in Goffman's example, refutes the invigoration of another's gaze. Shared emotional experiences escape access as eye contact, a fundamental somatic function of empathy, flounders. The empathic exchange becomes unreachable. The person in shame fails to connect with another and the external sense of dignity empathy perpetuates disappears. Being seen by the other in an empathic connection leads to respect and therefore a person experiences the self as dignified. Shame interferes. Yet empathy evokes an internal affective response of interest-excitement, that counters shame, and perpetuates self-worth, or an internal sense of dignity. The challenge for the shamed is to remain open and vulnerable to the possibility of an empathic connection.

12.7 Empathy: A Path to Restoration

Shame evidences the formation of a stigmatized self, which has some inherent and impassable defect or disgusting quality. The logic follows that the self contains an inherently evil or wrong, which as discussed earlier, contrasts with the logic of guilt that assumes fault in behavior or action. The recognition of the action—not the self—as the greatest component in wrongdoing inspires remorse in lieu of the visceral recoil in shame. Remorse for action moves a person closer toward an apology which mends the social bond, while shame, which provokes actions of withdrawal, disrupts the social bond. Shared emotional experiences revealed through empathic connections constitute the social bond.

Research has repeatedly shown that experiencing guilt has a positive correlation with the capacity for empathy, while the experience of shame induces the inverse (Tangney and Dearing 2002, p. 86). Empathy fosters the recognition that "our actions adversely affect others and it motivates us to take corrective steps to remedy the situation" (Tangney and Dearing 2002, 86). Shame, however, hinders the ability to identify a precipitating action; instead, fault points towards the self, which, believed deficient, can only remedy the situation by disappearing.

Guilt and empathy contribute to mutual growth, and the affective experience of guilt provokes remorse because of understanding the experiences of an injured other. Shame impairs the capacity for empathy. Shame perpetuates negative affect and additional shame, which rupture the empathic exchange, in part because the person in shame remains absorbed in his or her own experience and fails to imagine the emotional experience of the other. The shame-prone individual lacks empathy, while the guilt-prone individual possesses an empathic capacity (Tangney and Dearing 2002, p. 86). If internalized shame leads to a lack of self-worth or the perception of not having dignity, the external responses form others displayed as empathic exchanges cannot efficiently convey a sense of internal dignity. Cycles of shame and violence fall prey to this circular relationship—where shame perpetuates more shame and violence, towards the self and others. Within this scenario, feeling dignified and being treated with dignity, remains elusive, as in the modern United States penal system. Shame ultimately not only impairs an individual's internal sense of dignity, but it also disrupts the ability to treat another as dignified, offending dignity's external aspect.

Only a steadfast, non-judgmental approach to the other in empathy counters shame. However, shame itself, subversive to self-worth, interferes with the capacity for coordinated, affective communication. Shame interrupts balance between two people as it draws one to the other only to impede connection, yet this other, and the support provided through empathy, repairs shame and fosters dignity. Thus, empathy, while restricted by shame, plays an important role in the process of shame's amelioration.

The parallels between shame and empathy illuminate how human dignity can be restored both interiorly and exteriorly, in the social world. For instance, in shame, as in empathy, lies the dynamic related to being seen. Functioning within the visual realm, empathy requires at least the perception of one other person. In the theological framework, such seeing would entail witnessing in the other the *Imago Dei.*

Theologian Edith Stein calls this deep perception of one another as "co-seeing" (Stein 1989, p. 57). Co-seeing operates in the field of sensation between the self and the foreign other. I see the other, a foreign "sensing living body." This seeing composes the beginning of the empathetic connection, serving as a dual introduction, of the self to the self and of the other to the self. Or as Stein puts it, "I see myself as another or as another sees me. This makes empathy possible for me" (p. 63). Through the development of a new image, a new understanding emerges as a result of empathic projection. In the same vein, but in different terms, Welz discusses the *Imago Dei*, emerging specifically in Luther and Bonheoffer, not as an anthropological concept based on the nature or substance of the human, but rather as "continuity in relationality," created by God (2016, p. 157). This relational dependence manifests also in Ubuntu's notion of presuming that one's humanity links to another's. In all cases, internal dignity emerges from an external empathic exchange.

If the restitution of dignity requires relationality, then developing the capacity for or the availability to empathy is critical. An empathic connection, in lieu of hiding in shame, requires vulnerability and an uncovering inspired by an exchange between two people in the presence of trust. Instead of being aroused by a perception or a projection of a defect, compassion or love arouses empathy. The functional activation of shame and empathy respectively oppose each other. And yet, shame inhibits empathy.

In empathy, a caring other has the potential to counter diminishment. In shame, the experience of the self as unloved and unworthy constrains the capacity for empathy. Stein addresses this. She writes, "Only he who experiences himself as a person, as a meaningful whole, can understand other persons" (Stein 1989, p. 116). Taken seriously, this statement undergirds the importance of eradicating shaming and humiliating forms of punishment. Furthermore, empathic connection, crucial to human development, permits an experience of the authentic pride of self-worth, defined as pleasure in accomplishments or self-compassion. Hubristic pride, what Goffman calls a "false bravado," on the other hand, emerges from shame. Tangney and Tracy assert that "hubristic pride decreases empathy for stigmatized others, which leads to increased prejudice" and a greater likelihood of violence. On the other hand, authentic pride increases empathy for stigmatized others, which reduces prejudice" (2002, p. 461). In this case, empathy has an increased societal function. Empathy fosters the healing of prejudice which reduces violence and mitigates shame.

The mitigation of shame also functions as a result of shared laughter and gratitude, both indicative of the capacity for empathy. According to Thomas J. Scheff, shared laughter, "good-humored or affectionate laughter" can alleviate the most immediate experience of shame (1990, p. 172) forming an empathic connection. Such laughter, and the connection it creates, in Markovitz's terms, serves as a "weapon" in the maintenance of dignity (2016, p. 64). Empathy can also emerge from a primal gratitude, emblematic of the gratitude young children feel toward loving parents (Slote 2014, p. 73). All of the operations of empathy answer directly to the shame affect. Empathy expressed by another person modulates the affective experience of shame. In this empathic exchange, the diminished sense of self-worth, or lack of dignity, indicative of shame dissolves, and dignity materializes.

Restoration of dignity emerges after and as a result of empathic connection. In his work with refugees, Richard Mollica asserts that the trauma and shame stored and lived through as a refugee diminishes when an empathic ear, or listener is present,

Table 12.2 Parallels between shame and empathy

	Shame	Empathy
Sense Orientation	Visible	Visible
Conceptualization	Covering, hiding	Uncovering, being vulnerable
Location	Points inward	Exchange
Aroused by	Defect, failure	Love
Logic	Disappearing	Appearing
Consequences	Diminishment	Restores self-worth/givenness
Treatment of	Empathic Attachment (i.e. therapy)	Laughter/ Gratitude
Affect	Impedes empathy	Ameliorates shame

thus, in the restoration of a personal connection (pp. 115–120). For Mollica, participating in empathic connection leads to the healing process (2006). The healing process from trauma and shame can well be interpreted as the restoration of human dignity; internally, the self feels worthy, and externally this worth emerges when treated as dignified in the face of another (Table 12.2).

12.8 Conclusion

The dual concept of dignity as both inherent or internally developed and developed in response to external experiences such as being looked at and respected from the outside emerge in this analysis of shame and its affective amelioration through empathic connection. Human dignity from a theological perspective, as encapsulated in the concept of the *Imago Dei*, includes both an internal recognition of dignity and the experience of being seen as dignified (or as being created in the image of God). The same duality surfaces in the psychological framework: self-worth as dignity is both internally felt and externally ratified or extinguished as in the case of trauma.

External traumatic events violate dignity; the truncating of empathic connections or relationships of trust induce and exacerbate shame. Shame differs logically and structurally from guilt; however, even though it impedes empathy (where guilt does not), shame logically and structurally coordinates with empathy. Their sense orientation parallels each other—both take place in the visual field, or field of exposure. Their conceptualizations correspond: in shame one hides, in empathy one reveals oneself. Shame lies interiorly, and its amelioration comes from an exterior experience of empathic exchange. A defect arouses shame; empathy and love respond. Instead draining dignity, empathy attends to shame, ameliorates its affective impact, and results in a restoration of self-worth or dignity.

Shame and empathy act on each other like magnets. Profound or toxic shame repels empathy even when that empathy constitutes what a person in shame needs most. When that person can make eye contact, and allow the self to be seen, empathic connection ameliorates shame. From this relationality, an external act of having empathy or treating another as dignified restores internal self-worth or dignity.

References

Arel SN (2016) Shame, affect theory, and christian formation. Palgrave, New York
Center for Substance Abuse Treatment (US) (2014) Understanding the impact of trauma. trauma-informed care in behavioral health services. In: Treatment improvement protocol no. 57. Rockville (MD)
Cloitre, M., Cohen, L. R. & Koenen, K. C. (2006). Treating survivors of childhood abuse: Psychotherapy for the interrupted life. New York: Guilford Press.
De Rosis LE (1973) Self-esteem, dignity, or the sense of being. Am J Psychoanal 33(1):16–27
DeYoung P (2015) Understanding and treating chronic shame: a relational/neurobiological approach. Routledge, New York
Diagnostic and Statistical Manual of Mental Disorders: DSM-IV (1994). Washington, DC. American Psychiatric Association
Dickerson SS, Gruenewald TL, Kemeny ME (2004) When the social self is threatened: shame, physiology, and health. J Pers 72, no. 6 (December):1191–1216
Erickson E (1950) Childhood and society. Reprint; 1993. W. W. Norton and Company, New York
Erickson E (1959) Identity and the life cycle. 1959. Reprint; 1980. W. W. Norton and Company, New York
Gilligan J (2003) Shame, guilt, and violence. Soc Res 70(4):1150–1180
Gilligan J (1996) Violence: a national epidemic. Putnam, New York
Herman J (2011) Posttraumatic stress disorder as a shame disorder. In: Dearing RL, Tangney JP (eds) Shame in the therapy hour, pp 261–275
Herman J (1982) Trauma and recovery. Basic Books, New York
Hollenbach D (2014) Human dignity in catholic thought. In: Düwell M, Braarvig J, Brownsword R, Mieths D (eds) The Cambridge handbook of human dignity: interdisciplinary perspectives. Cambridge University Press, Cambridge, pp 250–259
Kirchhoffer DG (2017) Human dignity and human enhancement: a multidimensional approach. Bioethics 31:375–383
Ludy-Dobson C, Perry BD (2010) The role of healthy relational interactions in buffering the impact of childhood trauma. In: Gil E (ed) Working with children to heal interpersonal trauma: the power of play. The Guilford Press, New York, pp 26–43
Maibom HL (n.d.) The descent of shame. Fellows seminar. Princeton University Center for Human Values
Margalit A (2004) Ethics of Memory. Harvard University Press, Cambridge
Markovitz E (2016) Dignity. In: Levine SS (ed) Dignity matters: psychoanalytic and psychosocial perspectives. Karnac Books, London, pp 61–72
Miller William Ian (1997) The anatomy of disgust. Cambridge. Harvard University Press.
Mollica R (2006) Healing invisible wounds. Vanderbilt University Press, Nashville
Patterson, Orlando (1982). Slavery and social death: A comparative study. Cambridge. Harvard University Press
Perry, Bruce and Oprah Winfrey (2021) What happened to you? Conversations on trauma, resilience, and healing. London. Boxtree.
Rushdie S (1983) Shame. Random House, New York
Scheff T (1987) The shame-rage spiral: a case study of an interminable quarrel. In: Lewis HB (ed) The role of shame in symptom formation. Psychology Press, London, pp 109–149
Scheff TJ (1990) Microsociology: discourse, emotion, and social structure. University of Chicago Press, Chicago

Schore AN (2003) Affect regulation and the repair of the self. W.W. Norton & Company, New York
Schore AN (2016) Early shame experiences and brain development. In: Gilbert P, Andrews B (eds) Shame: interpersonal behavior, psychopathology and culture. University of Minnesota, St Mary's, pp 57–77
Sherin JE, Nemeroff CB (2011) Post-traumatic stress disorder: the neurobiological impact of psychological trauma. Dialogues Clin Neurosci 13(3):263–278
Slote M (2014) The roots of empathy. In: Snow NE (ed) Cultivating virtue: perspectives from philosophy, theology, and psychology. Oxford University Press, Oxford, pp 65–86
Stein E (1989) On empathy. Translated by Waltraut Stein. ICS Publications, Washington, D.C.
Tangney JP, Dearing RL (2002) Shame and guilt. The Guilford Press, New York
Tomkins SS (2008) Affect, imagery, consciousness. 4 vols. 1962. Reprint. Springer Publishing Company, New York
Tutu, Desmond (2004) God has a dream: A vision of hope in our time. New York. Doubleday
Welz, Claudia (2016) Humanity in God's image. London. Oxford University Press
Williams B (2008) Shame and necessity. 1993. Reprint. University of California Press, Berkley
Van der Kolk BA, van der Hart O, Janet P (1989) Breakdown of adaption in psychological trauma. Am J Psychiatr 146(12):1530–1540
van der Kolk, Bessel (2015) The body keeps the score. New York. Penguin

Chapter 13
Standing at the Threshold, Standing on the Edge: Intersections of Human Dignity and the Holocaust

Ron Roth

Abstract Any attempt to construct a historical account concerning the concept of human dignity is ultimately bound to reach the bewildering junction of 1945. The Universal Declaration of Human Rights of 1948, as well as the German Basic Law of 1949, has placed Human Dignity at the fore, introducing it as a fundamental right and value in need of reinforcement in the aftermath of World War II and the Holocaust. This chapter turns a spotlight on Israel, exploring another historical arena where Human Dignity and the shadow of World War II intersect in those formative years following the end of the war. This charged encounter produced a multi-layered discourse, which carried distinct features. As such, it was more intuitive and spontaneous than legal, and placed in a liminal area, between two contradicting concepts concerned with respect to the human- dignity and honor. The chapter examines three instances, which exemplify how those two different concepts constantly collide and transform while moving back and forth from the individual to the national, from trauma to catharsis, from the historic to the imagined. Thus, this chapter seeks to undermine the "conventional" discourse about human dignity, tending to describe human dignity as a coherent and homogeneous concept (indeed with various possible interpretations), and instead emphasizes human dignity's more fluid and unexpected character, changing and transforming within the ongoing discourse.

13.1 The "Recent Career" of Human Dignity

"It is an interesting fact," says Jürgen Habermas, "that it was only after the Second World War that the philosophical concept of human dignity... found its way into texts of international law and recent national constitutions."

Not surprisingly, Habermas (2010) finds this fact evidence of the Nazi atrocities' legacy, yet as he further presses:

R. Roth (✉)
Jerusalem, Israel
e-mail: ronroton@gmail.com

S. N. Arel et al. (eds.), *Probing Human Dignity*,
https://doi.org/10.1007/978-3-031-42437-3_13

> Is it only against the historical background of the Holocaust that the idea of human rights becomes... retrospectively morally charged... with the concept of human dignity? The recent career of the concept of human dignity in constitutional and international legal discussions tends to support this idea.

Habermas's association of the post-war career of human dignity and the Holocaust is far from unique. Many, for different reasons, have pointed to a linkage between the Holocaust, human rights, and human dignity—a linkage that became quite a common assumption, until being forcefully undermined in recent decades.

The most obvious context that draws attention to this alleged linkage is of course the Universal Declaration of Human Rights of 1948 (though it existed earlier in the United Nations Charter). Beginning in 1948, human rights and human dignity appear as "conjoined twins" (Schroeder 2012); and it is mainly from this time that human dignity came to be considered as a foundation of human rights. According to Habermas's historical observation, in the period that preceded World War II, human rights and human dignity—if invoked together at all—were not yet perceived as such close conceptual partners. However, their convergence during the aftermath of the war can be seen as the threshold of a new beginning—the beginning of a process in which human rights became a morally charged principle; where at the same time, human dignity was re-conceptualized to suit its new duty as the foundation of human rights. The Holocaust, in that context, is assumed to be the component igniting a chemical chain reaction, refining a new appreciation of human dignity, later bonded with human rights, and thus creating the contemporary human rights regime (see also: Fuh 2020). In other words, the claim is that the alleged waves of intellectual and moral shock produced by the Holocaust had actual influence on prominent post-war proclamations.

13.2 The Importance of Underrepresentation and De-Contextualization

An example of the view that draws strong connections between the Holocaust and post-war constitutive documents can be found in the claim that the Universal Declaration was influenced by the encounter between Holocaust survivors and Eleanor Roosevelt. The historian G. Daniel Cohen contends, in that regard, that Roosevelt's (2012): "... 'conversion' to human rights owes much to her personal encounters with Jewish displaced persons in Germany."

The evidence Cohen finds most convincing is Roosevelt's own reference to her encounters with survivors and the impression she received from them related to: "desperation about the dignity of the individual." Those personal contemplations are supported, in Cohen's view, by the involvement of some well-known Jewish figures as Raphael Lemkin, Hersch Lauterpacht, and Renee Cassin in the construction of the post war international legal order. Yet, despite Cohen's attempt to sketch a more profuse and complex linkage between the Holocaust and the post-war "human rights revolution" he could not refrain from concluding that this revolutionary emergence of human rights was a "loosely Holocaust-centric" one, and in fact, it: "constituted the first international site of Holocaust remembrance."

Other voices proclaiming this immediate post-war connection between the Holocaust and human rights are the sociologists Daniel Levy and Natan Sznaider. However, in an influential article published in 2004, Levy and Sznaider follow a different path in an attempt to construct what they call a "cosmopolitan memory" of the Holocaust. According to Levy and Sznaider, despite the fact that the Holocaust and human rights interconnectedness gained its recognition many years after the war, an actual affinity between them had existed all along, bubbling beneath the surface. Therefore, in spite of the fact that the Holocaust was overshadowed for many years—mainly by the political rivalries of the Cold War—post-war documents regarding genocide and human rights, including the Universal Declaration, can indeed be seen as a product of the moral revulsion it has generated. As Levy and Sznaider (2004) contend: "... we understand the diffusion of human rights norms during the last six decades as the distillation of changing modes of Holocaust memory."

The common ground for Cohen, Levy/Sznaider, as well as for others,[1] is the insistence on describing the Holocaust as influential, by utilizing its underrepresentation. Following that logic, for example, the minimal reference to the Holocaust during the Nuremberg trials does not necessarily indicate a lack of interest, unawareness, or an intentional disregard, but rather points to (Levy/Sznaider, 2004): "...the general unease that there was no existing legal language for the barbarous crimes the Nazis have committed...". Or, as was further claimed regarding Nuremberg, the Holocaust indeed formed the backdrop of the trials, though seemingly neglected, because: "The Jews were there. But they were standing in for humanity as a whole."

Following the line of this argument, we should assume that what was true for the Nuremberg trials of 1946 was also true for the Universal Declaration of 1948. By 1948, an initial version of Holocaust memory had already taken form and recorded for generations to come, even if, for political reasons, that memory was disguised in the Universal Declaration's preamble by the neutral expression: "...barbarous acts, which have outraged the conscience of mankind...".

Using a conspicuous non-appearance to support the silent omnipresence of Holocaust is, to say the least, speculative; and indeed, one that was heavily criticized. As Tony Judt (2005) noted:

> In retrospect it is the universal character of neglect that is most striking... For most Europeans, World War Two had not been about the Jews... and any suggestion that the Jewish suffering might claim pride of place was deeply resented. The Holocaust was only one of many things that people wanted to forget...

As Judt convincingly observes, open discussion about the Holocaust, not to mention recognition of its particular Jewish aspects, was neither an easy nor immediate outcome anywhere in Europe. In other words, albeit becoming at last, a: "...

[1]When making this close linkage between the Holocaust and the Universal Declaration on Human Rights, Levy and Sznaider rely on Johannes Morsink and his book on the Universal Declaration of Human Rights.

touchstone of a 'consciousness of catastrophe'..."(Torpey 2001), in the first decades following the war, the Holocaust was neglected in social and political dialogue. That the Holocaust was far from being an event with widespread recognition undermines the possibility that its horrors constitute a reason for the installation of Human Dignity as a central value in post war documents.

This basic line of thought, which sheds doubt on an early widespread Holocaust consciousness capable of anchoring moral lessons in international documents, is shared by historians such as Samuel Moyn (2015), Marco Duranti (2012) or David Mazower (2004). In a similar fashion, Aleida Assmann (2010) addresses the emergence of the Holocaust as a symbol of the 1980's, where:

> What had been treated as a footnote to the Second World War after 1945, now became a globally historical event, a rupture of civilization, the marker of a new epoch in the history of Humanity...

Notably, the tendency to postpone the emergence of Holocaust discourse in general, certainly its connection to human rights and human dignity, is correlated with its de-contextualization. The actual events consisting of the historical occurrence known as "the Holocaust" are thus increasingly losing their historic grip, while being transcended into a metaphysical dimension with pure universal meanings. In fact, instead of being considered only as the product of Holocaust discourse, human rights can be seen, in that perspective, as a prerequisite for Holocaust discourse, as Assmann observes:

> Through its link to universal human rights, the memory community of the trauma of the Holocaust can be globally extended.

Therefore, extending the local European lesson from the Holocaust into a transnational lesson that forms a global community of trauma, necessarily disconnects it from its direct historical experience, transforming it from history to memory. At this core of global memory, human dignity occupies a prominent place, functioning as the old-new moral foundation for humanity. In other words, human dignity is the embodiment of universal Holocaust memory, allowing for its further distillation into a set of universal, self-evident, moral norms (see also Fuh 2020; Krondorfer 2021, pp. 378–379).

13.3 Constitutionalism, Human Rights and the German Lesson

With the Universal Declaration, human dignity took a giant leap to the center stage of post-war international discourse. Yet, it is mostly against the backdrop of German Basic Law where the concept of human dignity was declared a supreme constitutional value and right, with concrete normative implications. Moreover, the well-known Article 1 of the German Basic Law, not only establishes human dignity as its master value but also declares it as an absolute and permanent human right that cannot be modified or balanced against other rights or values. Regarding this unique status of human dignity, Donald P. Kommers (1989) has indicated what he calls the "logical-theological" predilection of the Basic Law, which is defined by an objective hierarchical order of values. The most important of these values, the 'raison d'être' of the Basic Law, is the one of a free democratic basic order, based on human dignity (Kvistad 1999).

The first provisions of the Basic Law are saturated with heavy historical freight. The German Federal Constitutional Court itself referred to this historical relation (expressed already by founders of the German Federal Republic), acknowledging the connection between the emphasis on human dignity and the dehumanizing horrors of Nazism (Collings 2015). Yet, not only Nazi horrors have influenced the shaping of these provisions but also the specter of the Weimar Republic, the post-war division of Germany in 1945, and the beginning of the Cold War (Allinson et al. 2014, Krisch 1999). These historical experiences combined facilitated the transformative aspect of the Basic Law-making process and helped create a system of militant democracy, immune to internal subversion and founded on the dignity of the individual (Finn, 1991). As Kommers notes (1989):

> Many of the Basic Law's guaranteed rights provisions are word-for-word reproductions of the corresponding articles in the Frankfurt and Weimar Constitutions. The Bonn Constitution [i.e. the Basic Law], however "acknowledges" the pre-constitutional existence of these rights. Contrary to the prevailing legal positivism of the Weimar period, fundamental rights are not the creations of law. Rather, they are natural rights grounded in the concept of "human dignity."

In his exploration of German intellectual life after 1945, historian Sean Forner (2014) adds another angle to that story and, in particular, to the strong appearance of dignity in the Basic Law. He contends that the period following German defeat and occupation by the allies saw the formulation of: "... a vision of a democratic renewal"—a vision, which placed its emphasis on the intrinsic value of each person and his or her participation in the political community. He acknowledges that this view of the intrinsic worth of man was not an innovative idea, but one that was firmly embedded in distinct German cultural and political traditions (Eberle 2012). Human dignity, in that sense, is one idea (among others), rooted in German legal and political tradition, which emerged after the war to symbolize the anti-fascist essence of the German constitutional apparatus (Murkens 2013).

This early penetration of the concept of human dignity into German constitutional discussion after the war leaves little doubt that it reflects lessons drawn from the German experience under the Nazi regime. In fact, references to the ruins of war as an incentive for reaffirming human dignity were already incorporated into some of the initial constitutions of the eleven "states" (Bundesländer) later comprising West-Germany (Bendor and Sachs 2011; Sharples 2016). Forner also lays the renaissance of old democratic views centered in the individual to the incentive created by the Nazi experience. Yet, here also, the very presence of human dignity creates, as it seems, an irresistible temptation to associate it with the human suffering of others, strangers to the German experience of the war. It thus attributes the articulation of Holocaust attentiveness to its exposition in the Basic Law. As Peter Krüger (1999) argues:

> ...there was yet another deep impact on the national foundation of the Federal Republic. This was the Holocaust... This does not only mean the often emphasized anti-National Socialist consensus as a political basis for the Federal Republic but also... democratization based on adequate constitutional and institutional guarantees and on the inviolable dignity of man...

Krüger, though, provides no annotation or evidence that would support a view, which imbeds the Holocaust into the center of Germany's political metamorphosis in the postwar "Stunde null." [2] Perhaps for this reason, we find the attempt to find a different solution, by differentiating between the consciousness of the people and of the framers of the Basic Law. According to the abovementioned view, the delegates convening at Herrenchiemsee and in Bonn, allegedly isolated from the public they sought to represent, were those: "who had in full and basic knowledge rejected the evil of National Socialism and its crimes" (Neumann 2000). This acute alertness preceded the "historical anamnesis" of the German people in general, still unwilling or unable to face the historical burden of Nazi atrocities.

The controversy over human dignity in the Basic Law does not specifically relate only to the conundrum of awareness of Nazi atrocities and Jewish tragedy. For Samuel Moyn (2015), for instance, human dignity in post-war discourse should not be regarded as the emblem of a shift towards liberal democracy. In his opinion, human dignity evolved, in those decades, as a conservative constraint on liberal tendencies in the framework of Christian democracies. The highlighting of dignity in the German Basic Law and elsewhere, such as in the Irish constitution of 1937, according to Moyn, shows its usage as a signifier of natural law and Christian personalism, a prevalent trend in new national constitutions of the time: "...it seems fair to say that Germany's federal constitution in 1949 was part of a trend, localized wherever Christian democracy was strong... that founded new republics on—and limited them through—the morality of dignity." [3]

Disregarding the controversy over its conceptual origin, in post-war Germany, human dignity was anchored from the outset in its assertion as a supreme constitutional value. It may be true that the framers of Basic Law did not foresee its utilization as an independent judicial instrument by the German Federal Constitutional Court or its future liberal character. Nevertheless, it is the status of human dignity in the constitutional order that stands at the basis of this discourse. In a similar fashion, postwar declarative documents show that human dignity was embedded in discourse through an institutional, semi-constitutional path, fully realized later in international human rights conventions.

[2]The term "Stunde null" refers to the immediate aftermath of World War II in West Germany and was used mainly to mark the radical disengagement of West Germany from its Nazi past.

[3]Eberle (2012) also states Christian natural law as a major influence on the concept of human dignity embedded in the Basic Law. However, he sees this as only one of several major sources of inspiration, besides the Nazi trauma and various usages of dignity in German intellectual tradition. This fact was reflected, in his opinion, in the constitutions of various West-German Länder prior to the framing of a federal constitutional document.

13.4 Holocaust, Human Dignity, and Conventional Discourse

Here again, we should return to the process mentioned above, in which, according to Habermas, the post-war character of human dignity was intertwined with human rights and redefined by them. In the realm of global Holocaust memory, this process of restoration of human dignity was acknowledged as the redemptive response to the modern original sin of the Holocaust, while at the same time, human rights became the vehicle facilitating this restoration, thus epitomizing a new and possibly ultimate hope for humanity.

This narrative is relevant, of course, for those who draw a straight line between the rise of human dignity and human rights and an alleged early consciousness of the Holocaust. Yet, this is also relevant for those who claim to an early neglect of Holocaust memory, which later turned—through its de-historicization—into a memory capable of producing a universal moral lesson for humanity. Either way, human dignity, the Holocaust, and their interrelations were reduced to fit the measure of human rights desiderata.

This, however, is a problematic consequence. As we have seen, the view that discerns dignity as an immediate and direct response to the Holocaust encounters significant factual and historical difficulties. However, the view that acknowledges a much later linkage of human dignity with the Holocaust encounters a difficulty of its own, since it must first strip the Holocaust of its concrete historical context, in order to attribute it with unique qualities of timeless universal signification. Thus, both attitudes prefer to abandon the historical in favor of the a-historical or the meta-historical. Moreover, both attitudes share a problematic tendency to rely on a certain self-evident and stable character of human dignity. That character is conjoined with human rights and connected to the articulation of the Holocaust as an event of an unprecedented violation of those rights.

Against this background, I want to point out the specific case of Israel, which exemplifies the possibility of overturning the framework of conventional discourse. I contend that in the case of Israel, human dignity functions as a spontaneous, immediate expression rooted in the actual historical occurrence neither revolving around the cosmopolitan memory of the Holocaust nor intersecting with universal human rights. Instead, Isreal's case accentuates a particularistic and intimate character of the Holocaust.

13.5 Dignity Versus Honor

Before examining the distinctive Israeli features of a supposed relationship between the Holocaust and dignity, one must first spotlight a basic linguistic difficulty. This difficulty derives from the use of just one Hebrew word—"kavod"—to express the entire scope of what we can describe as modes of respect to the human (manifested in

English by the use of two typical phrases—honor and dignity), albeit this one word may refer to utterly different experiences and meanings. In this chapter, I am unable to explore the vast literature addressing dignity and honor and their distinguishing attributes in depth, but I will briefly sketch a few guidelines, essential for this particular discussion (see: Kamir, 2020).

Honor is characterized by its contra-universalism, focusing on a person's social recognition, measured against the fulfillment of his specific social practices. We should add another component emphasized in the research on "honor societies". In those societies, honor has an active social clout in the shape of a constant struggle to maintain one's place within a social structure. Honor discourse, therefore, will necessarily revolve around human strength, and one's capacity to occupy a social position and prevent humiliation on the part of potential rivals.

This stands in sharp contrast to the inherent nature of dignity, which has an utterly different view of man. As such, dignity is inherent in every human being and is independent of any social practices and perceptions. Moreover, it does not revolve around human strength but around human vulnerability, frailty, and dependence. The protection of human beings inspired by dignity-oriented thinking derives precisely from its awareness of human helplessness in confronting destructive powers. In fact, it was exactly this feature that, eventually, facilitated the recognition that the Holocaust redefined dehumanization and the violation of the dignity of man. In other words, telling the story of the Holocaust from the point of view of dignity must start with the acknowledgement of human defeat.

The Israeli example, in that sense, reveals a discourse that stretches between the two poles of dignity and honor. Moreover, unlike other instances I have discussed, in Israel the discourse did not take a juridical, constitutional, or declarative path. A good example is an 'almost-constitutional' Israeli document, composed just a few years after the Holocaust. This document, which was the most significant proposal for a constitution in Israel, was drafted (originally in English) in 1948 by Leo Kohn, constitutional law scholar, and served as the basis for constitutional discussions in the Israeli Knesset (parliament) until 1950, when the Knesset decided to postpone indefinitely the acceptance of a constitution. The first draft of the proposal, dated February–March 1948, stated the following (Kohn):

> The state shall ensure the sanctity of human life and uphold the dignity of man. There should be no penalty of death, nor shall anyone be subjected to torture, flogging or humiliating punishment. . .

As can be seen, the use of the term "dignity" was deliberately and exclusively limited in Kohn's draft to the prohibition of the death penalty, torture and humiliating punishment—and did not serve as an abstract moral value or a foundation for human rights in general. In his explanatory notes, Kohn further explicated this decision as standing:

> . . .on Hebrew spiritual ground. At a time when respect for the sanctity of life and the dignity of man has sunk to an unprecedented level, it is fitting that a Hebrew constitution should proclaim them afresh as the basis of civilized society.

According to Kohn, human dignity reflects the ancient creed of man's creation in the image of God. This creed was expressed by Kohn in the form of a constitutional prohibition of the death penalty and torture. Kohn (who was not a Holocaust survivor) saw this edict as rooted in Jewish moral and legal traditions, but probably was not inspired by the Holocaust, which is completely absent from his text. It is indeed possible to conclude from Kohn's text that he viewed the horrors of World War II—and the murder of Jews in particular—as reaffirming the Judeo-Christian belief in the sacredness of human life. However, his text does not reflect (not yet in any case) any interpretational dimension of the Holocaust as a moral earthquake; or a self-aware evaluation of it, as an unprecedented occurrence with universal dimensions calling for the re-sanctification of the dignity of man.

After the rejection of Kohn's proposal, the chance to incorporate human dignity in Israeli law had to wait until the passing of the Basic Law: Human Dignity and Liberty, in 1992. Even then, the concept of dignity in Israeli law was not inspired by the Holocaust (although it was certainly inspired by the German Basic Law). In the Israeli context, then, the intersection of dignity and the Holocaust should not be examined through constitutional or legal texts, but in extra-legal territory, in a liminal zone where dignity and honor take part simultaneously.

13.6 "Heroic Rebels and the Rest"

November 23, 1942 can be seen as the day that launched Holocaust memory discourse in Israel (during the pre-Israel "Yishuv"). Mass massacre, of course, was still raging in Europe without an end in sight. On this day, the Jewish Agency officially confirmed to the Jewish community of pre-state Israel what had until then only been rumors and unverified reports: European Jewry was in the midst of a systematic annihilation on a scale that had not been foreseen even in the darkest pre-war prophecies of doom. It is important to mention that while still an ongoing occurrence, the "Shoah" was already considered not only an unprecedented disaster, but an inconceivable humiliation. The Holocaust's perception as a transgression against Jewish honor facilitated the emergence of binary views on the reactions of the Jewish population. The main attribute of those who took part in armed resistance was heroism; in contrast, humiliation and disgrace were attributed to those who "marched to their death like sheep to the slaughter" (Gil 2009). The Warsaw Ghetto uprising, in that sense, became the ultimate symbol of resistance, with epic dimensions. Behind this mythologization, we find, inter alia, a certain perception regarding "Jewish fighting" (Yablonka 1999). Unlike the fighting in which Jews were "mere" participants—as members of partisan groups or soldiers in the allied armies—the armed resistance in Warsaw was organized by and for Jews. Therefore, it was perceived as restoring Jewish honor, what Israel Galili, a prominent figure in the

Yishuv leadership, defined as: "...the path of honor and resourcefulness of rebellion and national salvage."[4]

No wonder armed Jewish resistance during the Holocaust was overemphasized out of proportion to its actual place in reality. Thus, for example, the lion's share of the astonishingly small portion devoted to the Holocaust in the school text books of Israel's first decades was devoted to the issue of Jewish revolts. As one high school textbook, published in 1957 phrased it (Kirshenbaum 1965), the youngsters who revolted in the Warsaw Ghetto:

> Defended their people's honor that had been trampled... the brave stand of the Jews of the Ghetto compensated for the shameful surrender of the Jews being led to death camps.

The simile of Jews being pushed to their disgraceful death was thus contrasted to those few who, in this humiliating condition, maintained Jewish honor by armed rebellion against the Nazis. Closely tied to this last point, is the fact that armed resistance in ghettos was perceived as a triumph over Jewish-exilic characteristics, and a demonstration of Zionist-pioneering attitudes and ideals (Stauber 2007; see also Parvikko 2021, p. 144).

This memory structure of "heroic rebels and the rest" has been exhaustively described in literature concerning Holocaust memory in Israel. The commonly held view assumes that the rigid honor discourse was gradually softened and eventually abandoned in favor of a more complex understanding that acknowledged the heroism inherent in a variety of Jewish reactions and courses of action. However, this view fails to discern the appearance of an early and charged discourse of honor and dignity, related to this burning issue of Jewish conduct during the Holocaust. Examining this discourse reveals that it was not lack of awareness to aspects of the Holocaust violating human dignity, nor a disregard for the attempts to safeguard human dignity under the Nazis, which aroused the negative feelings toward the alleged passive reaction of Jews during the Holocaust. Rather, it was the apprehension that those attempts lacked honor (see also Arendt 2021, pp. 143–144). Nonetheless, the constant intersection of honor and dignity forced these two notions of respect for the human to transcend their static qualities, to collide, and to transform. I will now focus on three examples of dignity and honor intersections, relevant to Holocaust discourse that emerged in Israel in the early years of the State and discuss their meaning.

13.6.1 A Glance of Dignity: And Fast Retreat to Honor

The first example arises from a canonical text of Israel's first years, written by Yitzhak Sadeh, the commander and founder of the "Palmach" (combat units), the elite unit of the Yishuv's main military body (Haganah). In his text, Sadeh describes a night encounter he had with Holocaust survivors who landed on the shores of

[4]The text is from: Weitz (1996).

Palestine after disembarking from an illegal refugee boat and concentrates on the presence of a young woman, to whom he refers to as 'my sister':

> Darkness. On wet sand, my sister stands before me: filthy, tattered, wild haired, her feet are bare and her head is bowed. She stands and weeps. I know. Her flesh is branded: 'For Officers Only'... I know: evil people have tortured her and made her barren. And she weeps and says: Friend, what am I doing here? Why have you brought me here? Am I worthy that young healthy boys risk their lives for me? There is no place for me in this world...
>
> I embrace my sister, embrace her shoulders and tell her: you have a place in the world my sister, a very special place. Here in our land. And you should live my sister. Your feet have trodden the road of suffering, and tonight you have come home... [5]

Reading the above text makes clear why it came to be perceived as an icon of the patronizing attitude of the new Zionist Jew toward his exilic predecessor. The Holocaust, in that regard, stands as a definitive proof for the widening chasm between the masculine, self-reliant, and proud figure of the narrator, and the bowed, shattered figure of the woman he encounters. One sentence in particular in Sadeh's text arouses interest for its seemingly unnecessary presence. This is where Sadeh discloses the information regarding the woman's branded flesh, an enduring reminder of her forced serving as a prostitute for Nazi officers.[6] Idith Zertal (1998), addressing Sadeh's text with great fury, beholds this gaze at the woman's history of sexual abuse as another violation of her body. Furthermore, Zertal traces a latent message, according to which:

> ...the girl survived the Holocaust... because she did not defend the integrity and purity of her body... Her impurity, her defilement was her ticket to life... Her very survival, her being alive after the Holocaust, is a shameful to her... betrayal of her body, her femininity, and the betrayal of her people...

And proceeding to a more general inference Zertal concludes:

> The survivors, those now reaching Israel... survived because they, in some way, defiled and surrendered their bodies and souls to the perpetrators. In contrast, the righteous and decent Jews, who... preserved their physical and spiritual integrity, were obliterated from the face of the earth...

Zertal, so it seems, assumes Sadeh's homily as situated solely in the realm of honor and shame. As such, it is an encapsulated discourse, conducted in the form an internal dialogue among the new Jews of the land. The invasive inspection of the branded flesh by the narrator, in that sense, is designed to reaffirm his and his listeners' superiority by implementing identifying marks on others, those whose presence threatens the construction of a "young healthy" generation.

---

[5] The English translation of the text is from: Zertal (1998).

[6] As far as we know, such flash branding of Jewish women was not carried out by the Nazis, so Sadeh could not have met a woman marked as mentioned in his text. However, the poetic freedom he takes on this point probably reflects one of the common negative stereotypes regarding survivors, as people that survived due to immoral conduct on their part (such as, in our case, serving the Nazis as a prostitute).

This interpretation by Zertal, excludes, a priori, even the mildest existence of dignity elements in the text. And, while it is undeniable that views associating survival to the weaker moral character of the survivors did exist, Sadeh's text does not lack what seems as genuine empathy, even if Zertal prefers to completely revoke it. Furthermore, as Sadeh mentions the branded flesh, he does not refrain from mentioning the torture and humiliation the woman went through, that is to say, the violation of her individual dignity. To be sure, I am not stressing that while mentioning the defilement of the woman's body, Sadeh focuses himself on the ordeal she suffered. What I claim is that he is aware of that ordeal, acknowledging the violation and destruction of the human being standing next to him on the beach and serves as a witness to it. Yet, grasped within the sentiments of humiliated masculinity and shame, he quickly departs from those aspects of dignity back to the secure ground of manly honor and vengeance he aspires to arouse among his followers. Rather than tarnishing the survivors, the text teaches us about the rapid slide from a dignity discourse to one focused in honor. Moreover, by emphasizing his strong and honorable image, Sadeh, at the same time, redeems the sister from her shameful fate, as if infusing her with his honor and courage—an idea described more explicitly by Mordechai Shenhabi, the first proponent of the idea of a national memorial monument for the Holocaust: "tell of those who were burned to death, the children choked in the gas chambers, the raped mothers and sisters, the heroes who fought the desperate, courageous war for the honour of the Jewish people."[7]

13.6.2 Duality, Struggle and Transformation

Another example, described hereinafter, is one in which the intersection between honor and dignity in the realm of Holocaust discourse in Israel, ends in the rapid transformation of dignity discourse into honor discourse.

The ambivalence associated with aspects of dignity and honor is indeed traceable to the early days of Holocaust discourse in Israel, even if much more modest then, and as Stauber (2007) notes:

> ...alongside the criticism of the passive behavior of the Jews... there were also expressions of empathy for the ways in which the Jews managed to survive from day to day, and objections to any kind of moral distinction between those who rebelled and those who did not.

In fact, this duality of honor and dignity is found almost explicitly in the Martyrs and Heroes Remembrance Law 5713–1953—the law that founded "Yad Vashem" as Israel's Holocaust memory authority. In this law, both lie side by side:

> "The heroic stand of the besieged and fighters of the ghettoes, who rose and kindled the flame of revolt to save the honour of their people"; together with: "The sublime, persistent

[7] The text is from: Stauber.

> struggle of the masses of the house of Israel, on the threshold of destruction for their human dignity and human culture."

Unlike what came to be the general wisdom, the conjunction of heroes (who rebelled) next to martyrs (who did not) in the Remembrance Law was not intended to point to a moral distinction between the two groups. Quite the contrary, it aimed at granting legitimization to the ostensibly passive behavior of most of the Jewish population, by binding them together with the fighters. Thus, when addressing the Knesset for presenting this above mentioned bill (Protocol of Knesset, 12.5.1953), the historian Ben-Tzion Dinur, Minister of Education at the time, emphasized, as expected, the heroic rebels of the Warsaw Ghetto. Yet, on the other hand, he stated that:

> The first example of the heroism of the Jewish people was in its war to live ... it struggled day after day ... and this struggle of the people to maintain their human image under the circumstances of humiliation, abuse and torture, is an extraordinary heroic chapter...

Dinur, in accord with his particular holistic perception of Jewish history, wanted the term heroism to include both armed struggle and the daily struggle to survive and retain one's humanity, which he saw as parallel manifestations of Jewish courage and martyrdom. However, Dinur was not the only one holding these views, which some described as 'passive resistance' and others as 'spiritual heroism'. 'Passive resistance' serves here as a broad term for the individual struggle for daily survival, while maintaining human dignity and moral character. However, the fact that this struggle did not involve armed revolt situated it on the "wrong" side of the dichotomy between national disgrace and the epic rescue of Jewish honor. This view, correlating with the prevalent myth of Jews marching to their death without resistance, troubled Dinur as well as other intellectuals, educators, and public figures who perceived this myth as detrimental and prejudicial. The trouble was that preserving one's human dignity was not yet likely to arouse feelings of honor and respect, especially among the younger generation. As Shapira (1998) notes:

> The idea of passive resistance as a way of surviving or preserving human dignity did not at the time succeed in gaining respect in the collective memory.

Nevertheless, the expression 'passive resistance'—binding together heroism and attempts to safeguard human dignity—in itself suggests a possible solution to the problem. In an attempt to grant worthy respect to the masses of Jews struggling for daily survival, it was necessary to merge it into a story of heroism and national pride. For Dinur, and others, such as the prominent Zionist leader Berl Katzenelson, it was a natural observation, since for them Jewish courage could be expressed in different ways.[8] For others such as Marc Dvorzetzki—a doctor, educator, and Holocaust survivor from Vilna—it was a pressing need, an educational doctrine that must be endowed to the young generation for the sake of Holocaust memory (Nishmit 1960). By classifying the struggle to preserve individual dignity as heroism, the multitudes

[8] Stauber notes in that regard that already in 1947 attempts were made to speak about "different types of heroism."

of Jews annihilated without a fight were bestowed with a higher status, similar—even if not equal—to the one held by participants in revolts. That status allowed them to be honored instead of remaining the emblem of collective humiliation. As Amos Goldberg (2017) notes, the result of this endeavor was an artificial expansion of concepts of heroism and resistance, to the point that they incorporate almost every human action demonstrated by the Jews at that time. Yet, in that way, the image of the Jewish victim has been molded as heroic, autonomous and, to a certain and tragic degree, even victorious.

Through time, the heroic halo attached to the Holocaust has proven itself as a highly enduring perception, and it has remained a pivotal and self-evident element of Israeli Holocaust discourse until this very day. This outcome, though, may blur its inner inconsistency. For the inevitable consequence of crowning exertions to uphold human dignity as heroism transforms dignity discourse into an honor discourse. The human story of preserving the individual inner core is not disregarded but is translated into the honor dialect and has become an illustration of Jewish heroic conduct. Thus, we return to a discourse concentrating on safeguarding national honor and applauding the collective Jewish victory, while emphasizing every feature that was previously sketched as part of human honor. The paradoxical result is a discourse that sees national honor as manifested by the ability of Jews to retain their dignity under the conditions imposed by the Nazis.

As previously mentioned, however, dignity-centered discourse forgoes man's victorious stature in favor of man's hopelessness and vulnerability. Primo Levi (1959), in his classic memoir "If This Is a Man," written shortly after the war, emphasized this last point, by addressing the profound meaning of Nazi extermination project—the hideous metamorphosing of human beings into non-humans. As he describes in his book:

> The Russians can come now: they will only find us, the slaves, the worn out... to destroy a man is difficult, almost as difficult as to create one: it has not been easy, nor quick, but you Germans have succeeded... because we also are broken, conquered: even if we know how to adapt ourselves, even if we have finally learnt how to find our food and to resist the fatigue and cold, even if we return home.

Not only does Primo Levi refrain from portraying the victims as heroes, but he also even maintains that the capacity to physically survive does not exempt the victim from humiliation, shame, and emotional devastation (see also Volkova 2021, p. 76).

To a certain extent, this understanding is similar to remarks made by Aba Kovner, a leader of the underground in the Vilna ghetto and a partisan who became a symbol of Jewish armed resistance. In January 1942, Kovner was the first to insert into Holocaust vernacular the important phrase (employed originally in traditional Jewish liturgy)—'as sheep to the slaughter'—in a proclamation that called for Jewish uprising. Years later, though, Kovner became an advocate for the response by the masses of Jews to Nazi genocide, by emphasizing the inability of fathoming a fundamental aspect of their victimhood: "...before their final journey to death something even greater happened: they ceased living... how their souls were murdered before their bodies—that is what we have to study first...". [9]

Nevertheless, one clear consequence of the enfolding of dignity in heroism—thus annexing it to the honor discourse—is the corrosion of the message conveyed by the confrontation with dehumanization and its moral implications. Moreover, the following decades saw the emergence of a dignity-oriented discourse, which became a central element in contemporary Holocaust discussion. It has become an individualized discourse, focusing on private experiences and emotions, on the desperate and tragic struggle of individuals to remain alive and to adhere to their humanity. The everlasting heroism component, therefore, has led to an enduring and increasing dissonance within Israeli Holocaust discourse itself.

13.6.3 "A Nice Personal Death"

The third and final example emerging from the constant tension between honor and dignity in Israeli Holocaust discourse concerns an aspect completely concealed by the aforementioned amalgamation of Holocaust and heroism. This time the pendulum swings to the other side, and instead of turning dignity into honor, it turns honor into dignity.

As discussed above, the armed rebels, mainly in the ghettoes, came to be considered the emblem of Jewish resistance, the redeemers of Jewish honor in times of its most colossal breakdown. Expressions concerning the duty to redeem the nation's honor through armed insurgencies are already evident among members of the underground in the ghettos, and even more so among the survivors. A few prominent figures among those survivors, publicly expressed those views after the war—a view easily adopted by significant parts of the Yishuv and its leadership, reflecting in their eyes Zionist standards of action, thus reaffirming the myth regarding the multitudes of Jews who could have at least saved—if not their lives—their honor.

However, the embrace of those survivors by the Yishuv, disguised the more complex message they conveyed. The deep conscious gap here lies in the fact that although for members of the Yishuv fighting seemed as the natural and healthy reaction to collective humiliation, for survivors it was their final path to attain national honor and individual dignity, simultaneously.

Historian Dan Porat (2004), in his research on Holocaust education in Israel, attributes the sharp distinction between the rebels and most of Jewish population to the fact that in the public imagination:

> Holocaust victims lacked individuality; they acted as a passive mass. All Jews, secular and religious, men and women, children and elderly, appeared in textbooks as an undifferentiated and anonymous crowd under the single heading: 'the Jews'. The rebels,

[9]The quote is from: Stauber.

> however, were granted with active individuality; they chose their destiny... the victims acted as... a herd. They accepted their destiny, their death... without hesitation.

Porat is of course not mistaken when making this claim. Yet, he fails to mention the possibility that the rebels themselves viewed the uprising as a way to regain their individuality, as a way to re-experience their existence as autonomous and sovereign entities. A perspective of this sort should not be necessarily understood as criticizing the passivity of the rest of Jewish population, but as an independent individual path for safeguarding one's dignity. Moreover, this claim does not contradict the fact that participants in armed resistance saw their action as saving Jewish honor. Rather, in the exceptional and extreme circumstances of ghetto liquidations, the natural performance of honor—manifested by actively joining the "duel" and returning fire—merged with the determination to keep one's humanity by exercising autonomy. In support of Kren and Rappoport's (1981) psycho-historical analysis, describing participation in armed revolts as a way of therapy, I contend that joining the revolt was fueled by individual internal motivation. However, in their article—following Franz Fannon's observations—Kren and Rappoport focus on violence as the means for psychological relief and self-redemption. My focus is not on the euphoria gained by exercising violence towards the enemy, but on realizing the self as an autonomous agent, achieved in that particular case through violent means. Moreover, in a paradoxical way, this realization was simultaneously accompanied by a strong sensation of defeat. Thus, according to Zivia Lubetkin (1957), a well-known figure of the resistance in Warsaw, who arrived in Palestine in 1946, the uprising was generated out of the desire for:

> a nice personal death, that will be both a revenge and a rescue of the nation's honor...

As can be seen, in her description Lubetkin includes the three ingredients of armed resistance during the Holocaust: national honor, revenge, and "a nice personal death," as a way to regain individual autonomy and dignity while acknowledging defeat and destruction. Unlike the use of violent measures as therapy, the use of violence to reclaim human autonomy is contingent, not an end in itself, and serves as another manifestation of the struggle for individual dignity. However, this dignity is intertwined with the desire to fight a rearguard action for the sake of collective Jewish honor.[10]

---

[10]A reflection of this complexity can be found in: Nishmit (1960), p. 12. This book was one of the first handbooks for teaching about the Holocaust in Israel (which mainly contains bibliographic material for teachers), where different examples of armed Jewish resistance in ghettoes and camps are gathered under the title: *"The Jewish struggle for Human dignity and Jewish honor"*.

13.7 Conclusion

The aim of this chapter is to suggest a possible new reading of human dignity and the discourse surrounding it. The aftermath of World War II described here can be seen as the threshold of the concept of human dignity and the discourse surrounding it, in a few respects. The first focuses on the penetration of human dignity into the central declarative and constitutional documents of the post-war era. The second is connected to an alleged affinity between human dignity, now tightly bound with human rights; and the Holocaust, representing the ultimate and total denial of human dignity. Different views have been expressed as to whether such an immediate connection between human dignity and the Holocaust is real or imagined. These views all examine the relations between the Holocaust and human dignity, while describing human dignity as a static and homogeneous concept. In doing so, they abandon the examination of human dignity itself, as a dynamic concept influencing the discourse in a certain society, but at the same time, influenced by that discourse. The examples brought here concerning Israel, suggest a different kind of linkage between human dignity and the Holocaust, considering human dignity not as a well-known value in need of reaffirmation, but as a concept constantly undergoing change and transformation, a value that is captured in an inner struggle between dignity and honor. Moreover, this analysis of human dignity discourse could be applied to other examples, thus suggesting a new understanding of human dignity discourse, not confined to the conventional legal and theoretical boundaries, but as an authentic expression of deep currents and tensions within society.

References

Allinson M, Leaman J, Parkes S, Tolkiehn B (2014) Contemporary Germany: essays and texts on politics, economics and society. Routledge, New York

Assmann A (2010) The holocaust – a global memory? Extensions and limits of a new memory community. In: Assmann A, Conard S (eds) Memory in a global age: discourses, practices and trajectories. Palgrave Macmillan, Basingstoke, pp 97–117

Bendor AL, Sachs M (2011) The constitutional status of human dignity in Germany and Israel. Isr Law Rev 44:25–61

Cohen GD (2012) The Holocaust and the "human rights revolution": a reassessment. In: Iriye A, Goedde P, Hitchcock WI (eds) The human rights revolution: an international history. Oxford University Press, New York, pp 53–71

Collings J (2015) Democracy's Guardians: a history of the German Federal Constitutional court 1951–2001. Oxford University Press, Oxford

Duranti M (2012) The Holocaust, the legacy of 1789 and the birth of international human rights law: revisiting the foundation myth. J Genocide Res 14:159–186

Eberle EJ (2012) Observations on the development of human dignity and personality in German constitutional law: an overview. Liverpool Law Rev 33:201–233

Finn JE (1991) Constitutions in crisis: political violence and the rule of law. Oxford University Press, New York

Forner S (2014) German intellectuals and the challenge of democratic renewal: culture and politics after 1945. Cambridge University Press, Cambridge, p 2014
Fuh D (2020) Human dignity. In: De Lauri A (ed) Humanitarianism: keywords. Brill, Leiden
Gil I (2009) Teaching the Shoah in history classes in Israeli High Schools. Isr Stud 14:1–25
Goldberg A (2017) Trauma in first person: diary writing during the Holocaust. (Trans. Shmuel Semoneta and Avner Greenberg). Indiana University Press, Bloomington
Habermas J (2010) The concept of human dignity and the realistic utopia of human rights. Metaphilosophy 41:464–480
Judt T (2005) Postwar: a history of Europe since 1945. Penguin Books, New York, p 2005
Kamir, O (2020). Basic Law: Israel as Nation-State–National Honor Defies Human Dignity and Universal Human Rights. Israel Studies 25(3): 213–227.
Kirshenbaum SL (1965) Toldot am Israel be-dorenu (The history of Israel in our time), vol 2. Dvir, Tel-Aviv
Kohn L. Constitution proposal (page 7 to the explanatory notes), ISA C-281/5
Kommers DP (1989) The basic law of the Federal Republic of Germany: an assessment after forty years. In: Merkl PH (ed) The Federal Republic of Germany at forty: union without unity. New York University Press, New York, pp 133–159
Kren GM, Rappoport L (1981) Resistance to the Holocaust: reflections on the idea and the act. In: Bower Y, Rotenstreich N (eds) The Holocaust as historical experience: essays and discussion. Holms and Meier Publishers, New York, pp 193–222
Krisch H (1999) The changing politics of German national identity. In: Merel PH (ed) The Federal Republic of Germany at fifty: at the of a century of turmoil. Palgrave Macmillan, Basingstoke, pp 33–42
Krondorfer B (2021) Holocaust memory and restorative justice. CrossCurrents 71:373–405
Krüger P (1999) The Federal Republic as a nation state. In: Brady JS, Crawford B, Wiliarty SE (eds) The postwar transformation of Germany: democracy, prosperity and nationhood. University of Michigan Press, Ann Arbor, pp 339–356
Kvistad GO (1999) Building democracy and changing institutions: the professional civil service and political parties in the Federal Republic of Germany. In: Brady JS, Crawford B, Wiliarty SE (eds) The postwar transformation of Germany. University of Michigan Press, Ann Arbor, pp 63–93
Levi P (1959) If this is a man. Trans. Stuart Woolf. The Orion Press, New York
Levi D, Sznaider N (2004) The institutionalization of cosmopolitan morality: the Holocaust and human rights. J Hum Rights 3:143–157
Mazower M (2004) The strange triumph of human rights, 1933-1950. Hist J 47:379–398
Moyn S (2015) Christian human rights. University of Pennsylvania Press, Philadelphia
Murkens JEK (2013) From empire to union. Oxford University Press, Oxford
Neumann M (2000) Remembrance and political reality: historical consciousness in Germany after the genocide. New Ger Crit 80:17–28
Nishmit S (1960) Ha-shoah ve-hamered (The Holocaust and the resistance). Kibbutz Lochamei Ha-Getaot
Parvikko T (2021) Arendt, Eichmann and politics of the past. Helsinki University Press, Helsinki
Porat DA (2004) From the scandal to the Holocaust in Israeli education. J Contemp Hist 39:619–636
Protocol of Sitting 227 of the Second Knesset (12.5.1953), 1310
Schroeder D (2012) Human rights and human dignity – an appeal to separate the conjoined twins. Ethical Theory Moral Pract 15:323–335
Shapira A (1998) The Holocaust: private memories, publics memory. Jew Soc Stud 4:40–58
Sharples C (2016) Postwar Germany and the Holocaust. Bloomsbury Academic, New Delhi
Stauber R (2007) The Holocaust in Israeli public debate in the 1950s: ideology and memory. Trans. Elizabeth Yuval. Vallentine Mitchel, London
Torpey J (2001) Making whole what has been smashed: reflections on reparations. J Mod Hist 73: 333–358

Volkova B (2021) Forms of exile in Jewish literature and thought. Academic Studies Press, Boston
Weitz Y (1996) Hamemad hapoliti shel zichron ha-Shoah be-shnot ha-chamishim: (The Political Dimension of Holocaust during the 1950s). Iyunim Multidiscip Stud Isr Modern Jewish Soc 6: 271–287
Yablonka H (1999) Survivors of the Holocaust: Israel after the war. Trans. Ora Cummings. Macmillan Press, London
Zertal I (1998) From catastrophe to power: Holocaust survivors and the emergence of Israel. University of California Press, Berkley, p 1998
Zivia Lubetkin (1957) Achronim al ha-choma (The last ones on the wall). Ein Harod

Part V
Human Dignity and Ubuntu (Including Recent Reflections on COVID-19)

Chapter 14
Human Dignity and Ubuntu in Eviction Law

E. J. Marais

Abstract This chapter considers the implications a stronger emphasis on human dignity and the African notion of ubuntu (which focuses on the dignity of an individual *and* that of the community) may have on how eviction disputes are decided in South Africa today. It analyzes how human dignity and ubuntu could assist courts in reconciling the tension between the interest unlawful occupiers have in their homes (which is sourced in the constitutional right not to be evicted arbitrarily from one's home) and an owner's right to undisturbed possession of her property (which is encapsulated in the constitutional right against arbitrary deprivation of property). My hypothesis is that there are two advantages if courts were to more pertinently consider the constitutional values of human dignity and ubuntu when they reconcile the tension between the interests at hand. First, they enrich the reconciliation process by expanding the range of factors courts may consider when deciding whether it would be just and equitable to grant an eviction order. Second, ubuntu provides a strong normative foundation for the obligation the courts have placed on owners who are unable to evict unlawful occupiers forthwith, namely that they must temporarily accommodate them on their land, free of charge, while the state searches for alternative accommodation. Ubuntu also reveals the limits of this obligation, especially in cases where owners are required to house unlawful occupiers for unreasonably long periods.

14.1 Introduction

The chapter analyzes the role human dignity and the African notion of ubuntu could play in eviction law, which forms part of South African property law. (Property law, in turn, is part of the field of private law, which concerns itself with the legal relationships between private parties.) Eviction law concerns instances where landowners, many of whom in South Africa are still white, institute legal proceedings to

E. J. Marais (✉)
University of Johannesburg, Johannesburg, South Africa
e-mail: ernst.marais@wits.ac.za

S. N. Arel et al. (eds.), *Probing Human Dignity*,
https://doi.org/10.1007/978-3-031-42437-3_14

evict mostly black unlawful occupiers from their land in accordance with their right, as owners, to have undisturbed and exclusive possession of their property. In terms of South African property law, the point of departure during apartheid was that the subjective circumstances of unlawful occupiers play no role in such disputes (Van der Walt 2009, pp. 53ff). These subjective circumstances touch on the human dignity of occupiers, as evicting them might render them homeless, thereby undermining their dignity through their losing their homes and being forced to live on the street. Because the law usually strongly protects ownership of land, non-owners (like unlawful occupiers), had to prove that they had permission to be on the land to prevent eviction (Van der Walt 2009, pp. 53ff). Absent such permission, so the reasoning of South African courts and scholars typically went during this era, a court must grant exclusive possession to the owner as a natural consequence of ownership (Van der Walt 2009, pp. 53–54). Property law did not afford courts a broad discretion to refuse an eviction order based on the occupiers' subjective circumstances or the impact that such an order may have on their livelihood (Van der Walt 2009, pp. 53–54). Under the Constitution of the Republic of South Africa, 1996 ("the Constitution"), courts now have such a discretion.

With this legal history as a background, I examine the implications human dignity and ubuntu may have for the application of this new discretion courts have to refuse an eviction order based purely on the subjective circumstances of unlawful occupiers. Much has been written on how the competing interests in this setting (i.e. the home interest unlawful occupiers have in the land they occupy *vis-à-vis* the owner's interest in having undisturbed possession of her property) should be reconciled in terms of this discretion (Pienaar and Kotzé 2018; Muller 2011; Van der Walt 2009, Chaps. 1–3 and 5; Liebenberg and Goldblatt 2007; *Government of the Republic of South Africa v Grootboom* 2001 (1) SA 46 (CC) paras 23 and 83). These two interests find expression in two fundamental rights, namely Sect. 26(3) of the Constitution ("[n]o one may be evicted from their home, or have their home demolished, without an order of court made after considering all the relevant circumstances") and Sect. 25(1) of the Constitution ("[n]o one may be deprived of property except in terms of law of general application, and no law may permit arbitrary deprivation of property"). According to the Constitutional Court, when two fundamental rights are in conflict the responsibility of courts—in resolving the dispute at hand—is not to identify which right should trump the other. Rather, courts must resolve the dispute in a way that protects both rights and gives effect to them simultaneously and as optimally as possible (see *Port Elizabeth Municipality v Various Occupiers* 2005 (1) SA 217 (CC) par 23 ("*PE Municipality*"); Van der Walt 2012, pp. 153–168). Yet, thus far courts and scholars have not explored the implications human dignity and ubuntu hold for this reconciliation process in detail. Ubuntu, a notion unique to sub-Saharan Africa, entails that human beings are only able to become fully human (i.e., to realize their human dignity) by relying on other members of their community (Bennett 2018, pp. 35–36). My hypothesis is that paying more attention to human dignity and ubuntu when eviction cases are adjudicated has two advantages. First, these notions enrich the process of reconciling the tension between the competing rights at hand. Expanding the range of factors courts may consider when exercising their discretion as to whether to grant an eviction order or not, enhancing and improving the process of reconciling an unlawful occupier's home interest in the land with an owner's right to exclusive possession of her land. Second, and more pertinently, ubuntu provides a cogent normative basis for the obligation courts place on an owner when they refuse to grant owners an immediate eviction order. This obligation entails that an owner must temporarily accommodate the occupiers on her land, free of charge, until the state (or another landowner) provides him/her with alternative accommodation. Ubuntu directly underscores this obligation and indicates its limits.

In this chapter, to establish a foundation for the analysis, I offer a brief background of the historical and legal contexts of evictions during apartheid. In the second section, I outline how evictions occurred during apartheid, and then briefly discuss two seminal eviction judgments from the constitutional era. These cases illustrate how the constitutional dispensation broke away from the eviction regime followed during apartheid and direct the focus in section three on how human dignity and ubuntu are understood in South African law. Addressing how these notions feature in the cases under discussion reveals the rather limited role they (especially ubuntu) have played in these decisions. Section four, in turn, discusses the various sources of law in South Africa which govern legal disputes and explains why human dignity (as a fundamental right) does not directly feature in eviction disputes. The sources of law include the fundamental rights in the Constitution, legislation which gives effect to these rights, human dignity as an enforceable right (Sect. 10 of the Constitution) and a constitutional value (Sect. 1(a) of the Constitution), and ubuntu, itself a constitutional value. I emphasize how considering human dignity and ubuntu more pertinently in eviction disputes may assist courts in reconciling the interests of landowners with those of unlawful occupiers in a more holistic fashion. I argue further that there might be instances where ubuntu requires the state to assist owners who are required to house occupiers on the land (for free) for unreasonably long periods. The assistance should take the form of the state compensating such owners while the state searches for alternative accommodation, during which time the occupiers remain on the land without having to pay the owner. The chapter ends by briefly explaining how ubuntu requires an amendment to current eviction legislation to provide for the compensation mentioned and how ubuntu possibly also features in another part of private law, addressing the wider implications this notion may potentially have outside South Africa.

14.2 Historical and Legal Contexts

14.2.1 Evictions During Apartheid

An owner's right to have exclusive possession of her property is traditionally described as the most essential entitlement of ownership (Van der Walt 2009, pp. 36–37) or "stick" (in Anglo-American legal terminology) in the bundle of rights that constitutes ownership (see *Yee v City of Escondido* 503 US 519 (1992) at 528). Van der Walt (2009, Chap. 2) describes this view as the "rights paradigm." It flows from classic liberalism, which regards ownership as an absolute and exclusive right that can accommodate limitations, though such limitations are usually temporary in nature and require strong and overriding justification (see Birks 1985; Van der Walt and Dhliwayo 2017; Van der Walt 2009, p. 15).

Under the rights paradigm, the point of departure, at least in principle, is that an owner is entitled to exclusive possession of her property unless a non-owner can prove a countervailing right in the property (i.e., land) that derives from the owner's consent, such as a limited real right (i.e. a servitude or easement) or a personal right (i.e. a lease contract) (Van der Walt 2009, pp. 53–54 ff). Several legal systems have moved away from this absolute conceptualization of ownership by introducing measures to protect the interests of weaker parties, namely lessees and even unlawful occupiers (see, for instance, Van der Walt 2009, pp. 77–167 and his discussion with reference to developments in German law, Dutch law and the law of England and Wales). Yet, ownership as an absolute and exclusive right formed the essence of property law in South Africa up until the dawn of democracy in 1994.

During apartheid, an owner's right to exclusive possession was applied in an abstract, a-contextual manner that did not consider the subjective circumstances of those persons with no rights in land (like unlawful occupiers) or what impact eviction might have on them (Van der Walt 2009, pp. 146–147 ff). The only time an owner would not prevail was basically when the non-owner had a right in the property granted to her by the owner.

The weak position of non-owners was intensified by legislation aimed at promoting the state's policy of grand spatial segregation based on race (Van der Walt 2009, pp. 60ff). Apartheid statutes deliberately made it difficult, if not impossible, for black persons to acquire secure rights in land (like ownership or even lease agreements) in parts of South Africa reserved for occupation by white persons (Van der Walt 2009, p. 60). In terms of apartheid legislation introduced during the first decade of the twentieth century and thereafter, roughly 87% of South Africa was "reserved" for occupation by white people (who then made up about 20% of the population; today white people constitute just over 9% of the population) while the remaining 13% of the country was reserved for occupation by black people (Pienaar 2014, pp. 82–93). Given that most job opportunities were located in the major urban centers (basically all of which were in the white areas), thousands of black people migrated to the outskirts of these cities to earn a living. This migration, which was both a result of and a threat to the state's project of grand spatial segregation (see *Port Elizabeth Municipality v Various Occupiers* 2005 (1) SA 217 (CC) at par 10), resulted in the establishment of large informal settlements (called "squatter camps" during apartheid), where people were crammed together and lived in poverty, on the outskirts of cities. Black persons in these settlements lived in informal homes (referred to as "shacks" during apartheid) which they constructed with corrugated iron, wood and plastic sheets. Today there are still hundreds of thousands of South Africans, most of whom are black, who live in these appalling conditions.

The notorious Prevention of Illegal Squatting Act 52 of 1951 ("PISA") made the eviction procedure even more swift than the one found in property law and criminalized what it termed "illegal squatting" on private or state land. Section 3B(1)(a) of PISA permitted landowners—and state bodies—to demolish the informal homes of so-called "squatters," and to remove the materials of which these homes consisted from the land, without a court order. These parties could also evict "squatters" from the land, although actual eviction did require a court order (Sonnekus and Neels 1994, pp. 176, 183–184). These steps could be taken irrespective of any hardship the unlawful occupiers would have to endure, such as being rendered homeless or having their property destroyed during a forced eviction (Muller 2013). The result was a grave assault on the human dignity of black people, as this Act caused immense suffering and initiated a vicious cycle of occupiers' evictions; as a result, these occupiers had to settle on another piece of private or state land to make a living, making them prone to eviction again (see *Port Elizabeth Municipality v Various Occupiers* 2005 (1) SA 217 (CC) par 10). Scholars estimate that approximately 3.5 million people were displaced through forced evictions in South Africa between 1960 and 1983 (Van der Walt 2009, p. 2 footnote 5; Liebenberg 2010, p. 269).

14.2.2 Evictions Under the Constitution

The Constitution, which was adopted in 1996, recognizes the injustices which occurred during apartheid and seeks to "[h]eal the divisions of the past and establish a society based on democratic values, social justice and fundamental human rights" (see the preamble to the Constitution). Given the undignified and degrading way unlawful occupiers were treated during apartheid in the eviction context, it comes as no surprise that the Constitution has a fundamental right specifically dedicated to evictions, namely Sect. 26(3) (i.e., no one may be evicted from their home or have their home demolished without an order of court, which may only be granted after a court has considered all relevant circumstances). This provision must be understood in the context of the brief historical background provided above. The purpose of Sect. 26(3) is to advance the human dignity of unlawful occupiers in a very specific setting, namely protecting them from arbitrarily losing their homes without an order of court (Liebenberg 2010, p. 270; Fox 2007). Parliament enacted legislation to give effect to this fundamental right, namely the Prevention of Illegal Eviction from and Unlawful Occupation of Land Act 19 of 1998 ("PIE"). This Act also gives effect to Sect. 25(1) of the Constitution, which provides that property holders may only be deprived of property (i.e., their property may only be interfered with) in terms of law of general application, and no law may permit arbitrary deprivations (Muller 2011).

Section 26(3) and PIE constitute a decisive break with the old eviction order, which consisted of the rules of property law and PISA. The main aim of that Act was to prevent illegal squatting of land, while PIE's primary objective is to prevent illegal eviction. PIE furthermore seeks to prevent the unlawful occupation of land, as is evident from its title, though this purpose is secondary to its mentioned primary objective. The Act's two goals, which seem to entail a dichotomy, should be understood as a "constitutionally-inspired commitment ... to never again subject unlawful occupiers to the inhumane and degrading treatment of forced evictions that characterised apartheid land law" (Muller and Marais 2020, p. 123).

PIE provides both procedural and substantive protection to unlawful occupiers. In terms of the former, PIE determines how eviction proceedings are to take place and which parties should be joined to the case (see Sect. 4(2) of PIE; Muller and Liebenberg 2013). The substantive aspect concerns factors courts must consider when deciding whether it is just and equitable to grant an eviction order. The factors are found in sections 4(6)–(7) and 6 of the Act. The former two subsections deal with evictions by private landowners, including the state in its capacity as a landowner, while the latter provision governs evictions at the instance of a state organ. The difference between subsections (6) and (7) is that the latter concerns evictions where the occupiers have been living on the land for more than 6 months before the owner institutes eviction proceedings. It should be noted that the substantive protection under the Act does not give unlawful occupiers any rights (especially not property rights) in land. It rather entails an immunity (Van der Walt 2009, pp. 39–40), which tempers an owner's otherwise strong right to have exclusive possession of her property, which now flows from Sect. 25(1) of the Constitution.

The unifying theme of sections 4(6)–(7) and 6 is that a court may only grant an eviction order if it is of the opinion that it is just and equitable to do so. Courts therefore have a discretion, based on justice and equity considerations, whether to grant an eviction order. This discretion, which did not exist in eviction law during apartheid and does not form part of property law, amounts to a major qualification of an owner's right to have undisturbed possession of her property. The discretion may only be exercised once a court takes account of all relevant circumstances, which is done by reconciling the competing rights involved (i.e., the right of the unlawful occupiers under Sect. 26(3) of the Constitution with the right of the owner under Sect. 25(1) of the Constitution). Both subsections in Sect. 4 require courts to consider the rights and needs of the elderly, children, disabled persons, and households headed by women. PIE specifically mentions these persons, as they are typically the most vulnerable in the eviction context. A court should be hesitant to grant an eviction order if these persons are amongst the occupiers, especially if granting an eviction order will render them homeless. Requiring these marginalized persons to live on the street would cause particular hardship for them, thereby resulting in a grave insult to their dignity.

14.3 Human Dignity and Ubuntu in South African Law

14.3.1 The Meaning of Human Dignity

Section 26(3) of the Constitution and PIE dramatically altered South African eviction law by replacing the contravention-paradigm, which operated under property law and PISA, with a human-rights paradigm (Pienaar 2014, p. 668). This section outlines the new human-rights paradigm by focusing on the meaning of human dignity and ubuntu. It also reveals the rather limited attention these concepts received in the two eviction cases under discussion. It then lays the foundation, upon which section four then expands, for my argument that considering these notions more pertinently may enhance the process of reconciling the competing interests of owners and unlawful occupiers in a more holistic manner, one that expands the range of considerations courts may consider when deciding whether it is just and equitable to grant an eviction order.

Before delving into the meaning of human dignity, it is first necessary to say something about the different manifestations dignity has in South African law. In South Africa, human dignity is a fundamental right (Sect. 10 of the Constitution) and a founding constitutional value (Sect. 1(a) of the Constitution). In actual fact, human dignity can operate as a first order rule, a second order rule, a correlative right, and as a value or grundnorm (Woolman 2005, p. 19; Currie and De Waal 2013, p. 253). In a given case, it is possible for human dignity to apply in all these forms (Woolman 2005, p. 19). In *PE Municipality* and *City of Johannesburg Metropolitan Municipality v Blue Moonlight Properties 39 (Pty) Ltd* 2012 (2) SA 104 (CC) ("*Blue Moonlight*"), the Constitutional Court mainly relied on human dignity as a constitutional value to interpret and apply PIE (see *PE Municipality* at par 10, 12–13, 15, 17–18, 29, 39, 41–42; *Blue Moonlight* at par 2, 84). One might wonder why the court did not rely on human dignity, as a fundamental right, directly to vindicate the rights of the parties to the dispute. The reason why the court did not directly apply the fundamental right to human dignity is addressed in section four below. For now, it suffices to say that parties to a case may not invoke the more general fundamental right to human dignity to adjudicate their dispute when more specific fundamental rights (like sections 26(3) and 25(1) of the Constitution) are applicable, especially when there is legislation that gives effect to these rights. This is why the Constitutional Court in these two cases used PIE as the source of law to vindicate the rights of the parties at hand. With this in mind, the meaning of human dignity in South African law may be addressed.

Section 10 of the Constitution provides that "[e]veryone has inherent dignity and the right to have their dignity respected and protected." The formulation of the provision reveals that dignity is inherent in every human and is not acquired from the Constitution itself (Ackermann 2012, p. 95). At the same time, human dignity is also a foundational value of the South African constitutional order (Sect. 1(a) of the Constitution) which informs all other fundamental rights (Ackermann 2012, p. 98). Sect. 10 must be read with sections 7(2) and 8(1) of the Constitution (Ackermann 2012, p. 95). The former stipulates that the state "must respect, protect, promote and fulfil the rights in the Bill of Rights," while the latter provides for direct horizontal application of rights in the Bill of Rights. This means that not only the state but also private parties and juristic persons are bound by the fundamental rights (and their obligations) in the Bill of Rights, which includes the right to human dignity.

Though difficult to define in precise terms, human dignity (for purposes of South African law) refers to the "value and worth of all individuals" (see *National*

Coalition for Gay and Lesbian Equality v Minister of Justice 1999 (1) SA 6 (CC) par 28) or "inherent human worth" (Ackermann 2012, pp. 97–98). This inherent worth entails that humans are the bearers of an innate right to be respected and valued (Woolman 2005, p. 17). The Constitutional Court understands human dignity in the Kantian sense, namely that human worth is impaired when persons are treated as mere objects and not as ends in themselves (Ackermann 2012, pp. 99–100; Bennett 2018, pp. 54–55; Woolman 2005, p. 6; Currie and De Waal 2013, p. 251).

The right to human dignity (along with the right to life) is the most important of all human rights (see *S v Makwanyane* 1995 (3) SA 391 (CC) par 144) and is the source of all other specialized fundamental rights (see *S v Makwanyane* 1995 (3) SA 391 (CC) paras 144 and 328), which include sections 26(3) and 25(1) of the Constitution. As an enforceable right (in sect. 10 of the Constitution) and constitutional value (sect. 1(a) of the Constitution), human dignity requires that the fundamental rights should not only enjoy protection against unjustified state interference (i.e. negative protection) but also that state power must be used to promote the dignity of all people (i.e. positive realization) (Currie and De Waal 2013, pp. 350–251; Liebenberg 2005, p. 1). The understanding of dignity explained above (especially in terms of its horizontal applicability and Kantian content) reveals why the Constitutional Court in *PE Municipality* and *Blue Moonlight* relied on it—as a constitutional value—when it applied PIE. The fact that human dignity operates horizontally means it binds private parties, which—in turn—entails that landowners must treat unlawful occupiers as ends in themselves and not as mere objects. In other words, when landowners wish to evict unlawful occupiers, their dignity (especially if they may lose their homes upon eviction) plays a significant role when a court is called upon to decide whether it would be just and equitable to grant an eviction order. Though the court in the two cases under discussion did not refer to these elements of dignity in express terms, considering them more pertinently may aid the process of reconciling the competing interests under PIE, while also providing further justification for the outcomes of these cases. Indeed, from how the court applied PIE in those cases, it is possible to draw conclusions as to how the unarticulated elements of human dignity featured in the decisions and the role they played in their outcomes.

One cannot deny the fact that the dignity of the occupiers would have been impaired if they were required to vacate the land forthwith, as they would either have had to move to unsuitable alternative accommodation (in *PE Municipality*) or have been rendered homeless (in *Blue Moonlight*). Having a home (even a temporary one) is central to leading a self-fulfilling, dignified life, (see *Dladla v City of Johannesburg* 2018 (2) SA 327 (CC) par 43; Radin 1982; Fox 2007) which means that the loss of a home should be avoided as far as possible, especially in instances where occupiers have been living on land for an extended period. PIE, through giving effect to sections 26(3) and 25(1) of the Constitution, also gives effect to the human dignity of both unlawful occupiers and owners by providing a framework (or constitutional matrix) whereby courts may only grant an eviction order if granting such an order is just and equitable after considering all relevant circumstances. The framework of PIE reveals the impact public law (which concerns itself with the vertical relationship between the state and legal subjects) has on the private law (which deals with the horizontal relationship between private legal subjects) of property and weakens the public law/private law divide. Considering the human dignity of the parties to eviction disputes more pertinently reveals that evicting the occupiers straightaway would have negatively have impacted their dignity, specifically in the form of losing their homes. This view supplements the court's reasoning under PIE. Had the eviction occurred, the owners in *PE Municipality* would have regained possession of their land, which they did not intend to put to productive use (see *PE Municipality* at par 59). Thus, their human dignity would not have been promoted through having the land returned to them, as the presence of the occupiers did not impact on any plans they had for the land. In *Blue Moonlight*, the new owner (a juristic person or company) wanted to put the building to commercial use, but this would have occurred at the expense of the occupiers' dignity, who would have had to live on the street if the court granted the eviction order without the state having to provide alternative accommodation. Here the implications of the court's reasoning, again without the court using the dignity framework directly, are that the impact on the dignity of the occupiers (in terms of losing their housing interest) would have been more severe when compared to how the dignity of the owner would have been affected (i.e., being unable to obtain an eviction order immediately so as to use the building for commercial purposes). This view finds support in the court's ruling that "[t]here is no competing risk of homelessness on the part of Blue Moonlight [the company], as there might be in circumstances where eviction is sought to enable a family to move into a home" (see *Blue Moonlight* at par 39).

Though a greater emphasis on human dignity might not have changed the outcomes in these cases, such a focus would have provided a more holistic approach for the court in exercising its discretion while providing a stronger justification for these outcomes. The fact that the court in both instances temporarily permitted the occupiers to remain on the owners' land without them (or the state) having to pay the owners for the accommodation is noteworthy, as landowners are usually paid (at least in property law) when they accommodate persons on their land (such as with a lease agreement). In this context, the African notion of ubuntu is particularly valuable, as ubuntu explains two things. First, it shows why courts may deny or suspend the granting of immediate eviction orders to owners. Second, it reveals why owners may then be expected to provide free temporary accommodation to unlawful occupiers (i.e. to share the property with the occupiers: see Dyal-Chand 2013 and Van der Walt 2016, pp. 212–213 ff) while the state searches for alternative accommodation. The value of ubuntu here lies in the fact that it accentuates the obligation that rests on owners in a way that the Western conception of human dignity might struggle to do.

14.3.2 The Meaning of Ubuntu

Ubuntu is a moral theory (Metz 2011, pp. 535ff) and an ethical value (Mokgoro 1998, pp. 17–18) which is indigenous to sub-Saharan Africa. Ubuntu finds expression in the saying *umuntu ngumuntu ngabantu*, which is usually translated as "a person is a person [through] other people" (see *Dawood v Minister of Home Affairs* 2000 (3) SA 936 (CC) par 30 footnote 42; Kamga 2018, p. 626; Bennett 2018, p. 28; Nkosi 2018, pp. 3–6). Bennett (2018, p. 33) defines ubuntu as "the affirmation of an individual's humanity by accepting that others are equally human, and by being willing to share the world with them."

Ubuntu embodies a philosophy of humaneness, personhood, and morality between members of a community (see *S v Makwanyane* 1995 (3) SA 391 (CC) par 308; Bennett 2018, p. 33; Nkosi 2018, pp. 3–6). Ubuntu concerns sharing, co-responsibility and the mutual enjoyment of rights by all people (see *S v Makwanyane* 1995 (3) SA 391 (CC) par 224). This concept also places an obligation on each individual to realize certain goals *vis-à-vis* the community, namely expressing care, compassion, tolerance, reciprocity, respect, harmony, while maintaining and strengthening the community (Ackermann 2012, p. 112; Bennett 2018, p. 32; Nkosi 2018, pp. 3–6). This obligation flows from the supposition that an individual is incapable of becoming fully human without relating to (and relying on) other persons (Bennett 2018, pp. 35–36; Nkosi 2018, pp. 3–6).[1] The dignity of each person and the dignity of the community are central to this concept, as ubuntu regards the life of another person as valuable as one's own (see *S v Makwanyane* 1995 (3) SA 391 (CC) par 225). Treating others in an undignified and inhumane manner is therefore at odds with ubuntu (see *S v Makwanyane* 1995 (3) SA 391 (CC) par 225).

Ubuntu should be understood outside the Hohfeldian rights/duties legal framework (Hohfeld 1917) which concerns the duties persons without rights have towards right holders (such as the duty of unlawful occupiers to refrain from interfering with a landowner's right to exclusive possession of her property under the rights paradigm), and may instead—as mentioned above—be conceptualized in terms of relationships between people without references to who has a right in the property (see Bennett 2018, p. 47 and compare Nedelsky 1993). The interests of the individual are considered *from the perspective of the community of which the individual forms part* and not solely from the perspective of the individual, as is characteristic in Western thinking regarding human dignity (Bennett 2018, pp. 35–36; *PE Municipality* at par 37). The latter view underpins the responsibility ubuntu places on individuals towards other members of the community, as explained above (Bennett 2018, p. 47; Nkosi 2018, pp. 3–6). This responsibility resonates with the social obligation owners have towards non-owners in terms of constitutional property

[1]There may be interesting links between this aspect of ubuntu and Fineman's vulnerability and resilience theory, which emphasizes the inherent dependance of humans (Fineman 2017, pp. 142–143). However, such an investigation is beyond the scope of my chapter.

theory, namely how owners may use and enjoy their property, the limits of ownership, that the law may sometimes expect owners to share their property with others and the fact that property, as a legal and social institution, serves the public good. [2]

Ubuntu is a central feature of South Africa's democracy and the Bill of Rights (see *PE Municipality* at par 37; *Blue Moonlight* at par 38; *Barkhuizen v Napier* 2007 (5) SA 232 (CC) par 51; *Bhe v Magistrate, Khayelitsha* 2005 (1) SA 580 (CC) par 45, 163). Ubuntu assumes the role of a constitutional value and informs human dignity, both as an enforceable right and as a constitutional value (Bennett 2018, pp. 93–94; Ackermann 2012, p. 111; *PE Municipality* at par 37). Ubuntu combines individual rights with a communitarian philosophy and is a unifying motif of the Bill of Rights (see *PE Municipality* at par 37). Ubuntu also informs our understanding of existing rights and duties in the Bill of Rights (Bennett 2018, p. 49). The Constitutional Court in both *PE Municipality* and *Blue Moonlight* cited ubuntu when it interpreted PIE's provisions (see *PE Municipality* at par 37; *Blue Moonlight* at par 38). Yet, the court did not comprehensively explain the implications ubuntu has for the cases at hand, nor did it explain how it relates to human dignity (to which sections 26(3) and 25(1) of the Constitution, as well as PIE, give effect). It is therefore necessary to unpack the consequences ubuntu may have for eviction law in more detail.

The first step is to elaborate on the relationship between ubuntu and human dignity (Bennett 2018, pp. 51 ff; Cornell 2010; Mokgoro and Woolman 2010). Both concepts demand respect for the inherent worth of human beings (Bennett 2018, p. 56) and have a communitarian element (Ackermann 2012, pp. 79–80; Bennett 2018, p. 57). Yet, there are sufficient differences between the Western conception of dignity and ubuntu to justify using ubuntu as an independent constitutional value (Cornell 2010; Mokgoro and Woolman 2010). This is because the Western notion of dignity, which has a more individualized focus, does not place the same emphasis on the individual's embeddedness in the community and, as a result, on the welfare of the community (Bennett 2018, pp. 57–58; Cornell 2010). Ubuntu, in contrast, attaches greater significance to the wellbeing of the community (Kamga 2018, p. 626). This element of ubuntu opens the door to reconciling the competing interests of parties to an eviction case in a manner that is more community-oriented

[2] There seems to be similarities between an individual's responsibility towards the community under ubuntu and the social obligation that rests on owners—in terms of which property serves the common good—as well as the sharing of property: see Article 14(2) of the German Basic Law of 1949, *Shoprite Checkers (Pty) Ltd v MEC for Economic Development, Eastern Cape* 2015 (6) SA 125 (CC) paras 47–48; *PE Municipality* at par 16; Alexander (2009); Dyal-Chand (2013). There are possible, and as yet unexplored, links between the dignity (as understood in terms of ubuntu) of unlawful occupiers and owners in the eviction context and the marginality argument of Van der Walt (2009, 2014), the social-obligation norm of Alexander (2009), the sharing theory of Dyal-Chand (2013), the property and personhood theory of Radin (1982), and the vulnerability and resilience theory of Fineman (2017) (especially as applied to the unlawful land occupation context by Fox O'Mahony and Roark 2022), which indicate to what extent property and non-property interests should enjoy protection in the eyes of the law. An investigation of these relationships falls outside the scope of my chapter.

and focused on sharing, one which incorporates the obligations individuals have towards other members of the community and *vice versa*. The importance of the community for ubuntu must be distinguished from Marxism, though, where the individual's interest is "subordinate to the greater good of society" (Bennett 2018, p. 52).

The latter point touches on one of the main criticisms against ubuntu. The argument is that the emphasis on the community amounts to majoritarianism, which loses sight of the individual's interests and her fundamental rights (Metz 2011, p. 533; Bennett 2018, pp. 38–39). [3] This criticism is unfounded, however, as the well-being of the individual "is realised *in* and *through* the community." (Bennett 2018, p. 38 (my emphasis)). For ubuntu, the welfare of the individual is as important as the welfare of the community (Bennett 2018, p. 52). Therefore, the concept is about simultaneously promoting the self-fulfillment of the individual *and* the community and not ranking one over the other (Bennett 2018, p. 38). The next section below expands on the other positive implications ubuntu may have for the adjudication of eviction cases.

14.4 Reconciling the Tension Between the Interests of Owners and Unlawful Occupiers of Land through the Lens of Human Dignity and Ubuntu

14.4.1 The Relationship Between Different Legal Sources Under a Single System of Law

The previous section sets out the meaning of human dignity and ubuntu and shows that these notions could have received more attention in *PE Municipality* and *Blue Moonlight*. It also provides a glimpse of how these values enhance the process of reconciling the tension between the rights of unlawful occupiers and those of owners. This section builds on how the meaning of human dignity and ubuntu may enrich the adjudication of eviction disputes. Yet, such enhancement must occur in a way that complies with the constitutional methodology followed when various sources of law apply to a given case. For instance, we see property law principles, sections 26(3) and 25(1) of the Constitution, PIE as well as the values of human dignity and ubuntu all featuring simultaneously in eviction disputes. How human dignity and ubuntu, as constitutional values, fit into the combination of legal sources must thus first be explained before turning to the advantage a stronger emphasis on these values may have in eviction disputes. This constitutional

[3] Ubuntu is also criticized for, amongst others, being unworkably vague and unsuited for modern society due to its pre-colonial morality. See Kamga (2018), pp. 634–635; Metz (2011); Bennett (2018), pp. 36ff; Nkosi (2018), pp. 6–8 for sources and arguments against these objections.

methodology also reveals why litigants to eviction disputes may not invoke the right to human dignity (as a fundamental right) directly to vindicate their rights.

South African law is a mixed-legal system (as it was influenced by Roman-Dutch civil law and English common law) and is composed of a complex combination of legal sources. These include the Constitution, pre- and post-constitutional statute law, case law precedent, uncodified common law (of which private law and, hence, property law form part) and indigenous law. The Constitution, which is supreme law, stipulates that "law or conduct inconsistent with it is invalid, and the obligations imposed by it must be fulfilled" (Sect. 2 of the Constitution). Courts are allowed to test the constitutionality of law and conduct and must declare such law or conduct invalid in so far as it is inconsistent with the Constitution (Sect. 172(1) of the Constitution). The constitutional values of human dignity, equality, and freedom (Sect. 7(1) of the Constitution) are central to both the interpretation of all fundamental rights (Sect. 39(1) of the Constitution) and the constitutional project of realizing a society based on democratic values, social justice, and fundamental human rights (see the preamble of the Constitution; Henderson 1998).

Chapter two of the Constitution, namely the Bill of Rights, has a range of fundamental rights, many of which would be familiar to constitutional lawyers around the world. These include, for instance, the right to human dignity (Sect. 10), the right to life (Sect. 11), the right to equality (Sect. 9), and the right against arbitrary deprivation of one's property (Sect. 25(1)). The Bill of Rights also contains rights not typically found elsewhere, which were necessitated by South Africa's apartheid history. These rights include the right of freedom of movement and residence (Sect. 21), the right to be free from slavery, servitude and forced labor (Sect. 13), the right to have access to adequate housing (Sect. 26(1)), and the right not to be arbitrarily evicted from one's home (Sect. 26(3)).

The relationship between the different legal sources, particularly the right to human dignity *vis-à-vis* other fundamental rights, and relationship of these sources to the common law, is complex. For example, several sources of law (including different fundamental rights) may apply to a given dispute. The question is whether litigants are then free to base their arguments on the source that best favors their cases. An unfettered choice in this regard may undermine the transformative goals the Constitution seeks to achieve under a single legal system, namely promoting (instead of undermining) all the rights in the Bill of Rights optimally (Van der Walt 2012, pp. 32ff, 91–92, 102–104; Van der Sijde 2022, Chaps. 1–2). For example, in *Brisley v Drotsky* 2002 (4) SA 1 (SCA) ("*Brisley*") the respondent (who was the lessor) sought an eviction order against the appellant (the lessee) due to non-payment of the lease amount. The appellant relied on Sect. 26(3) of the Constitution (for unexplained reasons she did not rely on PIE) and argued that because of the personal circumstances of herself and her family and the hardship the eviction would cause them, the eviction order should not be granted. The respondent, in turn, relied on the common law (i.e., property law) to obtain an eviction order, in terms of which a landowner essentially only has to prove ownership when seeking to evict someone (*Chetty v Naidoo* 1974 (3) SA 13 (A) 20; Van der Walt 2009, pp. 43–44). The Supreme Court of Appeal dismissed the appellant's argument and granted an eviction order in terms of the common law, ruling that Sect. 26(3) is not sufficiently clear as regards the grounds on which the court may refuse an eviction order if an owner satisfies all the common-law requirements for eviction. The outcome of the case—which illustrates the strong protection ownership still enjoys in the rights paradigm and the dangers of giving litigants an unrestricted choice regarding the source of law they may invoke—would arguably have been differently if the appellant relied on PIE and not on Sect. 26(3) directly (compare Van der Walt 2009, pp. 43–46).

Given the very real danger an arbitrary choice of legal source poses, namely by realizing negative features (in the form of subverting fundamental rights), as arguably happened in *Brisley* (Van der Walt 2009, pp. 45–46), the Constitutional Court in later cases laid down two subsidiarity principles to govern the choice of law in a given dispute (Van der Walt 2012, pp. 107–108ff). These principles ensure that the dispute is adjudicated under the legal source that best promotes the positive characteristics the Constitution envisions for the whole legal system, namely by optimally advancing and vindicating the fundamental rights at hand (Van der Walt 2012, pp. 32ff, 91–92, 102–104). Two of these positive characteristics lie at the heart of this chapter, namely the right against arbitrary eviction from one's home (Sect. 26(3)) and the right against arbitrary deprivation of one's property (Sect. 25(1)). The question is therefore how to optimally reconcile these competing rights in eviction cases in terms of the single-system-of-law principle.

The two subsidiarity principles referred to in the previous paragraph derive from the single-system-of-law principle, which the Constitutional Court laid down in *Pharmaceutical Manufacturers Association of SA: In Re Ex Parte President of the Republic of South Africa* 2000 (2) SA 674 (22) at par 44. There, Chief Justice Chaskalson held that all law, including statute law and the uncodified common law, "derives its force from the Constitution and is subject to constitutional control." The implications of this principle are far-reaching and are discussed extensively elsewhere (see Van der Walt 2012; Van der Sijde 2012, 2022). Suffice to say that this principle guides the choice of law in legal disputes, as this choice has important systemic implications for a single legal system, namely whether the fundamental rights at hand are properly promoted and protected (Van der Sijde 2012; Marais 2018, pp. 186–188). Litigants are thus not free to choose the source of law that best suits their case, as the choice of law (and its application) must promote these positive features.

Of the two subsidiarity principles, only the first one is relevant for present purposes. The first principle entails that litigants may not directly invoke a fundamental right to find a cause of action when legislation has been enacted to give effect to that right (Van der Walt 2012, p. 36). In other words, litigants to an eviction dispute may not rely directly on either Sect. 26(3) or Sect. 25(1) of the Constitution to find a remedy in an eviction dispute, as PIE gives effect to these constitutional provisions. By way of logical extension, litigants may also not base their claim on any other fundamental right (such as the right to human dignity in Sect. 10 of the Constitution) to find a cause of action, as PIE gives effect to the applicable fundamental rights at hand (Marais and Muller 2018, pp. 770–771). They may only rely directly on the particular constitutional provisions themselves, in terms of the proviso to the first principle, if they challenge the constitutionality of the Act for not properly giving effect to the fundamental rights at hand (Van der Walt 2012, p. 36).

The two subsidiarity principles hold important implications for the relationship between property law, PIE, sections 26(3) and 25(1) of the Constitution, the right to human dignity (as a fundamental right) and the constitutional values of human dignity and ubuntu. PIE was specifically enacted to give effect to sections 26(3) and 25(1), while expressly excluding the common law when dealing with evictions where unlawful occupiers live on land in both urban and rural areas (see *Ndlovu v Ngcobo* 2003 (1) SA 113 (SCA) par 20). The first subsidiarity principle, therefore, indicates that cases pertaining to eviction must be adjudicated under this Act. Litigants may therefore not directly invoke Sect. 26(3), Sect. 25(1), the fundamental right to human dignity or the common law (as the landlord did in the *Brisley* case) to find a cause of action, unless they want to challenge the Act for not adequately giving effect to either Sect. 26(3) or Sect. 25(1).

The focus now turns to human dignity and how it relates to the mentioned legal sources. In *Dawood v Minister of Home Affairs* 2000 (3) SA 936 (CC) at par 35, Justice O'Regan described the multifaceted nature of human dignity as follows:

> [h]uman dignity ... informs constitutional adjudication and interpretation at a range of levels. It is a value that informs the interpretation of many, possibly all, other rights. ... Section 10 [the right to human dignity], however, makes it plain that dignity is not only a *value* fundamental to our Constitution, it is a justiciable and enforceable *right* that must be respected and protected. In many cases, however, where the value of human dignity is offended, the primary constitutional breach occasioned may be of a more specific right such as the right to bodily integrity, the right to equality or the right not to be subjected to slavery, servitude or forced labour. (Original emphasis.)

The fact that a litigant's Sect. 10 right to human dignity is infringed (as might be the case for unlawful occupiers in an eviction dispute when a court grants an eviction order and there is no alternative accommodation available to them) does therefore not automatically mean that the dispute should be decided in terms of this fundamental right. If it is possible to dispense with the case under a "more specific [fundamental] right", the case should be decided in terms of that right instead of the more general right of human dignity (see *Jaftha v Schoeman* 2005 (2) SA 140 (CC) par 21; *Government of the Republic of South Africa v Grootboom* 2001 (1) SA 46 (CC) par 83; *Nokotyana v Ekurhuleni Metropolitan Municipality* 2010 (4) BCLR 312 (CC) par 50). There are two reasons for this approach: (i) all fundamental rights derive from the general right of human dignity, and (ii) the above approach of Justice O'Regan (like the two subsidiarity principles) finds support in the *eiusdem-generis* principle, which entails that when there is a choice between a specific law and general law, litigants must frame their arguments in terms of the specific law and may not rely on the general law to find a cause of action (Van der Walt 2012, p. 36; Currie and De Waal 2013, p. 253; Marais 2018, pp. 187–188). The first subsidiarity principle thus explains why courts may not adjudicate eviction disputes in terms of human dignity as a fundamental right. Yet, this prohibition does not prevent courts from invoking human dignity and ubuntu as constitutional values when interpreting and applying the applicable source at hand, which is PIE in the eviction context.

14.4.2 A Stronger Emphasis on Human Dignity and Ubuntu in Eviction Disputes

As mentioned before, in *PE Municipality* and *Blue Moonlight* the Constitutional Court relied on the constitutional values of human dignity and ubuntu to interpret the provisions of PIE and to give content to the justice and equity enquiry courts must engage in when deciding whether to grant an eviction order (see *PE Municipality* at par 33–38; *Blue Moonlight* par 38). Justice Sachs found that ubuntu obliges courts to infuse the elements of compassion and shared concern into the law when deciding whether it is just and equitable to grant an eviction order (see *PE Municipality* at par 37). The fact that the Constitutional Court refused to grant the eviction order reveals the centrality human dignity and ubuntu played in reaching this decision, even though Justice Sachs did not explain the full implications of these values in his decision. Had the eviction order been granted, the occupiers would have had to move to an area unsuited to their needs, which would have undermined their dignity (in the form of requiring them to leave their homes in what seemed to be a relatively safe area near their job opportunities and children's schools to settle in a crime-ridden area far from these amenities). Simultaneously, it would have frustrated ubuntu by undermining the self-fulfillment of the occupiers (as members of the greater South African community of which the owners form part), while the self-fulfillment of the landowners would seemingly not have been promoted, as they did not wish to make any use of the land except for evicting the occupiers. The court's application of PIE, which required the owners to accommodate the occupiers on their land—free of charge—until the state could provide them with suitable alternative accommodation, resonates strongly with the obligation individuals have towards the community in terms of ubuntu. Ubuntu requires owners (as individuals) to express care, compassion and tolerance towards members of their community. Treating these members (i.e., the unlawful occupiers) in an inhumane way (namely evicting them and requiring them to live in an area unsuited to their needs, while the landowners do not intend to use the land) is contrary to ubuntu.

Although Justice Sachs relied on ubuntu in reaching the outcome in *PE Municipality*, he did not explicitly ground his decision on the obligation owners have towards unlawful occupiers in terms of ubuntu. This obligation takes the form of requiring owners (as individuals) to promote the well-being of unlawful occupiers (as the community) by allowing them to remain on land free of charge for a limited period (i.e., sharing the land with them). Explaining the implications of *PE Municipality* in this manner, which the court did not do, provides a basis for the obligation the court placed on the owners, given that this obligation constitutes a significant departure from the position in pre-constitutional property law. The significance of the departure lies in the fact that owners are no longer able to claim exclusive possession of their property as a mere "natural" consequence of ownership. The fact that they may be required to accommodate the unlawful occupiers temporarily (based solely on the hardship the eviction might have on the occupiers) without receiving payment from either them or the state entails a "significant qualification of and perhaps even a challenge to the rights paradigm" (Van der Walt 2009, p. 123). Owners usually only grant permission to non-owners to stay on their land against some form of payment, like rent. It is questionable whether the court would have been able to recognize this obligation in terms of the Western view of human dignity, which lacks the particular emphasis ubuntu places on the well-being of both the individual and the community. In this sense, ubuntu aids courts in deciding whether (and, if so, how) to grant an eviction order in future eviction cases and, importantly, also reveals the limits of the obligation resting on owners.

The Constitutional Court in *Blue Moonlight*, with reference to its earlier decision in *PE Municipality*, reiterated the importance of human dignity, as understood in terms of ubuntu, when courts decide whether it is just and equitable to grant an eviction order. Yet, the court there again applied PIE without expanding in detail on how human dignity and ubuntu inform this Act. One of the main differences between *PE Municipality* and *Blue Moonlight* is that, in the latter case, the court granted the eviction order but suspended its coming into operation for 8 months to enable the local authority to provide the unlawful occupiers with alternative accommodation near the building. The private landowner was required to house the occupiers on its land free of charge for this period. Like in *PE Municipality*, the fact that no compensation was payable to the private landowner (either by the unlawful occupiers or state) may be explained in terms of the obligation ubuntu places on owners. Interestingly, this obligation also finds support in another element of ubuntu, namely restorative justice (Ackermann 2012, p. 113; Metz 2011, p. 547). Restorative justice here entails preventing past injustices, such as evicting people without any regard for their well-being, from recurring by achieving harmonious resolutions to disputes (Bennett 2018, p. 79).

The Constitutional Court has made it clear that an owner cannot be expected to provide free accommodation to unlawful occupiers indefinitely, though (see *Blue Moonlight Properties* at par 40 and 97). Stretching the obligation to such an extent would infringe an owner's right against arbitrary deprivation of property under Sect. 25(1) (see *Blue Moonlight Properties* at 30–41; *Living Africa One (Pty) Ltd Ekurhuleni Metropolitan Municipality* (A5019/2022) [2023] ZAGPJHC (11 August 2023) unreported judgment ("*Living Africa One*")), which encapsulates her right to undisturbed possession of her property. At the same time, it would amount to the state unjustifiably shifting its constitutional responsibility to provide adequate housing to those in need (in terms of Sect. 26(1) of the Constitution) onto private owners (see *President of the Republic of South Africa v Modderklip Boerdery (Pty) Ltd* 2005 (5) SA 3 (CC) par 45). A further consideration, one which is yet to receive recognition from the Constitutional Court, is ubuntu. As seen earlier, ubuntu requires that the self-fulfillment of an individual and the community be promoted simultaneously; the self-fulfillment of one may not be ranked over the other. By expecting an owner to house unlawful occupiers free for indefinite (and perhaps even overly long) periods, the owner's obligation would become too heavy and may end up undermining her dignity at the expense of promoting the dignity of the occupiers. This assessment finds support in the purpose of property in constitutional law.

Property is protected in constitutional law because it is a means to an end, namely to "secure for its holder a sphere of liberty in the economic field in which he or she can lead a self-governing life" (see *Shoprite Checkers (Pty) Ltd v MEC for Economic Development, Eastern Cape* 2015 (6) SA 125 (CC) par 54, quoting from the English translation of BVerfGE 24, 367 (1968) (the *Deichordnung* case)). Property promotes individual self-fulfillment and thus enables persons to lead dignified lives (see *Shoprite Checkers* par 50 and compare Michelman and Marais 2018, pp. 127–129). Justice Froneman explains the link between property and dignity as follows: "[property's] function of personal self-fulfillment . . . is not primarily to advance economic wealth maximization or the satisfaction of individual preferences, but *to secure living a life of dignity in recognition of the dignity of others.*" (see *Shoprite Checkers* par 50 (my emphasis)).

If an owner is unable to evict unlawful occupiers for an indefinite period, her ability to lead a self-fulfilling life may be undermined. The presence of unlawful occupiers on land effectively sterilizes the use of that part of the owner's land. As such, it could be financially ruinous to an owner (especially one who is not wealthy) if she depends on the property to earn a living and is now expected to house the occupiers while receiving payment from neither them nor the state. Stated in terms of dignity and ubuntu, the self-fulfillment (i.e., dignity) of the owner in such a case is frustrated at the expense of promoting the dignity of the occupier(s).

Whether an owner's self-fulfillment or dignity in the holding of property will be frustrated and, if so, to what extent, depends on the type of property at hand. Radin argues that people require control of resources (i.e., property) to achieve proper self-development or to promote their human flourishing (see Radin 1982, pp. 957, 968–969; Radin 1993, pp. 1, 5–6 and compare Alexander 2009, p. 749). In her view, owners enjoy strong protection against property limitations (an example is when they are unable to evict unlawful occupiers for their land immediately) when their property is located close to the personal sphere of the owner (like a home), while lesser protection is afforded to property located further away from this sphere (i.e. land used for commercial purposes, and especially land held for purely speculative purposes or not even being used at all) (Radin 1982, p. 959; Van der Walt 2011, p. 103; German and South African constitutional law follows an approach comparable to Radin's theory: see *Shoprite Checkers* par 50; Michelman and Marais 2018, pp. 134–135 and the sources they cite). She describes the former type of property as personal (or constitutive) property, while the latter is known as a fungible property (Radin 1982, p. 960; Radin 1993, p. 2).

Interferences with personal property entail more severe limitations of an owner's human dignity, as it will amount to a greater subversion of an owner's self-fulfillment. The opposite holds for infringements of fungible property, where limitations of such property would have a lesser impact on her dignity, as would be the case in instances like *PE Municipality* and *Blue Moonlight*. For instance, when unlawful occupiers occupy an owner's family home, which is personal property, this would greatly undermine such owner's self-development or dignity. Here a court would probably either grant an eviction order relatively easily, perhaps even without there being alternative accommodation available to the occupiers, or assist the owner through ordering the state to compensate her (see the next paragraph below). When dealing with vacant land (as in *PE Municipality*, for instance) or land which an owner (in the form of a juristic person) still intends to use for commercial purposes (as in *Blue Moonlight*), the property is fungible in nature. This means the subversion of the owner's self-development would not be as severe when compared to how evicting unlawful occupiers without there being alternative accommodation for them would undermine their self-fulfillment. Thus, applying dignity and ubuntu more pertinently to an eviction dispute would look as follows: reconciling the human dignity of owners of fungible property (who are temporarily prevented from fully using their property) with that of unlawful occupiers (in losing their homes) reveals that the occupiers' dignity will probably be undermined more drastically if a court grants an eviction order without there being alternative accommodation available to the occupiers. The added value of placing stronger emphasis on human dignity and ubuntu in this context is that these values (especially given the community-centeredness ubuntu) provide a cogent normative foundation for the obligation owners of fungible property have towards unlawful occupiers.

Yet, in instances where owners are required to accommodate unlawful occupiers for unreasonably long periods, the obligation becomes too heavy to justify. Here the owners' dignity is sacrificed to protect that of the occupiers. In these cases, the state must restore the equilibrium between the dignity of the owner and that of the occupiers by compensating the owner for her sacrifice. In *President of the Republic of South Africa v Modderklip Boerdery (Pty) Ltd* 2005 (5) SA 3 (CC), for instance, a landowner was granted an eviction order which—it later turned out—was impossible to enforce. The impossibility of enforcing the eviction order was due to the huge number of unlawful occupiers on the land (around 40,000 at one point), the unaffordability of evicting them (the cost of hiring a private eviction company to evict the occupiers was higher than the value of the land they were occupying), the occupiers threatening the police who wanted to evict them with violence, as well as the fact that they had nowhere else to go. Here the Constitutional Court ordered the state to pay so-called "constitutional damages" to the owner for the infringement of his constitutional rights. Even though the case was decided under the right to access to courts (Sect. 34 of the Constitution), and not under sections 26(3) and 25(1) of the Constitution (or with reference to human dignity or ubuntu), the outcome here—as with *PE Municipality* and *Blue Moonlight*—may be explained in terms of ubuntu. Interestingly, the Johannesburg High Court in *Living Africa One* recently awarded constitutional damages to a landowner where the municipality failed, for an unreasonably long period, to provide temporary alternative accommodation to unlawful occupiers occupying the owner's land. The landowner obtained an eviction order in 2014, provided that the municipality provide temporary alternative accommodation to the unlawful occupiers. It failed to provide such accommodation for about 8 years. The court ruled that this long delay infringed the landowner's rights under sections 25(1) and 34 and ordered the municipality to pay constitutional damages to the landowner for the continued unlawful occupation of its land.

These judgments underscore the fact that the obligation an owner has towards unlawful occupiers in terms of ubuntu, even when her dignity is attenuated due to the property being fungible (the land which the occupiers lived on in *Modderklip* seems to have been an unused part of the owner's farm, while in *Living Africa One* the owner wanted to develop the land on which the occupiers lived), is limited. The decisions imply that the dignity of both the owner (as an individual) and that of the unlawful occupiers (as the community) must be promoted optimally and simultaneously. This type of promotion links up with how the Constitutional Court conceptualizes how the reconciling process between sections 26(3) and 25(1) of the Constitution should take place in terms of PIE. Reconciling the competing rights at hand in terms of ubuntu provides a clearer picture of why the state may be expected to pay constitutional damages to owners in certain instances. Constitutional damages, which are sourced in Sect. 38 of the Constitution, are damages courts may award to persons whose constitutional rights are infringed and where no other effective remedy exists to vindicate those rights (*Modderfontein Squatters, Greater Benoni City Council v Modderklip Boerdery (Pty) Ltd* 2004 (6) SA 40 (SCA) par 43; *Fose v Minister of Safety and Security* 1997 (3) SA 786 (CC) par 69). Thus, a solution in the eviction context is to pay constitutional damages to an owner who is unable to evict occupiers, like in *Modderklip* and *Living Africa One*. Awarding these damages to the owner restores the equilibrium between the dignity of the owner and occupiers, as ubuntu requires. Yet, constitutional damages will only be awarded in exceptional circumstances. For instance, in *Blue Moonlight* the Constitutional Court refused to award such damages to the owner, even though the occupiers have been on the land for 5 years from 2006 (when the owner instituted eviction proceedings) to 2011 (when the Court handed down its decision). The court's reason for refusing to award compensation was because the owner knew of the presence of the occupiers in the building and proceeded to purchase it nonetheless. Yet, *Living Africa One* shows that a court may award constitutional damages to a landowner if the municipality delays in providing alternative accommodation for an unreasonably long period.

Even though *Modderklip* dealt with the unique situation where the owner was unable to enforce the eviction order, ubuntu probably requires that something like constitutional damages should also be available to owners who have to endure occupiers on their land for unreasonably long periods while the state looks for alternative accommodation (compare Kruger 2014; Pienaar and Kotzé 2018; Fick 2021). This is then indeed what recently happened in *Living Africa One*., although the court there did not invoke ubuntu. Though it is easier to make this argument with regard to personal property, the same probably holds—albeit to a lesser extent—when property is fungible in nature (like in *PE Municipality*, *Blue Moonlight*, and, especially, *Living Africa One*). Whether owners affected by long periods of unlawful occupation may claim constitutional damages is currently one of the most pressing matters in South African eviction law (Kruger 2014; Pienaar and Kotzé 2018). In this regard the *Living Africa One* decision is a significant development, the implications of which will surely draw attention from scholars and other courts. Having to accommodate the occupiers for such periods could sterilize an owner's investment and thus be financially ruinous, as mentioned earlier (see, for example, *Occupiers, Berea v De Wet NO* 2017 (5) SA 346 (CC) par 80). Such an eventuality would undermine an owner's dignity, while upholding the dignity of occupiers. The extreme homelessness in South Africa, where the majority of the population still does not have access to adequate housing, is a huge societal problem (given the country's apartheid history), and as such, individual owners cannot be expected to shoulder the burden of providing long-term free accommodation to unlawful occupiers without any assistance from the state. This view finds support in the ruling that the state cannot shift its responsibility to provide housing to private individuals (see *Modderklip* at par 45). Viewed through the lens of ubuntu, requiring owners of fungible property to accommodate unlawful occupiers without cost on a temporary basis is justifiable. Yet, what is to be done when the period of accommodation becomes unreasonably long? A solution is to restore the equilibrium between the dignity of the owner and that of the occupiers by spreading the cost of accommodating them amongst all tax-paying owners, namely by compensating the affected owner (through awarding constitutional damages to her) from the state fiscus, which the court adopted in *Living Africa One*. Such an approach promotes the self-fulfillment of both owners and unlawful occupiers optimally, as owners may then use the compensation to recuperate any losses they suffered from having to accommodate the occupiers.

14.5 Conclusion

Despite the fact that the human dignity of unlawful occupiers of land was irrelevant when owners wanted to evict them during apartheid, their dignity now plays a key role in the discretion courts exercise when deciding whether to grant an eviction order. The dignity of these occupiers finds expression in the constitutional right that no one may be evicted from their home without an order of court, which may only be granted after considering all relevant circumstances. This right, which recognizes the importance of the home interest to the dignity of all persons, must be reconciled with a landowner's right to have exclusive possession of her property, which is sourced in the fundamental right against arbitrary deprivation of property. Being unable to evict unlawful occupiers forthwith results in a tension between these rights. PIE, which sets out the circumstances courts must consider when deciding whether it is just and equitable to grant an eviction order, gives effect to both these competing fundamental rights, which—in turn—are specialized manifestations of the right to human dignity. Although human dignity (as a fundamental right) does not apply directly to eviction cases, considering how PIE reconciles the tension in terms of the constitutional values of human dignity and ubuntu more pertinently provides two advantages.

First, human dignity and ubuntu enrich the process whereby courts reconcile the tension by expanding the range of factors courts may consider when adjudicating eviction disputes. These factors pertain to the dignity of both owners and unlawful occupiers and inform the justice and equity investigation courts must engage in when deciding whether to grant an eviction order. Human dignity and ubuntu provide additional support for the outcomes in *PE Municipality* and *Blue Moonlight* and offer helpful guideposts for courts when they decide future eviction disputes. Second, ubuntu provides a strong normative basis for the obligation the Constitutional Court has placed on owners when eviction is not ordered forthwith. The community-oriented element of ubuntu explains why the law may require owners to accommodate unlawful occupiers on their land temporarily without cost while the state searches for alternative accommodation. It is questionable whether courts would have been able to create this obligation solely in terms of the Western understanding of human dignity, which places more emphasis on the individual. Nonetheless, ubuntu also reveals the limits of the obligation: owners cannot be expected to house occupiers for unreasonably long periods without payment, as their own dignity would then be undermined at the expense of promoting the dignity of the occupiers. One way to restore the equilibrium between the dignity of owners and that of the occupiers is for the state to pay so-called "constitutional damages" to owners, which allows them to recuperate losses suffered due to the continued unlawful occupation of their land. It is significant that the Johannesburg High Court recently adopted this approach in *Living Africa One*.

Constitutional damages should take the form of what is known in German law as "equalization payments" (Van der Walt 2011, pp. 270–282; Bezuidenhout 2015). These payments are made to owners where property limitations (in terms of the state's police power to regulate the use and enjoyment of property in the public interest) have disproportionate impacts on one or a small group of owners (Van der Walt 2011, pp. 270–282; Bezuidenhout 2015). Such payments are normally sourced in legislation and are meant to prevent the property limitation (caused in the eviction context by either failing to evict the occupiers for reasons beyond the owner's control, like in *Modderklip*, or requiring an owner to accommodate unlawful occupiers on her land for an unreasonably long period, like in *Living Africa One*) from infringing Sect. 25(1) of the Constitution and therefore being unconstitutional (Van der Walt 2011, pp. 270–282; Bezuidenhout 2015). PIE will probably have to be amended to permit courts to make such awards, as the Act currently does not provide for payment of this form of compensation. When such payments will be due, and how they are to be calculated, are matters that require further attention. However, after *Living Africa One* it remains to be seen if such an amended will take place.

More work is needed on the role human dignity and (especially) ubuntu play in other parts of private law (see, for instance, Nkosi 2018 for a discussion of the role of ubuntu in the law of contract). South African mortgage law, which is also part of property law, is an area of law where such an investigation may yield interesting results. In terms of the mortgage law regime that applied up to 2005, mortgagees (or creditors) had an almost unqualified right to sell mortgaged or hypothecated homes in situations where mortgagors (or debtors) were unable to repay their loans (see, for instance, Brits 2016, pp. 68–105). The impact the sale in execution of the home would have on the livelihood of the mortgagor was completely irrelevant. In light of Constitutional Court decisions—where the court also relied on Sect. 26(3) of the Constitution—and certain legislative interventions, courts may now only permit a mortgaged home to be sold in execution if there are no other reasonable ways for the mortgagee to obtain repayment of the loan (see Brits 2016, pp. 68–105 and the sources he cites). (An example of such an alternative is for the mortgagor to repay the loan at reduced monthly instalments over a longer period.) If viable alternatives exist, the mortgagor's home may not be sold in execution. The obligation that now rests on mortgagees, namely that they must accept these alternatives and are no longer entitled to have the mortgaged home sold in execution as a mere "natural" consequence of their mortgage right (which is a limited real right), seems to share features with the obligation in eviction law, as sourced in ubuntu.

Although ubuntu is unique to sub-Saharan Africa, this notion may have wider application. This is due to its connection with human dignity, which—in turn—is central in most constitutional democracies. Ubuntu entails a stronger emphasis on the communal element in society, one which is not as prevalent in the Western understanding of dignity. Incorporating this communal focus into the understanding of dignity elsewhere has the potential to ensure more creative (and fair) outcomes in disputes between those who have property and those who do not. Poverty, homelessness, and displacement are global problems which need to be resolved in a human-rights oriented way. Ubuntu could provide valuable insights into what the law may expect from landowners and those without property in realizing a more just and egalitarian world.

Acknowledgement I am indebted to Prof Gustav Muller (University of Pretoria) for reading and commenting on an earlier draft of this chapter. A special word of thanks goes to Prof Letlhokwa Mpedi (University of Johannesburg) and Prof Muna Ndulo (Cornell Law School), and his students, for inspiring me to investigate the present topic. I am grateful for the feedback from the anonymous peer reviewers, whose generous comments greatly helped improve the chapter. Thanks also go to Mr. Tola Olowolafe and Ms. Joyce Phiri for providing technical and research assistance. Finally, I thank the National Research Foundation for financial support that made research for this chapter possible. Remaining errors are mine.

References

Ackermann L (2012) Human dignity: lodestar for equality in South Africa. Juta, Cape Town

Alexander GS (2009) The social-obligation norm in American property law. Cornell Law Rev 94: 745–820

Barkhuizen v Napier 2007 (5) SA 232 (CC)

Bennett WT (2018) Ubuntu: an African jurisprudence. Juta, Cape Town

Bezuidenhout K (2015) Compensation for excessive but otherwise lawful regulatory state action. Unpublished LLD thesis, Stellenbosch University

Birks P (1985) The Roman law concept of dominium and the idea of absolute ownership. Acta Jur:1–37

Brits R (2016) Real security law. Juta, Cape Town
Cornell D (2010) Is there a difference that makes a difference between ubuntu and dignity? South Afr Public Law 25:382–399
Currie I, De Waal J (2013) Human dignity. In: Currie I, de Waal J (eds) The bill of rights handbook. Juta, Cape Town, pp 250–257
Dawood v Minister of Home Affairs 2000 (3) SA 936 (CC)
Dladla v City of Johannesburg 2018 (2) SA 327 (CC)
Dyal-Chand R (2013) Sharing the cathedral. Conn Law Rev 46:647–723
Fick S (2021) Compensating landowners? The state's (limited) duty toward landowners indelayed eviction matters. Potchefstroom Electron Law J 24:1–35
Fineman MA (2017) Vulnerability and inevitable inequality. Oslo Law Rev 4:133–149
Fox L (2007) Conceptualising home: theories, law and policies. Hart Publishing, Portland
Fox O'Mahony L, Roark LM (2022) Squatting and the state - resilient property in an age of crisis. Cambridge University Press, Cambridge
Henderson AJH (1998) Putting section 1 to work: some preliminary thoughts on the first of the founding provisions of the new Constitution. South Afr Law J 115:215–222
Hohfeld WN (1917) Some fundamental legal conceptions as applied in judicial reasoning. Yale Law J 26:710–770
Kamga SD (2018) Cultural values as a source of law: Emerging trends of ubuntu jurisprudence in South Africa. Afr Hum Rights Law J 2:625–649
Kruger M (2014) Arbitrary deprivation of property: an argument for the payment of compensation by the state in certain cases of unlawful occupation. South Afr Law J 131:328–364
Liebenberg S (2005) The value of human dignity in interpreting socio-economic rights. South Afr J Hum Rights 21:1–31
Liebenberg S (2010) Socio-economic rights – adjudication under a transformative Constitution. Juta, Cape Town
Liebenberg S, Goldblatt B (2007) The interrelationship between equality and socio-economic rights under South Africa's transformative Constitution. South Afr J Hum Rights 23:335–361
Living Africa One (Pty) Ltd Ekurhuleni Metropolitan Municipality (A5019/2022) [2023] ZAGPJHC (11 August 2023) unreported judgment
Marais EJ (2018) Narrowing the meaning of 'deprivation' under the property clause? A critical analysis of the implications of the constitutional court's Diamond Producers judgment for constitutional property protection. South Afr J Hum Rights 34:167–190
Marais EJ, Muller G (2018) The right of an ESTA occupier to make improvements without an owner's permission after Daniels: Quo vadis statutory interpretation and development of the common law? South Afr Law J 135:766–798
Metz T (2011) Ubuntu as a moral theory and human rights in South Africa. Afr Hum Rights Law J 11:532–559
Michelman FI, Marais EJ (2018) A constitutional vision for property: Shoprite Checkers and beyond. In: Muller G, Brits R, Slade B, van Wyk J (eds) Transformative property law – festschrift in honour of AJ van der Walt. Juta, Cape Town, pp 121–146
Modderfontein Squatters, Greater Benoni City Council v Modderklip Boerdery (Pty) Ltd 2004 (6) SA 40 (SCA)
Mokgoro YM (1998) Ubuntu and the law in South Africa. Buffalo Hum Rights Law Rev 4:15–23
Mokgoro YM, Woolman S (2010) Where dignity ends and ubuntu begins: an amplification of, as well as an identification of a tension in, Drucilla Cornell's thoughts. South Afr Public Law 25: 400–407
Muller G (2011) The impact of section 26 of the Constitution on the eviction of squatters in South African law. Unpublished LLD thesis, Stellenbosch University
Muller G (2013) The legal-historical context of forced evictions in South Africa. Fundamina 19: 367–396
Muller G, Liebenberg S (2013) Developing the law of joinder in the context of evictions of people from their homes. South Afr J Hum Rights 29:554–570

Muller G, Marais EJ (2020) Reconsidering counter-spoliation as a common-law remedy in the eviction context in view of the single-system-of-law principle. Tydskrif vir die Suid-Afrikaanse Reg 1:103–124
Nedelsky J (1993) Reconceiving rights as relationships. Rev Const Stud 1:1–26
Nkosi S (2018) Ubuntu and South African law: its juridical transformative impact. South Afr Public Law 33:1–20
Nokotyana v Ekurhuleni Metropolitan Municipality 2010 (4) BCLR 312 (CC)
Pharmaceutical Manufacturers Association of SA: In Re Ex Parte President of the Republic of South Africa 2000 (2) SA 674 (CC)
Pienaar JM (2014) Land reform. Juta, Cape Town
Pienaar JM, Kotzé T (2018) Application of single system of law and subsidiarity: Constitutional damages as effective relief within the eviction paradigm. In: Muller G, Brits R, Slade B, van Wyk J (eds) Transformative property law – festschrift in honour of AJ van der Walt. Juta, Cape Town, pp 341–372
Radin MJ (1982) Property and personhood. Stanford Law Rev 34:957–1015
Radin MJ (1993) Reinterpreting property. University of Chicago Press, Chicago
Sonnekus JC, Neels L (1994) Sakereg vonnisbundel. Butterworths, Durban
Van der Sijde E (2012) Reconsidering the relationship between property and regulation: a systemic constitutional approach. Unpublished LLD thesis, Stellenbosch University
Van der Sijde E (2022) Property regulation – an integrated approach under the Constitution. Juta, Cape Town
Van der Walt AJ (2009) Property in the margins. Hart Publishing, Portland
Van der Walt AJ (2011) Constitutional property law. Juta, Cape Town
Van der Walt AJ (2012) Property and constitution. Pretoria University Law Press, Pretoria
Van der Walt AJ (2014) The modest systemic status of property rights. J Law Prop Soc 1:15–106
Van der Walt AJ (2016) Sharing servitudes. Eur Prop Law J 4:162–222
Van der Walt AJ, Dhliwayo P (2017) The notion of absolute and exclusive ownership: a doctrinal analysis. South Afr Law J 134:34–52
Woolman S (2005) Dignity. In: Woolman S, Bishop M, Brickhill J (eds) Constitutional law of South Africa, Chapter 36. Juta, Cape Town

Chapter 15
Dignity, Freedom of Expression and the Battle over Hate Speech: A Case Study in Post-Apartheid South Africa

Roxan Venter

Abstract The purpose of this chapter is to explore dignity (both as a right and as a value) and the right to freedom of expression in order to show the interdependence of these concepts in the South African context. Indicating the role that the value of human dignity plays regarding the transformation of the South African constitutional system is the first step in crossing the threshold in illustrating the imbrication of dignity and freedom of expression. Then the chapter attempts to show the interrelatedness of the right to freedom of expression and democracy, while also showing how these concepts give effect to the value of human dignity referencing various examples in the South African system. Next, the chapter explores whether recently proposed South African hate speech legislation unjustifiably infringes on the right to freedom of expression in an effort to protect the right (and the value) of human dignity. The chapter raises the, perhaps unpopular, opinion that hate speech in South Africa is already regulated by existing legislation (PEPUDA) and the common law, and that the creation of a new statutory crime of hate speech is therefore unnecessary. Finally, the chapter highlights that the battle over hate speech can only be resolved if the value of human dignity takes center stage in the debate. The chapter attempts to develop a new perspective that advocates for a disambiguity and centralization of human dignity and *ubuntu*, pushing past the threshold established by the South African legal system during apartheid, in order to develop new paradigms which expand and underscore human dignity.

15.1 Introduction

The importance of human dignity, either as a right or as a value, within the South African democratic system cannot be overstated. Ever since the adoption of the Constitution of the Republic of South Africa Act 200 of 1993 (the Interim Constitution) and later the current Constitution of the Republic of South Africa of

R. Venter (✉)
University of Johannesburg, Johannesburg, South Africa
e-mail: rventer@uj.ac.za

S. N. Arel et al. (eds.), *Probing Human Dignity*,
https://doi.org/10.1007/978-3-031-42437-3_15

1996 (hereafter the Constitution), the value of human dignity (as well as the other constitutional values guaranteed in Sect. 1 of the Constitution, which include the values of freedom, equality, non-racialism, non-sexism and the rule of law) has played an integral role in shaping and changing South African society and legal order. The value of human dignity however is at the heart of this fundamental change. In the context of the Interim Constitution, Etienne Mureinik compares the Constitution with a bridge which should ensure South Africa's transition from a "culture of authority" to a "culture of justification" (Mureinik 1994, p. 32; also see the Post-amble of the Interim Constitution). The value of human dignity was the main driving force behind the ambition and purpose of the 1996 Constitution, which may be seen as *transformative constitutionalism*. Pierre De Vos and Warren Freedman point out that the South African Constitution needs to be viewed as a document "written in response to the social, economic and political history of South Africa" and, furthermore, that the South African Constitution is a document "committed to social, political, legal and economic transformation" (De Vos and Freedman 2014, p. 27). Transformative constitutionalism therefore means that a particular system "attempts to transform its society from one deeply divided by the legacy of a racist and unequal past into one based on democracy, social justice, equality, dignity and freedom" (De Vos and Freedman 2014, p. 27). In order for South African society and legal order to become transformed, however, South African society had to become an open and transparent one where thoughts and opinions could be shared openly and where the activities of government were open to public scrutiny, debate, and criticism. An open and transparent society, as envisaged by the 1996 Constitution, is closely related to the protection of the right to freedom of expression, because there can be no transparency where free expression is stifled.

The freedom to share one's thoughts and opinions with others is closely related to what it means to be human, while the freedom to take part in political activities of government and to have one's voice heard on political and other matters are also connected to the recognition of one's equal worth as a person and a citizen of a particular country. In both instances, human dignity supports the political and non-political aspects of the entrenched right to freedom of expression because these types of expression relate to inherently human ways of expressing one's self.

The chapter attempts to develop a new perspective that advocates for a disambiguity and centralization of human dignity and *ubuntu*, pushing past the threshold established by the South African legal system during the apartheid regime, in order to develop new paradigms which expand and underscore human dignity. The purpose of this chapter is therefore to explore the interrelatedness of the value of human dignity and the right to freedom of expression and democracy in order to show their interdependence by using the South African democracy as a case in point. This is done by indicating what role the value of human dignity plays with regard to the right to freedom of expression. Then it is shown how the right to freedom of expression contributes to democracy and gives effect to the value of human dignity with reference to various examples within the South African system. Next, the chapter explores whether recently proposed South African hate speech legislation unjustifiably infringes the right to freedom of expression in an effort to promote the value human dignity. The chapter also addresses the, perhaps unpopular, opinion that hate speech in South Africa is already regulated by existing legislation (PEPUDA) and the common law, and that the creation of a new statutory crime of hate speech is therefore unnecessary. Finally, the chapter argues that the criminalization of hate speech is against the value of human dignity and the concept of *ubuntu*, as well as the spirit of reconciliation on which the South African constitutional order is founded. The chapter concludes that the approach of criminalization of hate speech should therefore not be followed. Ultimately, the chapter argues for an interpretive paradigm shift in legal thinking on human dignity, freedom of expression and democracy in order for the South African legal system to cross its conceptual threshold into new territory and to really embrace the constitutional values. Crossing this "dignity threshold" would move the South African legal system from "an ethic of apartheid to an ethic of *ubuntu*."

15.2 Dignity as a Constitutional Right and Value and the Right to Freedom of Expression and Democracy

In terms of the South African Constitution human dignity is both seen as a foundational value (s 1 of the Constitution) and a substantive right (s 10 of the Constitution). Sect. 1 of the Constitution expressly provides that the democratic state is founded on certain values—including human dignity, freedom, equality, non-racialism, non-sexism, and the rule of law. The inclusion of human dignity as a value in the South African Constitution has various purposes. As a value, human dignity is used when interpreting and giving effect to other constitutionally guaranteed rights and when interpreting and developing the common and customary law, while also playing a role in the limitation of rights in terms of the general limitation clause which may be found in Sect. 36 of the Constitution. Section 39 (1) of the Constitution expressly provides for the use of the value of human dignity in the interpretation of rights by stating that a court "must promote the values that underlie an open and democratic society based on human dignity, equality and freedom" when interpreting the Bill of Rights. Section 39(2) provides that when interpreting any legislation, or when developing the common or customary law, "the spirit, purport and objects of the Bill of Rights" must be promoted. In turn, section 36, also known as the general limitation clause, provides that rights may only be limited to the extent that it is "reasonable and justifiable in an open and democratic society based on human dignity, equality and freedom." Human dignity as a value is therefore used quite frequently in South African human rights litigation.

Apart from being a foundational value, human dignity is also an enforceable right in terms of the South African Bill of Rights. Infringements of human dignity as a right, however, tend to overlap quite frequently with the limitation of other protected rights, and because of the principle of subsidiarity, constitutional claims need to be brought in terms of a more specific right (if such right is guaranteed in the Bill of Rights) rather than a more general right. For instance, if a law were to limit a person's right to freedom of expression by prohibiting political criticism, the limitation would limit both the right to freedom of expression and the right to human dignity. The principle of subsidiarity however means that the individual in this example should base his claim for infringement on the right to freedom of expression, rather than the right to human dignity, because the law specifically targeted a *specific right*, in other words the right to freedom of expression. In a constitutional matter, therefore, a claimant would only directly rely on human dignity as a substantive right when there are no other expressly guaranteed rights involved on which to base a claim (see in general De Vos and Freedman 2014, pp. 458–461). The *value* of human dignity however must always be promoted when interpreting *any right* in the Bill of Rights. Therefore, human dignity must be considered in the context of freedom of expression. When the exercise of free expression limits another person's right to human dignity, the infringement will quite possibly also limit the infringed party's right to equality, or even other constitutionally protected rights. Although the infringed party would not be able to rely directly on dignity as a right (due to the principle of subsidiarity as explained above) a court would nevertheless be able to consider dignity as a *value* when determining whether hate speech occurred or whether (and to what extent) the right to freedom of expression may be limited. This discussion therefore focusses on the concept of human dignity as a *value* rather than a *right*.

Some scholars do not agree with the concept of dignity as a constitutional value—referring to it as a vague concept whose application is too wide to be usefully applied (see in general Wermiel 1998). The South African Constitution, however, expressly refers to the value of human dignity and this value must therefore be interpreted, and applied (Chaskalson 2011, p. 1382). The 1996 Constitution recognizes everyone's "*inherent* dignity," which asserts that respect for individual human dignity flows from "life itself, and is not a privilege granted by the state" (Chaskalson 2000, p. 196). The constitutional affirmation of inherent human dignity confirms South Africa's commitment to constitutionalism in the post-apartheid era, while also aligning the South African legal system with various international instruments such as the African Charter on Human and Peoples Rights and the Charter of the United Nations (Chaskalson 2000, pp. 196–197). Arthur Chaskalson points out that respect for human dignity, as well as the other founding values (including freedom, equality, non-racialism, non-sexism, supremacy of the constitution, and the rule of law), is essential in accommodating conflicting interests in society (Chaskalson 2000, p. 201). According to Chaskalson, this is so because dignity informs the "content of all rights and plays a role in the balancing process" so that different rights and values can be brought in harmony (Chaskalson 2000, p. 204). Chaskalson concludes that if South Africa wants to give full force to the transformative goal of the Constitution, the foundational values that underlie it must be interpreted consistently with this goal (Chaskalson 2000, pp. 204–205).

Traditional liberal legal thinking considers rights from a distinctly abstract and individualistic perspective focusing on "on rights-bearing human beings devoid of social relationships and outside of contextual reality" (Albertyn and Goldblatt 1998, p. 251). Cathi Albertyn and Beth Goldblatt point out, however, that critical theorists reject this individualistic approach to human rights, supporting the view that individuals are "rooted in their social context" (Albertyn and Goldblatt 1998, p. 251). This social context is especially noticeable where categories of persons have experienced gross human rights violations based, for instance, on a group attribute such as race—highlighting the *communal* elements of human dignity. Consequently, human dignity is not only a value in the context of *individual* human rights protection, but human dignity can also address years of systematic *communal* discrimination. Due to the communal character of human dignity, Susie Cowen points out that, because humans are social beings, "it makes little sense to speak of the worth of human beings in isolation" (Cowen 2001, p. 50). The communal nature of human dignity is also visible in indigenous African legal thinking. In the South African context, the value of human dignity is interpreted in the context of the indigenous African concept of *ubuntu* (Chaskalson 2011, p. 1387; also see Albertyn and Goldblatt 1998, p. 269). *Ubuntu* is akin to the value of human dignity but more specifically focuses on dignity as a communal concept—protecting communal rights and interests (S v. Makwanyane, see separate judgments from para 224, 263 and 308; Cowen 2001, pp. 50–51; Cornell and Van Marle 2005, p. 205; see generally Kamga 2018, pp. 627–635). Serges D Kamga argues that *ubuntu* was instrumental in the transition process from apartheid to our new democratic dispensation (Kamga 2018, p. 634). The value of human dignity, as well as the related indigenous concept of *ubuntu*, therefore plays an integral role in the interpretation and application of the South African Bill of Rights, transformative constitutionalism and propelling its legal system over the "dignity threshold" into a conceptual framework based on dignity. In order to breach the established conceptual legal thresholds, the value of human dignity and *ubuntu* need to be embraced in order to move the South African legal order from "an ethic of apartheid to an ethic of *ubuntu*."

Due to the important role that the value of human dignity, and the concept of *ubuntu*, played in South Africa's constitutional transformation from an apartheid state to a democracy, and the continued use of the value of human dignity as an interpretive mechanism, there is a definite connection between democratic government and values. Theoretically, various elements underpin the concept of "democracy" (Venter 2018a, pp. 53–64). [1] Considering the ethical and value-oriented element of democracy helps to show the connection between democracy and dignity. Some theories of democracy define democracy according to principles of "majority rule" and "popular control." Although the will of the people is an important element of democratic government, the will of the majority is by far not the only

[1]These elements of, or approaches to, democracy are as follows: the constitutional element, substantive element, procedural element, process-oriented element and the ethical and value-oriented element.

consideration. Claes G Ryn, for example, argues for an ethical and value-oriented approach to democracy:

> An ethical theory of democracy looks for more in the celebrated principle of majority rule than the idea that a numerically superior portion of a people is entitled to greater influence over public decisions than a numerically inferior one (Ryn 1978, p. 10; Venter 2018a, p. 62).

The mere fact, therefore, that a government has the support of the majority of the population does not necessarily mean that this society and its government supports and promotes desirable norms or values (Venter 2018a, p. 62). The "moral quality of the collective will of a state's citizens, and not the quantity thereof" should therefore be regarded as conclusive (Venter 2018a, p. 62; Hallowell 1954, p. 120). In order to ensure the *quality* of the collective will of a society, constitutional norms and values, which already enjoy recognition, should be promoted within the democratic system by means of interpreting existing constitutional rules in the light of these values (Venter 2018a, p. 63). Fortunately, the South African legal system is well suited to this approach, since Sect. 1 of the Constitution has expressly included a list of constitutional values underlying our new democratic order, as stated above, human dignity being among the most prominent. These constitutional values (referred to above) must be promoted, according to Sect. 39 of the Constitution, when interpreting any provision of the Bill of Rights, when interpreting any legislation, or whenever the common or customary law is developed. Furthermore, Rassie Malherbe and Michelle van Eck argue that democratic norms and values need to be instilled in procedures and mechanisms that regulate government activities and actions in order to ensure an effective democracy (Malherbe and Van Eck 2009, p. 221; Venter 2018a, p. 63). Accordingly, this entails the creation of a democratic culture among a state's citizens and government officials, where the members of society have the right and responsibility of keeping government officials accountable by means of "protests and pickets, freedom of expression and freedom of the media" (Malherbe and Van Eck 2009, p. 222; Venter 2018a, p. 63).

The right to freedom of expression and the democratic nature of government are closely linked. While democracy protects the right to freedom of expression, so too the right to freedom of expression ensures the maintenance of a democratic legal order. The well-known theoretical approaches to freedom of expression, which justify freedom of expression's importance and protection, include the search for truth theory, marketplace of ideas model, and the democracy theory (see Venter 2016, pp. 219–234; Greenawalt 1989, p. 130; Barendt 1985, pp. 8, 14; Carmi 2007, pp. 970, 973; Rautenbach and Venter 2018, p. 392). The democracy theory forms the link between the right to freedom of expression and democracy. The democracy theory not only serves as justification for the protection of the right to freedom of expression, but also emphasizes values that underlie a democratic system. In terms of the democracy theory, all citizens have the right to be fully informed about all political matters within a state and must be able to make sense of these matters by means of public discourse. This means that citizens should freely and effectively be able to partake in the democratic processes of the state (Venter 2016, pp. 225–230; Carmi 2007, pp. 971–972). At first glance, this would seem to suggest that political freedom of expression enjoys a higher degree of recognition and protection than other types of expression that do not necessarily contribute anything to a state's political discourse (see Sadurski 1999, p. 21). Expressing one's views on a political level gives recognition to an individual's equal dignity and worth as a citizen of a state, while expression on non-political matters gives recognition to an individual's right to human dignity and self-worth on a personal level. Recognition and protection of both types of expression therefore promotes different aspects of the value of human dignity, while also promoting the democratic nature of the state. Consequently, a wider value-based approach to the interpretation of the democracy theory seems to recognize and protect all types of expression. If freedom of expression were therefore to be viewed within the context of a constitutional democracy based on certain values, as is the case in South Africa, the protection of all types of expression may be justified along those lines. In other words, all types of expression enjoy recognition and protection if the specific type of expression (either political or non-political) contributes to the promotion of the values of human dignity, freedom, and equality, which underlie the South African democracy (s 1 of the South African Constitution; Venter 2016, pp. 227–228).

The intersection of the concepts of democracy, expression, and values can therefore be summarized as follows: a democracy is more than a system based on majority rule, which prescribes how governments should function and which makes provision for political participation of citizens in government processes (Venter 2016, pp. 227–228). Democracy encompasses all these characteristics (in other words, majority rule, prescribed government processes, and political participation of its citizens, among others) but should especially be regarded as a system that is based on constitutional values—such as the value of human dignity. In so doing, we cross the "dignity threshold" to a legal system based on a conceptual framework founded on human dignity. The promotion of these constitutional values (human dignity, freedom, equality, among others) lead to the promotion of the democratic nature of the state. Expression would therefore be worthy of protection if the expression contributes to the promotion of the values that underlie democracy.

The discussion above has indicated the link between democracy, the value of human dignity, and the right to freedom of expression. The protection of freedom of expression by means of the value of human dignity relies on a specific understanding of democracy—in other words that it is a system of government which is based on various values (human dignity, freedom, equality, among others). Human dignity in the South African context may however be used to either protect or limit freedom of expression depending on the facts of the particular case. This is further discussed below. The next part of the chapter considers some examples of instances of expression that affect human dignity and democracy in South Africa.

15.3 Examples Illustrating the Effect of Human Dignity on Freedom of Expression in the South African Democracy

The value of human dignity may have both a protective and limiting effect on the right to freedom of expression within a democracy. The effect of human dignity on freedom of expression can be illustrated by considering the role of the right to freedom of expression within three spheres of government in South Africa, namely the executive, legislative, and judicial authority. In the context of legislative authority, the legislature protects individual (and collective) freedom of expression by means of the Constitution and also in terms of other legislation. Section 16 of the South African Bill of Rights guarantees the right to freedom of expression. Section 16(1)(*a*)–(*d*) provides that each person has the right to freedom of expression, which includes the freedom of the press and the media, the freedom to receive and impart information and ideas, freedom, of artistic creativity, academic freedom and freedom of scientific research. By extensively including various types of expression, the constitutional drafters wanted to afford the right to freedom of expression the best possible protection (Venter 2018a, p. 65). The constitutional provision however also limits this right in order to promote the value of human dignity. The Constitution goes further and expressly excludes some types of expression from the protective ambit of the Bill of Rights (Venter 2018a, p. 65). The excluded types of expression does not enjoy constitutional protection as such expression undermines the constitutional values and the rights of others.

The drafters of the Constitution chose to expressly exclude certain types of expression from constitutional protection. Section 16(2)(*a*)–(*c*) of the Constitution provides that protected expression does not extend to propaganda for war, incitement of imminent violence, or the advocacy of hatred (also called "hate speech") based on the grounds of race, ethnicity, gender or religion which constitutes incitement to cause harm. These forms of expression were expressly excluded to give effect to the transformative goal of the new constitutional order and to attempt to address the gross human rights violations, especially regarding the rights to equality and human dignity, that occurred during South Africa's apartheid era. George Barrie agrees with this interpretation when he argues that the main reason for the exclusion of hate speech (and the other types of excluded expression) from constitutional protection is because of the serious infringement of human dignity suffered by those who are affected by the excluded instances of expression (such as hate speech for example) (Barrie 2013, pp. 700, 706–707). The constitutional provisions therefore both protect and limit freedom of expression in the pursuit of promoting the value of human dignity. In the South African context, and for example in the German context with regard to the Holocaust (although not expressly provided in the German Constitution), the reason for the exclusion of these types of expression is that these instances of expression undermine the human dignity of others (Venter 2016, p. 280). The exclusion of certain types of expression, such as Holocaust denial (in Germany) or hate speech (in South Africa), clearly traverse the "dignity threshold," supporting an approach that underscores human dignity. Other examples of states with constitutions that expressly exclude certain types of expression are Zimbabwe (Sect. 61(5) of the Constitution of the Republic of Zimbabwe, 2017), Kenya (Sect. 33(2) of the Constitution of the Republic of Kenya, 2010) and Fiji (Sect. 17(2) of the Constitution of the Republic of Fiji, 2013). Many states have however opted not to exclude these types of expression *expressly* from constitutional protection, but they leave it to the courts to decide how, or even if, such expression should be limited. The United States of America is one such example. In the United States, a more liberal and individualistic approach is taken to the protection of the right to free speech. Consequently, it is more difficult to limit the right to free speech, for example on the grounds of hate speech. According to Guy Carmi, the American approach to free speech protection and hate speech is explained by the "minimalist account" argument regarding the relationship between dignity and the right to freedom of speech (Carmi 2007, pp. 976–979). In short, the "minimalist account" argument regarding dignity and free speech focusses on the rights of the speaker and not the rights of the audience (Carmi 2007, p. 976). Therefore, when considering the limitation of a speaker's right to free speech, the effect of the speech on the audience is considered less important than the speaker's interest in expressing him or herself. Although the American courts have developed exceptions to this approach, such as the "clear and present danger" test developed in Brandenburg v. Ohio regarding incitement to cause harm, American courts remain protective of the right to free speech (Venter 2016, p. 292).

Another popular view in American jurisprudence is that speech should not be stifled, since the only remedy to offensive speech should be more speech and debate. This view is well illustrated by the court in Snyder v. Phelps where the Supreme Court remarked:

> Speech is powerful. It can stir people to action, move them to tears of both joy and sorrow, and – as it did here – inflict great pain. On the facts before us, we cannot react to that pain by punishing the speaker. As a Nation we have chosen a different course – to protect even hurtful speech on public issues to ensure that we do not stifle public debate (par 4 of the main judgment).

These counter arguments against the limitation of certain instances of freedom of expression do not consider the central role that the value of human dignity plays with regard the South African Bill of Rights. Expression that infringes upon the right of human dignity of individuals or that is contrary to the underlying constitutional value of human dignity will not enjoy protection in South African law, regardless of the effect of the limitation of the speech on the speaker. Expressly excluding hate speech, as well as the other types of expression that undermine dignity, from constitutional protection is therefore justified because this promotes the values underlying the South African Constitution and furthers the transformative goals of the new constitutional order—placing the values of dignity and the indigenous concept of *ubuntu* at the center of its conceptual legal framework.

Other South African legislative provisions also protect and limit the right to freedom of expression. Expression entails not only the right to share information and ideas but also the right to receive the information and ideas shared by others. The legislature protects this aspect of the right to freedom of expression by means of legislative provisions such as the Promotion of Access to Information Act 2 of 2000 (Venter 2018a, p. 67). Sharing certain types of information also enjoys express protection. For instance, disclosures made by employees to journalists about malpractices in the workplace are expressly protected by the Protected Disclosures Act 26 of 2000 (Venter 2018a, p. 67).

Protection (and limitation) of expression is sometimes also connected to the type of person or institution exercising the right. For example, the media and the press are extensively protected by legislation but limited to a certain extent, by means of legislative regulation. The Independent Communications Authority of South Africa Act 13 of 2000 (which protects the independence of the public communications authority), the Electronic Communications Act 36 of 2005 (which protects and regulates electronic communications and electronic communications services), the Media Development and Diversity Agency Act 14 of 2002 (which establishes the Media Development and Diversity Agency and promotes media development and diversity by redressing marginalization and exclusion of disadvantaged communities and promotes their access to media), the Imprint Act 43 of 1993 (which regulates all printed material) and the Films and Publications Act 65 of 1996 (which contains regulations regarding the classification of films and publications) are just some examples of legislation relating to the press and the media.

Other constitutional measures related to freedom of expression and public participation in government in South Africa are elections, referendums, and public hearings regarding proposed legislation. These are excellent mechanisms to allow citizens to participate in government processes and air their grievances without recourse to violence or public protests. The referendum mechanism, however, is sadly neglected and underutilized in South Africa (ss 84(2)(*g*) and 127(2)(*f*) of the Constitution; Venter 2018a, p. 71). Referendums on legislative and policy issues may be called by the President in terms of Sect. 84(2)(*g*) of the Constitution, in terms of an act of Parliament. Unfortunately, the South African Parliament has not yet adopted any legislation making provision for referendums, which means that this mechanism cannot be used. Public hearings and comments of the public on proposed legislation however give the public ways to let their voices be heard on policy decisions and impending legislative provisions proposed by government (Venter 2018a, pp. 74–82). In these instances, except for referendums, public participation and protection of political expression promotes the human dignity and equality of a state's citizens, while also promoting other constitutional values such as openness and responsiveness.

Public control mechanisms, such as freedom of the press and the media, play an important role in enforcing the ethical rules and standards applicable to the members of the executive authority. The South African constitutional order expects a high degree of ethical behavior of members of the executive authority. Apart from the values in Sect. 1 of the Constitution, section 195(1)(*a*) of the Constitution provides that certain specific values and principles underlie the public administration. The public administration of the state must therefore develop and uphold high ethical standards of conduct (Venter 2018b, p. 323). The Executive Members' Ethics Act 82 of 1998, as well as the Prevention and Combating of Corrupt Activities Act 12 of 2004, have important roles to play in this regard. These pieces of legislation create enforceable ethical rules and standards to keep government officials responsible and accountable. Freedom of expression of individuals, the media and the press is an important mechanism of public control which contributes to the uncovering of corruption and maladministration in government and therefore has an important function in enforcing these (ethical) values (Venter 2018b, pp. 323–325). Indirectly, all constitutional values are undermined when corrupt activities occur within the government of a state. A government that truly cares about the dignity, equality, and freedom of its citizens would therefore perform their governmental functions with due diligence, care, and according to the required ethical standards. Public control mechanisms, such as freedom of the press and the media, therefore have the dual effect of ensuring governmental accountability, as well as the promotion of the constitutional values, including human dignity, freedom, equality, the rule of law, and openness in government.

There should be transparency within the judicial branch of government, and individuals should have access to certain types of information. Access to courts, broadcasting of court proceedings, fair and public hearings, access to court documents, and the use of court interpreters, are some aspects that are related to freedom of expression within the judicial branch (Venter 2018b, pp. 327–342). These aspects, such as access to courts and broadcasting of court proceedings, either enable individuals to take part in court proceedings, which gives effect to their right to free expression and promotes the values of dignity and equality, or enables others to see that justice is being served, which promotes the free expression of others, access to information, and the values of openness and transparency in government.

15.4 The Proposed Criminalization of Hate Speech in South Africa

15.4.1 Current Legislative Framework Regarding Hate Speech

Given South Africa's painful history of discrimination, hate speech is specifically excluded from constitutional protection. The human dignity of individuals is especially affected by instances of hate speech, and human dignity is expressly protected in the Constitution (or some such). Currently, hate speech in South Africa is not a crime but an unprotected type of expression. Apart from Sect. 16(2) of the South African Constitution, which excludes hate speech from the protective ambit of the right to freedom of expression, section 10 of the Promotion of Equality and the Prevention of Unfair Discrimination Act 4 of 2000 (PEPUDA) provides the definition of hate speech:

> . . .no person may publish, propagate, advocate or communicate words based on one or more of the prohibited grounds, against any person, that could reasonably be construed to demonstrate a clear intention to be hurtful, to be harmful or to incite harm, to promote or propagate hatred.

PEPUDA defines a prohibited ground as "race, gender, sex, pregnancy, marital status, ethnic or social origin, color, sexual orientation, age, disability, religion, conscience, belief, culture, language, birth and HIV/AIDS status" or "any other ground" as a ground

> . . .where discrimination based on that other ground causes or perpetuates systemic disadvantage, undermines human dignity, or adversely affects the equal enjoyment of a person's rights and freedoms in a serious manner that is comparable to discrimination on the aforementioned grounds (s 1 of PEPUDA the definition of "prohibited grounds").

A complaint of hate speech may be brought before the Equality Court for expressing views that could be construed as hate speech. Section 21 of PEPUDA provides limited remedies to a complainant including, the granting of an interim order, an order restraining the conduct complained of, the payment of costs, and an unconditional apology. The Equality Court could also refer a matter to the Director of Public Prosecutions for the institution of criminal charges in terms of other appropriate legislation or the common law in certain circumstances (s 21(2)(*n*) of PEPUDA).

Although the provisions of PEPUDA have been criticized for including more prohibited grounds regarding hate speech than the Constitution itself, the court in South African Human Rights Commission v. Qwelane held that the provisions did not necessarily fail the Sect. 36 limitations test because more grounds were included in the Act than in terms of Sect. 16(2) of the Constitution. The court argued that this is so because the harm that Sect. 10 of PEPUDA sought to address, outweighs the interests of the speakers in such cases (Qwelane, para 63; also see Botha 2018 for a discussion of the case).[2] In South African Human Rights Commission v. Khumalo, the Equality Court criticized the court's judgment in the Qwelane case where it stated that "incitement" was not a prerequisite for speech to be regarded as hate speech. The Equality Court argued that this approach would effectively make the test for hate speech in terms of PEPUDA much wider than the test provided by the Constitution (Khumalo: para 83). In Afriforum v. Malema, the court argued that the real test for hate speech is "neither the historical significance thereof nor the context in which words are uttered, but the effect of the words, objectively considered, upon those directly affected and targeted thereby" (238I). The historical context regarding hate speech however is one of the reasons that the drafters of the Constitution chose to exclude certain types of expression from the protective ambit of the Constitution

[2]See also the decision of the Constitutional Court in Qwelane v. South African Human Rights Commission 2021 6 SA 579 (CC), where the court found that the word "hurtful" as used in sect. 10 of PEPUDA in relation to hate speech is too vague, which means that it could put an unjustifiable limitation on the right to free expression. Consequently the court declared the section unconstitutional. For a discussion of the case see Laubscher (2022).

in the first place—it is therefore not advisable to take words and phrases out of context and merely consider the "objective" effect of the speech involved.

Hate speech as such is not a crime in terms of PEPUDA. The common law however does provide a remedy regarding instances of expression that seriously affect the dignity of others. Prosecution in terms of the common law crime of *crimen injuria* is still possible if all the elements of the crime have been satisfied by the particular exercise of expression. *Crimen injuria* is "a wrongful act designedly done in contempt of another, which infringes a person's personal rights of safety, security, or privacy, or his dignity or reputation" (Claassen 2018 (online version)). The sentences and fines imposed with regard to *crimen injuria* may however be an indication that the proposed punishments in terms of the new hate speech legislation is perhaps too severe.[3] The question is, therefore, whether a new separate crime of hate speech is necessary, given that hate speech could be prosecuted in terms of the common law.

15.4.2 *The Offence of Hate Speech in Terms of the Prevention and Combating of Hate Crimes and Hate Speech Bill*

One of the main purposes of the Prevention and Combating of Hate Crimes and Hate Speech Bill [4] is to give effect "to the Republic's obligations in terms of the Constitution and international human rights instruments concerning racism, racial discrimination, xenophobia, and related intolerance, in accordance with international law obligations." [5] Furthermore, the Hate Speech Bill aims to "provide for the offence of hate crime and the offence of hate speech and the prosecution of persons who commit those offences; to provide for appropriate sentences that may be imposed on persons who commit hate crime and hate speech offences..." and "to provide for the prevention of hate crimes and hate speech." The preamble of the Hate

[3] In S v. Seluma (2015 JDR 1578 (GP)) the court imposed a prison sentence of 3 months for the crime of *crimen injuria,* which resulted from insults which violated a person's dignity. In S v. Prinsloo (2014 JDR 1444 (SCA)) the court imposed a fine of R 6000.00 or 12 months imprisonment, wholly suspended for 5 years, in circumstances where an accused had used a derogatory racial slur during an altercation.

[4] Hereafter the Hate Speech Bill, B9-2018, published in the *Government Gazette* No. 41543 of 29 March 2018.

[5] These international law obligations may be found in the following instruments: the Declaration adopted at the United Nations World Conference against Racism, Racial Discrimination, Xenophobia and Related Intolerance held in Durban ("the Declaration") (World Conference against Racism, Racial Discrimination, Xenophobia and Related Intolerance held in Durban from 31 August to 8 September 2001, A/CONF.189/12 https://undocs.org/A/CONF.189/12 (17-1-2019)); the International Convention on the Elimination of All Forms of Racial Discrimination ("the Convention") (General Assembly resolution 2106 (XX) of 21 December 1965); and the International Covenant on Civil and Political Rights (General Assembly resolution 2200A (XXI) of 16 December 1966).

Speech Bill refers to the values in sect. 1 of the Constitution which, for purposes of this discussion, is relevant because it shows that the Bill attempts to give effect to these values by limiting certain types of expression that infringe these values. The question remains, however, whether the Bill has succeeded in this task or whether the provisions are over-inclusive.

Regarding South Africa's international law obligations, the Bill may be criticized as being too strict with regard to criminalizing certain types of expression. The Rabat Plan of Action on the Prohibition of Advocacy of National, Racial or Religious Hatred that constitutes Incitement to Discrimination, Hostility or Violence ("Rabat Plan") is an appendix to the Annual report of the United Nations High Commissioner for Human Rights ("Annual Report"). The Rabat Plan of Action is a guide to the implementation of the international prohibition of "any advocacy of national, racial or religious hatred that constitutes incitement to discrimination, hostility or violence" (Rabat Plan, par III). According to the Action Plan, restrictions that are imposed on expression should be "clear and narrow" in their definition and should only be in response to a "pressing social need" (Rabat Plan, para 18). The restrictions that are imposed should be the least intrusive measure available, not overly broad and should not "restrict speech in a wide or untargeted way" (Rabat Plan, para 18). Consequently, all restrictions are to be proportionate in order to ensure that "the benefit to the protected interest outweighs the harm to freedom of expression, including with respect to the sanctions they authorize" (Rabat Plan, para 18). I therefore argue that the criminalization of hate speech (as defined by the Bill) cannot be regarded as the least intrusive method to combat this type of harm.

South Africa's current measures against hate speech, in terms of PEPUDA, are less intrusive than criminalizing hate speech. South African law excludes hate speech from constitutional protection and have provisions that regulate hate speech, without criminalizing it. The provisions of the Hate Speech Bill therefore do not seem to comply with the aforementioned international guidelines. There is a vast difference between expressly excluding certain types of expression from constitutional protection and placing a criminal prohibition on those types of expression. The Hate Speech Bill contains various problematic provisions, particularly regarding its definitions, vagueness, over-inclusiveness, harsh sentences and lack of defenses against a charge of hate speech. These issues are discussed below.

The definitions contained in the Bill are problematic. Section 4(1)(*a*) of the Bill provides that any person is guilty of the offence of hate speech if that person

> ...intentionally *publishes, propagates or advocates anything or communicates* to one or more persons in a manner that could reasonably be construed to demonstrate a clear intention to (i) be *harmful* or to incite *harm*; or (ii) promote or propagate *hatred*, based on one or more of the following grounds... (my own emphasis)

The Bill further defines "communicates" (within the context of the definition above) to include the following: "(a) display; (b) written, illustrated, visual or other descriptive matter; (c) oral statement; (d) representation or reference; or (e) an electronic communication." The definition of hate speech in the Bill therefore differs from the definition of hate speech in the Constitution, as *incitement of harm* is not required in terms of the Bill—words need merely be "harmful" in order to qualify as hate speech. If "incitement of harm" is not required to qualify as "hate speech," the application of the Bill becomes too wide. If the Bill therefore comes into force, this would mean that mere insults could be criminalized. In addition, the Bill fails to define key elements of the crime of "hate speech." For example, the Bill does not define what the "promotion or propagation of hatred" entails. If action words, such as "promotion" or "propagation," are not defined, prosecution becomes problematic, as it is unclear whether a person's action(s) comes down to "promotion" or "propagation" of hate speech. Further, the definition of "hate speech" in the Bill does not require that the "harmful" words be "hateful." As a matter of logic, "hatred" is an essential element of the crime of hate speech and should therefore form part of the definition of the crime of hate speech. Consequently, the Bill is excessively vague and its deficiencies very serious. If the Bill is adopted, this vagueness could make the enforcement of its provisions arbitrary and cause legal uncertainty. Furthermore, the Bill's application is much too wide increasing the possibility for misinterpretation. If the application of the Bill is too wide, also referred to as "over-inclusiveness," individuals may be prosecuted for instances of expression that are not hateful, but merely insulting. Over-inclusive hate speech rules may stifle free expression and this would offend the value of human dignity and limit the rights to free expression and human dignity, among others.

The provision in Sect. 4(1)(*b*) of the Bill, further illustrates this over-inclusiveness:

> ...[a]ny person who intentionally distributes or makes available an electronic communication which that person knows constitutes hate speech as contemplated in paragraph (a), through an electronic communications system which is—(i) accessible by any member of the public; or (ii) accessible by, or directed at, a specific person who can be considered to be a victim of hate speech, is guilty of an offence.

The provision aims to address the distribution of messages containing hate speech by electronic means, including social media. The number of comments, pictures and other messages on social media, shared without thought (and therefore unintentionally), challenges the state's ability to effectively enforce this prohibition. The state would have the extremely difficult, if not impossible, task of determining which persons intentionally distributed electronic communications containing the alleged hate speech and which persons did so unintentionally. There may also be hundreds, if not thousands, of potential perpetrators involved—which would further complicate matters for the state.

The punishments that the Bill prescribes after successful prosecution on a charge of hate speech are also problematic. Successful prosecutions of hate speech may, for example, attract a prison sentence of up to 3 years for a first offender, while subsequent convictions attract a prison sentence of up to 5 years. This seems excessive when compared to the much lighter sentences usually imposed for convictions in terms of the common law crime of *crimen injuria* referred to above.

The Bill also does not make provision for many defenses with regard to an accusation of hate speech. The only defenses against a charge of hate speech are included in Sect. 4(2) namely: *bona fide* artistic creativity; academic or scientific inquiry; fair and accurate reporting, and the *bona fide* interpretation or espousing of any religious tenet, belief, teaching, or writings. These defenses in Sect. 4(2) could not easily be used in the case of "mindless sharing" of electronic messages containing hate speech on social media. The only possible defense in such a case would be to prove that the action of sharing the message containing the alleged hate speech was not done "intentionally"—which is not always easy to prove. The Bill's lack of defenses for a charge of hate speech means that the Bill affords the state a substantial amount of control over social media—stifling freedom of expression and, ultimately, also human dignity. While the protection of the value of human dignity is a worthy objective, I do not believe that creating a new crime of hate speech is the best remedy to do so. PEPUDA already regulates hate speech (without criminalizing it), and there also exists a common law crime which can be used to prosecute instances of expression that comply with the elements of the crime of *crimen injuria*. I therefore argue that creating a new crime is unnecessary, because there are already mechanisms in place that can deal with the problem of hate speech without wasting time on drafting new legislation that merely complicates the matter even further. Even if the purpose of the new Hate Speech Bill was only to better regulate hate speech in South Africa, the Bill's provisions are much too vague and wide to do so adequately. In addition, I argue that the non-criminalization of the unprotected types of expression (hate speech, incitement to violence, propaganda for war), and following the route of an apology and compensation when a person is found to have committed one of these forms of expression instead, is an approach that is more in line with reconciliation, dignity, and *ubuntu*. Reconciliation (instead of retribution) and the indigenous value of *ubuntu* are two concepts that have been adopted and advanced in the post-apartheid era in order to transform our society—both reconciliation and *ubuntu* focus on forgiveness and the airing of grievances, instead of on retribution and punishment. The criminalization of hate speech would therefore be a step backward, away from crossing the "dignity threshold" into an era where dignity and *ubuntu* take center stage.

15.5 Concluding Remarks and Recommendations

Uncovering the role of the value of human dignity with regard to the right to freedom of expression in the South African democratic system highlights the importance of dignity and expression in transforming South Africa's legal system into a constitutional democracy. Investigating the role of human dignity in this chapter (and the book as a whole) occurs in tandem with situations "at the threshold," in other words where the use of the value of human dignity and the concept of *ubuntu* is used in response to great societal crises, individual hardships or human rights violations, where human dignity becomes an ethical and legal dilemma.

In terms of the South African Constitution, human dignity is given a prominent status as both a right and a constitutional value, and this prominence emphasizes

South Africa's commitment in addressing the gross violations of human dignity which occurred during the apartheid regime. I have shown that human dignity plays a critical role in the theoretical approaches to both democracy and freedom of expression, supporting the value based approached to democracy, which emphasizes that certain constitutional values should be promoted in the performance of government actions and decision-making and that citizens and institutions (such as the press and the media) should enforce the government's adherence to these values by means of freedom of expression.

With regard to freedom of expression, the democracy theory (which serves as justification for the protection of freedom of expression), entails that a particular type of expression would be worthy of protection if it contributes to the promotion of the values that underlie democracy—such as human dignity. If a particular instance of expression undermines any of the constitutional values, it may not be worthy of protection and should therefore not enjoy constitutional protection within the context of the limitation clause contained in Sect. 36 of the South African Constitution.

Furthermore, I have highlighted various examples of the interrelatedness of democracy, freedom of expression, and the constitutional value of human dignity within the South African context, using South African examples where human dignity serves as justification to protect or limit freedom of expression within the various branches of government. For example, I considered public participation with regard to the legislative and the executive authority, as well as access to courts and court documents, the broadcasting of court proceedings, and court interpreters with regard to the judicial authority. Certain types of expression in South Africa, such as hate speech, propaganda for war and incitement of imminent violence, have however been expressly excluded from the protective ambit of the Constitution. This is so, not only because these types of expression undermine the constitutional value of human dignity, but also because the exclusion of these types of expression furthers the transformative goals of the Constitution given South Africa's historical background of discrimination.

I questioned whether recently proposed South African hate speech legislation unjustifiably infringes the right to freedom of expression in an effort to protect human dignity, arguing that, although the proposed Hate Speech Bill attempts to promote human dignity and equality and give effect to various international law obligations and provisions, it fails on three accounts. First, assuming that such a Bill is necessary at all, the Bill has gone much further than is needed in order to address the hate speech problem. If better regulation is indeed the purpose of the Bill, a more precise regulation of hate speech is needed, not a vague and over-inclusive piece of legislation that does not provide adequate defences to a charge of hate speech. Second, the Hate Speech Bill is wholly unnecessary. This is because hate speech is already regulated by PEPUDA and the common law crime of *crimen injuria* (if all the elements of the crime are satisfied). Wasting time and resources on the drafting, adoption, and implementation of a new piece of legislation regulating hate speech is unnecessary. Third and more importantly, however, criminalization of hate speech is incompatible with the South African Constitution's commitment to human dignity, reconciliation and the concept of *ubuntu*. The criminalization of hate speech would therefore be a step backward, away from crossing the "dignity threshold" into an era where dignity and *ubuntu* take center stage. Hate speech, however, remains a serious problem in South African society and needs to be addressed—the criminalization of hate speech is perhaps just not the ideal way of doing so. The approach of criminalization does not accord with the reconciliatory approach that South Africans adopted after the end of the apartheid regime. The South African constitutional order's commitment to reconciliation, the indigenous value of *ubuntu*, and the value of human dignity rather suggests the opposite approach to hate speech—that of an apology, not retribution. Ultimately, it is the value of human dignity that should remain triumphant in the battle over hate speech, because this value lies at the heart of freedom of expression, dignity, and democracy as such. This chapter, therefore, argues for a new perspective that advocates for a disambiguity and centralization of the concept of *ubuntu*, in order to push past the "dignity threshold" established by the apartheid legal system in order to develop new legal paradigms that expand and underscore human dignity. Such a paradigm shift would force the South African legal system to cross the "dignity threshold" into new territory, to really embrace its constitutional values in order to move from an ethic of apartheid to an ethic of *ubuntu*.

References

Albertyn C, Goldblatt B (1998) Facing the challenge of transformation: difficulties in the development of an indigenous jurisprudence of equality. South Afr J Hum Rights 14:248–276

Annual report of the United Nations. High Commissioner for Human Rights available at https://www.ohchr.org/Documents/Issues/Opinion/SeminarRabat/Rabat_draft_outcome.pdf. Accessed 30 June 2023

Barendt EM (1985) Freedom of speech. Clarendon Press, Oxford

Barrie GN (2013) The divergent constitutional approach to hate speech in South Africa and the United States. TSAR 2013:697–707

Botha J (2018) Of semi-colons and the interpretation of the hate speech definition in the Equality Act. Obiter 39:526–546

Carmi GE (2007) Dignity – the enemy from within: A theoretical and comparative analysis of human dignity as a free speech justification. Univ Pa J Constit Law 9:957–1001

Chaskalson A (2000) Human dignity as a foundational value of our constitutional order. South Afr J Hum Rights 16:193–205

Chaskalson A (2011) Dignity as a constitutional value: a South African perspective. Am Univ Int Law Rev 26:1377–1407

Claassen RD (2018) Dictionary of legal words and phrases. LexisNexis, Durban. (Online version)

Cornell D, Van Marle K (2005) Exploring ubuntu: tentative reflections. Afr Hum Rights Law J 5: 195–220

Cowen S (2001) Can dignity guide South Africa's equality jurisprudence? South Afr J Hum Rights 17:34–58

De Vos P, Freedman W (2014) South African constitutional law in context. Oxford University Press Southern Africa, Cape Town

Declaration adopted at the United Nations. World Conference against Racism, Racial Discrimination, Xenophobia and Related Intolerance held in Durban ("the Declaration") (World Conference against Racism, Racial Discrimination, Xenophobia and Related Intolerance held in

Durban from 31 August to 8 September 2001, A/CONF.189/12 https://undocs.org/A/CONF.189/12. Accessed 30 June 2023
Greenawalt K (1989) Free speech justifications. Columbia Law Rev 89:119–155
Hallowell JH (1954) The moral foundation of democracy. University of Chicago Press, Chicago
Independent Communications Authority of South Africa Act 13 of 2000
International Convention on the Elimination of All Forms of Racial Discrimination ("the Convention") (General Assembly resolution 2106 (XX) of 21 December 1965)
International Covenant on Civil and Political Rights (General Assembly resolution 2200A (XXI) of 16 December 1966)
Kamga SD (2018) Cultural values as a source of law: emerging trends of ubuntu jurisprudence in South Africa. Afr Hum Rights Law J 18:625–649
Laubscher R (2022) Overview of Constitutional Court judgments on the bill of rights - 2021. TSAR 356:364–365
Malherbe R, Van Eck M (2009) The state's failure to comply with its constitutional duties and its impact on democracy. TSAR 2009:209–223
Media Development and Diversity Agency Act 14 of 2002
Mureinik E (1994) A bridge to where? Introducing the Interim Bill of Rights. South Afr J Hum Rights 10:31–48
Powers, Privileges and Immunities of Parliament and Provincial Legislatures Act 4 of 2004
Prevention and Combating of Hate Crimes and Hate Speech Bill B9-2018, published in the Government Gazette No. 41543 of 29 March 2018
Promotion of Access to Information Act 2 of 2000
Promotion of Equality and the Prevention of Unfair Discrimination Act 4 of 2000
Protected Disclosures Act 26 of 2000
Qwelane v. South African Human Rights Commission 2021 6 SA 579 (CC)
Rabat Plan of Action on the Prohibition of Advocacy of National, Racial or Religious Hatred that Constitutes Incitement to Discrimination, Hostility or Violence, appendix to the Annual report of the United Nations High Commissioner for Human Rights available at https://www.ohchr.org/Documents/Issues/Opinion/SeminarRabat/Rabat_draft_outcome.pdf. Accessed 30 June 2023
Rautenbach IM, Venter R (2018) Rautenbach-Malherbe Constitutional Law. LexisNexis, Durban
Ryn CG (1978) Democracy and the ethical life: a philosophy of politics and community. Louisiana State University Press, Baton Rouge
Sadurski W (1999) Freedom of speech and its limits. Kluwer Academic Publishers, Dordrecht
Venter R (2016) Demokrasie en die Reg op Vryheid van Uitdrukking (Democracy and the Right to Freedom of Expression). Unpublished LLD thesis, University of Johannesburg, South Africa
Venter R (2018a) The role of freedom of expression in a democratic system (part 1). TSAR 2018: 52–87
Venter R (2018b) The role of freedom of expression in a democratic system (part 2). TSAR 2018: 308–366
Wermiel SJ (1998) Law and human dignity: the judicial soul of Justice Brennan. William Mary Bill Rights J 7:223–239

Chapter 16
Reclaiming African Dignity through Ubuntu and Decolonization as Dangerous Memory

Nontando M. Hadebe

Abstracts Africans (The term 'African' in this paper is used in a generic sense and is not meant to be monolithic and should not be interpreted as reducing the complexity of African histories, identities, differences, and diversity into a single narrative. It is used pragmatically to address the shared history of colonialism, racism, and hegemony of western knowledge particularly in former colonies in Sub-Saharan Africa.) have resisted centuries of oppression, conquest, and exploitation designed to strip them of their human dignity. The struggles for liberation and independence drew inspiration from multiple sources including pre-colonial traditional practices and beliefs that affirm the dignity and value of African lives. As memories of a different reality of dignity, these traditional practices and beliefs constitute so called "dangerous memories" capable of disrupting the status quo and inspiring resistance to oppression and redefinition of lives and identities on their own terms. Ultimately, this leads to a restoration of human dignity which is crucial to healthy group identities. In this chapter, "dangerous memories" will be discussed using the example of the African cultural resource of "*Ubuntu*" as a basis for anthropologies of resistance and human dignity drawn from African knowledge systems. Examples of applications of *Ubuntu* for transformative purposes that restore human dignity will be discussed in dialogue with decolonial movements, "decolonization" being another example for "dangerous memories" or memories that challenge the hegemony of western knowledge which inferiorizes indigenous knowledge, undermining agency and human dignity of all Africans particularly marginalized groups such as women. The restoration and sustenance of the human dignity of all Africans requires the intersection of dangerous memories with the decolonial call to the critical appropriation of African precolonial knowledge marginalized by the hegemony of western knowledge through the lens of marginalized groups.

N. M. Hadebe (✉)
University of Free State, Johannesburg, South Africa
e-mail: noehadebe@gmail.com

S. N. Arel et al. (eds.), *Probing Human Dignity*,
https://doi.org/10.1007/978-3-031-42437-3_16

16.1 Introduction

> All human beings are born free and equal in dignity and rights. They are endowed with reason and conscience and should act towards one another in a spirit of brotherhood (UDHR, Article 1).

> Everyone is entitled to all the rights and freedoms set forth in this Declaration, without distinction of any kind, such as race, colour, sex, language, religion, political or other opinion, national or social origin, property, birth or other status. Furthermore, no distinction shall be made on the basis of the political, jurisdictional or international status of the country or territory to which a person belongs, whether it be independent, trust, non-self-governing or under any other limitation of sovereignty (UDHR, Article 2).

The United Nations Declaration of Human Rights (UDHR) was adopted by the United Nations General Assembly on December 10, 1948, and represents "the first comprehensive agreement among nations as to the specific rights and freedoms of all human beings."[1] According to the preamble of the UDHR, the basis of human rights is the "recognition of the inherent dignity and of the equal and inalienable rights of all members of the human family."[2] Accordingly, human rights are based on the inherent dignity of every human being without exception. Therefore, all human beings are entitled to rights.

It was the gross violations of human rights including genocide of the Second World War that led to the drafting of the UDHR by western countries, presenting to the rest of the world the basis of human rights for all. Leary explains the significant impact of the exclusion of many nations as follows:

> The lack of influence of major non-Western cultures in the early drafting of international human rights has been cited as a serious deficiency in the development of a universally acceptable concept of human rights. The rich cultures of Asia and Africa express matters of human dignity in terms other than "rights". Many of these cultures, in contrast value a sense of community and stress duties of family and community more than they emphasize individualism and rights (1990, p. 16).

Non-western countries including Africa challenged an underlying individualistic anthropology evident in the UDHR. A process of critique and reformulation ensued, one that reflected the communal understanding of personhood common to African worldviews. These worldviews came to fruition in a contextualized version of the human rights declaration called the *Banjul Charter* (1981). The significance of this act of protest and agency was its affirmation of precolonial indigenous beliefs and knowledge as the basis of a distinctive African anthropology, generally understood as more communal and without a rigid centralized authority. Communality and group participation in decision making, opposing the centralized and top-down construction of the western model, creates societies with a level of cohesion, absent of the constitution of a political society within which ethnic, cultural, and racial origins combine and overlap (Wa Mutua 1995, p. 348).

---

[1] http://www.udhr.org/history/question.htm#_Toc397930427.

[2] United Nations Universal Declaration of Human Rights http://www.un.org/Overview/rights.html.

Bujo describes the practice of the decentralized community participation as palaver which is the "uninterrupted interpretation of established norms, which have to be adapted to different situations in order to do justice to the community in its task of promoting life" (Bujo 1998, p. 56). In order to draw from this life orientated system of knowledge flourishing well before the UDHR in Africa, this essay employs a methodology of looking to past memories as epistemological sources for strength, restoration of dignity, and the redefinition of identities for the group, for all Africans including marginalized groups such as women.

The retrieval and remembrance of the past as a resource for liberation and restoration of human dignity emerges in the conception developed by Johann Baptist Metz[3] that the destruction of memory, effected by a colonized Africa, led to the systematic deprivation of power. But for South Africa, and helped along by the Banjul Charter as well as the Freedom Charter, [4] enaction of a reverse, forming an identity becomes possible with memory's arousal (1980, p. 66). The move from destruction to identification constitutes what Metz and others refer to as 'dangerous memories' of oppressed groups that ultimately enable such groups to resist oppression. Within 'dangerous memory' lies the hope of freedom and power that liberates people from oppression and provokes change, principles which operate equally within the African notion of *Ubuntu*. Therefore, as will be argued in this chapter, cultural beliefs such as Ubuntu form part of the 'dangerous memories' of an anthropology liberated from colonialism, constituting the basis of human dignity as it is rooted in the traditions and beliefs of Africans. Further, the Banjul Charter emerges from these dangerous memories as it challenges the universal claims of hegemonic European knowledge. Hence the simultaneous appropriation of African beliefs such as *Ubuntu* and the challenge to the hegemony of western knowledge as argued by decolonial theories are essential components in the ongoing struggle for the restoration and sustenance of the human dignity of Africans. This argument will be further developed in this chapter beginning with a definition of dangerous memories, *Ubuntu* and decolonization in relation to the human dignity of Africans.

16.2 Dangerous Memories

In their article entitled "Education and the dangerous memories of historical trauma: narratives of pain, narratives of hope," Zembylas and Bekerman (2008) define dangerous memories as they operate within the field of education corroborating

[3] Johann Baptist Metz developed his definition of dangerous memories in response to the failure of academic theology in Germany to respond to Nazism and Hitler. Metz framed dangerous memories theologically attributing the experiences of Jesus as the full expression of the liberating power of dangerous memories.

[4] The *Freedom Charter* represented a vision for a united, non-racial and democratic South Africa and was ratified at the Congress of the People in Kliptown, Soweto on 26 June 1955. Accessed 20/3/2023 https://www.sahistory.org.za/article/congress-people-and-freedom-charter.

with scholars in theology, such as Johann Baptiste Metz and Sharon Welch, who consider dangerous memories within a liberative, religious framework. For Zembylas and Bekerman, dangerous memories are,

> ...disruptive to status quo which is the hegemonic culture of strengthening and perpetuating existing group based identities. Group based identities are usually essentialized, static and tribalistic because they are built on the notion of separating 'us' (the good) and 'them' the bad. [...] The danger is in the practice of remembering the past in new ways that are disruptive to taken-for granted assumptions about a group's identity; such ways establish new understandings of personal and collective identities that enable solidarity (2008, p. 127).

African endurance of colonialization and apartheid reflect the hierarchy of group identities based on inequality where blackness was the 'inferior other' in opposition to whiteness as 'the superior other.' Colonialism was a "relationship of domination between an indigenous (or forcibly imported) majority and a minority of foreign invaders" legitimated and sustained by three fundamental beliefs (Osterhammel 2004, p. 16). First, the belief in the irreconcilable differences between colonizers and colonized reflected "the notion that non-Europeans differ utterly and essentially from Europeans was a cornerstone of colonialist thought" (Osterhammel 2004, p. 107). Racism and western superiority are the byproduct of this theory of radical difference. Second, these differences led the colonists to justify their conquest and subjugation of colonies as an ethical imperative commonly referred to as 'white man's burden'. Third, colonists claimed that the administrative structure of colonialism brought order to what was perceived to be a chaotic existence (Osterhammel 2004, p. 107). Many missionaries shared these colonial assumptions, and it was this "ideological identification of the missionary enterprise with the colonial regimes that generated a crisis of identity amongst the African converts" (Mugambi 2002, p. 23). The quest to 'civilize' and 'Christianize' Africans resulted in the vilification and rejection of African religions, cultures, and systems of knowledge constituting violations to the personhood and dignity of Africans.

Hence the exploitation and oppression from so called efforts to 'civilize' or 'Christianize' profoundly undermined the human dignity of Africans and brought great suffering at all levels: physically, mentally and spiritually. Solidarity in suffering empowered communities to engage in resistance, agency, and redefinition of their own identities. Drawing from the writings of Metz, Welch, and Zembylas and Bekerman fosters an understanding of suffering, linked to dignity, understood through the definition of dangerous memories. Metz's calls for solidarity with those who suffer based on listening to their pain and retrieving their memories from histories of suffering: "There are memories in which earlier experiences break through the center point of our lives and reveal new and dangerous insights for our present. Such memories are like dangerous and incalculable visitants from the past (Metz 1972, p. 15). These memories call for a "praxis of memory grounded in solidarity with the suffering of others" (Zembylas and Berkerman 2008, p. 130). These dangerous memories disrupt the status quo created by those with the power to write history and reveal the stories of pain and oppression of those who are victims of history. Without solidarity with those who suffered, the dangerous memories become sources of 'hatred and violence' (2008, p. 131) violating the dignity of both oppressor and oppressed. Welch puts solidarity in terms of communion and energy evoked by being in relation that steadies the strength required for resisting oppression (Welch 1988).

In the South African context, for instance, racial oppression in the form of Apartheid and colonialism shaped the identities and power relationships among all race groups that perpetuated difference and inequality. These historical constructions of group status and difference continue to operate in post-Apartheid South Africa and need to be confronted as an integral part of the struggle against all forms of oppression and privilege. Without this confrontation, efforts at dividing South African from the rest of Africa will proceed, eroding dignity and dividing people. A needed first step is an encounter with 'dangerous memories' that empower people to join, in communion, the struggle for justice.

The Truth and Reconciliation Commission (TRC), established by the government of national unity in South Africa on 19 July 1995, represents an innovative restorative justice process that confronted the dangerous memories of brutality and violations of rights and dignity from the Apartheid era through appropriating principles drawn from legal framework as well as African religious beliefs such as *Ubuntu* and Christian beliefs such as justice, forgiveness and reconciliation. The TRC described its process and mandate as follows:

> While seeking to establish responsibility for many of the devastating wrongs suffered, the TRC sought the whole truth and in so doing, to reconcile victims, and perpetrators and to help establish a just society. It was the firm belief of the TRC that unless a society exposed itself to the truth, it could harbor no possibility of reconciliation, reunification and trust (TRC 1998, Vora and Vora 2004, p. 2).

The second characteristic of dangerous memories cited by Zembylas and Berkerman (2008) elaborates further on the liberative aspects as follows:

> Dangerous memories fund a community's sense of dignity because they empower those who challenge oppression and injustice. For Welch dangerous memories are a people's history of resistance and struggle in the face of oppression. They bring to the surface stories of injustice and mark how recognizing past wrongs may endanger the continued acceptance of injustice and thus propel people to acts of resistance (p. 132).

Dangerous memories emerge here as empowerment in the struggle for justice in African contexts. Two movements manifest this notion of dangerous memories giving birth to liberative praxis and therefore power: the Black Consciousness Movement (BCM) from South Africa and the philosophy of Negritude from Franco-phone colonized countries.

Steve Biko the founder of BCM realized that the internalization of racism by Africans was a stumbling block to liberation and therefore promoted black pride as the first step in restoring dignity. Therefore, the mission of BCM was "to infuse the black community with a new-found pride in themselves, their efforts, their value systems, their culture, their religion and their outlook to life" (Stubbs 1978, p. 49).

He identified the weapon of the oppressor as the mind of the oppressed:

> The most potent weapon of the oppressor is the mind of the oppressed. So as a prelude whites must be made to realize that they are only human, not superior. Same with Blacks. They must be made to realize that they are also human, not inferior (Stubbs 1978, p. 49).

Similarly, the restoration of black pride as the first step in the liberation of Africans is also reflected in the Negritude movement which emerged in Paris among African and West Indian students in protest against the French method of colonialism that promoted and enforced assimilation into French culture and citizenship yet did not accord Africans the same rights as French natives (Ahluwalia 2006, p. 231). In protest, Africans returned to their roots and traditions and sought to rediscover their past, their black roots, and African heritage:

> They 'sought to reverse the representations ascribed to them and to turn those negative identities into positive images.' Negritude became a cultural-political movement that had as its driving force, the rejection of the imposition of French culture through a countermovement that promoted pride in African culture and physical aspects of black heritage. The movement believed that it was 'returning to black people a humanity that had been denied to them by centuries of denigration and brutalization which reached its apex through the colonial process (Ahluwalia 2006, p. 231).

These two examples of resistance and struggle for African dignity based on precolonial past represents how memories of past pride and affirmation of dignity became a source for resistance against imposition of colonial culture. An example for one of the legacies from African culture which has already been alluded to is Ubuntu.

16.3 Ubuntu

Ubuntu is an ambiguous term in the sense that its meaning is known around the world and understood, yet its definition by scholars remains elusive and contradictory (Dolamo 2013; Hailey 2008). Understanding the concept in its fullness requires a return to the language from which it is derived. Afterwards, considering the etymology of the word and comparing different definitions will permit a description of an anthropology based on *Ubuntu* as a source of restoring and sustaining the dignity of Africans.

Scholars including McDonald (2010) start with a definition of the word *Ubuntu* in its original language including variants in other African languages.

> Morphologically Ubuntu is an Nguni term with phonological variants in many African languages including mudu in Kikuyo, iumuntu in Kemeru, bumuntu in Kisukuma, vamuntu in ShiTonga, bomoto in Bobang and gimuntu in Kikongo (p. 141).

In the Nguni language, *Ubuntu* consists of two words in one that is prefix '*ubu*' and stem *'ntu'* which together mean "being and becoming" and "being as oneness and wholeness" (McDonald 2010, p. 141). At the heart of *Ubuntu* is the description of humaneness; in other words, to be human is to be humane: "it is to affirm one's humanity by recognizing the humanity in others and on that basis establish humane relationships with them" (Ramose 2002, p. 231). The relationship between community and personhood is expressed in the phrase *'umuntu ngumuntu ngabantu,'* a person is a person through or because of others. The implication of the well-known phrase is that the community and the individual are united in an interdependent relationship. Bujo elaborates further when he articulates a difference between western individualism and African communitarianism:

> The human being does not become human by cogito (thinking) but by relatio (relationship) and cognatio (kinship). The fundamental principle of this ethics is not cogito ergo sum (I think, so I am), but rather cognatus sum ergo sum (I am related, so I am) (Bujo 1998, p. 54).

Bogmba (2004, p. 298) further elaborates on *Ubuntu* as follows:

> The concept 'ubuntu' means 'humanity' or 'humanness'. These concepts are important because people share a common humanity. As a philosophy, it upholds individuality and community together. It also promotes the exercise of individual responsibility for the good of the person and the rest of the members of the community. Central to the concept is the idea that relations and transactions that take place among people should be undertaken humanely, in light of values that people share in a given community (Bogmba 2004, p. 298).

The idea that "transactions that take place among people should be undertaken humanely" also emerges in the UN Charta. The deduction remains: A human right is not only an individual right; its worth as a right rests in the idea that it is invoked in relation to others, thus requiring interaction. An African anthropology adds depth to this assumption and fleshes out the requirements of the interaction. *Ubuntu* holds together individual and communal identity without sacrificing either or reducing identities to any of these. The two are connected in dialectical inextricable relationships so that there can be no personhood without community and no community without persons. The concept of community also bridges the past, present, and future as well as all of creation: the past represents ancestors 'the living dead;' the present consists of 'the living,' both human and the remainder of creation, and the future is understood as 'the yet to be born.' The inclusion of creation as an integral part of community has led advocates for environmental justice in Africa to adopt *Ubuntu* as an ethic for just relations between humans and nature/creation described below:

> In *Ubuntu* ethic, there is no conception of anthropocentricism, as humans and nonhumans are moral counterparts. The ethic articulates the human interconnectedness and dignity which an individual has towards other beings. This depicts life as wholeness, as life extends to the environment and past and future generations.

Community also extends to the founding of African Traditional Religions (ATRs) which are the basis of African culture. Mbiti describes the communal nature of ATRs as follows: "African religions are communal in origin, practice and propagation. It has no founder like Moses, Confucius, Buddha, Jesus, or Muhammed."

The absence of a singular leader disperses power to the group, disrupting the status quo and destabilizing authority. The subversive memories of the victims of history come to the fore in Ubuntu, which signifies then a dangerous memory, not only in its liberative praxis as a memory of conflict but also in its constituting "a memory of hope, a memory of freedom and resistance" (Welch 2007, p. 370).

Ubuntu reflects precolonial traditional beliefs and practices that uphold the dignity and value of African lives—signifying hope, signifying freedom. Hence, Ubuntu becomes a tool for resistance against dehumanization and is a resource for affirming the tradition of human rights and dignity in African cultures.

The Banjul Charter which as discussed in the introduction is a contextualization of the Universal Declaration of Human Rights by Africans to reflect African anthropology based on traditional beliefs. For example, article 2 of the Charter states that each person has the duty to,

> Preserve and strengthen positive African cultural values, in his relations with his fellow beings and in his relations with society in the spirit of tolerance, dialogue and consultation and in general to contribute to the promotion of the moral well-being of society.

The insistence on duties to community is consistent with the philosophy of *Ubuntu* and traditional African beliefs that combine individual rights with communal duties which is also reflected in the preamble of the Charter: 'the enjoyment of rights and freedom also implies the performance of duties" (p. 14).

As stated earlier, *Ubuntu* represents indigenous knowledge stored in culture, beliefs and practices. Mbiti notes that African Traditional Religions (ATRs) have no written text but have oral traditions infused into every aspect of life including language, ritual, art, song and proverbs (2005, p. 8). This type of knowledge and transmission is different from the scientific paradigm of western knowledge and is one of the reasons for the marginalization of indigenous knowledge which is a form of violation against the dignity of Africans. Whitt (2009) describes western knowledge as anti-pluralistic and suspicious of knowledge outside of its paradigm:

> The dominant knowledge system tends to embrace an anti-pluralism, a lack of receptiveness to alternative epistemologies, to other ways of knowing the world. Other knowledge systems are usually reduced to "superstition the very antithesis of knowledge." This is especially so for knowledge systems employing forms of knowledge transmission that are regarded as suspect—such as the stories and ceremonies upon which indigenous communities heavily rely on (Whitt 2009, p. 32).

However despite power and privilege that sustain the hegemony of western knowledge, African indigenous knowledge, particularly *Ubuntu,* continues to be a significant resource to contemporary challenges that violate or compromise the dignity of African lives. For example Banda (2019) critically appropriates *Ubuntu* in response to the commodification of human identity that results in the 'thingifying of human identity'(2) and "creation of human identity that undermines human solidarity and interpersonal human connections" (4). The *Ubuntu* ethic as discussed earlier emphasizing the communitarian and relational identity of human beings provides an alternative response to the issues of commodification. Banda (2019) further cautions against romanticizing *Ubuntu* citing contrary views from woman scholars who point to entrenched patriarchy and marginalization of women found in African communities upholding *Ubuntu* ethics,

> Feminist and womanist scholars have decried the overly masculine nature of ubuntu, which makes it oppressive and exclusive (Chisale 2018:1, \4; Manyonganise 2015:2).

Manyonganise (2015:3) declares 'ubuntu is exclusive' and cites several instances where the notion of ubuntu is used to segregate and oppress women (p. 6).

The outcry by women against cultural practices steming from indigenous knoweledge, that undermine their rights and human dignity, led to the issuing of the *Maputo Protocol* which is a development from the Banjul Charter focusing on the protection of women's rights in Africa against cultural practices that violate their rights. The next section on decolonization will further strengthen the role of indigenous knowledge in the promotion of the dignity of Africans particularly through the lense of marginalized groups including women.

16.4 Decolonization

"Decolonization demands the valuing of Indigenous sovereignty in its material, psychological, epistemological, and spiritual forms" (Sium et al. 2012, p. v). This definition of decolonization as the affirmation of indigenous knowledge was echoed by university students in their struggle for decolonial education. In South Africa, students have defined decolonization as "the adoption of a curriculum that includes African writers and ideas, as well as a culture of learning that addresses racism and other forms of exclusion against black students in universities" (Ra'eesa Pather 2016). The students further argued as follows: "Our own thinking as Africans has been undermined. We must have our own education from our own continent. Eurocentrism does not serve our interests culturally, socially, economically. It does not resolve the issues of Africa. The current curriculum dehumanizes black students" (Nonxuba 2016).

The cry by students is echoed in not only higher institutions of learning but workplaces, media, and all aspects of life where western hegemonic knowledge has sought to exclude and marginalize African traditional beliefs and cultures represented in indigenous knowledge. Mbembe (2015), in agreement with Whitt (2009) quoted earlier, argues that the problem is not western knowledge per se but the assumption that western knowledge constitutes universal and legitimate knowledge at the expense of other systems of knowledge. He explains the double nature of this problem as follows:

"The Eurocentric canon attributes truth only to the western way of knowledge production" considering this as universal and also "represses anything that is articulated, thought and envisioned outside of these frames" (Mbembe 2015).

The solution is not 'either' 'or' but 'both' 'and' which means embracing all forms of knowledge in the concept of pluriversity which Mbembe defines as:

A process of knowledge production that is open to epistemic diversity. It is a process that does not necessarily abandon the notion of universal knowledge for humanity, but which embraces it via a horizontal strategy of openness to dialogue among different epistemic traditions. To decolonize the university is therefore to reform it with the aim of creating a less provincial and more open critical cosmopolitan pluriversalism (2015).

An "open critical cosmopolitan pluriversalism" recognizes and acknowledges that indigenous knowledge is a site of struggle and contestation too as noted in the previous section particularly by groups who trace their oppression to interpretations of beliefs and practices of pre-colonial Africa. These groups include women, differently abled persons, and sexual minorities. Kanyoro defines culture as a double edged sword that is a "creed for community identity on one hand and on the other hand the main justification for difference, oppression and injustice" (2002, p. 13). In relation to women: "All questions regarding the welfare and status of women in Africa are explained within the framework of culture" (2002, p. 18). Often women's rights are denied in the name of preservation of pre-colonial culture by those in power. Similar dynamics can be observed in the appropriation of pre-colonial beliefs and practices to justify the marginalization of sexual minorities. The dangerous memories of life affirming practices that affirm dignity for all such as *Ubuntu* become resources for liberation not only for marginalized groups but also for helping communities live up to the ethos of dignity implied in the practice of *Ubuntu*. Pluriversalism as critical appropriation of indigenous knowledge through the experiences of marginalized groups provides the means of realizing the vision of human rights and dignity for all through precolonial African traditions and beliefs such as *Ubuntu*.

16.5 Conclusion

The struggle for dignity and human rights has been a long and hard for Africans. Yet against all odds they have resisted all forms of dehumanization and violations of dignity from slavery to colonialism and apartheid. The resources for the struggle came from dangerous memories of pre-colonial past of traditions and beliefs that affirmed dignity and pride. These memories became "liberating over against the controls and mechanisms" of the dominant white, colonial consciousness and it's "abstract ideal of emancipation" (Metz 1972, p. 19).

Ubuntu embodies emancipation in its material, tangible form through relationships. *Ubuntu* constitutes the resource that continues to drive all forms of resistance against violations of human dignity as well as promote new forms of dignity that affirm the anthropology of communion and interdependence which is essential for the flourishing of African communities. The restoration and sustenance of the human dignity of Africans requires both dangerous memories and an affirmation of its sources in African beliefs and cultures marginalized by the hegemony of western knowledge.

References

Ahluwalia P (2006) Negritude and nativism. In: Ashcroft B et al (eds) The post-colonial studies reader, 2nd edn. Routledge, London, pp 230–232

Banda C (2019) The privatised self? A theological critique of the commodification of human identity in modern technological age in an African Context Professing Ubuntu. HTS Teol Stud/Theol Stud 75(1):10. https://doi.org/10.4102/hts.v75i1.5288

Bogmba EK (2004) Reflections on Thabo Mbeki's African renaissance. J South Afr Stud 30(2): 291–316

Bujo B (1998) The ethical dimension of community: the African model and the dialogue between north and south. Pauline Publications Africa, Nairobi

Dolamo R (2013) Botho/ubuntu: the heart of African ethics. Scriptura J Context Hermeneut South Afr 112(1):1–10

Hailey J (2008) Ubuntu: a literature review. Tutu Foundation

Kanyoro MRA (2002) Introducing feminist cultural hermeneutics. In: An African Perspective (Introductions in Feminist Theology 9). Sheffield Academic Press, Sheffield. Online: https://citeseerx.ist.psu.edu/viewdoc/download?doi=10.1.1.459.6489&rep=rep1&type=pdf

Leary VA (1990) The effect of western perspectives on international human rights. In: An-Nacim AA, Francis MD (eds) Human Rights in Africa: Cross-cultural perspectives. Brookings Institution, Washington, DC, pp 15–30

Mbembe A (2015) Decolonizing knowledge and the question of the archive. Africa is a Country. Online: https://wiser.wits.ac.za/system/files/Achille%20Mbembe%20-%20Decolonizing%20Knowledge%20and%20the%20Question%20of%20the%20Archive.pdf. Accessed 30 June 2023

McDonald DA (2010) Ubuntu bashing: the marketisation of 'African values' in South Africa. Rev Afr Polit Econ 37:139–152

Metz JB (1972) The future in the memory of suffering. In: Metz JB (ed) New questions on God. Herder and Herder, New York, pp 9–25

Metz JB (1980) In: Smith D (ed) Faith in history and society: toward a practical fundamental theology. The Seabury Press, New York

Mugambi JNK (2002) Christianity and African culture. Acton Publishers, Nairobi

Mutua MW (1995) The Banjul Charter and the African cultural fingerprint: an evaluation of duties. VA J Int Law 35:339–380

Nonxuba A (2016) What is decolonised education? Politics Web. 25 Sept 2016, Online: http://www.politicsweb.co.za/news-and-analysis/what-is-decolonised-education

Osterhammel J (2004) Colonialism. Translated from German by Shelley L. Frisch. Markus Wiener Publishers, Princeton

Pather R (2016) Students in New York rise up in solidarity with #FeesMustFall. Mail and Guardian. 18 Oct 2016. Online: https://mg.co.za/article/2016-10-18-students-in-new-york-rise-up-in-solidarity-with-feesmustfall/. Accessed 30 June 2023

Ramose MB (2002) The philosophy of ubuntu and ubuntu as a philosophy. In: Coetzee PH, Roux APJ (eds) Philosophy from Africa, 2nd edn. Oxford University Press, Cape Town, pp 230–238

Sium A et al (2012) Towards the 'tangible unknown': decolonization and the indigenous future. Decolon Indigen Educ Soc 1(1):1–13

Stubbs ACR (1978) Steve Biko. I write what I like. A Selection of his writings. Bowerden Press, London

Vora JA (2004) The effectiveness of South Africa's truth and reconciliation commission. J Black Stud 34(3):301–322

Welch S (1988) For the trumpet shall sound: protest, prayer, and prophecy—conference proceedings Aquinas Center of Theology. Spiritual Today 40:10–29

Welch S (2007) Dangerous memory and alternate knowledges. In: Lawrence BB, Karim A (eds) On violence. Duke University Press, Durham, pp 362–376
Whitt L (2009) Science, colonialism, and indigenous peoples: the cultural politics of law and knowledge. Cambridge University Press, Cambridge
Zembylas M, Bekerman Z (2008) Education and the dangerous memories of Historical trauma: narratives of pain, narratives of hope. Curric Inq 38(2):125–154

Chapter 17
Gently, But Firmly: Human Dignity and Public Responses to COVID-19

Benjamin Davy

Abstract The chapter deals with three aspects of the relationship between human dignity and the COVID-19 pandemic of 2020. One, the growing body of academic journal articles on COVID-19 shows remarkable appreciation of human dignity as guidance for public responses to the pandemic. Two, the "corona triage" (Lübbe, Corona triage. A commentary on the triage recommendations by Italian SIAARTI medicals regarding the corona crisis, 2020) can be regarded as a modern version of the trolley problem (Thomson, Yale Law J 94:1395–1485, 1985) when the differentiating valuing of human lives is combined with ideas about killing and letting die: Human dignity demands that corona triage situations be avoided. Referring to Ubuntu, the sub-Saharan version of human dignity, the chapter demonstrates why "flattening the curve" (social distancing, mouth-nose-coverings, travel restrictions, lockdowns) was a collective effort to protect human dignity and also a manifestation of human dignity. Three, the protests against public responses to COVID-19—often associated with contempt for the government, scientists, and media—should not be explained only with disdain for "covidiots." Rather the loss of agency imposed by COVID-19 rules encroached on human dignity.

17.1 "Every Life Matters" and the COVID-19 Crisis

17.1.1 COVID-19 and Plural Conceptions of Human Dignity

By March 2020, the COVID-19 crisis raged in Northern Italy and started to spread throughout Europe. What began as an infection in a seafood market in the Chinese City of Wuhan turned into a pandemic. In Italy, doctors were forced to withhold ventilators from elderly patients with existing conditions so they could go to younger

B. Davy (✉)
TU Dortmund University, Dortmund, Germany

University of Johannesburg, Johannesburg, South Africa
e-mail: benjamin.davy@udo.edu

S. N. Arel et al. (eds.), *Probing Human Dignity*,
https://doi.org/10.1007/978-3-031-42437-3_17

Fig. 17.1 Jedes Leben ist wertvoll—*Every life matters* (Bielefeld). Poster by Katjes and Karsten Thormaehlen. © 2020 B. Davy

patients with higher life expectancy (Mounk 2020). The doctors followed a guideline on ethics in intensive care (SIAARTI 2020). The "corona triage" (Lübbe 2020) was born.

In May 2020, Katjes, the third-largest German candy company, launched a poster presenting the face of an elderly lady and the slogan "Jedes Leben ist wertvoll—*Every life matters*" (see Fig. 17.1). The poster reminded Germans of the reason why many cities and countries all over Europe shut down social and economic activities, education, and culture for several months: to protect the healthcare system as well as members of a COVID-19 risk cohort.

To avoid a misunderstanding, an explanation must be added. The slogan "every life matters" has a history prior to COVID-19 in Germany. Katjes had used the slogan for many years to advertise their vegan candy. In 2020, however, the police killings of George Floyd, Breonna Taylor, and many more Black persons fueled the rightful indignation of the *Black Lives Matter* movement (Boisseron 2023; Gallicano et al. 2023). In the United States, white supremacists used phrases such as "*All lives matter*" in protest against BLM. The Katjes poster displayed all over Germany was, as far as the author knows, not at all meant as a comment on the police killings of Black persons (even if the poster was sadly insensitive to the *Black Lives Matter* movement).

This chapter examines the relationship between human dignity and public responses to the COVID-19 crises. Plural conceptions of human dignity exist, and dignity has been called "amorphous" and "potentially unbounded" (Daly 2021, p. 25). I find the following four conceptions particularly helpful:

- Human dignity means "that every person has inherent equal worth" (May and Daly 2020).
- Human dignity is protected by a decent society "if its institutions do not act in ways that give the people under their authority sound reasons to consider themselves humiliated" (Margalit 1996, pp. 10–11).
- Ubuntu, the Sub-Saharan moral principle of human dignity and humaneness emphasizes that dignity entails a moral obligation to social solidarity (Davy 2020, pp. 15–17; Hadebe, in this volume; Mabovula 2011; Marais, in this volume).
- Human dignity also pertains to the "successful presentation of the self (gelungene Selbstdarstellung)" (Luhmann 1965, p. 68; translation BD).

In light of the plural—and sometimes contradictory—conceptions of human dignity, this chapter discusses public responses to the COVID-19 crises with regard to the inherent equal worth of every person, the causing or avoiding of humiliation, the moral obligation to social solidarity, and the dwindling opportunities for a successful presentation of the self during the pandemic.

I am limiting my examination of the relationship between human dignity and public responses to the COVID-19 crises to the year 2020. In Germany, during 2020, two pandemic waves infected more than 1.7 million persons and killed more than 33,000 persons (RKI 2020). Inevitably, the pandemic and public responses to COVID-19 (Saha et al. 2022) put great pressure on human dignity, ranging from the patients denied treatment in crowded hospitals to children denied access to schools and friends (Kirchhoffer 2020; Lombart et al. 2022; May and Daly 2020). As the COVID-19 crisis develops over time, other aspects than the ones that were significant in 2020 may emerge as important. Problems, perceptions, and solutions will shift with the growing number of vaccinated persons. This chapter does not discuss the COVID 19 pandemic after December 2020.

17.1.2 "Human Dignity and Rights Need to be Front and Centre"

In 2020, the number of patients in need of intensive care rose above the threshold of available intensive care units. The corona triage commenced. COVID-19, in combination with healthcare systems weakened by decades of austerity and commercialization, compelled doctors to put differentiating values on human lives. Choosing between who would be saved and who would be let die, encroached upon human dignity (Deutscher Ethikrat 2020, pp. 3–4; Hong 2020; Kirchhoffer 2020; Kumm and Walen 2014; Riva and Petrini 2020). Human dignity demanded that healthcare systems be protected from being overloaded and understaffed. Human dignity demanded that human lives were not valued as superior or inferior.

Social distancing and lockdowns exacted a huge toll from families staying at home, owners of closed businesses, and furloughed nonessential workers. Protecting human dignity by defending healthcare systems and individuals at risk from COVID-19—plausible from a viewpoint emphasizing public health—compromised the "successful presentation of the self" (Luhmann 1965) and resulted in the super-spreading of human dignity conflicts. Ms. Michelle Bachelet, UN High Commissioner for Human Rights, asserted that human dignity and human rights should guide public policies against the COVID-19 pandemic (OHCHR 2020):

> Lockdowns, quarantines and other such measures to contain and combat the spread of COVID-19 should always be carried out in strict accordance with human rights standards and in a way that is necessary and proportionate to the evaluated risk. . . . COVID-19 is a test for our societies, and we are all learning and adapting as we respond to the virus. Human dignity and rights need to be front and centre in that effort, not an afterthought.

Perhaps human dignity needed "to be front and centre" (OHCHR 2020) in public responses to COVID-19, but how effectively did or could have human dignity guide public responses? In this chapter, I discuss how well human dignity helped protect the threshold of healthcare systems in 2020 and how dignity conflicts tested the limits of social solidarity. Three questions guide the discussion:

- What did the emerging COVID-19 literature say about human dignity?
- Did the protection of human dignity legitimize lockdowns, social distancing rules, and other efforts to flatten the curve?
- Did human dignity help clarify why dignity conflicts resulted in opposition to lockdowns, social distancing rules, and other efforts to flatten the curve?

All answers to the three questions are, of course, tentative. In the course of the pandemic, it became clear how ephemeral knowledge and convictions are. This is why the chapter should be read more like a diary than a regular academic text.

17.2 Human Dignity at the Margins of the Emerging COVID-19 Literature

17.2.1 Quantitative Aspects

During 2020, COVID-19 literature emerged as a new literature genre that was made temporarily available for free by leading publishers. Digital COVID-19 repositories have been offered, for example, by Brill (2020), Cambridge University Press (2020), Elsevier (2020), Oxford University Press (2020), SpringerNature (2020), Taylor & Francis (2020), and Wiley (2020). Many publishers stopped the service by 2022.

The pandemic, in combination with social media and the Internet, has created a substantial conversation within just a few months. The rapidly growing body of academic literature on COVID-19 proved that writing about the virus fomented a new genre. COVID-19 literature was different from many academic publication cultures. And COVID-19 articles in medicine had much more in common with COVID-19 articles in, for example, social studies or ethics (e.g., speed, rapid review, open access) than with regular articles in medicine.

Although the new genre contributed mostly to natural science, medicine, and public health, a survey of articles (often pre-print online publications) in English on COVID-19 and human dignity confirmed a conversation at the margins of the emerging literature. By the end of October 2020, the COVID-19 collection made available by leading publishers contained 79 scientific publications which mention "COVID-19" and "dignity."

Most of these articles were in medicine or healthcare (28), law (20), ethics or religion (13), and social studies (10). Not counting the words used in titles, abstracts, and bibliographies, the articles together contained the word "dignity" 420 times and "lockdown" 400 times.

Other words that could be expected were used less: "triage" (180), "allocation" (104), "mask" (145), and "social distancing" (101). Regarding COVID-19 and human dignity, many articles addressed measures to curb the spreading of the virus (lockdown: 33 articles; social distancing 32 articles; mask: 24 articles) and the allocation of scarce medical equipment (allocation: 31 articles; triage: 15 articles). Several articles dealt with vulnerable individuals and groups (26): Black persons, children, migrants, the mentally ill, refugees, senior citizens.

17.2.2 Qualitative Aspects

What did the emerging COVID-19 literature have to say about human dignity? Quite often, human dignity was mentioned only in passing (which was the main reason for the number of hits). Some of the texts, however, dealt with human dignity extensively. The following seven examples (in alphabetical order) illustrate the scope of deliberation in the COVID-19 literature:

- Davy (2021) considered social (or physical) distancing and the spatiality of COVID-19 from the perspective of cultural bias. The paper explored the significance of distance and proximity for human dignity. Having to keep 6 ft. apart from others, wear a mouth-nose-covering in public, or work from one's home office while simultaneously organizing homeschooling and household work may affect human dignity. Simmel (1906, p. 453) asserted the existence of a sphere "into which one may not venture to penetrate without disturbing the personal value of the individual." This sphere is the spatial manifestation of human dignity, sometimes called personal space. In 2020, social distancing rules greatly re-shaped this sphere, often with considerable consequences.
- Dhungana (2020) reflected on human dignity, Nepali cross-border migrants returning from India, and COVID-19. From the perspective of development

studies, human dignity is considered in the frame of Nussbaum's capabilities approach which focuses on "ten capabilities" which "all are held to be part of a minimum account of social justice" (Nussbaum 2006, p. 75). In March 2020, the Nepali government closed the border to India in order to prevent community transmission by Nepali migrant workers re-entering the country. Dhungana (2020, p. 3) concluded that the Nepali government exposed the stranded migrant workers to humiliation amounting to a violation of their dignity.

- Kirchhoffer (2020) discussed human dignity and the allocation of scarce medical resources during the COVID-19 crisis. The paper argued that "a proper conceptualization of human dignity can help guide ethical decision-making during COVID-19 and similar critical care crises" (Kirchhoffer 2020). As in an earlier book (Kirchhoffer 2013), the Director of the Queensland Bioethics Centre distinguished inherent dignity from acquired dignity. An overwhelmed healthcare system would violate the dignity of patients as well as doctors and other caregivers. Kirchhoffer (2020, p. 4) suggested that autonomy be limited when an individual was objectively morally wrong:

  > Based on adequate information and cognizant of the moral meaning of my actions, the morally right conception of self-worth might lead me to the recognition that the morally appropriate thing for me to do is to not start or to end a treatment that has no proportionate benefit or is overly burdensome.

  This view was relevant for the allocation of scarce ventilators and other medical equipment as it enabled doctors to end the treatment of COVID-19 patients, who failed to see that a continuation of their treatment is futile. The moral deliberation must have appeared "abstract" or "academic" to healthcare givers.

- May and Daly (2020) presented a comprehensive account of dignity rights and various issues that need to find legal answers in times of COVID-19: Employment, immigration, criminal justice, domestic violence, intellectual property, and environmental protection. May and Daly (2020) regarded human dignity as a "frame" for difficult policy decisions:

  > Dignity in law doesn't answer all the questions. It doesn't tell us whether quarantines should last longer or whether helping people return to work should take precedence. It doesn't tell us whether younger generations or older generations or future generations should be privileged at the expense of others. ... In other words, when multiple dignity claims are at stake, dignity itself doesn't tell us how to balance. But it does help frame how we should think about the questions. It reminds us that all legal and policy decisions should cherish human life and protect the quality of human life so that all people can live with dignity.

- Meier et al. (2020, p. 219) examined rights-based approaches to deal with infectious diseases:

  > Human rights law offers international frameworks to facilitate accountability for social justice in efforts to prevent, detect, and respond to infectious disease. Instrumental to human dignity, human rights address basic needs and frame individual entitlements, conceptualising international imperatives to uphold a universal vision of global justice.

According to the authors, many responses to the COVID-19 pandemic (such as lockdowns or travel restrictions) violated human dignity unless they were based on scientific evidence (Meier et al. 2020, pp. 227–228). They recommended restrictions on the autonomy of individuals who flout social distancing rules (Meier et al. 2020, p. 229). The authors even found another dimension to human dignity and the pandemic related to the dignity of "individuals of Asian descent" threatened by stigmatization "with the label of the 'Chinese virus'" (Meier et al. 2020, p. 230).

- Odigbo et al. (2020) constituted a research article (awaiting peer review) on COVID-19 lockdowns (mostly in Africa and Asia) and human rights abuses:

  > COVID-19 lockdowns and curfews' enforcement by law enforcement officers contravened some peoples' fundamental human rights within the first month. Security forces employed overt and immoderate forces to implement the orders. The lockdown and curfew enforcements were not significantly respectful of human life and human dignity. (Odigbo et al. 2020)

- Saunders (2020) was an Oxfam Discussion Paper on COVID-19 and human rights. Here, human dignity was regarded as one of five "principles" to fight the pandemic (Saunders 2020, pp. 4–5). Other "principles" were equality/non-discrimination, participation, proportionality, and freedom of expression/assembly/information. Saunders (2020, p. 5) asserted:

  > Protecting the dignity of people suffering from COVID-19 poses enormous challenges to health and social care systems. Dignity requires states, businesses and individuals to avoid stigma and hatred during and after the pandemic.

  Saunders (2020, p. 13) also related human dignity to Nussbaum's capabilities approach.

The qualitative examples illustrated that academics quickly applied their expertise to the new pandemic. The experts solved new problems by recognizing which previous solutions might help. The fusion of prior knowledge and uncertainty about the new coronavirus produced a peculiar epistemic dynamic:

- Living in an overcrowded apartment can be humiliating, yet COVID-19 added a grave health threat to poor housing and pressure on personal space caused by working from home, home schooling, and loss of privacy (Davy 2021).
- The dignity of migrant workers is often compromised, but the Nepali border closing due to COVID-19 increased the pressure on the human dignity of migrant workers (Dhungana 2020).
- The allocation of scarce medical resources poses problems to healthcare systems all the time, but the shortage of medical equipment in some regions in 2020 put the human dignity of elderly patients and stressed healthcare workers in the limelight (Kirchhoffer 2020).
- Human dignity always serves as a "frame" for all public policy decisions; this was underscored during the COVID-19 pandemic (May and Daly 2020).

- Human dignity is also frail during an HIV/AIDS or Ebola pandemic, but the COVID-19 crises lent urgency to a chapter about human rights and responses to infectious diseases (Meier et al. 2020).
- Human rights abuses occur on a daily basis in most countries, yet the pandemic offered another reason to focus on abusive law enforcement (Odigbo et al. 2020).
- Avoiding stigma and hatred helps respect and protect human dignity; the same was true during the COVID-19 pandemic (Saunders 2020).

The epistemic dynamic suggested sound science. By applying long-established knowledge to a new and frightening global threat, scientists ascertained the role of human dignity in guiding policymakers, healthcare workers, and the public through the COVID-19 crisis. But was their assertion correct? In the remainder of the chapter, I explore whether human dignity proved to be a useful concept to understand and endure a pandemic. On the one hand, I examine whether human dignity helped legitimize efforts to flatten the curve (17.3). On the other hand, I discuss dignity conflicts that emerged from measures introduced to flatten the curve (17.4).

17.3 Protecting the Threshold of the Healthcare System

17.3.1 Social Distancing and Other Ways to Flatten the Curve

One of the slogans associated with the year 2020 and COVID-19 demanded: "Flatten the curve!" The slogan referred to the relation between increasing numbers of new infections, the percentage of severely ill patients, and the capacity of the healthcare system. Hospital beds in intensive care wards, ventilators, and health personnel were scarce. Flattening the curve accounted for the scarcity of resources needed to combat the pandemic and to treat all patients needing intensive care (Roberts 2020):

> The ideal goal in fighting an epidemic or pandemic is to completely halt the spread. But merely slowing it—mitigation—is critical. This reduces the number of cases that are active at any given time, which in turn gives doctors, hospitals, police, schools and vaccine-manufacturers time to prepare and respond, without becoming overwhelmed.

Social or physical distancing, washing hands, wearing mouth-nose-coverings ("masks"), and following sneezing etiquette became the strategy of choice to limit the community spreading of COVID-19. Other ways to flatten the curve included the avoiding of non-essential travelling and large gatherings. The most intense non-pharmacological intervention to flatten the curve were lockdowns of restaurants and bars, theaters and fitness clubs, churches and community centers, shops, and schools.

COVID-19 is an insidious disease. Persons infected with the new coronavirus displayed no, mild, or severe symptoms. Even infected persons with no symptoms spread the virus ("silent spreaders"). Between an infection that resulted in severe symptoms and the need to commence intensive care several weeks could transpire.

The combination of silent spreading and time delay turned out to be a challenge for healthcare systems. For many weeks after the first wave had subsided, the coronavirus spread through various communities with low numbers of patients requiring intensive care. In the summer of 2020, politicians as well as the public misinterpreted this as proof that the worst was over and restrictions were unnecessary. In November 2020, the number of patients requiring intensive care increased rapidly. Once the threshold to the exponential growth of the number of new infections had been passed, intensive care units were flooded with patients in need of ventilators and qualified personnel. To "flatten the curve" meant to avoid that the pandemic reached a point when there were more severely ill patients than hospital resources to treat every one of them.

17.3.2 COVID-19, the Corona Triage, and the Trolley Problem

17.3.2.1 Favoring Higher Life Expectancy?

The *Società Italiana di Anestesia Analgesia Rianimazione e Terapia Intensiva* issued a guideline, later removed from the website, to doctors in intensive care wards (SIAARTI 2020). In case of extreme scarcity of medical equipment, the guideline advised to treat the COVID-19 crisis with utilitarian triage criteria. The guideline considered the life of elderly patients as less valuable than the life of younger patients with a higher life expectancy (SIAARTI 2020):

> Come estensione del principio di proporzionalità delle cure, l'allocazione delle risorse sanitarie in un contesto di grave carenza (shortage) deve puntare a garantire i trattamenti di carattere intensivo ai pazienti con maggiori possibilità di successo terapeutico: si tratta dunque di privilegiare la 'maggior speranza di vita'.
>
> As an extension of the principle of 'care-proportionality', in a context of severe shortage, the allocation of health resources must aim at guaranteeing intensive treatments to those patients with greater possibilities of therapeutic success: it is, therefore, a matter of favoring the 'higher life expectancy.' (translated by Stefano Cozzolino)

The SIAARTI guideline created an inconsistency with established triage rules. It advised to treat patients merely based on a higher life expectancy. This often meant that the treatment of younger patients was given preference over the treatment of older and very old patients. But the person or persons with the greatest life expectancy may not even have required intensive treatment (Lübbe 2020, p. 2).

The SIAARTI guideline raised the question about whether one human life may be sacrificed for another human life if the sacrificed life was expected to have lasted a shorter duration than the saved life. The guideline distinguished between lives more worth or less worth saving. From which moral principle drew the guideline its recommendation? Presumably, the guideline relied on the ethics of self-defense or a state of emergency.

The ethics of necessity as legitimation of self-defense or emergency measures have a long tradition in philosophy. Immanuel Kant discussed whether the victim of a shipwreck in imminent danger of drowning may push another person from a plank to safe oneself (Kant 1797, pp. 41–42). The act would exercise *ius necessitates*, Kant wrote, the law of necessity: saving one's own life from a life-threatening situation by killing somebody else is illegal, but not punishable. Kant explained this with the basic principle of the law of necessity: *necessitas non habet legem* (necessity knows no law). The adage *necessitas non habet legem* is sometimes used to legitimate governmental actions in a state of exception or emergency (Agamben 2005, pp. 24–31). In most countries, COVID-19 responses did not amount to a state of emergency, and the rule of law prevailed (Kersten and Rixen 2020). In many countries no triage laws existed, and the state left the sovereignty over "bare life" (Agamben 1998) to medical and ethical associations.

Even if one accepted the necessity defense, Kant's shipwrecked killer was far from the situation in hospitals in Northern Italy in early 2020 (or hospitals in Saxony in late 2020). The SIAARTI guideline did not excuse patients with a high life expectancy for killing patients with a less promising life expectancy. The guideline addressed doctors and health personnel in intensive care units overwhelmed by more COVID-19 patients than could be treated. They were supposed to decide, who was going to live or let die, by allocating scarce ventilators and medical staff to some and not to others. Ethically, the "corona triage" (Dufner 2021; Lübbe 2020) resembled not the necessity defense, but the so-called trolley problem.

17.3.2.2 The Corona Triage as Trolley Problem

The term "trolley problem" was coined by Judith Jarvis Thomson in a Yale Law Journal article. Thomson contemplated an ethical dilemma introduced by Philippa Foot (1967/2002, pp. 23–24). The trolley problem combined the question of valuing human lives with the choice between killing and letting die (Thomson 1985, p. 1395):

> Suppose you are the driver of a trolley. The trolley rounds a bend, and there come into view ahead five track workmen, who have been repairing the track. The track goes through a bit of a valley at that point, and the sides are steep, so you must stop the trolley if you are to avoid running the five men down. You step on the brakes, but alas they don't work. Now you suddenly see a spur of track leading off to the right. You can turn the trolley onto it, and thus save the five men on the straight track ahead. Unfortunately, Mrs. Foot has arranged that there is one track workman on that spur of track. He can no more get off the track in time than the five can, so you will kill him if you turn the trolley onto him. Is it morally permissible for you to turn the trolley?

Thomson claimed that many would find it morally permissible to save the five by killing the one. But what about the doctor, who had the duty to save the lives of five of her patients in dire need of organ transplants when no suitable organs were available. But a young and healthy man sat in the waiting room, a perfect donor. Would it be permissible for the doctor to kill and cut up the young man to save five lives? Thomson (1985, p. 1396) said no. Why would it be so difficult to find five lives more valuable than one life? The—possible—difference between letting die and killing did not seem an explanation (Thomson 1985, p. 1401; Malm 1989).

The corona triage posed a trolley problem (Mounk 2020). The following translation may be helpful. In the corona triage, the five track workmen (or the five transplant patients) of Thomson (1985) represented a severe COVID-19 patient with a higher life expectancy than another severe COVID-19 patient (represented by the single-track workman ... or the young man in the waiting room). The problem was not limited, however, to severe COVID-19 patients in different age groups and with or without existing conditions. Doctors postponing elective surgery because the medical resources were needed by severe COVID-19 patients had to resolve a trolley problem, too (Shao 2020).

Thomson did not explicitly link the trolley problem to human dignity; however, I believe that the two are interconnected. At one point, Thomson referred to the Kantian idea of human dignity as treating other persons always as an end, never as a means only (Thomson 1985, p. 1401). But the Kantian reading of human dignity failed help understand why the trolley problem and human dignity are connected. Doctors, who gave the last ventilator to a young mother of four and denied it to a senior COVID-19 patient, did not treat the senior patient "as a means only." Elderly patients excluded from intensive care in the face of scarcity were not "means" for anything; they were merely excluded from care.

Still, the link between human dignity and the trolley problem was strong. A person deciding to save five lives by taking one life made a differentiating judgment on the value of human lives (Kumm and Walen 2014, pp. 71–77). Such a judgment encroached on the concept of human dignity where "every person has inherent equal worth" (May and Daly 2020, p. 1).

The *Deutsche Ethikrat*—the German council on ethics—linked the problem of allocating scarce medical resources during the COVID-19 pandemic directly to human dignity (Deutscher Ethikrat 2020, p. 3):

> The Basic Law (*Grundgesetz*) sets out a binding framework for medical ethics, too. The guaranteeing of human dignity necessitates egalitarian equality and thus provides for corresponding basic protection for all against discrimination. For the state – the direct addressee of fundamental rights – the principle of indifference to the value of life likewise applies: it is prohibited to evaluate human life, never mind devalue it. Any direct or indirect differentiation of the state with regard to the value or duration of life and any associated regulation by the state resulting in the unequal allocation of chances of survival and risks of death in acute crisis situations is inadmissible. Every human life enjoys the same protection. This means that not only differentiations based on gender or ethnic origin are prohibited. The state must also refrain from classifying lives on the basis of age, social role and its assumed 'value' or a predicted lifespan.

The ad-hoc-recommendation, even if it presented a strong moral argument, was legally weak. German case law on human dignity is erratic. The council implicitly referred to a judgment by the German Federal Constitutional Court regarding the use of armed force against a civil aircraft kidnapped and weaponized by terrorists. The terrorists intended to pilot the aircraft, packed with passengers, into a large crowd of persons on the ground. Following the September 11 attacks, the German legislator authorized the use of armed force against such an aircraft (*Luftsicherheitsgesetz*). The court squashed the law because the balancing of human lives against each other (crew and passengers versus persons on the ground) contradicted the right to life in conjunction with the guarantee of human dignity (German Federal Constitutional Court 2006, para 130):

> [T]he legislature may not . . . give authority to perform operations . . . vis-à-vis people who are not participants in the crime . . . As missions of the armed forces of a non-warlike nature, they are incompatible with the right to life and the obligation of the state to respect and protect human dignity.

With respect to the corona triage, the German Federal Constitutional Court (2021, para 128) ruled in favor of persons with disabilities, who were not protected against triage discrimination. The court asserted the lawmakers' duty to establish criteria, but ruled out specifically to distinguish some human lives as superior, others as inferior: "Certainly, respect for human dignity prohibits any weighing of life against life" (German Federal Constitutional Court 2021, para 128). Lawmakers will find it difficult to comply. Discussing the constitutional aspects of the COVID-19 pandemic, Mathias Hong asserted that valuing and weighing human lives may be inevitable. Hong did not suggest, however, that human lives be valued in a differentiating fashion. The assertion is based on the questionable distinction between killing and letting die (Hong 2020):

> When distributing scarce rescue resources it can be a legitimate goal to maximize the number of lives saved. The ban on balancing life against life, following from the right to human dignity, is therefore more comprehensive for the right to life as a right not to be killed, directed against the state, than for to the state's duty to protect one's life.

The strongest case in favor of corona triage based on semi-utilitarian principles has been made—cautiously—by Kirchhoffer (2020). Individuals can come "to a morally right decision to forgo medically futile treatment" and in times of resource scarcity, "distributive justice requires that the dignity of concrete (not hypothetical) others be included in moral consideration of withholding and withdrawing treatment, with the help of adequate information from clinical advisors" (Kirchhoffer 2020, p. 3). Interestingly, Kirchhoffer's argument reflected a position close to the SIAARTI guideline. Like others, he assumed that triage situations occurred. But did the COVID-19 crisis legitimize triage? Did doctors face a trolley problem?

The community spreading of a virus that could have been prevented by flattening the curve (until the effective vaccination of a large part of the population) was not comparable to a mass shooting, a large-scale toxic accident, colossal flooding, or other natural or man-made disasters (Lübbe 2020):

> Not every scarcity, even if it is existential, is classified as a disaster. Only in the event of a disaster – a suddenly emerging situation in which masses of people in need exceed by far the amount of resources regularly kept in place – the procedure known as 'triage' has established itself. This also includes a mass influx of wounded persons in wartime. The traditional rule here is to use resources in such a way that as many people as possible survive.

In the second half of 2020, the shortages of medical resources in Germany were not caused by an unforeseen disaster. The COVID-19 crisis arose from and was exacerbated by two circumstances. One, decades of austerity and the commercialization of healthcare increased the threshold for treating patients in a pandemic. Two, exposure in nursing homes, prisons, and refugee camps as well as the ignorant, careless, or selfish behavior of some individuals caused community spreading. Inappropriate communications by politicians, the prioritization of the vast part of the economy, and inconsistent COVID-19 regulations contributed to the second wave. These circumstances did not justify triage, they *caused* an untenable shortage of medical resources.

The COVID-19 pandemic was a terrible global tragedy, not a debate topic for a seminar on legal philosophy or applied ethics. Sophisticated "solutions" to the trolley problem did not help doctors and medical staff to make morally justified decisions on who was treated with scarce medical equipment and who was not. On the contrary, compelling doctors and medical staff to make life-or-death decisions was disrespectful of their human dignity (Kirchhoffer 2020). Expecting elderly patients or patients with existing conditions, whose continued treatment was medically indicated, to resign themselves to palliative care also violated human dignity (Saunders 2020, p. 5). These patients would have had "sound reasons to consider themselves humiliated" (Margalit 1996, pp. 10–11). Human dignity did not help deciding who may live and who must die. Yet, in a somewhat surprising way, human dignity offered guidance in the COVID-19 pandemic.

17.3.2.3 Flattening the Curve Avoided the Trolley Problem

Throughout 2020, ethics guidelines on corona triage were issued and revised. Apparently, most of the guidelines did not suggest that aggregated life expectancy be maximized: "Respect for the patient's will, fair distribution, and maximization of benefits based on chance of survival are at the heart of the recently issued triaging guidelines" (Joebges and Biller-Andorno 2020).

Considered from the perspective of 2020, more waves of COVID-19 and even corona triage were inevitable until the effective vaccination of a vast part of the population. The best—perhaps only—way to avoid the COVID-19 trolley problem and the severe violation of the human dignity of patients, doctors, and health workers was the strict maintenance of measures supposed to flatten the curve (Shao 2020). Measures ranged from wearing mouth-nose-coverings and social distancing to travel restrictions and partial or complete lockdowns (see Fig. 17.2).

Human dignity offered a convenient solution neither to the trolley problem nor the corona triage. But human dignity offered guidance to public policies and civic behavior. Human dignity demanded that corona triage, if possible, be avoided. The ad-hoc-recommendation of the German council on ethics presented an incomplete moral argument. The council derived from human dignity and the "principle of indifference to the value of life" that "the unequal allocation of chances of survival and risks of death in acute crisis situations is inadmissible" (Deutscher Ethikrat

Fig. 17.2 Flattening the curve. © 2020 B. Davy

2020, p. 3). So far, so good. The council continued to point out an "ethical corridor of solidarity and responsibility" (Deutscher Ethikrat 2020, p. 5). Inside the ethical corridor, decisions and actions concerning the COVID-19 pandemic must also take into account the "socio-psychological consequences," "economic consequences," and "elementary conditions of democratic culture" (Deutscher Ethikrat 2020, p. 6). The recommendation was incomplete because the council did not consider the relationship between human dignity and flattening the curve.

The relationship between human dignity and flattening the curve may be understood better when human dignity is conceptualized not merely as a right of the individual, but also as a moral obligation towards the community. Such a conceptualization draws from Ubuntu, the Sub-Saharan moral principle of human dignity and humaneness (Davy 2020, pp. 15–17; see chapters by Hadebe and Marais, in this volume). The word Ubuntu derives from the "Xhosa expression 'Umuntu ngumntu ngabanye abantu', which means that each individual's humanity is ideally expressed in relationship with others" (Mabovula 2011, p. 40). The phrase sometimes is translated as "I am because we are" (Rider 2016). Ubuntu differs from a Western understanding of human dignity in its emphasis on the communal over the individual. Ubuntu emphasizes the community, the Western concept of human dignity the individual.

Ubuntu in times of COVID-19 demanded social solidarity and altruistic behavior (Lubner 2020; Roberts et al. 2020; Wooldridge 2020). Physical distancing, wearing mouth-nose-coverings, and staying at home as much as possible were ways to practice Ubuntu. Flattening the curve, in other words, was a community effort to protect human dignity as well as an expression of human dignity (in the sense of Ubuntu). Human dignity, as a concept, explained why flattening the curve during the COVID-19 pandemic was an act of humaneness. Yet, the curve could not be flattened by any single person. Flattening the curve required a collective effort. Viewed through the lens of human dignity and Ubuntu, social distancing showed kindness and compassion. In this sense, human dignity gave meaning and purpose to a way of life that otherwise would have been an inhuman isolation.

17.4 Testing the Limits of Social Solidarity

17.4.1 Human Dignity and the Lack of Scientific Consensus

On September 28, 2020, one million patients had died worldwide from or with COVID-19 (Pérez-Peña 2020). On October 4, 2020, three professors from Harvard, Oxford, and Stanford respectively issued the *Great Barrington Declaration* (Kulldorf et al. 2020):

> Current lockdown policies are producing devastating effects on short and long-term public health ... with the working class and younger members of society carrying the heaviest burden. Keeping students out of school is a grave injustice. Keeping these measures in place until a vaccine is available will cause irreparable damage, with the underprivileged disproportionately harmed.

The *Great Barrington Declaration* recommended "focused protection" (Kulldorf et al. 2020): As "herd immunity" would build in the community, only "the old and infirm" required protection (e.g., frequent PCR testing in nursing homes, delivery of groceries to the vulnerable). As of December 31, 2020, the website of the *Great Barrington Declaration* claimed that the declaration had been signed by about 710,000 concerned citizens, 13,000 medical and public health scientists, and more than 39,000 medical practitioners (https://gbdeclaration.org/). The website also displayed a map showing that—in absolute numbers—the largest portion of signatories were located in the United States, the United Kingdom, and Germany. The website was discontinued because too many spoof signatures had been added.

On October 14, 2020, an online publication on the website of *The Lancet*, called the *John Snow Memorandum* (www.johnsnowmemo.com/) warned against pandemic strategies relying upon immunity from natural infections for COVID-19:

> Continuing restrictions will probably be required in the short term, to reduce transmission and fix ineffective pandemic response systems, in order to prevent future lockdowns. ... The evidence is very clear: controlling community spread of COVID-19 is the best way to protect our societies and economies until safe and effective vaccines and therapeutics arrive within the coming months. We cannot afford distractions that undermine an effective response; it is essential that we act urgently based on the evidence.

As of December 31, 2020, the website of the *John Snow Memorandum* claimed that more than 6900 scientists, researchers, and healthcare professionals had signed the memorandum.

With good reasons, Meier et al. (2020, pp. 227–228) emphasized that public responses to the COVID-19 pandemic (such as lockdowns or travel restrictions) violated human dignity unless they were based on scientific evidence. The demand for scientific evidence was difficult to fulfill, however, in the face of uncertainty and rapidly changing information.

The *Great Barrington Declaration* and the *John Snow Memorandum* epitomized the dilemma that plagued fighting COVID-19 from the beginning. The biopolitical interventions from experts on epidemiology, virology, and public health—dominating the public discourse since the WHO had proclaimed COVID-19 a pandemic—never fully gained the public trust indispensable for making effective public policy. Expert opinions and the daily announcement of numbers of infections and deaths sat well with a hierarchist worldview, but the hierarchist strategy hardly worked for the individualist, egalitarian, or fatalist biases (B. Davy 2021). Colombo (2021) asserted that corona defiance occurred because the tension between "biomedical knowledge" and "economic knowledge" simply neglected a social perspective. Consequently, societies worldwide grew more and more polarized. In the remainder of my chapter, I discuss how flattening the curve tested the limits of social solidarity: COVID-19 rules resulted in the super-spreading of dignity conflicts.

17.4.2 COVID-19 and the Super-Spreading of Dignity Conflicts

Lockdowns and social distancing rules tested the limits of social solidarity. Designed to protect the health system and persons at particular risk to die from COVID-19, lockdowns, social distancing rules, and other measures to fight the pandemic potentially threatened the human dignity of everyone affected. This was particularly true for persons already living on the margins: "The ability to live with dignity is threatened for people who are homebound or locked down in unsafe conditions, whether in institutional settings like prisons or in private settings where there is abuse or scarcity" (May and Daly 2020).

COVID-19 put the human dignity of homeless and poor persons under stress. Yet, threats to human dignity were not confined to persons already living on the margins; they were ubiquitous. The lockdown put enormous pressure on families: Parents had to combine domestic work, parenting, working from home, and home schooling. Children lost their agency and playground access. The duress of little privacy in overcrowded homes also affected human dignity. Physical distancing often resulted in amplifying social distance. Meeting other persons with their mouths and noses covered in public transport, shopping malls, or court rooms was an odd experience. Social distancing and staying at home required access to an adequate home and strong Internet. Also, being able to meet with family and friends merely in video conferences affected human dignity as well as the closing of nonessential businesses and workplaces. Not being allowed to earn money to put food on the table and to pay the rent greatly threatened human dignity.

As mentioned before, the *Great Barrington Declaration* was most popular in three countries: the United States, the United Kingdom, and Germany. The regional distribution of popularity coincided with the fact that opposition to COVID-19 rules was strongest in these three countries. On April 16, 2020, thousands of demonstrators created a traffic jam around the State Capitol in Lansing, Michigan, protesting the stay-at-home orders (Bogel-Burroughs and Peters 2020):

> Some had affiliations with the Tea Party and displayed the 'Don't Tread on Me' logo that was an unofficial slogan for the movement. At least one protester in Michigan waved a Confederate flag with the image of a gun. Others waved banners in support of Mr. Trump and protested Gov. Gretchen Whitmer, a Democrat who has been a target of Mr. Trump's ire, by chanting, 'Lock her up.'

The Lansing protest was one of many gatherings of angry citizens, who protested rules issued to fight COVID-19. In Texas, armed militia-style protesters helped businesses defy coronavirus lockdowns (Fernandez and Montgomery 2020).

In the United Kingdom, a survey found that COVID-19 lockdown rules were even more disruptive than Brexit: "People who didn't break lockdown are far more likely to think badly of those who did than leave voters are to think badly of remainers" (Booth 2020). An article in *The Guardian* framed the divide as a combat between lockdowners versus libertarians (McKie and Helm 2020):

> On one side there are the lockdowners. They think the only hope of triumphing over Covid-19 is shutdowns to bring numbers of cases back under control. ... On the other are the libertarians. They say we cannot return to those days because it would trigger an economic collapse and allow thousands of untreated cases of cancer, heart ailments and other diseases to mount.

In Germany, contrarian protesters ("Querdenker") against COVID-19 rules compared themselves to victims of the Nazis. The protesters dubbed politicians, who appeared in corona press conferences, or persons, who insisted on everybody wearing a mask in shops and on public transport, "Coronazi." A young woman, calling herself "Jana from Kassel," claimed to feel "like Sophie Scholl because I've been active in the resistance movement for months." At another *Querdenker* rally, a girl mourned her clandestine birthday party—she had to hide with friends because gatherings were prohibited during lockdown. The girl compared herself to Anne Frank (for both incidents see Hasselbach 2020). Also, mouth-nose-coverings—masks—were politicized and increasingly polarized the public (Blech and Blinda 2020):

> Those who don't wear them or even join protests against them, those who doubt their efficacy and thus question scientific consensus: They accept the risk of infection – and the risk of infecting others. The mask is a symbol of solidarity. Not wearing one is an expression of individual freedom or just plain selfishness. Families have been divided by the debate over the masks and friendships have been strained.

The publishers of the Oxford English Dictionary considered to choose "covidiot" as Word of the Year (Schuessler 2020). In 2020, covidiot became an umbrella term for lockdown protesters, mask refusers, anti-vaxxers, selfish hoarders, *Querdenker*, and others, who denied social solidarity during the pandemic. Even though I had little sympathy for "Jana from Kassel" and her likes, I believe that one conception of human dignity can explain why at least some "covidiots" had reasons to feel humiliated by social distancing rules, mask duties, and other measures to flatten the curve.

Niklas Luhmann defined human dignity as the successful presentation of the self. In his book on *Grundrechte* (basic rights), he explained how humans achieve dignity through communicating how they want to be seen by others (Luhmann 1965, p. 68; edited translation BD):

> Even more than 'liberty', 'dignity' is a concept of desire (*Wunschbegriff*) that – without mentioning the problem because this would cause a failure of presentation – describes the successful presentation of the self (*gelungene Selbstdarstellung*). Human dignity is by no means a natural property like intelligence. Also, dignity is not a 'value' which humans naturally 'possess' or 'carry inside themselves'. . . . Dignity must be crafted. Dignity is the result of a complex performance of self-presentation as well as the result of permanent social cooperation.

Luhmann's dignity theory was unorthodox. He believed that human dignity results from successfully communicating to the world how individuals define themselves. The eminent relevance of a successful presentation of the self had already been described by Goffman (1959), a book that Luhmann did not mention. Luhmann emphasized that social order emerged from sound and sociable communication. Therefore, to protect social order, human dignity must be respected and protected: "Humans have to be able to be seen by everybody!" (Luhmann 1965, p. 70; translation BD).

The mask or mouth-nose-covering, which became one of the symbols of the pandemic, modified and often severely obstructed a successful presentation of the self (see Fig. 17.3). Not being able to smile properly in public, but more importantly, not being able to breathe properly while working indoors reduced everybody's ability to lead a self-determined life in full. Lockdowns, working from home, permanent video conferences, travel restrictions, and other measures to flatten the curve severely damaged the successful presentation of the self. Luhmann's dignity theory did not excuse covidiots, but it explained why societies that emphasized the protection of human dignity as an individual right were prone to produce citizens with limited social responsibility and solidarity. In such societies, the successful presentation of the self was ranked highly—and sometimes misunderstood as an entitlement to endanger the health and lives of others.

COVID-19 policymakers often failed to account for the super-spreading of dignity conflicts they caused with their rules. Not recognizing these dignity conflicts contributed to protest and resistance against social distancing, masks, and lockdowns. Of course, not all mask refusers or *Querdenker* could have been persuaded by convincing and respectful explanations. But the pervasive contempt expressed for the "covidiots" deepened the social chasm and motivated "evil insurgency" (Davy 2019).

Fig. 17.3 Masks and distance modified the presentation of the self. © 2020 B. Davy

17.5 Conclusion

The COVID-19 pandemic created an enormous, perhaps exaggerated interest in human dignity (Safransky 2022, p. 429):

> As COVID-19's death-dealing blows along race and class lines brought systemic inequities into stark relief, dignity had emerged as a sort of keyword of the times. Globally, demands had grown for dignified housing, dignified work, dignified care, and, poignantly, the right to die a dignified death.

The comment is a bit sarcastic. As discussed throughout the chapter, human dignity fosters an understanding as to why the threshold of the healthcare system must be protected from overload during a pandemic. But human dignity also engenders an understanding of the limits of social solidarity. Despite the significance of human dignity as public policy guidance, public announcements or conversations rarely are framed as *dignity* discourses. This is prudent. Human dignity is a delicate topic, hardly suitable to explain to the public the responses to the COVID-19 pandemic. However, not being able to discuss COVID-19 responses in terms of human dignity is also disappointing. The supreme value of international human rights law (OHCHR 2020) and many constitutions proves inappropriate for the public debate about the corona triage, the flattening of the curve, or lost opportunities to successfully present the self. Perhaps Luhmann (1965, p. 68) is right, and human dignity must better be regarded "without mentioning the problem because this would cause a failure of presentation."

Fighting COVID-19 must be done gently: Since social distancing, mouth-nose-coverings, or lockdowns encroached on the human dignity of everybody, who lost agency to the public responses to COVID-19, these measures were more successful when explained properly, consistently, and transparently. Also, fighting COVID-19 must be done firmly. Half-hearted lockdowns or inadequate mask wearing caused huge economic and social cost without creating health benefits. If this chapter has a speculative message, it is this: Flattening the curve must be done gently, but firmly.

References

Agamben G (1998) Homo sacer. Sovereign power and bare life. Stanford University Press, Stanford

Agamben G (2005) State of exception. University of Chicago Press, Chicago, London

Blech J, Blinda A (2020) Tempers flare over German mask requirement. SPIEGEL International, August 19, 2020. Online: https://www.spiegel.de/international/germany/tempers-flare-over-german-mask-requirement-a-3edea99d-3563-43e6-8401-4671a6671816. Accessed 30 June 2023

Bogel-Burroughs N, Peters JW (2020) 'You have to disobey': protesters gather to defy stay-at-home orders. The New York Times, April 16, 2020. Online: https://www.nytimes.com/2020/04/16/us/coronavirus-rules-protests.html. Accessed 30 June 2023

Boisseron B (2023) Black ecology in COVID times. Black Scholar 53(1):35–49

Booth R (2020) Covid lockdown rules more divisive than Brexit, survey finds. The Guardian, September 11, 2020. Online: https://www.theguardian.com/world/2020/sep/11/covid-lockdown-rules-more-divisive-than-brexit-survey-finds. Accessed 30 June 2023

Brill (2020) COVID-19 collection. Online: https://www2.brill.com/COVID-19_Collection. Accessed 30 June 2023

Cambridge University Press (2020) Coronavirus free access collection. Online: https://www.cambridge.org/core/browse-subjects/medicine/coronavirus-free-access-collection. Accessed 30 June 2023

Colombo E (2021) Human rights-inspired governmentality: COVID-19 through a human dignity perspective. Critical Sociology 47(4–5):571–581. https://doi.org/10.1177/0896920520971846

Daly E (2021) Dignity rights. Courts, constitutions, and the worth of the human person. Updated edition. University of Pennsylvania Press, Philadelphia

Davy B (2019) Evil insurgency. Planning Theory & Practice 20(2):290–297

Davy B (2020) Human dignity: is there a place for it in planning? Transactions of the Association of European Schools of Planning 4:7–21

Davy B (2021) Social distancing and cultural bias. Journal of the American Planning Association 87(2):159–166. https://doi.org/10.1080/01944363.2020.1824617

Deutscher Ethikrat (2020) Solidarity and responsibility during the coronavirus crisis. Ad hoc recommendation. Online: https://www.ethikrat.org/fileadmin/Publikationen/Ad-hoc-Empfehlun-gen/englisch/recommendation-coronavirus-crisis.pdf. Accessed 30 June 2023

Dhungana N (2020) Human dignity and cross-border migrants in the era of the COVID-19 pandemic. World Development 136 (December). Online: https://www.sciencedirect.com/science/article/pii/S0305750X20303016?via%3Dihub. Accessed 30 June 2023

Dufner A (2021) Nutzen und Gerechtigkeit im Rahmen einer Corona-Triage. Bundeszentrale für politische Bildung, May 6, 2021. Online: https://www.bpb.de/gesellschaft/umwelt/bioethik/327159/nutzen-und-gerechtigkeit-im-rahmen-einer-corona-triage. Accessed 30 June 2023

Elsevier (2020) Elsevier's free research on the novel coronavirus (SARS-CoV-2) and COVID-19. Online: https://www.elsevier.com/connect/coronavirus-information-center. Accessed 30 June 2023

Fernandez M, Montgomery D (2020) Businesses chafing under Covid-19 lockdowns turn to armed defiance. The New York Times, May 13, 2020. Online: https://www.nytimes.com/2020/05/13/us/coronavirus-businesses-lockdown-guns.html. Accessed 30 June 2023

Foot P (2002) The problem of abortion and the doctrine of the double effect. In: Foot P (ed) Virtues and vices: and other essays in moral philosophy. Oxford University Press, Oxford, pp 19–32. (first published 1967)

Gallicano TD, Lawless O, Higgins AM, Shaikh S, Levens S (2023) The concentric firestorm: a qualitative study of Black Lives Matter activism and the COVID-19 pandemic. Journal of Public Relations Research 35(2):63–85

German Federal Constitutional Court (2006) Judgment of the First Senate, February 15, 2006, 1 BvR 357/05 – Aviation Security Act. English translation online: https://www.bundesverfassungsgericht.de/SharedDocs/Entscheidungen/EN/2006/02/rs20060215_1bvr035705en.html. Accessed 30 June 2023

German Federal Constitutional Court (2021) Order of the First Senate, December 16, 2021, 1 BvR 1541/20 – Corona triage. English translation online: http://www.bverfg.de/e/rs20211216_1bvr154120.html. Accessed 30 June 2023

Goffman E (1959) The presentation of self in everyday life. Anchor Books

Hasselbach C (2020) Coronavirus: How German protesters are trivializing Nazi-era persecution. DW (Deutsche Welle), November 28, 2020. Online: https://www.dw.com/en/coronavirus-how-german-protesters-are-trivializing-nazi-era-persecution/a-55753236. Accessed 30 June 2023

Hong M (2020) Corona-triage and human dignity. On the limits of balancing life against life. Verfassungsblog on matters constitutional, March 31, 2020. Online: https://verfassungsblog.de/corona-triage-and-human-dignity/. Accessed 30 June 2023

Joebges S, Biller-Andorno N (2020) Ethics guidelines on COVID-19 triage – an emerging international consensus. Critical Care 24. Online: https://ccforum.biomedcentral.com/articles/10.1186/s13054-020-02927-1. Accessed 30 June 2023

Kant I (1797) Die Metaphysik der Sitten. In: Quoted from Wilhelm Weischedel (ed) Werkausgabe, Vol VIII. Frankfurt/Main, Suhrkamp

Kersten J, Rixen S (2020) Der Verfassungsstaat in der Corona-Krise. C.H. Beck, München

Kirchhoffer DG (2013) Human dignity in contemporary ethics. Teneo Press, Amherst

Kirchhoffer DG (2020) Dignity, autonomy, and allocation of scarce medical resources during COVID-19. Bioethical Inquiry. Online: https://link.springer.com/article/10.1007/s11673-020-09998-3. Accessed 30 June 2023

Kulldorf M, Gupta S, Bhattacharya J (2020) The Great Barrington declaration. Online: https://gbdeclaration.org/. Accessed 30 June 2023

Kumm M, Walen AD (2014) Human dignity and proportionality. In: Huscroft G, Miller BW, Webber G (eds) Proportionality and the rule of law. Rights, justification, reasoning. Cambridge University Press, Cambridge, pp 67–89

Lombart B, Moïse L, Bellamy V, Landolfini V, Manifacier M-J, Mesnage V, Heilbrunn C, Pateron D, Andro-Melin A, Fain O, Carbonell N, Bourrier A, Thomas C, Libeaut D, Coichard C-G (2022) Alice Polomeni and Bertrand Guidet. Nursing Ethics 29(4):833–843

Lübbe W (2020) Corona triage. A commentary on the triage recommendations by Italian SIAARTI medicals regarding the corona crisis. Verfassungsblog on matters constitutional, March 16, 2020. Online: https://verfassungsblog.de/corona-triage-2/. Accessed 30 June 2023

Lubner M (2020) The spirit of Ubuntu is a tried and tested antidote for Covid-19. news24, September 24, 2020. Online: https://www.news24.com/news24/columnists/guestcolumn/opinion-the-spirit-of-ubuntu-is-a-tried-and-tested-antidote-for-covid-19-20200924. Accessed 30 June 2023

Luhmann N (1965) Grundrechte als Institution. Ein Beitrag zur politischen Soziologie. Duncker & Humblot, Berlin

Mabovula NN (2011) The erosion of African communal values: A reappraisal of the African Ubuntu philosophy. Inkanyiso 3(1):38–47

Malm HM (1989) Killing, letting die, and simple conflicts. Philosophy & Public Affairs 18(3): 238–258
Margalit A (1996) The decent society. Harvard University Press, Cambridge, London
May JR, Daly E (2020) Dignity Rights for a pandemic. Law, Culture and the Humanities. https://doi.org/10.1177/1743872120944515
McKie R, Helm T (2020) Lockdowners v libertarians: Britain's coronavirus divide. The Guardian, September 27, 2020. Online: https://www.theguardian.com/world/2020/sep/27/lockdowners-v-libertarians-britain-coronavirus-divide. Accessed 30 June 2023
Meier BM, Evans DP, Phelan A (2020) Rights-based approaches to preventing, detecting, and responding to infectious disease. In: Ecclestone-Turner M, Brassington I (eds) Infectious diseases in the new millennium, pp 217–253
Mounk Y (2020) The extraordinary decisions facing Italian doctors. The Atlantic, March 11, 2020. Online: https://www.theatlantic.com/ideas/archive/2020/03/who-gets-hospital-bed/607807/. Accessed 30 June 2023
Nussbaum MC (2006) Frontiers of justice. Disability, nationality, species membership. Belknap Press, Cambridge, London
Odigbo B, Eze F, Odigbo R (2020) COVID-19 lockdown controls and human rights abuses: the social marketing implications. Emerald Open Research (awaiting peer review). Online: https://emeraldopenresearch.com/articles/2-45/v1. Accessed 30 June 2023
OHCHR (2020) Coronavirus: Human rights need to be front and centre in response, says Bachelet. Online: https://www.ohchr.org/EN/NewsEvents/Pages/DisplayNews.aspx?NewsID=25668. Accessed 30 June 2023
Oxford University Press (2020) Access to OUP resources on COVID-19. Online: https://academic.oup.com/journals/pages/coronavirus. Accessed 30 June 2023
Pérez-Peña R (2020) Coronavirus deaths pass one million worldwide. The New York Times, September 28, 2020. Online: https://www.nytimes.com/2020/09/28/world/covid-1-million-deaths.html. Accessed 30 June 2023
Rider RA (2016) I am because we are. Tennessee Law Review 83(3):813–823
Riva L, Petrini C (2020) Ethics of triage for intensive-care interventions during the COVID-19 pandemic: Age or disability related cut-off policies are not justifiable. Clinical Ethics 16(3): 228–233. https://doi.org/10.1177/1477750920971803
RKI (Robert Koch Institut) (2020) Daily report, December 31, 2020. Online: https://www.rki.de/DE/Content/InfAZ/N/Neuartiges_Coronavirus/Situationsberichte/Dez_2020/2020-12-31-de.html. Accessed 30 June 2023
Roberts S (2020) Flattening the coronavirus curve. The New York Times, March 27, 2020. Online: https://www.nytimes.com/article/flatten-curve-coronavirus.html. Accessed 30 June 2023
Roberts B, Davids YD, Bohler-Muller N, Alexander K, Mchunu N, Majikijela Y (2020) The Ubuntu Nation? Changing views on social solidarity and the Covid-19 pandemic. Maverick Citizen, September 11, 2020. Online: https://www.dailymaverick.co.za/article/2020-09-11-the-ubuntu-nation-changing-views-on-social-solidarity-and-the-covid-19-pandemic/. Accessed 30 June 2023
Safransky S (2022) For a spatial politics of dignity. Dialogues in Human Geography 12(3):427–430
Saha A, Carreras M, Quak E-J (2022) Investigating initial policy responses to COVID-19: evidence across 59 countries. International Review of Applied Economics 36(5–6):762–791
Saunders J (2020) COVID-19 and human rights. States' obligations and businesses' responsibilities in responding to the pandemic. OXFAM Discussion Paper. Online: https://policy-practice.oxfam.org/resources/covid-19-and-key-human-rights-principles-in-practice-state-obligations-and-busi-621037/. Accessed 30 June 2023
Schuessler J (2020) Oxford's 2020 Word of the Year? The New York Times, May 13, 2020. Online: https://www.nytimes.com/2020/11/22/arts/oxford-word-of-the-year-coronavirus.html. Accessed 30 June 2023
Shao C (2020) The COVID trolley dilemma. The American Journal of Surgery. Online: https://www.ncbi.nlm.nih.gov/pmc/articles/PMC7224645/. Accessed 30 June 2023

SIAARTI (Società Italiana di Anestesia Analgesia Rianimazione e Terapia Intensiva) (2020) Raccomandazioni di etica clinica per l'ammissione a trattamenti intensive e per la loro sospensione, in condizioni eccezionali di squilibrio tra necessità e risorse disponibili. Online version retracted after July 2020. On file with the author

Simmel G (1906) The sociology of secrecy and of secret societies. American Journal of Sociology 11(4):441–498

SpringerNature (2020) Coronavirus (COVID-19) research highlights. Online: https://www.springernature.com/gp/researchers/campaigns/coronavirus. Accessed 30 June 2023

Taylor & Francis (2020) Online search. Online: https://www.tandfonline.com/action/doSearch?AllField=%22coronavirus%22+OR+%22COVID-19%22&content=standard&countTerms=true&target=default&pageSize=50&subjectTitle=&startPage=&sortBy=Earliest. Accessed 30 June 2023

Thomson JJ (1985) The trolley problem. Yale Law Journal 94(6):1395–1415

Wiley (2020) Covid-19: Novel Coronavirus Outbreak. Online: https://novel-coronavirus.onlinelibrary.wiley.com/. Accessed 30 June 2023

Wooldridge M (2020) Ubuntu should be at the centre of our response to Covid-19. Mail & Guardian, May 12, 2020. Online: https://mg.co.za/coronavirus-essentials/2020-05-12-ubuntu-should-be-at-the-centre-of-our-response-to-covid-19/. Accessed 30 June 2023

GPSR Compliance

The European Union's (EU) General Product Safety Regulation (GPSR) is a set of rules that requires consumer products to be safe and our obligations to ensure this.

If you have any concerns about our products, you can contact us on ProductSafety@springernature.com

In case Publisher is established outside the EU, the EU authorized representative is:

Springer Nature Customer Service Center GmbH
Europaplatz 3
69115 Heidelberg, Germany

Batch number: 10732090

Printed by Printforce, the Netherlands